STUDIES IN THE PSYCHOLOGY OF THE MYSTICS

By

JOSEPH MARÉCHAL, S.J.

Translated, with an Introductory Foreword, by

ALGAR THOROLD

MAGI BOOKS, INC.

33 Buckingham Drive   Albany, New York 12208

MAGI BOOKS, INC. EDITION, 1964

NIHIL OBSTAT
    THOMAS McLAUGHLIN, S. Th.D.,
        Censor deputatus

IMPRIMATUR
    EDM. CAN. SURMONT,
        Vicarius generalis

WESTMONASTERII
    DIE 14a JULII, 1927

First published by
BURNS, OATES AND WASHBOURNE, LTD.
C. BURNS & OATES LTD., 1927, 1964

Reprinted by
MAGI BOOKS, INC.
by special arrangement with
BURNS & OATES, LTD.

FOREWORD

FATHER JOSEPH MARÉCHAL, S.J., the author of the following essays, is Professor of rational and experimental psychology at the Jesuit Philosophical and Theological College at Louvain, and also gives an " interim " course of lectures on the history of modern philosophy. From 1904 to 1916 he taught general biology and human physiology, and during the War he also taught logic and epistemology, general metaphysic, and the history of philosophy. His course of preparation for these functions had included a four years' course of biology at the University of Louvain, at the end of which he took the degree of Doctor of Science, several years of special research in cytology and general physiology, in the course of which he published several important scientific monographs, followed by courses at various German Universities in nervous and mental pathology and legal psychiatry, " Mon but était double," writes Dr. Maréchal, " 1° Prendre un contact direct avec les méthodes de recherche scientifique, en mettant moi-même la main à la pâte, comme spécialiste; 2° me préparer indirectement à l'enseignement de la psychologie." And, he adds, in the same letter: " Vous voyez, cher Monsieur, que je me suis intéressé à des sujets assez divers, trop divers même: . . . . il y a cependant une certaine unité dans cette diversité; vous me comprendrez d'un mot: la mystique m'a toujours attiré comme couronnement de la métaphysique et de la psychologie; *c'est d'en bas, comme philosophe et comme homme de science que j'ai voulu l'envisager et que je me suis efforcé de la comprendre, très modestement.*"

Dr. Maréchal's other most important book is his philosophical treatise, *Le Point de Départ de la Métaphysique.* The three first and the fifth volumes of this great work, which articulates the lines of a Thomist epistemology against the background of Kantian idealism, and to a large extent in its terms, at all events in terms intelligible to modern philosophical students, have already been published. We may hope that this great work will soon be completed. Nevertheless, as Dr. Maréchal says, in the letter quoted above, mysticism is the completion and

iii

FOREWORD

the crowning of metaphysic, and it is in the volume now presented to the English reader that his most mature thought is contained.

I am very conscious of the defects of my rendering. A work of science which is also a work of literary art is doubly hard to translate. I have sacrificed everything to the achievement of as exact a version of the writer's meaning as lay within my power.

A. T.

CONTENTS

EMPIRICAL SCIENCE AND RELIGIOUS PSYCHOLOGY

CRITICAL NOTES[1]

SUMMARY

EMPIRICAL SCIENCE AND RELIGIOUS PSYCHOLOGY

WHAT end, it will perhaps be asked, can it serve still further to complicate the imbroglio in which at the time of the sixth Congress of Psychology[2] the discussion of religious phenomena became involved? And if it is felt to be absolutely necessary to dissipate inevitable misunderstandings, is not such a labour of Sisyphus amply represented on the Catholic side by certain studies already published?[3] This may be true; moreover, the objection is not very significant: their very banality will, it is hoped, justify the very few simple ideas which it is proposed to express here in as concise a form as possible.

Leaving on one side technical particularities—it is not here that the apple of discord lies, even in religious psychology— let us address ourselves in these pages to the examination of an absolutely fundamental problem of method, precisely that problem the solution of which in principle may have appeared to be the most appreciable fruit of the labours of the section of religious psychology at the Congress of Geneva: *should religious psychology be constituted, yes or no, on the type, by the methods and in conformity with the general postulates of the positive sciences?* Everyone from his own point of view—theologians, psychologists, physiologists, and independent enquirers—was convinced in perfectly good faith of the affirmative answer to this question. It was agreed: religious psychology was to be a " positive science," and, for my part, I gladly say, why not ? And yet, when I detect in the case of psychologists of different schools instinctive suspicions piercing the conciliatory varnish of the most sincere approximations, I begin to fear that the most profound divergencies will once more appear. And how can such divergencies between loyal and learned allies be explained, if not by a latent equivocation in the very terms of their pact?

It will, then, be worth while to examine this pact more closely. And as it rests entirely on the express purpose of treating

3

religious psychology as a *positive science*, we are faced with the preliminary necessity of precisely determining the meaning of this phrase.

I. THE OBJECT OF POSITIVE SCIENCE

The proper domain of positive science is that of explicit human experience expressed in definite facts and in their immediate co-ordination, or, if other terms are preferred, the proper object of positive science is the diversity of phenomena (in the rigorously critical sense of the word) and their synthesis.

To this exclusive competence of empirical science with regard to the phenomenon, to the " relative," is opposed the no less exclusive competence of metaphysics, with regard to the " transcendent," the " absolute."

Without wishing to dispute the justice of this delimitation of frontiers, now definitely acquired, it would seem, as far as philosophic criticism is concerned, that it is permissible to point out at once a condition of their tracing too important to be neglected with impunity.

The human and plenary act of " knowing "—the act which gives us a hold over the " real " whatever degree of reality be involved, the act which constitutes the inevitable antecedent of action—is evidently and without any doubt an act of judgement. Now this act, in spite of the plurality of the sources from which it is fed, synthesises their disparate contributions in a very close unity—so close, indeed, that that unity alone, as such, expresses our attitude before the " real."

What follows from this ?

That the partial modes of knowing which psychological analysis may be able to discover among the constitutive conditions of judgement cannot, in that isolated state, possess jurisdiction over the entire fulness of the " real " accessible to humanity : they only exhaust—in their intensive action—the proper object of human knowledge in their mutual conjunction.

Now, supposing that by a methodological artifice we succeed in isolating one from the other these modes of knowing in order to study separately those aspects of the real which correspond to them, it is quite clear that we must refrain from speaking purely and simply of the " real," before completing on our analytic data the harmonious synthesis which shall restore them to their natural unity. And it is also quite evident that after having thus isolated, by a kind of abstraction, one aspect of the

4

real, we cannot legitimately apply to other aspects observations or laws depending on that methodological abstraction itself.

A critical study, therefore, of the mutual relation of the different modes of knowing contained in the unity of the act of knowledge is obligatory for anyone wishing to make a legitimate analytic use of the content of knowledge.

Let us at present enumerate for reference the general elements the cohesion of which is implied in every act of human judgement.

They may be reduced to three.

First of all a diversity of purely empirical and relative elements, grouped in space and time. These are the " phenomena " belonging as much to internal as to external experience.

The second element, more exclusively formal, is a metempirical mode of synthesis. It consists in the compenetration of groupings of phenomena by the superior unity of concepts, or, if you will, in the representation of a more or less defined relation between the empirical conjunctions of phenomena and the absolute unity of *being*. It is unimportant whether this element of synthesis be called " active intellection," " total intellectual abstraction," " apperception," or " synthetic activity of the intelligence," since at bottom all these terms indicate the same operation of the spirit unifying and generalising its phenomenal content.

The third element, inseparable from the preceding ones, is of a particular nature, and is the specific characteristic of judgement. It is no longer merely the conception but the *absolute affirmation* of the relation of the empirical synthesis to the unity of being. By this affirmation the spirit takes up its position before the conceptual data and confers on them a logical or moral value. In this third stage—which is not really distinct from the second—we detect the proper movement of the human spirit, the expression of its intimate nature, effecting and affirming unity, because it points fundamentally towards the unity of Being, its inaccessible object, the end which ever escapes it.[4] But let us disregard this point of view which is in no way indispensable to the psychological deduction which we are here concerned to make. It is sufficient to note that the authentic human act of knowing, the judgement, whatever be the plan of *being* to which its two terms are referable, necessarily contains the *absolute* expression of a value, hence also of a reality.

What follows from this ?

A minimum conclusion which would seem to defy all controversy, but will bring us nearer to the object of this critical note. It follows that, in the problem with which we are occupied, two methodological attitudes only escape evident logical contradiction—(1) the radically agnostic attitude, which consists in a refusal to take sides for or against the psychologically inevitable affirmation of a value; (2) the frankly metaphysical attitude which respects the integrality of the essential conditions of human knowledge and recognises every value inevitably affirmed or postulated.

A " negative " empiricism would be intrinsically self-contradictory.

We arrive at a truism, it will be said. Without doubt; but the evidence of that truism grows only too easily obscure in practice, and it is decisive for the appreciation of the competence of the positive sciences.

It is, indeed, true that the sciences formulate themselves in propositions, which, considered as statements of judgements, necessarily express " values," and that these values themselves are founded on metaphysical principles by right prior to any particular science. But, strictly speaking, a man of science might envisage these statements less as laws than as recipes; I fully believe for my part that these generalised " recipes " still imply plenty of metaphysics, and that even the most empiricist of savants writes as much metaphysics as M. Jourdain wrote prose. But I will be generous and not pursue the discussion. It remains in any case that the pretension of confining oneself to positive knowledge—that is, of limiting oneself to the phenomenal order—involves a correlative renunciation of the act of judgement on the integrality of an objective fact. Scientific method—apart from a narrowly agnostic and pragmatist point of view—is therefore by itself incomplete and insufficient: it demands in order to make contact with reality the complement of some metaphysic or other.

Let us retain this conclusion which we have taken the trouble to justify, though it is hardly contestable—or, indeed, in theory contested—and take a step forward.

SCIENCE AND PSYCHOLOGY

II. THE MATERIAL AND FORMAL ELEMENTS OF EMPIRICAL SCIENCE

The object of " Science," the phenomenon, is the product of a methodic abstraction performed upon the real. Every strictly scientific statement remains, then, affected in its intimate value by a coefficient of abstraction which cannot be neglected. Let us not attempt for the moment to calculate this coefficient or determine the precise dose of reality which no doubt transpires in these affirmations; but let us rather analyse in themselves and in their co-ordination the empirical elements which are the material of science. Perhaps this enquiry confined to the experimental and relative field may appear of some use if brought into relation with the critical conclusion which we have drawn above.

The dialectical stages of the birth of the sciences, if looked at from outside and superficially, wear an appearance of schematic clarity, which leaves no room, it would seem, for any further problem. The savant, we are told, observes *facts*; from these *facts* he induces *laws*; finally, on these facts and laws he builds his theories. At the base of this triple operation in the irreversible order of its stages are the facts, an element strictly defined and directly observable; on the observation of the facts rests the generalising induction from which the laws, the standards of groupings and succession, are formed; and again, these laws are but the immediate and authentic generalisations of the facts from which they have sprung; on the other hand, they constitute the firm ground on which the edifice—less directly objective—of the theories is to rise.

Does this logical schematism faithfully describe the birth of experimental science in the concrete ? No doubt the observation of facts will always keep on some side a priority of right over induction and theory. Yet if we consider scientific research in practice, no longer in manuals but in laboratories, in clinics, or on the actual field of observation, we become easily convinced of the far from negligible anticipatory influence on observation itself exercised by induction and theory. And perhaps it may be maintained that scientific knowledge is built up simultaneously at its three dialectical stages, so much so that there is no scientifically observed fact that has not found its place from the first moment in a certain generalisation and a certain theoretical conception.

I proceed immediately to justify this assertion.

STUDIES IN THE PSYCHOLOGY OF THE MYSTICS

1. The Facts of Observation

(a) Generalising Assimilation and Qualitative Indetermination.

No more in the case of common-sense knowledge than in the case of scientific knowledge does the objective elementary fact reach in all its original purity the clear consciousness of the perceiving subject. The first contact of the object with the subject which becomes aware of it is enveloped from the first moment in a resurrection of manifold sensory memories. The existence of this " assimilation," performed at once on pure sensation by a whole psychological past which frames it, shades it, modifies it, alters or even dissimulates it, is one of the best established theses of experimental psychology: sensation only succeeds in crossing the threshold of consciousness, thus escorted and disguised. The mechanism of the observation of an objective event—abstraction being made even of the possible influence of emotional concomitants—is not, then, so very simple: the sensory phenomenon only becomes a conscious acquisition of the subject on the condition of finding a home, an acceptable relation in the framework of previous acquisitions; and if it be able in its turn to modify the framework into which it is introduced, it has nevertheless at first to adapt itself, if necessary, by deformation.

Such is the law of clear perception—or if you will of empirical apperception—which governs the whole domain of the sensibility and, everything considered, is but one section of the more general law of the unity of consciousness. It attests on the emergence of the first degree of sensory experience the close solidarity of the different levels of knowledge, since to observe a " fact " is at once to introduce it into a pre-existing mould, to class it to some extent, and to seize in it less its original and individual traits than those which it shares with other facts. Psychological assimilation is a kind of inchoative generalisation, effected in the individual representation, the image; it is, if one may say so, a sort of *concrete generalisation*.

The simple elementary psychological mechanism tends, therefore, to make predominate, in the sensorial image itself, the " type " over the " individual." To what extent will the individual be able to resist the levelling influence of the type ?

The individuality of particular facts in the inorganic world, less rich, less complex, and also less closely defined, has to make comparatively slight sacrifices to fit into the uniformity

8

of the type: the resemblance between the concrete data of our physical or chemical experiences and their qualitative prototypes is very great. On the other hand, the nature of the physico-chemical types organised in our knowledge depends as little as possible on the tendencies and interests of our personal life: our relative impartiality in this field guarantees there a very large objectivity of " assimilating types."

But if we go higher into the organic world, where the always complex objects instead of complacently exhibiting all the elements of their structure show the subject who is observing them only a limited number of characteristics of identity, how much wider grows the scope of psychological assimilation and how much less reliable its action ! In this case the assimilating types of direct knowledge are sometimes so vague that they cover, under the insignificant unity of one label, all sorts of discrepancies and incoherencies. A partial likeness, a chance analogy, easily mask fundamental divergencies. Think of the strange assimilations of popular zoology or physiology, or, for example, of the characteristics really perceived—I am speaking of sensory perception—in a quantity of diverse insects by an outsider on the one hand and an entomologist on the other. No doubt that the perception of the entomologist will be more precise and more detailed, because he has a larger number of better defined prototypes at his mental disposition. We shall see, however, that this advantage has to be paid for.

And as to psychological facts ? Are there any more elusive, more unattainable in their concrete reality ? First, as to those that occur in ourselves. Fundamentally speaking, in each of us, at every instant a single complete psychological fact unfolds itself. I mean that total attitude in which is gathered up all the polymorphic elements, both conscious and unconscious, of our minds: representations, feelings, wishes, actions, tendencies, etc. It is a difficult task to isolate any particular one of these elements in order to define and study it alone; those who have attempted the labour of systematic introspection for some definite purpose will tell us how partial is their success and what ingenious artifices represent the price they have had to pay for it. Nay, more, certain groups of complementary psychological elements never reach the threshold of consciousness dissociated: how, for instance, can we isolate pure sensation, spatial and temporal synthesis, apperception whatever be the idea we form of it ? The study of such elements is based not on objective dissociation, but on a gradually increasing abstraction.

9

STUDIES IN THE PSYCHOLOGY OF THE MYSTICS

If the psychologist—who is not a solipsist by vocation—passes from the observation of his personal states of consciousness to the psychological phenomena of his neighbours, he comes up against increasing difficulties. Ultimately, the physical, physiognomic, or verbal indications which he obtains from his patients are not psychological facts, but very inadequate signs of psychological states, in themselves purely personal and incommunicable. And since this very incomplete signalling system gets all its signification-value from its relations with the personal psychology of the signaller, it is not so very certain that the same somatic indication or the same expressed symbol really covers precisely the same internal fact in the observer and in the subject. The incertitude resulting from this, unimportant for the banal series of the more common psychological states, will increase with the complexity and the relative rarity of the phenomena being studied.

(b) Quantitative Indetermination.

A quantitative indetermination runs parallel to this qualitative indetermination of the facts of observation. A number of phenomena, principally in biology and psychology, are *de facto*, if not *de jure*, irreducible to measurement. And yet it would be easy to show that the ideal, legitimate or not, of scientific knowledge is the rigorous determination of each phenomenon in terms of space and time—in other words, the transposition of qualitative differences into quantitative relations. Every purely qualitative law is an approximative law. On the other hand, the most exact quantitative laws, apart from the fact that they always remain partially qualitative, themselves rest on approximate measurements: particular observations have always to be " corrected " by a certain amount, however small, in order to enter the curve which expresses the law. Now this correction, which works satisfactorily in physical laws, assumes in the attempts at measurement and statistics made in psychology a disquieting importance. I am not criticising the procedure: it is inevitable, but neither do I wish to forget how much latitude is left to the observer in the selection of his curve-type and his principle of correction by this numerical incertitude. We have seen that the facts of experience are partially constructed, incompletely generalised, often altered, and both qualitatively and quantitatively corrected. Must we not add—as daily observation shows us— that many events which affect our senses pass unperceived by us, and that several " perceived " facts are eliminated, considered as not having occurred, kept apart from our personal science ? . . . and this reflexion invites us to the examination of the particular conditions of the " scientific fact."

(c) Inchoative Interpretation.

The " scientific fact " is not the same as the " vulgar fact." Or, rather, this important proposition is badly stated: there is no such thing as a " vulgar fact " which can be opposed to a " scientific fact," because *every fact of human experience is at least rudimentarily scientific.* What does this mean ? That every fact from the moment of its perception attaches itself in our minds to some concept which exceeds it. In different degrees, and, above all, under different forms, every man from the crassest savage to the most subtle philosopher forms a certain conception of things: he admits possibilities, impossibilities, likenesses, types, standards, etc., in which his further experiences will have to find their place. No observer is without " prejudices," and no one ever allows " the facts to speak for themselves " purely and simply, it being indeed the nature of facts to be mute. What is true of all experience is if possible still more true of so-called " scientific " experience: a fact only becomes scientific in so far as it shows itself intelligible, logically classifiable in so far as it will cohere with the master lines of the whole edifice of the sciences. If the " new fact " does not at once appear co-ordinated with passed experiences and capable of subsumption under acquired categories, it will either pass almost unperceived, or it will be held, until fresh discovery is made, as unacceptable, suspect, doubtful, badly analysed, incomplete, etc. If it be strong enough and obstinate enough to cross the threshold of consciousness, it will perhaps force the barrier of hostile associations, but sometimes at the cost of compromises, and in doing so it will close a new barrier of prejudices against its further advance. No matter that these prejudices have their usefulness and even indirectly in a great measure protect the objectivity of scientific experience; it is, nevertheless, the fact—I am making here another point—that the fact of observation is only accepted as a " scientific fact " under their control.

Now in every science the scale of general principles—of " prejudices "—extends by a gradual degradation of tone from intangible axioms to changeable and provisional hypotheses; who can say in the concrete case, in this or that particular science, where the dividing line of these two groups passes ? The recalcitrant fact may be able to force its acceptance in spite of this or that hypothesis of detail; will it do so if it happens to collide with one of those customary views which habit has erected into an axiom ? What, indeed, will be its fate if it contradicts one of the most fundamental postulates of science ?

Let us illustrate this by some examples. Harmless instances of the eliminating influence of theory on observation are well known to those who have engaged in some special branch of scientific research. Here, for instance, is a biologist occupied in the reconstitution of a series of stages of cellular evolution. The objects of his observation are there before him juxtaposed in space; his problem is to discover, by the analysis of their internal structure, their chronological filiation. How often will he not pass by, without noticing it, some aspect of the object in no way suggested by his plan of observation, his " preconceived idea " ? Should some theoretical view occur to his mind which gives a meaning to such an aspect, he will not fail to see it at the first glance. Otherwise a structural peculiarity, to which his attention is nevertheless drawn, will be considered as accidental, non-significant, in short practically " eliminated," and occasionally the event will show that this aspect appeared negligible solely because it was misunderstood. This happens every day in various departments of science. Looking at the matter from a more general point of view, would one dare to say that such principles—be they true or false—as the fixity or the evolution of organic species, the necessity or the impossibility of spontaneous generation, the chemical law of definite proportions, the conservation of energy, the absolute determinism of empiric causation—have never influenced the actual observation of facts ? To maintain it would be as much a psychological heresy as an historical blunder. For nothing is easier than to detect such an influence even to-day in the perplexity, for example—to take obvious instances—in which the reality of metapsychical phenomena, not yet integrated in the body of science, leaves most psychologists and doctors; or in the sacrifice of historical testimony to which a too narrow criticism resigns itself in virtue of the principle of the elimination of the supernatural, or again in the smiling *a priori* incredulity with which certain savants, in other respects conscientious men, receive the mere occurrence of various marvellous and scientifically inexplicable facts, such as several of the miracles at Lourdes.

Why these misunderstandings and hesitations if not because there are no bare facts imposing themselves in their materiality as such at the base of science: if not because the fact enters science already big with its anticipated interpretation ? The part played by anticipated interpretation, as much as that played by indetermination which we have already noted, takes on an altogether special importance in psychology; for, on the one hand, psychology only lends itself with a bad grace, and very incompletely, to experimentation which, by turning a fact round in every direction, enables us to isolate it methodically; while, on the other hand, psychology touches more closely than other sciences certain intimate interests the consideration of which can hardly leave us impartial. It must also be said, without ambiguity, that with reference even to primordial facts the unanimity of professional psychologists will remain for a long time yet a pious and platonic desire: nothing is so equivocal, if you look closely at them, as such ordinary expressions as " consciousness," " sensation," " perception," " apperception," " forms of space and time," " intellectual abstraction," " idea," " volition," " feeling," " consciousness of action," " consciousness of liberty," and so on. If anyone thinks I exaggerate, I would beg him, in the interest of the progress of psychology, to solve immediately these two little problems: first, to extract the precise and universally accepted meaning of the above-mentioned terms and several others; secondly, to point out exactly the empirical elements which they indicate in the eyes of all.

(d) The Psychological Principle of the Above-Mentioned Particulars.

In the meanwhile, to resume the preceding pages, let us recall the first principle of this manifold influence of the form and the content of the spirit on the observation and principally on the scientific observation of facts. For a long time the fact has been noted—*scientia non est individuorum :* the pure individual as such is not the object of science. Perhaps I may be allowed to develop a little the meaning of this axiom.

In the intuition of the senses—the sole source of the diversity of our knowledge—the Ego and the non-Ego are equally concerned, and, one might say, mingled; the contact between the sensible object and the experiencing subject who models himself upon it is effected without medium, disjunction, or reflection. At this first moment of direct communion, the collaboration of the Ego and the non-Ego reaches its maximum of unity; knowledge is strictly concrete and individual. Such as it is, however, it cannot become more conscious and luminous than the nature of our sensibility permits. The Sense, not being a metaphysical faculty, knows neither subject nor object; it is relative, not absolute. Indeed, the first moment of the direct contact of object and subject in pure sensation still involves, from the point of view of knowledge, the non-distinction of the Ego and the non-Ego: their mutual relation—or, if you like, their common form—only emerges at the moment of the completion of that contact.

How can sensation penetrate into the clear consciousness and straightway manifest itself there as an object capable of being opposed to the subjectivity which knows it ? It is thanks to the synthetic activity of the intelligence that the sense-datum becomes an " object in itself " in a *concept*. For in the terms of the old scholastic adage, precisely those which make the datum an " object in itself "—*being, substance, quality, accident*, etc., are *sensibilia per accidens*—are not themselves objects of the senses, but of another faculty co-ordinated with the sensibility.

Let us now reflect on the presuppositions involved in the subsumption of the datum under a concept. The form of every concept is one of the general modes under which the empirical data are unified with reference to being. This unification is effected gradually with an increasing precision, through the scale of categories and by reducing the phenomena to imaginative schemes—that is to say, according to the rules of the constructive synthesis of the intimate sense, which are, as it were, the phenomenal linings of the categories.

The first plenary and complex—though obscure—contact with the real in sensation, gives place then, not only to a simple generalisation, but to an analysis, a breaking up, a progressive regrouping of the phenomena which were first experienced confusedly as an *ensemble*. In proportion as they affirm and define themselves as objects, they isolate themselves from each other, scattering all the originality concentrated in the intuition in which they first appeared; and not only do they isolate themselves, but they necessarily enter into new combinations and allow themselves to be captured by preconceived systematisations which form the armament that the spirit has contrived for itself. For sense data only penetrate clear consciousness as objects in so far as they are referred all at once, both to the fundamental permanent unity and to the actual empirical co-ordination of the consciousness. The formal and progressive objectivation of the data, or, if you prefer, the emergence of the non-Ego from the non-distinction of pure sensibility, is effected under the increasing influence of the intellectual activity, both analytical and constructive, of the knowing subject.

2. THE LAWS OF INDUCTION

(a) *Their Arbitrary Element.*

The material fact (*le fait brut*) presents no interest for science, unless it is susceptible of generalisation in the form of a law: the formulation of laws is the immediate business of the empirical sciences. Now, these laws are of two kinds: some express the constancy of certain groupings of characteristics, others the regular succession of various phenomena: the former are, on the whole, static; the latter, on the whole, dynamic. I say, " on the whole," because there is no adequate or irreducible distinction between these two groups of laws. In any case, they are found mingled together almost everywhere; for, ordinarily speaking, natural laws do not express a relation of sequence between one elementary phenomenon and another equally elementary, but rather a relation between an already complex *ensemble* of phenomenal conditions (pressure, temperature, magnetic state, etc.), and an object, that is to say from the empirical point of view, a grouping of manifold phenomena (a gas, a solid, a chemical composition, etc.). This more or less stable, more or less complex, grouping obtains recognition through a small number of distinctive characteristics which guarantee the presence of their associates.

This is the point at which the possibility of an arbitrary element is introduced into the construction of empirical laws. Such a possibility would be excluded if laws expressed nothing but elementary relations and immediate sequences. But even in the study of the inorganic world so complete an analysis of the elements involved is far from having been made. Analysis is still less advanced in biology, where the relations being more complex, the danger of self-deception on the meaning of certain coincidences and of erroneous generalisation from fortuitous juxtapositions is increased. Examples of such a misadventure are numerous. And in psychology where the same reason is *a fortiori* stronger, the danger increases.

But it will be said that the cause of error just indicated is, after all, but accidental and is derived rather from the imprudence of savants than from the postulates of science. Perhaps; with this corrective, and it is no negligible one, ·that it is precisely in the evitable processes of empirical knowledge that the imprudence of savants finds the gap which is its point of insertion. But inasmuch as our subject brings us to the point, let us examine the rôle and the value of the methodological postulate which all experimental science admits in the most formal way.

(b) The Postulate of Empirical Determinism.

1. *The Notion of Empirical Determinism.*—Determinism is the most fundamental postulate of all empirical science, for, without it, no generalisation is possible. It is necessary to understand exactly what it means.

Is determinism—as a postulate of science—merely a corollary of the principle of metaphysical causality ?

No. The principle of causality is absolute and allows no exception: every being must have its adequate justification from the point of view of the intelligence: if it is not fully intelligible in itself, it must find its complement of intelligibility in its causes, free or unfree; the relation of the effect to its cause is necessary and measured without any possibility of error by its definitely determined deficiency of being.

The principle of empirical determinism does not carry so far; its application is limited to the phenomenal world; it posits the invariability of the relation of concomitance or sequence between any given antecedent and its consequent. But this invariability does not by itself bear the character of *metaphysical necessity*, because the relation of two phenomena, even if it be constant, has nothing intelligible in it: the most diverse spatial and temporal combinations of phenomena can be equally well " conceived." And if the constancy of one or other such combination should invest it to our eyes with the characteristic of necessity, properly so called, the reason of this is not the phenomenal relation itself, but the coincidence, which would then be admitted, of that phenomenal relation with an ontological relation of causality. It should, however, be observed that to found the determinism of phenomenal relations on the presumption of a strictly corresponding delimitation of onto-logical relations is not only to base a possibly acceptable postulate on a certainly inexact supposition, but at the same time to open a large breach in experimental determinism itself; for the same metaphysic which would guarantee in certain cases the invariability of phenomenal associations by supposing them to be struck off, so to speak, by so many relations of ontological causality, on the other hand and with no less energy proclaims that identical combinations of phenomena may depend on many diverse ontological causes, among which free causes must also be counted.

The determinism of empirical causality cannot then bear the character of absolute and universal necessity, except at the price of an hypothesis not only unverifiable *de jure* and *de facto*, but even, as we shall see further on, intrinsically self-contradictory.

2. *The Contingency of Natural Laws.*—Will it be said that I am here following the thesis of M. Boutroux on the contingency of natural laws ? Certainly, there would be nothing in such an affiliation to displease me, if only I were sure of being rightly understood. In that case, indeed, I might blazon more ancient ancestors. Whatever may be the case, it would be difficult to contest the fact that wherever *internal finality* is perceived, a purely empirical determinism is transcended: the mutual relation of antecedent and consequent phenomena—analytic elements extrinsically grouped together—does not adequately express in an object its real profound activity, orientated as a whole, and organically one. Even in a case in which this profound activity is itself entirely determined by its relations to certain conditions, these conditions are not integrally represented by the formula of the corresponding empirical co-ordinations; and it is further necessary to distinguish the *experimental determinism*, or the invariability of phenomenal connexions, from the ontological determinism, which is causation properly so called, and depends on wider conditions.

These two determinisms are not, indeed, unconnected with each other: the former mimics the latter, and from the point of view of one looking at experience as a whole, tends to rejoin it. But, nevertheless, it remains true that the former is originally a methodological postulate and that, in any particular case, its coincidence with the latter is far from being guaranteed. Thus it is that, to my mind, a certain *alea*, a certain indetermination, or, if you like, a certain " contingency," always affects those empirical relations that we call natural laws.

Understood in this way, the " contingency " of natural laws will no doubt become accentuated in proportion as the internal finality or the total activity of an object emancipates itself from each of the empirical relations which it dominates, or, in other terms, in proportion to the growing complexity of the phenomena, the grouping of which betrays an active ontological unity. Less evident in the inorganic world, internal finality imposes itself—at least as a problem—in the study of the organic world. No doubt, many biologists imagine that they succeed in reducing it to a complicated intricacy of empirical, purely phenomenal relations identical with those which express the inorganic world; but such a " mechanicism " is neither an axiom nor an experimental deduction; it is purely and simply a theoretical hypothesis to which we will return later on. Other biologists, on the contrary, recognise in the living being harmonies and regulations which explode the too rigid shell of purely inorganic co-ordinations. Is not this merely to say, in other words, that the experimental determinism of inorganic phenomena does not apply to the phenomena—in appearance absolutely similar—which are developed in the living being ? Yet this relative suppleness of biological events remains compatible, if not with experimental determinism understood in a narrow sense, at least with ontological determinism: if our " phenomenal laws " become less precise when applied to vegetative being, in it there nevertheless exists, from the point of view of objective causalities, a veritable option between diverse possibilities.

But what is to be said of psychology, where it appears more and more clearly that the very complex synthesis of phenomena is not reached by the co-ordination of the lower elements involved, that is to say as the result of the mutual reactions of elementary phenomena, but rather " from the top," that is to say, under a formal influence which dominates and orientates the phenomena and which is no mere additional factor ? What can the absolute determinism of phenomena mean in this case ?

In proportion as mental organisation perfects itself, each element is increasingly subjected in its appearance, situation, and development to the heterogeneous influence of the *ensemble ;* and to the same extent it escapes the narrow determinism which would otherwise bind it to its neighbours. Every psychologist who recognises the indigency and insufficiency of pure associationism necessarily adopts the point of view which I have just indicated. The thesis would be still more evident—though more contested—if I rested it on the psychology of free will: a free option escapes at some point or other not only phenomenal but also ontological determinism.

3. *Determinism and Prevision.*—We may admit with Ostwald that the value of scientific generalisations is closely bound up with the previsions they permit. For in what does the generalisation of an empirical relation consist if not in raising it above temporal contingencies and thus transforming it into an anticipated vision of the future? Now it should be noted that prevision becomes less precise and less certain as one advances from the physical to the biological sciences and to psychology. Why is this? Is it only because the complexity of the phenomena often prevents us in biology and psychology from making an analysis sufficiently close to justify the formulation of true laws? Some savants hold this view. I think that this increasing imprecision has a profounder cause: the reason is that in biology and more particularly in psychology, as we have said, the partial antecedents and consequents made use of in the elaboration of laws become more and more the products of methodic abstraction; corresponding less and less to the ontological factors really in operation, they find themselves exposed in their *liaisons* to an increasing indetermination.

4. *The Legitimacy of the Postulate of Determinism.*—And yet the determinism of empirical laws is the necessary condition of the possibility of science, because every generalisation must necessarily be based on the invariability of certain relations. To abandon the postulate of determinism in relation to a particular order of objects is, for science, to proclaim its incompetence in the new field, and to limit itself by an impassable barrier. Is there not here some strange anomaly, and, if our preceding remarks on the insufficiency of determinism as applied to the whole of empirical knowledge are exact, does there remain for science no alternative but that of suicide or falsehood? Such a question rests on a very grave—and, unfortunately, very frequent—confusion of ideas, a confusion which we endeavoured to dissipate in the first pages of this study: people wrongly suppose that empirical science furnishes an intensively complete knowledge of the " real," when, as a matter of fact, it belongs entirely to the level of the " phenomenon " and only attains the aspect of the " real " which is relative to the knowing subject; in order to attain the " real "

as an object in itself, it is necessary to proceed further, with the collaboration of the adjoining sciences and of metaphysics, to a reconstruction which is, properly speaking, the task of " natural philosophy." I do not wish to insist on the difficulties which surround this task of synthesisation or on the very severe critical sense which should preside over it, and it would be discourteous to dwell on the very rudimentary " natural philosophy " professed by several savants who appeal to the " positive spirit "—men in whose eyes the secular effort of philosophical criticism remains non-existent.

Briefly, when we are dealing with theories, we will enquire how the sciences are built up, each with its own proper method, on the common base of determinism. Here let us merely note that the determinism which they postulate is not confined, in order to justify itself, to the exact and integral expression of the objective relations of phenomena: it is justified as a method as long as it suffices for practice. For, if the sciences unquestionably present in their conjunction with philosophy a speculative interest, and if they present us with at least an aspect of the real co-ordinated in their own fashion, it nevertheless appears that their immediate function is rather of the pragmatist order; they construct schemes of action, models of further experiences, which may " succeed " without on that account being perfect imprints of the ontological order.

There is, however, a certain relation between their success and their truth. The maximum of success—that is, of possible prevision—will no doubt correspond to a maximum of complete ontological value and to a maximum approximation to a true determinism. There is, then, nothing astonishing in the fact that the less " pragmatist " sciences like biology or psychology, in which the brutal and decisive control of experimental failure is often wanting, should also be those in which the speculative value of the postulated determinism appears more disputable.

Empirical determinism is much more an instrument of action than a part of philosophic speculation. Necessary from the point of view of method, it becomes not only arbitrary but often erroneous as soon as one endeavours to make it the expression of an ontological determinism. Indeed, its real bearing will be much more exactly appreciated by means of a rapid consideration of the place of " theory " in the constitution of science. Some repetitions must be excused; they are inevitable in an exposition the whole development of which moves round a single idea.

SCIENCE AND PSYCHOLOGY

3. SCIENTIFIC THEORY

(a) Theory in the Observation of Facts.

Man never behaves like an inert receiver before the exterior world which is offered to his investigation. From the moment of his first conscious contact with reality, he analyses and selects. The senses and the intelligence cut out and isolate phenomena, disengage relations, seize or create characteristic aspects in an objectively individual unity. And all this dissection, we have seen, operates in such a way as to reduce to the largest possible extent the originality of the object perceived into a sum of more modest elements already known and classed.

The procedure of "theory," less directly objective, thus insinuates itself into this first stage of scientific observation. The partial aspects of the object isolated from each other, and the system of relations stretched between them by the observer, do not necessarily correspond to the ontological elements existing in the object or to really distinct physical relations in it. The antecedent and consequent phenomena—the first scientific material to be erected—depend from the first for their delimitation and their definition on the subject as much as on the object, the latter being dismembered under the earliest pressure of the understanding which impresses the lines which its dislocation is to follow. But there is more: the object thus analysed is resynthesised by the man of science who has to consider it as a whole. And how is this reconstruction effected ? By the reintegration of the analytic elements, the partial phenomena in the profound unity from which they have issued ? No; this would be a task for a philosopher. The savant substitutes for the undivided unity of the object the frail and purely external system of phenomena and their perceived connexions. He replaces an intimate but polymorphous unity by an external but co-ordinated multiplicity. All the "objects" of empirical science are the products of synthesis by co-ordination.

(b) The Fundamental Process of the Theory.

Always, *au fond*, this process consists in a double inverse movement: the reduction of an ontological unity to a multiplicity of phenomena, followed by an intense effort to reach again the original unity by the mere co-ordination of these phenomena. An illusory effort, for unity of co-ordination is of a different nature to ontological unity which is its limit. Let reality be represented by a curve; the effort of empirical science to seize it adequately may be figured by a polygon approaching as its sides are multiplied nearer and nearer the curve, which remains inaccessible. Scientific theory is then essentially an approximate reconstruction of reality from outside, at the phenomenal level. But the elements employed as materials of reconstruction may be of very unequal value. And this point must now be considered a little more closely.

(c) Theory in the Induction of Laws.

In the simplest case—in which the part played by theory is reduced as much as possible—science limits itself to the substitution for the object, of the phenomenal outline presented by the object to direct observation. As such, however, the object remains an individual object: how can it, then, become an object of " science " ?

Evidently by stripping itself of everything in itself which is purely concrete and bound up with the present moment, retaining only what is general and hangs motionless above the stream of time. This general and stable content of the object is the *law* of its constitution and reactions. The *ensemble* of the phenomena and empirical relations characterising such and such an object will therefore pass from the concrete to the abstract—that is, will be conceived as identically realisable at any point whatever of space and any moment whatever of duration; now, this generalisation naturally cannot be made except by the sacrifice of certain descriptive particulars of the individual object, for if anything is certain, we may be sure that never are any two phenomena, however similar they may be, totally identical: even if the object remains inert and suffers no qualitative variation in the course of its duration, repeating itself identically in other exemplars, the subject, on the other hand, has necessarily become modified by living, for the subject is physically enriched by its incessantly growing past; consequently the phenomenon which is the limit of an object and a subject cannot have an absolutely similar replica. On this scarcely contestable point I may defer to the masterly and decisive demonstration of M. Bergson. The constitution of abstract types by the elaboration of individual phenomenal complexes marks, then, a second stage of the invasion, so to speak, of science by theory; this stage, moreover, is not in practice unconnected with the further stages. What are they?

(d) Theory in Further Generalisations.

Let us first observe that these further generalisations are but the logical development of the initial process—generalisation by the gradual reduction of qualitative differences. The first which had to be eliminated were those belonging to the diversity of individuals or individual reactions. Thus we were able to constitute, each under its general type, the first groupings of individuals. But from grouping to grouping, from general type to general type, qualitative difference continued to persist. How force this second line of defence of ontological originality and reduce it as well to the rule of a levelling determinism?

In the world of quantitative objects resemblances exist at different levels in different and manifold degrees: even at the extreme point of unlikeness, there still persists a common value of " quantity " with its relation to space and time. Empirical science, in its work of generalisation and of the extension of determinism, utilises these likenesses and this fundamental common value. Science will disaggregate the type—static or dynamic—into simpler elements, in such a way as to establish partial equivalences from one type to another. These simpler elements disaggregated from the *ensemble*—types of which they were but aspects—become in their turn the support of generalised relations. In the same way as individuals had been reduced to the condition of " particular cases " of the species, species themselves or more general types were brought back as far as possible to simple defined combinations of simpler elements, themselves obeying their own laws. At this stage causal determinism becomes interspecific and already holds in its vice the universality of phenomena. The goal and the term of this generalising analysis, followed by resynthesis, is indicated by Newton, in a celebrated passage, as belonging to the efforts of what he called " experimental philosophy ": it consists in discovering in the organised diversity with which the world presents us the *causas generalissimas*[5]—that is to say, the most simple and most general antecedents; or, in other words, those phenomenal aspects which are the most inseparable from *every* physical reality. The law of universal attraction seemed to him to express, with reference to material phenomena, one of these *causæ simplicissimæ*.

It is easy to see what is the "limit" to which the procedure we have sketched tends, and consequently what also is the theoretic ideal of empirical science: it is to push to the end the reduction of qualitative differences and to define each of them, from the humblest to the greatest, as a particular combination of purely quantitative elements, as a collection of material points and elementary movements, totally and exclusively determined with reference to space and time. In this way the theory would make use of the last and irreducible similarities, and the explanation of the world by empirical determinism would be complete. Evidently this limit is inaccessible in the same way as a mathematical "limit," and its ideal as defined is self-contradictory, for no one will ever be able to make the heterogeneous out of the homogeneous, the qualitative with the quantitative. But this impossible goal is nevertheless in the logic of the procedure, and aptly characterises its tendency. It shows why science, in proportion to its progress, tends to take a mathematical form, and also why mechanism seems to so many savants to be the only possible form of scientific theory. There is nothing in this theory but what is perfectly clear and entirely consequent. It remains to be seen whether reality can be fitted to it.

(e) The Theory and Reality. Its " de facto " and " de jure " Insufficiency.

No doubt that experimental reality fits in well enough in the domain of the physical sciences with the first degrees of the theoretical reconstruction which has just been described: here the transposition of the " real " into the " phenomenon " is as faithful as it can be and wears the prestige of " success." It is no longer quite the same when we reach the ultimate generalisations of the inorganic world; everyone knows the partial, relative, symbolic rather than ontological value of the great theories on the constitution and the fundamental reactions of matter: chemical atomism, Newtonian physics, electromagnetic theories; the experimental control of such syntheses as these in which induction is more and more giving place to hypothesis is too limited ever to become decisive. As H. Poincaré has rightly observed, the most opposed conceptions can, with a little complication more or less, in these cases become the bases of various but equally verified hypotheses.

In spite of everything, as long as we are concerned with

inert matter only, the insufficiencies and fluctuations of theory may perhaps be due solely to our ignorance of certain phenomena, to the far too incomplete analysis of antecedents which we formulate. But the method would be at least adequate to the purpose of human knowledge, and the empirical science of mere matter once complete would give us a very faithful image of this inferior order of realities; empirical determinism would, in the measure of its own perfection, approach causal, ontological determinism. Let us admit this, with this reserve however, that if qualitative differences exist in the inorganic world, empirical determinism is related to ontological determinism, in the same way as a variable is related to its limit, and not as a continuous achievement is related to its maximum term. But, as we have already insinuated, the cause of empirical determinism, and consequently the value of empirical theories, becomes infinitely more disputable in the domain of organic life where reigns an " internal finality," properly so called. How is the relation of this internal finality to theoretic determinism to be characterised ? One feature of the relation is enough for my purpose: organic finality with reference to phenomenal connexions is not a resultant, but, if one may say so, a " dominant." No doubt all the phenomena observed in the living being, each of them being taken in isolation, can be reduced to the phenomenological forms of the inorganic world; but, on the other hand, their associations, their combinations, if partially obedient to physico-chemical laws, seem always to escape them, if considered as a totality. This point may be reinforced by making use of the very penetrating analysis of the experimental characteristics of life that we owe to Hans Driesch, and we may remark that this irreducibility of vital manifestations affects precisely that very fundamental relation which, according to the determinist postulate, obtains between all phenomenal connections and space: in the living being, the geometrical ideal of determinism becomes evidently chimerical, since the most decisive characteristic of life is that the phenomena which it dominates are not totally predetermined with reference to space. I refer the reader to the well-known works of the eminent biologist-philosopher, and conclude that from the vitalist point of view, which I hold to be the true one, there cannot be an *integral* empiric science of life. Empirical theories explanatory of life, however useful they may be in other ways, remain affected by a radical insufficiency, an insufficiency not only *de facto*, but also *de jure*.

Let us mount a stage higher and consider psychological facts, the objects of internal observation. They reveal on analysis, side by side with the material element: the phenomena of the sensibility, a purely formal element: the intellectual synthesis of those phenomena. We may here consider the sensible phenomena as the elementary material of psychology, more or less analogously to the way in which inorganic phenomena constitute the primordial data of other positive sciences. That being understood, can one venture to say that these sensible phenomena are subject, like the others, to empirical determinism, and bound together by experimental laws in such a way that their pretended " intellectual synthesis " can be simply reduced to their resultant co-ordination ? To admit this is to admit the legitimacy of the most exclusive psychological associationism: a passive associationism founded on a purely physical causality. Now it is well known that many psychologists to-day are repelled by so narrow a mechanism and feel disinclined to throw overboard, in spite of their internal experience, the directing activity of the spirit and the efficacity of volition. But what is the alternative ? To admit that the principle of co-ordination of phenomena is in the mental order analogous to what it is in the biological order: a dominant and not a resultant.

There exists, moreover, between these two orders an essential difference. The purpose or the norm of biological co-ordination is a reality which can be empirically defined, a concrete " type " accessible when realised to direct observation: on the contrary, the ultimate term which defines the finality of psychology, the unifying purpose of the spirit escapes all phenomenal verification: it is transcendent: being no less than the complete integration of the spirit in Being. Such a goal can only be translated into empirical language by the term " becoming," by the movement which causes it to progress —*i.e.*, by the progressive co-ordination of the spirit gathering up the diversity of its content under the concept of the never attained unity of Being pure and simple. To propose to reduce this ideal of unity to phenomenal terms is exactly the same thing as to wish to exhaust the concept of Being by successive additions.

Thus mental synthesis is constantly performed under an influence which essentially escapes the forms of experimental determinism. What value, then, can be attributed to the psychological theories which postulate these forms ? If we consider them as hypothetical reconstructions of the spirit and symbols of its real constitution, they have no doubt a certain value; but they would be harmful if they duped us into objectifying them without preliminary criticism.

4. ABSTRACT SCIENCE AND EXPERIENCED SCIENCE

We have now critically reviewed the most fundamental conditions of the constitution of an empirical science considered in the abstract. But is such a science the " Science," concrete and living, which our contemporaries place on the pinnacle of their thought ? Apart from a few prudent and critical minds, most of the champions of " Science " understand by that word, not the careful application of the empirical method and the determinist postulate to the co-ordination of the relative aspect of the real, but the extension of that method to the total explanation of experience. Science thus becomes a way to " think the world," a *Weltanschauung*, a philosophy of which the fundamental axiom is the transposition of a methodological artifice into a necessity of things, of a partial point of view into an integral reality. Dare to opine that the " real " slips through the fictitious frames of determinism; that while it is always possible in theory to assign determined antecedents to any isolated phenomena, it is, nevertheless, equally impossible to build to the top an empirical theory of experience or " to make a curve with straight lines "; and that, consequently, empirical science not being self-sufficient, it were wise to remember sometimes that it has its natural frontiers, the tracing of which depends on other mental disciplines. Dare to maintain this at the bar of that " Scientism," conscious or unconscious, which while it has gone out of fashion with philosophers remains still so widely spread in other circles, there is a considerable chance that your judges will deny you the " scientific " spirit, because you do not admit beforehand with closed eyes the most arbitrary extensions of " scientific method." Let us frankly admit that in these circumstances, in spite of the sincerest desire for a sympathetic understanding, we must repeat: *Amicus Plato sed magis amica veritas*.

But, it may be objected, does not the limiting of the competence of the positive method risk by an opposite excess the arbitrary restriction of the domain of science ? In no way; for it no less remains the task of science in the eyes of all to extend as far as possible the empirical explanation of things;

we assign no limit to the inquirer's efforts, the phenomenal image of reality being in itself indefinitely perfectible. We only refuse to admit the adequation of reality and the phenomenon, and also, even on the phenomenal plan, of the one and original fact with the mechanism or the combination of factors, often indigent and pale, which scientific theory substitutes for it.

III. RELIGIOUS PSYCHOLOGY AS EMPIRICAL SCIENCE

We can now approach directly the question that has been our constant objective throughout the preceding pages: what are the conditions governing the constitution of religious psychology as an empirical science ?

A question of this kind, already delicate, as we have seen, in biology, still more delicate in ordinary psychology, becomes extremely difficult in religious psychology. Let us repeat that we are here considering principles alone, and that the technical examination of methods is reserved for further treatment.[6]

1. THE UNANALYSED FACTS (*Les Faits bruts*)

The *facts* of religious psychology are of a slightly special nature. It must, nevertheless, not be forgotten that the religious man or the mystic remains " human " even in his transcendental activity itself—*i.e.*, remains in continuity with the world of physical, biological, and psychological phenomena —to the laws and reactions of which he is up to a certain point subjected. The mystical state is escorted by an accompaniment of phenomena which have to be inserted, as well as can be done, in a pre-formed empirical framework. In a concrete case it will not be such an easy task to discover and appreciate at their right value such indisputable influences as temperament, climate, education, nationality, language, knowledge, mental habits, and so on. Religious psychology carries with it many difficulties which are common to it and the neighbouring sciences, but its special condition aggravates them still further. This is the fact which we have now to consider.

First of all, a religious phenomenon, if it sometimes closely resembles, apart of course from the difference of object, an ordinary psychological fact, presents when defined and intensified, exceptional, even abnormal, characteristics which tend to assimilate it to pathological facts. But this analogy, by which so many psychologising doctors have been duped, is purely superficial, for, on a closer examination, the strangest mystical phenomena appear to be co-ordinated under points of view which have nothing to do with delirium, and moreover prolong themselves in a very consecutive manner in practices and enterprises of high moral value most justifiable from the point of view of one who admits the fundamental truths of religion. We may add that the appearance of these strange phenomena is allied, more often than one may think, with a perfect psychological equilibrium, and on occasion with a most remarkable practical sense. Here, then, are facts (sudden conversions, illuminations, visions, ecstasies, clairvoyance, temptations, etc.) which do not easily enter our scientific framework, but whose classification, or maintenance outside classification, must depend on an analysis made in each particular case. It will be readily admitted that such an analysis will be easily influenced by preconceived opinions. The analysis, moreover, will be a still more delicate task if, when the whole fact is taken to pieces, it is found to contain certain definitely pathological elements: there is no doubt that many mystics suffered from a temperament nervous to the point of nervous disease and that, in consequence, their special states were bound to show traces of their physiological insufficiency. Did not Suarez admit that the failure of bodily strength in ecstasy was a mere physiological counterstroke quite distinct in itself from mystical grace ? The scope of this criticism would no doubt admit of extension. But to go from that to the application *en bloc* to mystics of the clinical *tableaux* of mental pathology is the same thing as to identify the analysis of a geologist with the separation of the elements of the soil effected by a gardener's spade. And in many cases the closest analysis will leave an abundant residue, impossible to classify medically. Another circumstance which aggravates the difficulty: the most characteristic religious or mystical facts escape experimentation. The observer finds himself reduced to their description and theoretical interpretation. And even when it is possible to outline by experimentation some secondary aspect of the fact, it remains very difficult to restore it to its true position in the *ensemble* of the mystical state observed. For example, the ecstasy which can be provoked in the hypnotic state, while it shows certain features resembling mystical ecstasy, differs from it completely on other points. Thus mystical phenomena *seem* to depend in the circumstances of their appearance on an influence which surpasses and dominates our known physiological and psychological laws.

Finally, the mere observation of religious facts, and particularly of mystical facts, is surrounded by very special difficulties. The essential in these facts is not the somatic phenomenology but the internal psychological state. It must also be added that very few psychologists have the opportunity of observing in satisfactory conditions even the external phenomena: in most cases they only know them by narrations, the tenor of which they have to criticise and the deficiencies of which they have to supply. But the internal facts? The mystic alone observes them directly: the psychologist works on statements. Suppose the auto-observation of the mystic well made and his testimony exact: this testimony—as we may judge from the writings of the great contemplatives themselves —is generally very incomplete, not only because it has not been written with the purpose of satisfying the curiosity of a psychologist, but principally because it is scarcely possible to describe completely an exceptional internal state. In daily life our descriptions are made up of suggestions which proceed to awaken in another intimate experiences analogous to our own. But mystical experience is not so banal that we are justified in presuming the psychologist to possess personal knowledge of states of this kind. Frequently, indeed, the psychologist is not himself gifted with a religious temperament. In such a case he will interpret the language of the mystic in the terms of reference of his own very limited experience, not to say of his own inexperience. He will have, with the personal materials at his disposition, to reconstruct the mystical fact before studying it, and this reconstruction will be partly conjectural, for what shades of meaning, what important features of the original may not escape him! And, frankly, even after a lengthy familiarity with the special literature of mysticism, in spite of knowledge of the technical value of expressions which puzzle the uninitiated reader, how often is one not reduced to suspend one's judgement and reserve one's interpretation! It is not so easy to know what the mystics say or wish to say.

But we have supposed that the written document is the exact direct expression of the writer's experience. Now it can hardly be said, in general, that these documents present objectively in their actual materiality the facts of internal observation: very often the facts described are facts already interpreted and classified in completely good faith. The mystic may have been mistaken as to the original fact; he may thus have substituted for the material fact the result of an immediate inference: the fact and its inchoative interpretation have, so to say, run together in his consciousness and reached it simultaneously; then, the fact to be described is of such a nature, that terms are lacking for its exact expression: the mystic supplies this insufficiency by an abundance of metaphors which give us a great deal more information on the affective state of the narrator than on the descriptive characteristics of the fact. Moreover, sometimes the mystic himself warns us not to take his metaphors too literally, and it is always a very delicate task to extract a precise meaning from them. It is evident that if the sincerity of the mystic is generally beyond doubt, this advantage is much less decisive on account of the multiplication of other chances of error.

2. Induction and the Theoretic Extension of the Determinist Postulate

To treat religious phenomena as " scientific facts " is, first of all, to undertake the task of *translating them into laws and of submitting them to an empirical determinism*. We have already sufficiently insisted in the preceding pages that this methodic operation falsifies the *real*, at least in biology and psychology, and therefore, at least to an equal extent, in religious psychology. But is it really certain that if the observer confines himself to a purely empirical point of view and has no intention whatever of defining " realities in themselves " it is possible legitimately to extend psychological determinism to the integrality of religious phenomena ? Are not these considered as simple phenomena irreducible on one side or another to the classification of natural common laws ?

Even the psychologist is permitted to remain perplexed before this question. Religious sentiment causes the psychological mechanism to act in such a special way and, on the other hand, the difficulty of disengaging in all its original sincerity the religious fact—a fact so intimate and so personal, so inexpressible and so unverifiable by experiment—is so great that we must doubtless renounce the hope of recognising in this matter even approximatively any particular determinism, nor can the " extrapolation " which would extend determinism to it be looked on as other than the most illegitimate and fallacious of inductions. The religious fact, more than any other, only enters science if interpreted, by the door of "theory." . . . But what shall this theory be ?

Has it been sufficiently observed how the religious fact, directly observed by the mystic and only reconstituted on testimony by the psychologist, is interpreted by the one and the other ? The direct observer, the mystic, interprets the phenomenon by partially withdrawing it from the purview of science, in virtue of a religious system neither contradicted nor affirmed by science, but in accordance with otherwise arguable metaphysical views; the psychologist, in his turn, reconstitutes and interprets it, making it an integral part of empirical science in virtue of a methodological postulate, the ultimate evaluation of which has nothing to do with science, but the absolute legitimacy of which would certainly be the contradiction of all metaphysics.

Interpretation for interpretation, which is the least irreproachable ? Both seek their inspiration and their criterion outside science, properly so called; only, while the criterion of the mystic *may* be true, that of the empirical psychologist is certainly false. Nor have we the resource of repeating here the scene from La Fontaine's fable of " The Oyster and the Litigants," and sending off both mystic and empirical psychologist, each with the shell of his personal appreciation, while reserving for ourselves the precious content of the pure and simple fact. The fact in this case, in so far as it is specifically religious ore, only enters our material of observation clinging to the inseparable alloy of an interpretation which either inserts it in empirical determinism or raises it above it.

But is not this to concede too much ? I hear the mystic protest. If he sometimes interprets, as he has the right to do, he nevertheless often claims to present in his written relations, immediate and objective observations. He does not deduce the transcendent character of his experiences—he touches, he has the intuition of it. . . . In the mystical union, it is the immediate contact of the Divinity, the direct vision of Being that he experiences. He distinguishes quite clearly between this culminating point and other visions—sensory, imaginative, symbolic visions which can be more easily handled by psychology; in union properly so called, the symbol vanishes, imagery fades, space disappears, multiplicity is reduced, reasoning is silent, the feeling of extension gathers itself together and then breaks down: intellectual activity is entirely concentrated in its intensity; it seizes without intermediary with the sovereign certitude of intuition, Being, God. That is what is being constantly repeated under different forms with more or less insistence on the affective accompaniment, with more numerous or fewer details on the phenomenal conditions of the preparatory phases, in the documents that come from the great contemplatives; from which it follows that it may, after all, be the case that the mystic really does experience . . . the Transcendental. Whom shall we believe ? The mystic murmuring his incommunicable experiences in a language incapable of their translation, but energetically affirming as a fact their transcendence ? Or the psychologist reduced to spelling out this language, the isolated sounds of which are perhaps known to him, but the antithetic contradictory form of which defying all empirical synthesis disconcerts or repels him ? A cruel alternative for the scientific spirit, for if the boldness of the mystic passes too far beyond our speculative timidities, how, on the other hand, repress a smile when the confusion of the psychologist, converted into a bourgeois daring, leads him to strip the mystic's descriptions of their transcendence so as to delimit as the object of his study a diminished state of prayer which he can better understand ? If the conflict here is not between science and truth, there is at least an acute conflict between two attitudes—which we suppose to be equally sincere: the charming spontaneity of an expansive devotion and the pedantic method of a simplifying scientism.

But may not " scientism " find its revenge elsewhere ? It does not cut a very good figure before the mystical union; what matters this inelegance (truth can dispense with elegance) if it drags after it marching to the step of determinism all the *other* so-called religious phenomena ?[7] We are not referring here to certain marvellous events, taken—rightly or wrongly— for miracles and attributed to the influence of this or that holy personage: these inexplicable facts, often well proved, have but an accidental relation with the religious or mystical life of the wonder-worker. The humbler phenomena of which we are here thinking are the direct and normal manifestations of sincere religious feeling: conversion to the faith and moral conversion; the special firmness of the adhesion to faith; constant purity of life, fidelity to a very elevated moral ideal, the interior touches of that " grace " of every moment, which makes the Good more luminous and sustains effort; the facility and attraction of prayer; the feeling of the nearness of the Divinity; serenity and force under trials; the specifically Christian humility of mind and heart—in short, the daily

C

religious life, imperfect with some, better organised and fuller with others, in certain cases still more penetrating and refined.

All these not strictly mystical phenomena in which the religious life manifests itself, may without contestation be described from the outside in empirical terms: the " types " of these phenomena enter without difficulty the moulds of psychological determinism. But here comes the difficulty. The psychologist, in order to arrange them in his categories, abstracts them from their actual sequence in the subject who experiences them, and strips them, no doubt quite unconsciously, of those fine shades which are invisible from outside, but which so strongly modify an internal state.

Now, how does the subject of these phenomena appreciate them ? His opinion may have some weight, and in any case deserves examination. We know that in these matters all religious men profess certain theoretical ideas which influence their appreciations: these appreciations will not, then, have a merely psychological value. Under this reserve, let us interrogate the subject on his spontaneous convictions. In so far as he lives an interior life of medium intensity he will tell us of his conviction of a constant compenetration of his action by the Divine action: this persuasion constitutes the greater part of his confidence in his moral future and of his firmness of conduct; when he prays he does not doubt, in practice, that God answers his prayer by the gift of more peace, light, and courage; when he acts, when he struggles to maintain his moral ideal, he believes himself to be leaning on a powerful arm which sustains him. Ask him, if you will, which of the two following hypotheses corresponds most completely to the *ensemble* of his internal experiences: the hypothesis of a supernatural action directing the whole of his intimate life and mingling itself with his own natural activity, or the hypothesis which would reduce this intimate life of his to be nothing but a mechanical combination of mental phenomena modified psychologically by the representation of a religious ideal. The reply is not doubtful; it may be read in the writings of the saints and of truly religious men; and the conviction which it expresses goes far beyond the exigencies of dogma on the subject of Grace.

From all this we wish to draw one conclusion only—namely, that not only the metempirical reality of the religious life, but even its phenomenology, the direct object of internal experience, may well be irreducible to psychological determinism.

34

In this case scientific method would have to admit a partial failure in the matter.

Once more, the dilemma is cruel for the psychologist: before the categorical affirmation of the transcendent character of mystical states and before the general conviction among those who live a Christian life of the active rôle played in their experience by Grace, what will he do ? It is his duty to observe from outside to the best of his ability and to endeavour to co-ordinate the observations he collects. Will he take literally the testimony of the only direct observers ? He can only do so at the cost of evading the categories of empirical science and determinism, of refusing to compute an empirical explanation of a given order of facts, of placing a limit to scientific method, and of recognising its radical insufficiency. On the other hand, shall he interpret the testimony he receives, shall he expurgate it, amputate it on the pretext of error or illusion ? By what right and in virtue of what principles ? And what further significance can belong to so mutilated a documentary basis ? Its value becomes subsidiary to that of the theories which have supplanted it.

3. The Attempts of Empirical Theory

Theories only ? No doubt; for there can be no question of opposing absolute " principles " to the observations or, if you will, the interpretations of mystics and religious souls. Empirical determinism, as we have sufficiently shown, is a method and not an unconditioned affirmation. All we are concerned with here is to know up to what point this method can be applied to specifically religious facts; and we have seen that it can in any case only be applied to them at the cost of a theoretical interpretation of the original documents. Let us now consider the principal theories concerned, and see whether, when weighed in the balance with mystical phenomenology, they will not seem to us too light.

The era of " medical " theories of the religious sentiment is virtually closed; let us hope, at least for the sake of the good taste of humanity, that it will not be reopened. The " bio-logical " theory—as he calls it—of Professor Leuba does not deserve to be confused with the preceding theories. The imagery adopted by this psychologist is no doubt biological; but under an appearance of " high-relief " and slightly brutal vigour, it manifests upon examination so deceptive a vagueness, that a professional biologist—may he be forgiven—can only see in it a poor parody of his methods. It is dangerous to play with words, the meaning of which, as soon as they are stretched beyond their proper subject, becomes analogical; and this is certainly the case with expressions like " Life," " Need," " Function," etc., when applied to the facts of mysticism. What can really be inferred from this analogy, if its law cannot be defined in empirical terms ? And to define it in theory is to prejudge the question. I can only truly conceive one *frankly* " biological " theory: it would establish equivalences between the phenomena of religion and those of vegetative life: Professor Leuba, if I understand him aright, tends as yet too timidly towards this ideal. If he feels he absolutely must wave the plume of biology, let him, since he wishes to remain logical, be in future less of a psychologist.

For a psychologist he is without contestation. He has done justice on more than one point to the mystics; and this relative perspicacity will always prevent his association with the Binet-Sanglés[8] of the past or the future. But his psychology, although it may have disengaged and translated into general formulas —formulas, however, which are partly contestable—the " fundamental tendencies of Christian mystics," appears to be without that fineness and certainty of touch which guarantee the object of observation from distortion. We do not know how Professor Leuba reads the mystics; but we shall not be alone in suspecting him of doing so through terribly simplifying spectacles when we hear him declare with reference to St Teresa, whom he proposes, and not without reason, as the most representative type of mystic, " that there is nothing in the life of the great Spanish mystic, not a desire, not a thought, not a sentiment, not a vision, not an illumination, which can lead one seriously to think of transcendent causes."[9] What ? Not even a problem for the psychologist ? The Professor has, then, all ready a completely satisfactory and adequate explanation of the whole moral and mystical life of the Saint ?

Let us see. He refers us himself to his articles in the *Revue Philosophique* (1902) and to M. Delacroix's last book. Let us leave M. Delacroix for the moment. What do we find in Professor Leuba's articles ? At the side of observations on the influence in the mystical life of certain biological and psycho-social tendencies, a meagre little theory of the higher mystical state characterised in his opinion by an acute impoverishment of the consciousness pushed in ecstasy to a complete absence of ideas (*aïdéisme*). Now, if there is a hypothesis contradicted by Christian mystical literature, it is certainly that of the absence of ideas: but in order to understand the mystics, it is necessary to read them integrally and not allow oneself to be hypnotised by a few formulas which occur only sporadically, and are unintelligible apart from their immediate or more distant context. Let us suppose, however, that Professor Leuba understands better than do the mystics themselves the characteristics of higher contemplation; in that case he should be able to explain to us in virtue of his theory the principal details of the contemplative illusion. A dissimulated absence of ideas (*aïdéisme*) interpreted by the mystic in a positive sense in virtue of his dogmatic or metaphysical prejudices; it is really too simple: and in order to be satisfied with such a theory, one must have a very vague idea of unitive contemplation, and have retained only the most abstract recollections of the mystics' writings. The explanation of Professor Leuba, as he proposes it, is manifestly insufficient and does not enjoy the slightest experimental probability. This is so, whatever be the " cause " and the " nature " of mystical states.

The fact remains that Professor Leuba, incapable of explaining these states by anything but a vague and unscientific hypothesis, cannot, we think, maintain that his attitude is dictated to him by a serious experimental probability: *au fond* his attitude is a-prioristic and has no foundation save the arbitrary principle of the unlimited jurisdiction of empirical determinism over the field of human experience. Moreover, he does not clearly draw in his writings the critical distinction between the phenomenal and the real.

Professor Leuba is hard on William James, whose religious psychology seems to him to lead to a " fiasco."[10] Perhaps it does, but we nevertheless find it superior to Professor Leuba's theory. Of James's Lectures on " Religious Experience " certain results will no doubt remain, such as the discredit thrown on a purely medical psychologism, and the feeling of the necessity of a more careful and more sympathetic study of the religious fact. As for the theory of the subliminal adapted from Myers which crowns James's studies, if it has the merit— for Professor Leuba it is a weakness—of leaving a door open to metaphysics and thus implicitly recognising the impossibility for empirical determinism of reaching the *fond* of the real, it is, from a scientific point of view, nothing but a rather vague hypothesis, more an interesting point of view than an instrument of methodical investigation. The subconscious of James complaisantly opens its vaults to all the explanatory elements that one may wish to bury in them so as to bring them out to the light of day at the convenient moment. Such a hypothesis necessarily adapts itself to the facts—it is so plastic: but it does not constitute what is called, in the strict sense, a scientific theory. It may perhaps become that when the uncertain zone of the subconscious has been completely defined and delimited. In the present state of affairs nothing is harder to define psychologically than a " subconscious element," and, as will be readily understood, no agreement reigns on this point between specialists who are keener about things themselves than about the fictitious unity of a word.

We have already said elsewhere all the good that we think of M. Delacroix's studies on mysticism. Their author conceives the mystical fact—and the religious fact, in general—in the forms of empirical determinism, abstraction made of all transcendence. He, moreover, does not confuse the problem of integral reality, which is a philosophical problem, with the problem of empirical, purely phenomenal, explanation, which is the proper theme of science. Only he retains the conviction that this (empirical) explanation may be as complete in religious psychology as it is in the other sciences of matter or spirit: neither more nor less; the religious phenomenon, if it is more complex, has no special privilege.

M. Delacroix has over Professor Leuba the advantage of justifying this point of view—in itself arbitrary—by a much more carefully studied and more delicate attempt at interpretation. Not only is his analysis of mystical facts finer and more careful, but the methods of theoretical synthesis which he employs have at least a preliminary justification in ordinary psychological experience. In his opinion the successive stages of the mystical life are connected together in each subject in conformity with an internal determinism, the mechanism of which is for a good part subconscious. But these stages, far from being phases of dissociation, of insanity, or impoverishment, are, on the contrary, noteworthy in the case of the great Christian mystics for a progressive enrichment of the consciousness and the personality. This enrichment occurs through a better co-ordination of ordinary psychological elements without the addition of specifically new experiences. This is, we think, M. Delacroix's view.

We cannot refrain from setting this recognition by M. Delacroix of a law of progress in the mystic side by side with the very interesting declaration which he made in a later communication to M. l'Abbé Pacheu:

" No doubt, I think that religion can be explained in a human manner like science or art: but I also think that the great works of man are penetrated and borne on by a spirit which surpasses each moment of humanity taken apart, and that thus there is in humanity a movement which surpasses it: this might be interpreted in a religious sense, but does not attach itself in my thought to any positive religion."[11]

Doubtless, this does not imply any religious faith, but it does imply the insufficiency of empirical determinism to express integrally essentially human phenomena, mystical and other. Determinism moves between equivalences of combination, and, pushed as far as it will go logically, can do no more than stereotype for each instant of duration a system of relative positions of defined elements: determinism is essentially immobilist, for, unobserved, it reduces successions to co-existences; the very passage from one state to the immediately following one escapes it.[12] Now time is surely a phenomenon of internal experiences, and psychologists know how easy it is to reduce it to terms of space.

But there is more: all duration is concrete; succession is not an empty figure of speech: it is the transition from one state to another state—it is an *orientated* succession. What does the determinism of natural laws teach us with reference to this transition and this orientation ? Nothing but the respective connection, at each instant, of the observed internal variations of the system under consideration. I know that if a particular point has varied, the system will have taken such and such a form; if another point has been displaced, the total equilibrium will have been modified in some other definite way. But which point will vary, and what will be the antecedent of the variation ? Determinism can only indicate this by treating my particular system as part of a more general system. Let us, then, consider at once the whole system, which theoretical determinism obliges us to consider as a " closed system "; why should it vary at any particular one of its points ? What is the natural law which gives me, as a particular instance of its operation, this determining variation ? From the point of view of empirical determinism, each element is at each instant in fixed relations with all the others: the system is rigid. If it becomes deformed, if the following moment differs from the preceding one, it is in virtue of " something else," of something which expresses itself in terms of human consciousness as " tendency " (*tendance*), and may be timidly translated by sucn dynamical expressions as: force, living force, actual or potential energy, etc. Here is a second phenomenon—qualitative variation in time—which is not totally explained by empirical determinism. Determinism explains still less the harmonious progress and the connected evolution of a system —that is, a system in which each partial development occurs in dependence on the totality of developments. Now the development of the mystical consciousness—we will willingly include the religious consciousness in general—is dominated in Christianity, at all events, by a teleology which overflows its particular phases. M. Delacroix admits this teleological disposition of the phenomena of the mystic's life and quotes in this connexion, without however making them his own, the very fine reflections of Maine de Biran, on the collaboration of the organic factors, of free activity and sovereign Grace. But to admit this teleology is to admit that the preceding moment has been not merely *replaced* but *surpassed* by the following moment, it is to disengage in the phenomenal co-ordinations which express mystical experience, a formal element, a mode of connexion, irreducible to empiric determinism; it is to discover in the relative and the phenomenon the negative indication of another plan of " explication "; in short, it is to pass your hand to the metaphysician.

Does M. Delacroix's thought go as far as that ? I do not pretend that it does, and it would be, no doubt, indiscreet on my part to endeavour to reconstitute such a conclusion by deduction in order to attribute it to him. But I hold as certain that the failure of experimental determinism to explain integrally the facts, as much in biology and ordinary psychology as in religious psychology, manifests not only our accidental ignorances, but the partial incompetence of scientific methods. Now if the incompetence of these methods is *evident* in relation to the general psychological form of religious experience, by what right can we invoke the *presumption* of their competence in order to deny to the transforming Union the descriptive characteristics which the great contemplatives unanimously attribute to it ? And in a more modest sphere, will the speculative interpretations formulated, also so unanimously, by religious souls of their interior states and of the rôle of Grace still appear so evidently absurd, when observation itself has forced us to break the iron circle of empirical determinism ?

It is, moreover, well known that it is possible to admit metaphysical realities, even a religious finality of the world, and yet to refuse to accept the strictly supernatural. But that distinction does not preoccupy us much in this essay, in which we are only enquiring whether scientific method furnishes a complete empirical explanation of religious facts. We have seen that that method does not furnish such an explanation. That is all. The problem of their special phenomenology presents itself, then—partially at least—outside the frontiers of science. How will it be resolved ?

4. SOME TYPES OF EXTRA-SCIENTIFIC SOLUTIONS OF THE PROBLEMS OF RELIGIOUS PSYCHOLOGY

A priori, there appear to be three types of positive, affirmative solution: First of all, the solution which reintroduces the problem in a roundabout way into science. This is the point of view of metaphysical scientism, of materialism, if you wish to call it so, for which empirical determinism is the actual and ultimate expression of things. Once this universal competence has been decreed, it is necessary that psychological phenomena, religious or otherwise, should accommodate themselves to it. If they are recalcitrant, they will be forced under the yoke of a theory which will retain its value, no longer from its power of experimental control, but from an *a priori* principle. The experimental insufficiencies of the theory thus become negligible.

Another point of view: psychology emerges from the psycho-physiological determinism which it transcends. The strictly scientific method loses its jurisdiction over the *total* psychological activity of the mystic or of the religious man, but solely because there exists no science of " liberty " as a partial factor of the mystical life. This is more or less the point of view of M. Récéjac in his thesis on *Les Fondements de la Connaissance Mystique* (Paris, 1896). Perhaps M. Delacroix, if he made his profession of metaphysical faith, would, in spite of his much greater *finesse* of psychological analysis, place himself with M. Récéjac.

This solution opens a wider field to explanatory hypotheses than the preceding one. It corresponds to the conception of a human mysticism, very elevated but purely natural, the summit of which would consist in an intense unification of the self in an excessively condensed intellectual activity with perhaps sometimes at its climax a loss of consciousness. Does Christian mysticism, viewed from outside in its own phenomenology, necessarily oblige us to transcend this psychological schema? Due reserve being made as to the nature of the underlying causality, a Catholic might admit that it does not: he then sacrifices the " letter " of numerous mystical documents, and is bound to explain psychologically, by the combination of common elements, the whole experimental side of states of union. If he is looking for a theory he will not find at the present moment a more complete one than that of M. Delacroix. Such as it is, however, it hardly deserves the name of a scientific hypothesis; indeed, its intrinsic experimental probability is too feeble and its pragmatist value null; it is rather an ingenious and conscientious illustration of the systematic application of the psychological point of view to the study of mysticism.

A third solution is held by the majority of Catholics. Starting from the principle, admitted on other grounds, of the reality of the supernatural and of the active rôle of Grace, this solution proves itself to be more respectful than the preceding ones of the " letter " of mystical and merely ascetical texts. According to it the religious life would, even in its phenomenology, be constantly influenced by supernatural grace—the grace of light and moral force. This influence, however, would insert itself into the series of psycho-physiological determinism without directly violating it in our eyes; for the empirical effects of grace, considered in isolation, hardly ever transcend the apparent power of natural causes. The abstract " type " of the religious phenomenon, apart from mystical union, remains psychological. The higher mystical states alone would definitely transcend the level of ordinary psychology, not only as regards their causation or their ontological nature, but even as regards their experimental type. They would truly consist, as the interested witnesses affirm, in an *intellectual intuition of Being*, which supposes that God Himself, by a sovereignly benevolent *initiative*, substitutes Himself for presentations derived from the senses and unveils Himself for an instant to the soul.[13] It is easy to see why, if this hypothesis be true, the states of higher contemplation are—as the Christian mystics insist— not only unpredictable, *i.e.*, they transcend empirical determinism, but also inaccessible to human effort, *i.e.*, they also transcend by reason of one of their elements—the Divine Self-presentation—the scope of individual liberty.

IV. GENERAL CONCLUSIONS

It only remains for us to resume and formulate certain conclusions which may be drawn from the preceding pages.

To ask whether religious psychology can be constituted as an empirical science comes in practice to putting one of the three following questions:

1. Is the procedure of empirical science applied to religious facts sufficient to lay hold of them in their reality? (Ontological or philosophical point of view.)

2. Is the religious fact, considered from a relative point of view as a phenomenon, reducible *de jure* to an empirical theory, complete in its own order? (Point of view of empirical theory or of science.)

3. Should the religious fact be treated by scientific methods —*i.e.*, provisionally studied by the psychologist as an ordinary psychological fact which would be submitted to experimental determinism? (Point of view of research.)

Let us successively consider these three points of view.

1. THE ONTOLOGICAL POINT OF VIEW

And, first of all, the ontological point of view. It is evident that scientific method, since it limits itself to phenomena, will never give us more than a partial view of reality: as we have already remarked, it reaches the relative aspect only of the real. Reality itself in the measure to which it is accessible to us can only be encountered at the point of convergence of all the sciences relating to a given object: empirical sciences, metaphysics, and even, if necessary, theology. Why is this so? Because the integral reality, a limited and abstract portion of which is the proper object of each of these sciences, can only be reconstituted by the synthesis of all the scattered fragments to which it has been reduced.

" Very well," it will be said, " but the remark is wholly superfluous, because no particular opinion as to their ontological reality, their nature and their causes is implied in speaking of the empirical science of religious facts. It is perfectly allowable to make, on the common ground of psychology, complete abstraction of the philosophical problem which would separate enquirers." Forgive the sincerity—perhaps the unpleasant sincerity—of our reply. In pure theory, certainly, that is so: a strictly critical attitude *would* enable the enquirer to separate the point of view of empirical science from that of philosophy. But why dissimulate the truth? This critical attitude, hard to maintain, is tolerably rare; and we Catholics can hardly hope to find it maintained by all those who discuss from a different point of view the religious problem: many of them will endeavour to impose on us, in the name of science, a " scientist " metaphysic, which we have the right to find somewhat rudimentary: and they will excommunicate us in the name of science, not only when we express, on our side, dogmatic beliefs (which, however, we do not pretend to base on exclusively scientific grounds), but also when we recall them to the respect of certain frontiers which can only be crossed in the name of positive science by an abuse of logic. If we complain, the retort is prompt and triumphant; it consists under different forms of throwing in our faces one of two maxims dazzlingly evident: science is not merely that pale method of co-ordination which philosophical criticism would confine to the " phenomenon "—*it is the scientific conception of the universality of things (die wissenschaftliche Weltanschauung)*. " True " science is, then, a metaphysic: why is it not always admitted so clearly? . . . The second axiom lays down that spiritualist convictions have a necessarily injurious *contre-coup* on the application of scientific method, because they create *prejudices essentially restrictive of science :* quite different consequences follow the profession of materialist metaphysics or an empiricist philosophy.

This last charge—which aims at no less than fixing on every Christian psychologist a radical incompetence on certain subjects—introduces us to the examination of the two points of view which remain to be considered: that of empiric theory and that of research.

2. THE POINT OF VIEW OF SCIENTIFIC THEORY

Is the religious fact, as regards its phenomenology, adequately explicable by a strictly scientific theory founded on the basis of empiric determinism?

Let us remind ourselves once more that a Christian's beliefs only bind him in the ontological field: purely scientific theory as such remains a matter of indifference to religious faith, because it is, up to a certain point, independent of metaphysics.[14]

SCIENCE AND PSYCHOLOGY

There remain, however, certain relations between the metaphysical or religious attitude of an enquirer and his choice of a scientific theory which require precise definition.

Let us first of all lay down that scientific theory or explicative hypothesis *cannot be purely arbitrary*. Modern savants have no doubt re-acted against the excessive severity of Newton towards pure hypotheses: still, they demand that, failing speculative probability, a scientific hypothesis should show itself useful for research.

(a) *The Grounds of Scientific Theory in Religious Psychology*.

1. *Internal Experimental Probability*.—How can a *completely* empirical theory of religious phenomena find its justification ?

In the assistance which it brings to experimentation ? But, precisely, religious or mystical states are not, as yet at least, experimentable. A *general* theory with primarily " technical " aims would to-day be premature and superfluous, if not impossible. Theory in religious psychology must remain then, before everything, speculative. Whence can we draw its legitimacy ? From its internal probability ?

Such a probability in the empirical sciences may be drawn from two distinct sources. First of all, the real object for which the theory substitutes a sum of antecedents is often itself accessible to experimentation: supposing that the conditions recognised as necessary and sufficient for its appearance are precisely those foreseen by the theory, the equivalence in practice of the object and its hypothetical substitute would be the guarantee of a certain equivalence in intimate constitution. Unfortunately, the most characteristic religious facts are totally irreducible to such an experimental confrontation: no theory provides the recipe, even in an approximative sense for their provocation. A second source of probability for an empirical theory, failing the deliberately provoked observation of the object itself, lies in the possibility of knowing sufficiently completely by experimentation the value of each of the partial antecedents or of the simple relations invoked by the theory. By verifying each joint, so to speak, of the constructive theory itself, one can judge " from below " (*par en bas*) of its degree of aptitude to represent the real model, in spite of the fact that the model can never be realised to the extent that we could wish in the conditions postulated by the theory; the completed image, if it appears faithful

45

enough in design and *capable* of realisation, will at least play correctly the part of the object in our thought, and will thus acquire a more or less considerable probability.

Can purely psychological theories of religion and mysticism perhaps claim this second sort of internal probability ? It must be recognised that even on the hypothesis of the purely psychological nature of the higher mystical state, such an effort of theoretical reconstruction, making use as it does of materials too imperfectly known, would not really succeed in reaching this level. M. Delacroix's theory, which is much the most satisfactory of any, only gets as far as ecstasy at the price of an " extrapolation " which nothing experimental justifies: the mechanism of the " shortened discourse," or of the " *simili-intuition* " of normal life, in any case too superficially analysed, combined with the little that is known for certain of the sub-consciousness, have to undergo in order to meet the curve of mystical intuition a most disconcerting amplification and intensification. Evidently M. Delacroix finds this procedure tolerable, but we do not doubt that he founds the legitimacy of his hypothesis on anything rather than its experimental probability.

Moreover, strictly speaking, this kind of probability is limited to the explanation of objects themselves certainly belonging to the same order as their theoretically postulated antecedents, such as the explanation of a movement resulting from the combination of various virtual and partial displace-ments. The moment that a serious doubt hangs over the nature of the objects, it casts its shadow over the explanatory theory itself, the effort of which is *perhaps* radically vain. Such would be the case in our opinion of a purely empiric theory, of, say, vegetative life, or in the psychological order, of a mental synthesis and liberty. We have shown how these activities, which nevertheless transpire in the phenomenal order, escape the forms of an empirical determinism, which is the funda-mental condition of all scientific theory. The possibly radical impotence of the theory betrays itself equally in the presence of religious facts, and principally that of mystical union: for if it is difficult to prove that mystical union is trans-cendental and supernatural, it is absolutely impossible to demonstrate the contrary; indeed, the contrary can only be " supposed " if mystical documents are " interpreted " in a sense which is certainly not that of their authors. Let us, then, admit that from the point of view of psychology alone, the nature of higher contemplation remains a problem. How, then,

" categorically " assimilate any theoretic reconstruction with an original of such doubtful signification ?

Our conclusion will be that purely psychological theories of the higher mystical state cannot rest on any experimental probability. What basis have they then ? Nothing but a presumption of competence decreed *a priori*. But on what grounds ?

2. *The General Presumption of Competence.*—The principle of the economy of thought of M. Mach, if it was not always formulated in the same manner in the past, has been admitted at all times by philosophers as far as its meaning goes. It may be said to have profited by an implicit agreement based on a common need. No doubt that, from a metaphysical point of view, every constatable variation in the phenomenal world, even when it did not exceed the power of causes near at hand, might also, strictly speaking, be the immediate effect of a superior cause, the scope of which exceeding that of humbler causes would contain it " eminently " in the language of the School. How escape this tiresome possibility which rendered perpetually doubtful the frontiers of the " Physics " of the past, the science of sensible realities ? It was commonly agreed to adopt a helpful methodological artifice, which may be formulated in these terms : *let us not appeal to superior causes where more proximate causes appear to be sufficient*, to the first cause where the effect to be accounted for is not beyond the scope of second causes; or : *science confines itself to defining the sufficient causes of sensible realities;* or again, in more general terms : *it cannot be right to explain by the greater what can be sufficiently explained by the less.* This last formula transferred from the ontological domain, in which the " Physics " of the Ancients moved, to the phenomenal, to which modern sciences are confined, practically means : let us not give up the search for the simplest antecedents, and let us aim at the reduction of new phenomena to phenomena already known : *the presumption is in favour of the reducibility of every new phenomenon ;* its irreducibility ought to be positively demonstrated, it would constitute an exception at the same time as a complication.

How demonstrate such an irreducibility ? By the successive failure of the theories that are tried ? No, for such failures merely show the absence of experimental probability attaching to those theories : another perhaps will succeed, and there is nothing moreover to prevent the investigator who takes advantage of the presumption formulated above, from contenting himself provisionally with an insufficient theory.

(b) *Experimental, Metaphysical and Theological Counter-Indications.*

But there are other possible sources of this proof of irreducibility. The object itself may show itself in its *experimental* character incompatible with empirical determinism; such is the case in my opinion with life, vegetative or psychological. Is it also the case with specifically religious facts on a new and altogether special ground? Perhaps it is; but we will not impose on any one the opinion that it is indeed so: all that we can say is that the mystics affirm it energetically.

Other sciences directed to a more general object might for their part limit by their *certain* conclusions the merely *presumed* competence of empirical science. The sciences here relevant are metaphysics and theology. What says metaphysics in the matter of religious psychology? That God, the first cause, is not controlled in his action by the determinism of empirical causality which has no absolute value; it follows that miracle, and the direct communication with God in ecstasy and the supernaturality of religious acts, cannot be taxed *a priori* with impossibility. The teaching of metaphysics is thus here more or less negative: it puts on one side in favour of a hypothetical " transcendental experience " the objection arising out of a false metaphysics negating the supernatural. Is theology (we speak of Catholic theology and for those only who, like us, recognise its authority) any more explicit? A reply cannot be given in a word, and several distinctions must be made.

First of all, Catholic dogma affirms the ordinary intervention of Grace in the Christian's religious activity, with the purpose not only of rendering his actions supernaturally meritorious, but also of showing him the right path, of exciting and sustaining his good will. The *elevation* of the action become naturally meritorious has a very real signification, but is not directly expressed in the phenomenal or empirical order; on the other hand, stimulating and assisting Grace is necessarily exercised in the empirical order. However, while the *fact* of this influence is incontestable for every Catholic, the *mode* of its exercise cannot be determined with equal certitude: sufficiently certain data are wanting to the two theological problems, the solution of which would decide the question: we shall proceed to verify this.

May not the influence of stimulating and assisting Grace, instead of being itself an immediately supernatural cause, function perhaps through the intermediary, providentially ordained *ad hoc* from the beginning of things, of the ordinary psychological causal series? To this problem we should reply with the majority of theologians in the negative, on grounds, however, of mere probability, and we would not condemn[15] the partisans of a psychological theory of the *experimental* effects of Grace, on the condition that they reserve the question of a strictly religious finality of those effects—a supernatural finality in their first origin, God, and in their goal, salvation.

The second theological problem arising out of the empirical action of Grace may be stated as follows: supposing that the immediate causality of stimulating and assisting Grace *is* supernatural, is it *experimentally demonstrable as such*? To this question, if it is intended to refer to isolated supernatural acts, we do not hesitate to reply in the negative. Every isolated religious act—making abstraction from mystical states properly so-called—may be theoretically reduced to ordinary psychological elements: a psychological theory of the Christian life is therefore, speaking absolutely, possible. But is it probable? An ambiguous question. Distinctions are necessary. From the integral point of view of the "real"? Certainly not. From the point of view of purely theoretical co-ordination of phenomena in the framework of natural laws? Yes and no, according to the idea which has been formed on other grounds of the empirical causality of Grace. From an exclusively experimental point of view? From this point of view it is acceptable in my opinion so long as it is limited to the explanation of isolated facts and partial attitudes; it becomes improbable—or rather insufficient—if extended to the whole movement, the total orientation of the Christian's life.

Has Theology a definite and clear doctrine on higher contemplation, on mystical union?

Theology admits as certain—in the sense that the profession of another opinion would be " temerarious "—not only the possibility but the existence of extraordinary communications between God and the human soul. It would take too long to develop here the reasons for this thesis. On the other hand, apart from the indirect influence of this general affirmation, no absolute guarantee is offered of the spiritual states and revelations of this or that mystic in particular. The approbation given by the Church to various writings of contemplatives does not involve any assurance of this nature, as Benedict XIV formally declares. Here then, again, theology merely gives a general indication, giving us rather an orientation in a field of possibilities, than dealing with any concrete facts.

Nevertheless, by grounding a modest argument on this vague contribution of theology, we shall be in a position to block out the following conclusions:

1. The action of Grace in the ordinary Christian life has *probably* an empirical value, manifested rather in general effects than in particular details.

2. Speaking generally, special communication with God in the mystical union is not an illusion. However, no particular case is specially guaranteed; but it is probable that the most approved mystics, whose writings have had a wider influence on Catholic piety, have not been mistaken to any considerable extent as to the phenomenology and nature of their states.

Is this decisive enough to justify us in barring the road to a psychological theory in the scientific domain, even if it be insufficient, of higher contemplation? I think not. Perhaps, however, we should make a great mistake in forming our personal point of view, to despise the suggestions of theology and the divinations of traditional piety: without bringing us full light, they have the very appreciable advantage of keeping us in closer contact, and, so to speak, in sympathy with the original documents which we have to utilise: when all is said, thanks to the modest and always reformable " prejudice " with which they inspire us, we run less risk of misunderstanding important shades of thought or feeling of the mystics themselves, while a premature psychological theory would certainly involve such sacrifices.

In any case, as we have observed elsewhere,[16] the point of view of the mystics when describing the state of Union is not so foreign to psychological plausibility. Introspection can always discover in the human intelligence an ever active tendency towards the close unification of the Ego and its empirical content, ranging itself under an ideal type of unity which is no other than Being itself. If the spirit of man is not condemned to a perpetual becoming, it ought to be able to reach some day the limit towards which it tends with the whole weight of its nature. Now this limit—the unity of Being— is heterogeneous to the unity of co-ordination. As long as the intelligence has not been emancipated in its apprehension of its object from the multiplicity of fragmentary presentations which is the law of its exercise here below, it will continue to tend on its endless journey to an inaccessible unity. But should that law one day be suspended by the presentation or the direct revelation of Being, the soul would pass to its limit, that is, the instantaneous integration of its indefinite progression. Is such an integration—which supposes the concourse of a Being distinct from the soul—either probable or even possible? Pure psychology has no solution of the problem of which we do not find in our internal experience the adequate data: but it at least shows that the discursive movement of the intelligence is entirely directed towards a goal—is it an illusion?—which is precisely that very direct possession of Being claimed by the Christian mystics: the pale and fugitive anticipation here below of the enduring possession of the next life. And so a place is found for the intellectual intuition of contemplatives if not in psychology, at least in its immediate prolongation.

Let us resume what has been said before passing to a final category of conclusions.

No purely psychological theory of religious facts being able to justify a claim to experimental probability, it is necessary to look outside the limits of psychology for a criterion which shall enable us to form by anticipation of eventual experiences a judgement as to the extent to which it is legitimate to apply empirical theory in these matters. Some, non-believers in general, find this criterion by attributing a presumption of competence to scientific methods: we have criticised this point of view, which may be called the " *scientific prejudice*," without excessive severity. Others, with whom I rank myself, will be more impressed than the former with the weakness of that presumption; it will even seem to them that the possibilities thrown open by metaphysics and the probabilities suggested by theology, without peremptorily establishing the incompetence of scientific methods, destroy at least the presumption of their competence. I have here expressed as loyally as I can the " *Catholic prejudice* " as I conceive it to exist.

Prejudice for prejudice! Each investigator will defend his own. And it seems very difficult to disengage oneself from this position, unless indeed, after having refrained from posing the problem of the real in religious psychology, one proceeds to decline this second problem (which we have just examined) of the *right* of a purely psychological theory to give a complete *empirical explanation* of religious facts. It is true that this problem, posed apparently on an empirical ground, does but dissimulate its realist nature, because it can only be solved *a priori*, by an absolute affirmation or negation of competence. The opposition of " prejudices " which we have mentioned, and which seems to us inevitable, is foreign to " experimental science " properly so called: all hope, then, is not lost of finding in " science " a sphere of conciliation.

3. THE POINT OF VIEW OF RESEARCH

Divided from the point of view of the " real," divided also from the point of view of " explicative theory," there appears nothing to prevent psychologists studying the religious fact from joining forces in the domain of " Research." We do not disagree: if nothing is concerned but to push as firmly as possible the investigation of facts, to extend as far as possible under the control of experimentation the postulate of determinism; to synthesise phenomena from a theoretical point of view only in so far as the synthesis sums up past and prepares future experience, if in a word nothing is concerned save the loyal application to the greatest possible extent of a " method," without any pronouncement on its theoretical limits, then indeed there subsists no ground of conflict. Catholic and non-believing psychologists can collaborate without the slightest *arrière-pensée*. And such an alliance is rightly made on a scientific basis, for science in the modern and critical sense of the word is before everything a " method." Method no doubt easily transforms itself into doctrine, but at the same moment " science " has become a " philosophy."

Unfortunately, all men are born philosophers. And too many of our savants (non-believers or believers) possess this flaw unconsciously. One sees them at every point taking headers into the real, forgetful or ignorant that in doing so they frequently cut a very poor philosophical figure, and that, on the other hand, a grain of sound and sincere philosophy, teaching them to distinguish the relative from the absolute, would replace them in their rôle of men of science. For one has to be a bit of a philosopher in order on occasion to abstain from philosophising.

Let me confess, however, that I await with complete scepticism the eventuality of a conversion to philosophic criticism of savants *en masse*. It is better to allow as well as one can for certain divergences; the unanimous and complete agreement of psychologists theoretically possible in the limited sphere of research is practically illusory even then. May I refer in this connection to the first part of this article ?   Men will continue not only to philosophise, which is permissible, but to philosophise underhand under the flag of science.   Science will not itself become any more objective and the criticism of contributions will certainly remain more difficult; but what is to be done ?   At least sincere and serious researches, even when inspired by very different theoretical points of view, will bring from their different sides new and utilisable elements.   The truth, which is not empirical, will be gradually disengaged, and that the more quickly, the more conscious both writers and readers become of the critical notion of the proper object of science.

We have gone a good way round, and here we are again at our starting-point.

NOTES

[1] This study first appeared in the *Recherches de science religieuse*, Paris, 1912, No. 1.
We shall deliberately abstain from loading these pages with bibliographical indications which, in order to be coherent, would have to be excessively developed, and would in any case be superfluous for our readers.   They will read between the lines and detect without difficulty the influence of the classics of philosophy and of theoretical science, also various reminiscences of contemporary thinkers who have made a specially noteworthy contribution to the criticism of scientific thought, such as Mach, Ostwald, Duhem, H. Poincaré, Reinke, Driesch, Le Roy, Blondel (we may specially refer to some excellent pages, too little known, of *L'action*), Boutroux, Bergson, and others. We ought also to refer to psychologists, but the list would be long and not very significant.   On the other hand, authors who have specialised in religious psychology need only slight mention; apart from W. James we will name only Höffding, Leuba, Delacroix, and Pacheu.   We may add that bibliography has appeared to us in the case of the present article of very secondary importance: the reflections which we put forward are those which occur spontaneously, if the student's attention is awake, on personal contact with the methods and literature of science.

[2] Cf. Sixth International Congress of Psychology, *Rapports et comptes rendus*, Geneva, 1910.

[3] Such as the articles of M. Pacheu.   Since these pages were written, M. l'Abbé Pacheu has published a new book treating of a subject akin to our own: *L'expérience mystique et l'activité subconsciente*.   We think, however, that the present article does not reproduce it, since the standpoints are different.

[4] See S Thomas Aquinas, *Summa contra Gentiles*, iii, cap. 37-63, and P. Rousselot, *L'intellectualisme de S Thomas*, Paris, 1908.

[5] I. Newton, *Optice*, lib. iii, quaest. 31, p. 329, Lausanne and Geneva, 1740.

[6] Several of the assertions which will be formulated without comment in the course of these pages have been developed and justified in the article, " On the Feeling of Presence in Mystics and Non-Mystics," below.

[7] In this study we leave completely aside the psychology of the divine Founder of the Christian religion. Certain profane hands have attacked this ideal figure during recent years with a heaviness that carries its own punishment with it. Other studies have been at the same time more psychological and in better taste, such as a recent work of Sanday, which has been most judiciously criticised by M. Léonce de Grandmaison. See *Recherches de science religieuse*, 1911, pp. 189 ff.

[8] A psychiatrist of this name perpetrated in 1909 a pseudo-psychological study of the Founder of the Christian Religion. Binet-Sanglé's book was called *La Folie de Jésus*, and *non ha alcun valore* according to Professor De Sanctis, *La Conversione Religiosa*, Studio Bio-psicologico, p. 13. [Translator's Note.]

[9] Sixth International Congress of Psychology, *Reports*, Geneva, 1910, pp. 132-33.

[10] The word is Professor Leuba's.

[11] J. Pacheu, *L'expérience mystique et l'activité subconsciente*, Paris, 1910, Appendix, p. 306.

[12] We cannot delay over this statement, which to-day hardly stands in need of justification. For the proof we refer the reader to the well-known pages of M. Bergson on the " cinematographic method " of the human intelligence.

[13] It will be understood that we are speaking here only of the *summit* of the mystical states.

[14] St Thomas, following the Greeks, makes profession of this independence in regard to astronomical theories, the only ones which in his day corresponded exactly to what we now call " scientific theories." See Commentary *De Coelo et Mundo*, lib. ii, 17, and *Summa Theol.*, Ia IIae, 32, 1 ad 2.

[15] Remember the theses of G. Vasquez on the supernatural *in se* and *quoad modum*.

[16] See especially the two studies below : " On the Feeling of Presence in Mystics and Non-Mystics," and " Some Distinctive Features of Christian Mysticism."

ON THE FEELING OF PRESENCE IN MYSTICS AND NON-MYSTICS[1]

SUMMARY

INTRODUCTION.

FIRST PART

DATA FURNISHED BY NORMAL AND PATHOLOGICAL PSYCHOLOGY

I. FIRST PRECISE NOTIONS TO BE APPLIED TO THE CONSIDERATION OF THE PROBLEM. THE JUDGEMENT OF REALITY AND THE JUDGEMENT OF PRESENCE.

II. THE JUDGEMENT OF REALITY IN SEVERAL "GROUPS OF FACTS."

    1. *True Hallucinations.*
    2. *Pseudo-Hallucinations and Intermediate Cases.*
    3. *Illusions of Perception.*

III. DISCUSSION OF THESE CASES.

    1. *The Judgement of Reality is not,* originally, *a* Conclusion, *even an Implicit One.*
    2. *Nor is it the Immediate* Result *of a Structure of Representations.*
    3. Negative Hallucinations *and Feeling of* Unreality.
    4. *The* Affective Connexions *of the Judgement of Reality.*

        (*a*) Belief and interest.
        (*b*) Belief and will.
        (*c*) Insufficiency of phenomenalist empiricism.
        (*d*) Participation of the life of the emotions in the affirmation of reality.
        (*e*) Attention and belief.

    5. Difficulty *of Co-Ordinating the Elements of the Problem* if *the* "Judgement of Reality" *is Secondary and Resultant.*

IV. INVERSION OF THE TERMS OF THE PROBLEM.

    1. Realism *is* Primary *and cannot be Reduced to more Elementary Conditions.*
    2. *Rise of* Doubt *and of the* Demand for a Synthesis *of Representations and Affections.*
    3. Secondary Modes *of Emergence of the Judgement of Reality. The Whole Complex of Facts is Explained by* One of the Fundamental Laws *of the Human Mind.*

V. VIEW OF THE GENERAL PSYCHOLOGY OF INTUITION AND AFFIRMATION. DEEP REASON OF THE LAWS TO WHICH APPEAL IS MADE.

STUDIES IN THE PSYCHOLOGY OF THE MYSTICS

SECOND PART

APPLICATIONS TO MYSTICAL KNOWLEDGE

I. THE ESSENTIAL AND ACCESSORY IN THE MYSTICAL STATES.

II. INTERMEDIARIES BETWEEN ORDINARY KNOWLEDGE AND THE HIGHER MYSTICAL STATE. THEIR PSYCHOLOGICAL MECHANISM.

1. *Sensible Visions.*
2. *Imaginary Visions.*
3. *Laws of the Hallucinatory Spatialisation of a Representation.* Spatialised " *Intellectual* " *Visions.*

III. INTUITION OF A TRANSCENDENT PRESENCE IN THE HIGHER MYSTICAL STATE. NATURE OF THIS INTUITION.

1. *The* Problem.
2. Mystical Intuition outside Catholicism.

   (*a*) *Neoplatonism.*
   (*b*) *Yogism.*
   (*c*) *Buddhism.*
   (*d*) *Musulman mysticism. Sufism.*
   (*e*) *Contemporary profane or pantheistic mysticism.*
   (*f*) *Ecstasy of Contemporary Protestants.*

3. Mystical Intuition *in the* Great Orthodox Catholic Contemplatives. *Its* Descriptive Characters.
4. Discussion.

   (*a*) *Preliminaries.*
   (*b*) Statement and criticism of certain *opinions of psychologists.*
   (*c*) *The Conditions of* any *legitimate* explanatory *hypothesis.*
   (*d*) Psychological *legitimacy* of a metempirical hypothesis *which respects the letter of the mystical documents.*

ON THE FEELING OF PRESENCE IN MYSTICS AND NON-MYSTICS[1]

INTRODUCTION

IT is the purpose of this essay to set down a few reflections suggested by a problem on which psychologists have not as yet shed much light. The impression of the *presence of an object* is one of our most ordinary experiences. On close examination, however, it appears complicated with so many varying elements, and comes before our notice in such widely differing circumstances, that its analysis speedily becomes difficult, if not impossible. It is easy, therefore, to understand the puzzled and hesitating tone of a short note which William James[2] devotes to the specially baffling case where the quite clear feeling of a presence is found dissociated from any concomitant sense-impression. Cases of this kind are, as a matter of fact, by no means rare. James himself, a little later, in the course of his *Gifford Lectures* on Religious Experience,[3] quotes a fairly long list of them from the special point of view with which he was then dealing.

The problem, in fact, has long been presented in all its urgency by every page of that richly diversified psychological repertory which lies in the archives of orthodox or heterodox mysticism. Now that these archives have become the object, even on the part of the most completely " non-religious " enquirers, of increasingly frequent and proportionally less superficial researches, the psychological riddles they conceal have begun one by one to come to light, and to excite a keen curiosity.

M. Henri Delacroix, in his *Études sur l'histoire et la psychologie des grands mystiques chrétiens*,[4] has encountered in his turn the problem indicated by James. Though we cannot agree with all the conclusions of M. Delacroix, we are pleased to find in his new book that serious spirit of enquiry and that sympathy with criticism which are still the most indispensable conditions for a correct understanding of the questions approached. It is not, however, our intention here to undertake an examination of M. Delacroix's work, nor even merely of the appendix thereto,

57

entitled *Sentiment de présence ;* we shall limit ourselves in the following pages to grouping together certain elements which will enable our readers to consider in greater detail the problem presented by that work, and to place it rightly. And for ourselves—we will at once confess—it presents itself especially as a function of Catholic mysticism; it is our desire, from a preliminary examination of profane documents alone, to suggest solutions, possibly diverse in character, which will enable the laws and analogies of psychology to be accepted in a strictly mystical connection. But the reader will excuse us from claiming, any more than James or M. Delacroix, to " provide a definitive solution of this little problem,"[5] which, modest though it may seem, has none the less a close connection with several more profound questions.

FIRST PART

DATA FURNISHED BY NORMAL AND PATHOLOGICAL PSYCHOLOGY

I. FIRST PRECISE NOTIONS TO BE APPLIED TO THE CONSIDERATION OF THE PROBLEM. THE JUDGEMENT OF REALITY AND THE JUDGEMENT OF PRESENCE

The feeling of presence is not wholly different in kind from that of reality. In fact, the character of *reality* which the *immediate* perception of an object carries with it is for us confused with the feeling of that object's presence. To say, in the real meaning of the word, " this sheet of paper is present to me," is equivalent to saying " it is actually accessible to my senses, I see it, I am touching it." Later on we shall have to analyse all that this equivalence implies; for the moment we are content with stating the relationship between the two notions of *presence* and of *immediately perceived reality*.[6]

The ascertainment of this relationship will enable us to connect our own enquiries with preceding ones, and to make use of the results and hypotheses which have long been recorded in classical works on psychology.

Everyone instinctively grasps the difference between a direct sensation and a pure imaginative representation, the *Wahrnehmung* and the simple *Vorstellung*. Why does the one carry with it the note of reality, of actual presence, while the other, even though identical in content, lacks this character ? What is it, in short, which distinguishes " this table " which I see or am touching from " this table " which I imagine ?

Most modern psychologists reply, following Hume, that it is a " persuasion," a *belief* which invests the sensation of " this table " with its affirmation of reality, without also investing the pure representation therewith. In what, then, does this belief consist ? It is, says James Mill, wholly resolvable into association.[7] It is primordial, and not susceptible of further analysis, John Stuart Mill maintains.[8] These criteria, adds A. Bain, are too purely intellectual; a represented object manifests itself as *real* when it at once calls forth some exercise of our activity upon it; the belief in its reality is " an incident of our intellectual constitution . . . not made up, in the first instance, by either activity or emotion, but is largely magnified by both."[9] " In its inner nature," writes W. James, " belief, or the sense of reality, is a sort of feeling more allied to the emotions than to anything else."[10]

This belief, which distinguishes sensation from pure representation, is assimilated by James to the judgement of reality, the " affirmation " of Brentano; " every object," says the latter, " touches consciousness in two ways : as a simple representation, and as affected by affirmation or negation."[11] By the mere fact of its presentation to the mind, the object raises the question of its reality, and calls for some mental attitude, a Yes, a No, or doubt. The " Yes " is the judgement of reality, the " belief " of James—perhaps it would be better to say that it is the translation of this affective belief into the intellectual field. But if the judgement of reality be founded *immediately* on a sense-perception, it will be at the same time a judgement of presence : " I *see* this sheet of paper; it *exists*; it is *there*." And this judgement, once more, will be original and incapable of analysis.

It would, however, be rather too simple to distinguish a perception from a representation solely by the fact that the former is a representation accompanied by a belief, which is at the same time accompanied by an *affirmation* of reality. From the standpoint of pure description, we can distinguish several momentary steps in the process which ends in full perception of reality—steps indissolubly united and rendered possible the one by the other.[12]

We must remember that man, in whom the understanding collaborates with all the operations of consciousness, does not in his personal experience possess any " sensation " in the pure state; he may define in the abstract, but he does not experience in an isolated state that simple and direct touch of the sense-impression by itself, without a concept, without an intellectual synthesis to put it in its place, without a judgement to support it and set it as object over against the thinking subject, without " reflection " to relate it to the Ego. It therefore comes to pass that, as soon as we become conscious of our attitude towards the problem of a sensible object's reality, the original and immediate contact of our knowing faculties with that object is already entangled in a complex set of co-ordinated operations; to which of these elements, which it is so difficult to separate from one another, is the decisive influence on our final affirmation of reality or unreality, subjectivity or objectivity, to be attributed?

I see my pen running over my paper; it is there " present " to me, in the strictest sense. This apparently simple judgement presupposes a mass of elementary sensations, associated in a spatial synthesis, distinguished from other groupings, incorporated, so to speak, in their place in the flux of my psychological life, connected up with my possibilities of action, " apperceived,"[13] that is to say, grasped by virtue of an act of attention (whatever the nature of it may be), gathered together into the unity of a concept, and only as such introduced as subject into a direct existential judgement, then lastly—by setting this complex unity over against my thinking sub-jectivity—explicitly affirmed as an object that is immediately present to me.

We can already, then, by means of a summary analysis, make clear to some extent the approach to our problem. The *judgement of presence* properly so called affirms a *spatial relation* between a subject and an object; it presupposes the affirmation, which logically precedes it, of the *distinction between subject and object* on the one hand, and of their *reality* on the other. This judgement of reality is itself based upon the *more elementary mental processes* which determine it. For us the delicate point is, not so much the search for the conditions that establish a spatial relation between subject and object, as that for the determining conditions of the more general judgement of immediate *objective reality*. Since the judgements of immediate reality which we shall have to examine in the first part of this work are at the same time judgements of presence, we shall use the two expressions indiscriminately; to differentiate between them more exactly at the start would hamper us.

THE FEELING OF PRESENCE

From this rapid analysis we will draw two principal consequences, which will oblige us to go further.

First of all, the judgement of reality, the direct existential judgement, presupposes antecedents which bring it about. If we seek to make this judgement, Brentano's " affirmation," itself the characteristic of (real) sensation as opposed to pure (imaginary) representation, we are but marking time, or arguing in a circle. The judgement of reality is a synthesis which is not justified solely by itself. But what are its determining antecedents ? Must we go back to the original sense-impression in order to discover them ? Or are they, on the contrary, to be found among the retinue of cognitive and affective reactions which accompany this impression, and which are capable, strictly speaking, of being separated from it ?

Another consequence, which likewise resolves itself into a question.

It is evident that James Mill, Bain, etc., from the very manner in which they mark the distinction between a sensation and an image, presuppose identity of nature between free representation and sensation[14]—the characteristic note of the latter being in reality extrinsic and, if we may so put it, of the extra-representative order. But what can be the value of such a characteristic note ? How does it come to be attached to what does not of itself, by hypothesis, bear the mark of objective reality ?

It will be remarked how much greater this difficulty becomes for those psychologists who, having affirmed the identical nature of a sensation and a mental image, shut the knowing subject up within himself, and having posited as a principle the antecedence of subjective to objective knowledge, find themselves in difficulties at having to discover the reason or impulse which determines us to go forth out of ourselves towards the object. Now this fundamental point of view, which might be called a " psychological subjectivism," is—explicitly or implicitly—that of most modern authors, however they may explain the passage from the order of pure representation to that of reality. We shall have to estimate and distinguish later the legitimate and the insufficient elements in their conception. Let us first of all attempt to come to rather closer grips with our problem itself.

STUDIES IN THE PSYCHOLOGY OF THE MYSTICS

II. THE JUDGEMENT OF REALITY IN SEVERAL "GROUPS OF FACTS"

Sense-perception marks its objects with a token of reality and immediate presence. If the bond between this token, which in the case of man is translated into a judgement, and the psychological state which we define as sense-perception, were exclusive and indissoluble, there would be nothing to prevent our seeing in it an original and primitive connection defying every attempt at further analysis. Unfortunately the feeling of present reality is attached to psychological states other than sense-perception; and reciprocally, sense-perception sometimes appears unreal.

1. TRUE HALLUCINATIONS

A healthy man sees with his eyes, and has no doubt of what he sees; the subject of pure hallucination likewise sees, and likewise has no doubts. The compelling feeling of a present reality, therefore, is not the exclusive appanage of external sensation; it may be grafted on to that purely central phenomenon, the hallucinatory image. And it is to be noted that, in the majority of mental maladies, as also during the passing intoxication caused by belladonna, cocaine, santonin, nitrous oxide, ether, alcohol, opium, hashish, etc., or even simply under the influence of the passage of an electric current, the conviction of reality is remarkably intensified, and may attach itself to the most fantastic representations. True hallucination, for one who is subject thereto, assumes all the characters of true perception. It would be superfluous to support so classically commonplace a statement by examples. Let us rather at the moment enquire what characteristics differentiate from a simple mental image, not only external sensation merely, but indifferently either a hallucinatory image, or that direct sensorial image which Taine, perhaps wrongly, called " true hallucination."

" The opinions of psychologists and psychiatrists as to the difference between perceptions and free representations vary most diversely," writes G. Störring.[15] He classifies these psychologists in three groups. The majority, uncompromising associationists, perceive nothing but differences of intensity in the imagery which at any moment fills the field of consciousness; let a simple representation acquire an abnormal access of intensity, and it at once becomes hallucinatory—that is, it takes on the character of true perception. For others—among them Fechner[16]—the difference in question is specially marked by the constraint which a perception or hallucination, but not a simple image, causes in the knowing subject; the latter depends in part on the subject's voluntary activity, the former give rather an impression of receptivity, of passivity; they impose themselves. Others again, especially the psychiatrists, add a new characteristic—that is, the retinue of muscular and visceral sensations associated with a perception or hallucination, but absent or curtailed in the case of pure representations.

It is indeed true that these various characteristics normally accompany the feeling of perceived reality; they do not, however, as can be shown from facts, constitute its necessary and sufficient conditions. Moreover, the first of them (relative intensity), the only one that is strictly internal, is manifestly inadequate to the problem before us; the second (the constraint experienced) expresses a mode of sensation, but unfortunately does not furnish a criterion of universal application, and moreover, if taken in all strictness, would involve a *petitio principii*, for the constraint experienced can only be a criterion of external reality if it is perceived as submitted to from without; unless the " judgement of reality " which accompanies the sense-perception is always the conclusion of a ratiocination, an hypothesis which we shall examine later; the third characteristic (associated internal sensations), which some add to the other two, is purely extrinsic to the external sensation which it ought to specify, a sufficiently grave drawback; we will see whether it can in spite of this furnish a satisfactory basis for a " judgement of reality."

Wundt admits no radical psychological distinction between sensation and representation; this distinction, in his eyes, belongs to logic; the greater or less intensity of the representation has nothing to do with the matter. " The restitution of the concept of ' representation ' (*Vorstellung*) to images of the memory (as opposed to free imaginations), as in general all differentiation of the content of consciousness based on the immediate presence or absence of real objects, is null and void from the psychological standpoint, seeing that it uses as its principle of distinction a characteristic which is not psychological but logical, and one which tends to the admission of psychological differences which do not in reality exist."[17] Yes, but it still remains to elucidate the origin of our existential judgements and to explain that immediate impression of present reality which perpetually mingles with our representations. We shall return to this matter shortly; first of all let us collect a few more data.

2. PSEUDO-HALLUCINATIONS AND INTERMEDIATE CASES

Between sense-perception and true hallucination on the one hand, and pure representation on the other, there intervenes a class—perhaps it would be better to call it a scale—of phenomena which have been known at all times, but sympathetically studied for hardly fifty years past: this is the group called by Baillarger (1845) *"psychic hallucinations."* " It is important," writes J. Séglas, " to distinguish from true hallucinations the phenomena described under the names of *false hallucinations* (Baillarger), *pseudo-hallucinations* (Hagen, Kandinsky, Hoppe), *apperceptive hallucinations* (Kahlbaum). It must be remarked, however, that these terms are not exact equivalents. Each author designates and includes different facts among them." Séglas, then, distinguishes more precisely three categories, covered—rightly or wrongly—by the names given above. The second is of special interest to us; it " comprises those phenomena for which Kandinsky reserves more particularly the name pseudo-hallucinations. These are phenomena partaking at the same time of the nature of ordinary sensorial mental representations and of hallucination, representations vivid, animated, exact, stable, spontaneous and incoercible, thus approximating to true hallucinations, but not, like these latter, creating an appearance of objective reality. They are lacking in that character of *exteriority* which Baillarger rightly looked upon as inherent in sensorial hallucinations."[18]

It seems to us that we must not, under penalty of leaving a large number of cases " unclassified," take this lack of the " character of exteriority " too strictly. We would prefer to say merely: lacking in the character of *complete objectivity*. For though it is true that the subjects often declare that they " see with the inward eye " or " in their head,"[19] though it is likewise true that pseudo-hallucinatory images are often " in no wise in relation with the field of vision," it is true also that in certain cases the image seems not merely localised, but in a normal relation with the other objects which occupy the field of vision; it is *spatially* objectivised as an image, and it lacks nothing to become completely hallucinatory save the character of independent reality. We shall shortly meet with examples of this.

Störring makes use of the case of pseudo-hallucinations to show the insufficiency of the differential criteria that are generally applied to distinguish true hallucinations from pure representations. He justly remarks that the intensity, the character of constraint, the associated impressions, may be as highly accentuated in pseudo-hallucination as in true hallucination or perception. And thence he arrives at the following conclusion: " The objective character of visual perceptions as opposed to the subjective character of pseudo-hallucinations—and the same might be said of representations in general—rests on the fact that the content of the perception appears to the individual as located in the space apprehended at a given moment, and manifests a constant and experimentally known dependence on the movements of the sense-organs and of the whole body."[20] This is all very well; but who will agree that the simplest of our judgements requires so much learned psychology in its immediate antecedents ? And even if we were willing to apply this highly-developed standard to check our spontaneous judgements of reality, it is to be feared that a number of quite clear cases of pseudo-hallucination would find their way—with every right—into the class of true hallucinations and of perceptions.

It is true that we cannot push any classification to extremes without flouting to some extent the law of the continuity of phenomena. Here are a few intermediate cases, which we would prefer to include among pseudo-hallucinations, although they seem very closely to approach complete hallucinations. In fact they usually take place during the progressive degradation of an hallucination, or inversely, during the passing of a pseudo-hallucination into complete hallucination.

" Hallucinations most often produce an illusion of complete objectivity, so much so that instructed subjects affirm in their convalescence that they have heard the voices their cerebral affection has called forth as clearly as they hear the physician speaking at the moment." " Sometimes, however, the patient has doubts as to the reality of the hallucination. Thus, a woman attacked with alcoholic delirium, who believed that she saw butterflies and tried to catch them, declared, as soon as she had grasped the imaginary objects in her hand, that it was all unreal."[21] If we are not mistaken, this case, analysed in the light of analogous cases, shows, at a given moment, the clear spatial externalisation—clear enough to have been responsible for the illusion of reality—of a simple image afterwards recognised as such.

Inversely, when a representation tends to become completely hallucinatory, it may provoke a feeling of spatial localisation, and even inchoatively that of independent reality, in very varying degrees.

Störring[22] reports a case, studied by Friedmann, in which the alternate dwindling or accentuation of an obsessing image carried with it the affirmation or negation respectively of its objective reality. In a general way it is well established that obsession may become hallucinatory. Pitres and Régis quote the case of a patient of Séglas, " overcome, at the sight of a rabid dog, with an obsessing fear of rabies. When the crisis overtook him, during his sleepless nights, he used to see dogs in his room. One day, overcome by his crisis in the street, he even began to fly before an imaginary mad dog which he believed he *saw* at his heels; he cried out, to the astonishment of passers-by, who for their part could see nothing."[23] In the establishment of the " hallucinatory obsession " we meet with every degree of externalisation and objectivisation of the image that we could wish for.

Wigan, in his work, *A New View of Insanity*, relates a very instructive case, quoted by Taine.[24] It is that of an English painter, and is recorded as follows: " When a sitter came, I looked at him attentively for half an hour, sketching from time to time on the canvas. I wanted no more; I put away my canvas and took another sitter. When I wished to resume my first portrait, I took the man and set him in the chair, where I saw him distinctly as if he had been before me in my own proper person—I may almost say more vividly. . . . When I looked at the chair I saw the man. Gradually I began to lose the distinction between the imaginary figure and the real person; and sometimes disputed with sitters that they had been with me the day before. At last I was sure of it; and then—all is confusion. I lost my senses, and was thirty years in an asylum."

This painter, then, perceived a clear image, perfectly localised, fixed in its place amongst real objects. The spatial externalisation was as complete as it could be, in spite of his consciousness of the unreal character of the externalised representation. It is true that the affair came to a bad end and led to complete hallucination, but the conclusion does not do away with the intermediate states.

THE FEELING OF PRESENCE

Stout, after mentioning this case, backs it up with a description of a state of confusion artificially brought about in himself. " Under the influence of a large dose of haschisch," he says, " I found myself totally unable to distinguish between what I actually did and saw, and what I merely thought about. The value of this experience lies in the fact that I was throughout able to observe my own mental state."[25]

Let us mention a last example, taken from our own observations. The subject, a rather nervous person, does not seem at all a likely candidate for Bedlam. In a state of complete wakefulness, during sleepless nights, he sees a well-known face model itself more or less vaguely near his bed. One element alone is always extremely definite—that is, the spatial localisation; the image does not follow the movement of his eyes, but remains fixed in one spot at a measurable distance. The subject has never had any inclination to take this image for a real object; at most the increasing precision of the features thus represented has created the " inchoative " and slightly disturbing impression of a present reality. We consider this as a case of pseudo-hallucination with complete spatialisation of the image.

M. Delacroix, in the book mentioned at the beginning of this article,[26] refuses—rightly, we think—to share M. Bernard-Leroy's scruples as to the reality of this group of pseudo-hallucinations. This group is neither more nor less homogeneous than most other psychological groupings; the unity of a " social reason " always remains a little artificial. On the whole, the criticisms of M. Bernard-Leroy seem to us, though true, irrelevant. It is, strictly speaking, possible, and even probable, that pseudo-hallucination can be reduced to a type of *interpreted* ordinary hallucination, or of likewise *interpreted* simple representation; but the interpretation in this case is too characteristic of the mental state we are classifying to forbid our basing a systematic delimitation thereon. We shall continue, therefore, without hesitation to speak of pseudo-hallucinations.

3. Illusions of Perception

We find an example of the inevitable inexactitude of psychological groupings in a last order of facts, which we will describe in a few words as " illusions " of sense-perception, as opposed to hallucinations. While an hallucination is a " perception without an object," an *illusion* is only an *alteration* of a real perception, and hence always presupposes an exciting cause from without, a nucleus of sensation. This distinction, introduced by Arnold and explained in more detail by Esquirol, has caused difficulty to most of the more recent psychiatrists, for, on the one hand, how are we to *prove* that an hallucination does not always demand for its production an initial exciting cause coming from the sensorial apparatus, and, on the other hand, as Kraepelin remarks, " between these two forms of illusion (simple and hallucinatory) all possible intermediate varieties are to be found."[27] Moreover, a simple illusion—which no one would call an hallucination—comprises in reality a number of hallucinatory *elements*. That a hunter takes a tree-stump for a hare and prepares to shoot can result only from an over-hasty identification; but that he halts, that the image of the animal grows more definite under his eyes, is but the hallucinatory projection of a subjective representation. Who has not at a distance mistaken one person for another, recognised in the utmost good faith features formerly seen, and then, after a moment's distraction, been astonished at finding almost no physical basis for his error ?

This " inchoative pathology " of ordinary life would hand over the greater part of the lessons crudely prominent in glaring cases to a fairly close analysis. After all, is our most ordinary sense-perception absolutely free from some share of illusion, or even of hallucination ? We perceive at the same time both *more* and *less* than our simple sense-impression presents to us, by virtue of what Ampère called a phenomenon of " concretion ";[28] when a simple sensation reaches the consciousness it is already mingled with a store of memories and subjective representations to which the original sensorial nucleus communicates in some degree the consistency of reality. " The rapidity with which we perceive forms or sounds already known," Kraepelin writes, " is based essentially on the fact that all common and rapid impressions which our senses collect are immediately strengthened and completed by memory-images, usually, no doubt, justly, but very often to the detriment of truth. No one can fail to recognise to what a degree preconceived opinion holds even normal perception under its influence, especially when fairly vivid passions interfere with our clear and objective view of our surroundings. Even the calmest and most scientific observer is never absolutely certain that his perceptions will not adapt themselves in spite of himself to the theoretical views with which he embarks on the consideration of an object of study."[29]

Illusions—even those unobtrusive illusions which accompany normal perception—thus supply us with a new example of the objectivisation of pure images, and of the parallel failure to recognise authentic sensorial elements.

III. DISCUSSION OF THESE CASES

It will be useful at this point to consider in further detail the groups of facts which we have just set forth. Henceforth they will confine within narrower limits the problem of the conditions necessary and sufficient for the spontaneous emergence of the judgement of reality and of presence. Care must be taken not to confuse this psychological problem with the logical problem of the conditions which make such a judgement valid.

Neither the feeling nor the judgement of presence, as we have seen, is exclusively connected with sensation; the necessary determinant of this feeling, then, is not a characteristic of the sensorial image which opposes the latter to a simple representation, or, if the expression be preferred, a central image. It would seem necessary to look for this determinant either in an element common both to sense-perception and hallucinatory representation, or in their concomitants. Let us make the attempt.

1. The Judgement of Reality is not, originally, a Conclusion, even an Implicit One

Is not the feeling of present reality merely the affective accompaniment of the judgement of reality, itself the *conclusion* of a true process of reasoning, at least implicit ? Is the reality of an object *inferred* from a number of convergent indications ?

We must distinguish. There are, beyond doubt, judgements of reality which are the fruit—legitimately or not—of a reasoning process; they are those which suppose a preliminary questioning, in a reflex manner, of the reality of the object they affirm. But man does not play the Descartes or the Berkeley every day, even in regard to particular objects; and the judgements of objective presence which we make in the course of a single day of our lives are innumerable. Are they all the expression of the individual's reasoning, or at least the distant echo of a reasoning process performed by the race ?

No one, we think, will choose the former hypothesis, and condemn us to emerge from our Ego only by the tortuous defiles of psychological inferences, even supposing that from a collection of representations, known *in the first place* as subjective, the notion of an independent objective reality could in logical strictness be derived.[30] We think that there is an inextricable logical difficulty for anyone who starts with the principle that every affirmation is originally relative to the knowing subject. But however this may be, experience shows in our feeling of present reality and in the judgement into which it is translated an affirmation more elementary and immediate than a logical conclusion, even one arrived at summarily. There is nothing in our consciousness which resembles a syllogism or an enthymeme in the course of normal sense-perception; nor is there anything of the kind in an hallucinated subject; we reason only in order to free ourselves from a doubt. And what shall we say as to the growth of the feeling of the real, in many hallucinated persons, proportionally to the disso-ciation or decrease in the content of their consciousness ? Have they anything wherewith to pad out the premises of the ratio-cination " by exclusion " which is needed to give them the decisive assurance of an external reality ?

Is this assurance, in default of an actual inference, at least either a legacy from the subject's own past, or a laborious acquisition from far-off ancestors which has entered into the automatism of their descendants ? The judgement of reality would in this case have contracted a *stable association* with a collection of circumstances formerly bound up with its rational premises, allowing it to arise mechanically without the recalling of its true premises. Such, moreover, is the common lot of those familiar judgements whereof each of us can find examples in his own personal experience, and which, motivated and accepted with consciousness of their cause in the first place, end by laying direct hold on a few indications insufficient to form a rational justification of their application. The feeling and judgement of presence in each particular case would be the result of a previously acquired association, just as spatial perception constitutes for the empirical school the persistent residuum of experiences accumulated by the individual or the race.

This conception is open to the same theoretical objections

as the preceding one; however prolonged we suppose the experience of the individual or the species to have been, we do not see how, from internal representations *perceived solely as modifications of the subject*, the rational affirmation of the external object can arise, without peremptorily raising to the status of an external object the gap which subsists in our knowledge of subjective causal connexions. But here again let us remain on the ground of experience; the facts are hardly favourable to the hypothesis we are attacking. The circumstances in which the judgement of objectivity presents itself are so variable, that we really cannot see—if it be only the result of manifold experiences—how heredity or habit has been able to associate it with such capricious conditions of emergence. We will go further into this impossibility by examining a fresh hypothesis, which answers better to the position taken up on the present question by the majority of modern psychologists.

2. Nor is it the Immediate Result of a Structure of Representations

It might be that the judgement of immediate reality and the feeling which accompanies it were, not the consequence of a ratiocination formally undertaken on each occasion, or merely brought into the open by association, but rather the *direct result* —the instinctive result, if we may so express it—of mental activity co-ordinating a *complex assemblage of representations.* The problem of reality would thus come down to an examination of psychological antecedents; reality would answer strictly to certain *combinations* of mental presentations; and the vital enigma of the " apprehension of the object," translated into the descriptive language of the psychological mechanism, would be lessened or even completely disappear. We are here, it will be realised, touching on principles of methodology big with consequences:[31] let us proceed to a deliberate examination of the facts.

The following passage—borrowed from MM. Raymond and Janet, and, we hasten to add, far removed in its simplicity of expression from the usually more highly coloured psychology of M. Janet—seems to us to express typically enough the kind of explanation dear to psychological empiricism. " . . . That which distinguishes these three things—the imagination, the memory, and the real perception of an object or event—is simply the degree of complication and co-ordination of the different images whose systematic reunion constitutes the thought of that object or event. To think of an imaginary dog is to have in one's mind a system of images of the dog's colour, shape, voice—images few in number, and consequently lacking in precision and in association with each other. To remember a dog that one has really seen is to add more precise images to the former system—images of determined colour, associated in a more regular fashion. To see a real dog is to have the same phenomenon in the mind once more, not necessarily stronger, but much more complex, with a systematisation that is much better determined and imposes itself more forcibly. The confusion of these three first phenomena the one with the other may happen very frequently and easily through two mechanisms which can act separately, but which may also unite and act simultaneously. Let the higher phenomenon diminish in intensity, let it be less complex, less precise, and it approximates to the lower phenomenon. Let the lower phenomenon increase in complexity and coherence, and it will approximate to the higher. When the perceptions are feeble or insufficient, during sleep or the dozing state for example, the memories will seem realities. Inversely, if the memory becomes more complicated and exact, it becomes hallucination."[32]

It could not be more candidly stated that the notion of objective reality is a resultant of combinations of subjective images. It is the triumph of associationism. And yet, once more, how can we conceive that pure associations of phenomena perceived as subjective should at a given moment, merely by their co-ordination, create the feeling and affirmation of an objective reality ? Wundt, no doubt, would reply that the proper province of psychology does not extend beyond pure co-ordinations of representations and of feelings; that the problem of objective reality belongs to the logical order; that it is a fact that certain associative relations of representations are transformed in the mind into logical relations. " Reality is only given to us immediately in our representations."[33] The empirical relations which are imposed upon us by virtue of the very content of those representations become, when they have been once grasped by apperception, the immediate determinant, the *scheme*, as we may put it, of corresponding logical affirmations. The question, then, is to define, in its essential elements, the " scheme " of the " real." And we always find ourselves faced once again by the same problem; does this " scheme " emanate from a co-ordinated collection of representations, so that the affirmation of objective reality is connected not with the representations taken by themselves, but with their co-ordination ? Or, on the other hand, is it not—this " scheme "—infinitely more simple, and does not co-ordination play quite another part in the knowledge of the real ?

Let us say at once that there is unquestionably a very large portion of truth in the analysis of the " perception of objects " which we owe to the numerous psychologists who derive from the empiricist-associationist school.[34]

When a sense-impression strives to cross the threshold of consciousness, it finds the place occupied, the attention fixed elsewhere, the mind's whole activity shared between powerful and organised factions which dispute its leadership. The new impression has a hard task to force its entry; it must be robust enough to bring about a rupture of equilibrium in its favour, or else must take its stand on the natural alliances it discovers for itself with the dominant party; it must in any case harmonise with the tendencies and activities of the Ego. It is impossible, moreover, for the newcomer to enter without an escort of associated sensations, reawakened images, feelings or impulses. If isolated, it would disappear—stifled, contradicted, trampled down by rivals, before it could demand from our attention the regard which would at least for a moment give it full life. Hardly is it introduced into the clear field of consciousness when it comes up against a manifold check—a check from prejudices and memories; a check from concomitant and especially from tactile sensations; nothing appears so real as the " tangible ": while Berkeley[35] well calls the other senses " organs of anticipated touch," actual contact is a kind of taking possession of the sensible object. In short, the objective character of a sensation is the reward either of a victorious struggle or of an initial agreement. But is what results from this harmony, imposed or ready-made, indeed the *first investiture* of the character of objectivity ? Every distinct perception is normally accompanied by a certain co-ordination of the " empirical Ego "; but is its " index of reality " *derived* therefrom ?

The same question evidently arises in respect of pure hallucinations. The index of reality which affects them is considered by many psychologists as a pure resultant. " This notion of the complexity of the hallucinatory image and of the association of its various attributes," writes Séglas, " it is all the more important to recognise, because at the present day it has become, for certain authors, much more than its intensity, the real criterion of its objectivity (P. Janet, Souriau)."[36] Let the reader recall the passage of Störring we have quoted above (p. 65); the conditions for the feeling of objectivity there described really determine the problem, and in a certain sense are indeed observed. We think, however, that the feeling of presence arises, decisive and compelling, before their full realisation.

Thus we are now brought, after having recognised the portion of truth included in the associationist explanations, to emphasise some of their difficulties and insufficiencies.

If the feeling of presence is essentially a resultant of complex representations, whose very complexity, thanks to a high degree of co-ordination, to a perfect fitting together, brings with it at a certain moment the character of objective reality, it—this feeling—must therefore vary in direct proportion to the degree of coherence of the representative elements to which it is attached. Now this law is not strictly exact. For if there are, for example, cases of certain invalids in which the persisting delirium, highly " systematised," determines the form of their hallucination and subordinates to it the perceptions themselves, there are also others in which an isolated hallucination, an illusion of perception, penetrating the mental imagery by effraction, disturbs its original equilibrium, and becomes sometimes in its turn the groundwork of delirious ideas.[37] In alcoholic delirium, for example, it does not seem that the objective character of many hallucinations—such as the frequent visions of animals[38]—is always the crown of as many pre-established personal syntheses. Then how many hallucinations arise from a *dissociation* of the content of consciousness ! This fragmentation multiplies the partial syntheses; the content of these latter continues to be diminished; and it would truly seem that the tone of reality, far from coming to flower only at the summit of cleverly arranged psychological structures, merely awaits the relative isolation of the representations—even if they are simple and of small content—in order to lay hold of them. Think of that state of terminal confusion in which many serious insanities issue, actual mental disaggregation, misdirection of the sense of reality which performs the antics of a compass-needle gone mad.[39] Likewise again, that oscillating state at the beginning of intoxication, in which the most disparate hallucinations arise, disappear, return, and sometimes organise themselves in " variegated and fantastic " dances, whose unity is surely too loose to suffice to mark each of the associated elements with the stamp of reality.[40]

Let us not say then, *merely*, that the note of an object's reality is intensified proportionately to the richness and coherence of the system of images it represents. The richness and perfect adaptation of the content of a complex representation confer on it a certain *logical* guarantee of objectivity, but are not by themselves either indispensable or sufficient for the *original* emergence of the feeling and judgement of reality; poor, uncomplicated images, without positive co-ordination with the rest of the representations, may bring the hallucinated subject to a standstill, and give him an intense impression of reality, while, in pseudo-hallucination, a richer and infinitely better combined imagery, clearly localised in space, will not bring with it, even before having been contradicted by experience, any conviction of objectivity. If it be true, as Binet would have it, that " in the simplest act of perception there exists a process of reasoning brought about by habit in a subconscious manner," it must none the less be recognised that, at least outside the normal state, perception or the counterpart of perception may appear amid conditions which offer neither the elements of a *ratiocination*, even an implicit one, nor the complicated antecedents of a *resultant* objective " realisation."

We may be permitted to cite an example which will shed light at the same time on the power of assimilation of pre-existent mental syntheses and on the relative independence of the hallucinatory image. We bring it forward as an " illustration " and not as a " proof " of our thesis. The patient is a deranged subject, whose whole psychic life is under the control of a very complicated illusional system; one of the essential elements of this system consists in the presence, exploits, and queer migrations of intestinal worms. In the state of profound hypnosis the posthypnotic sight of a snake is suggested to the patient; and to furnish a connexion with the suggested hallucination, a rubber belt is stretched out before his eyes. On awaking, the patient's eye was at once fixed on the belt. But the latter at first gave rise to no hallucination; the mere word-suggestion emerged, and that in a purely negative form: " It is no snake," he kept on saying. His look, however, was constantly fixed on the belt, as if the eye was fascinated. . . . The expression of his face grows defiant: " It looks like a snake, but it must be dead." Then the dominating delusional system of the patient comes to the fore. " It looks dead," he repeats, " but my worms are alive; this is not alive. . . ." " The patient became more and more fixed on the belt, as if his eye were riveted to it. His face assumed a puzzled questioning look of doubt and uncertainty; evidently he could not decide what in the world that fascinating object could possibly be. Finally, a look of recognition, and also of terror, could be clearly seen coming over him; the percept was being gradually assimilated by the delusional system, and now the suggested hallucination began to develop rapidly (under the new form which the fundamental delirium imposed on it): ' I do not know what it is, but I am scared at it. . . . That thing must have come from somebody; and I am scared at it now. . . . I shall throw it away.' He threw the belt away, but picked it up soon, and looking fixedly at it, ended by becoming really frightened, and concluded: ' Maybe it is mine. . . . It is no snake, though; I have no snakes.' The patient could not see the belt as a snake, because his delusion was that he was possessed by worms, not by snakes."[41]

This case seems to us to show in detail, in an almost typical manner, the conflict of the present perception with the suggested hallucination and with the pre-existing delirious synthesis; none of the three elements has given way, but they have ended by fusing with each other. It will be remarked that the direct perception—profoundly changed and closely assimilated as it may finally have become—has inflexibly retained the index of reality throughout the apparent contradiction of the immediate fluctuations. The reality of an object, then, may impose itself even before its full identification and rational interpretation; but it is true that the consciousness tends to eliminate every representation that is obstinately incompatible with its internal unity. In the establishment of an hallucination there happens something analogous to what we have remarked in the development of a fixed idea: both of them may appear—at the term—as the resultant of a systematisation which they have in reality created. The fixed idea, no doubt, only develops on a favourable ground; but it does not always answer from the start to the deepest or best-organised tendencies of the subject; it passes through a period of " struggle for life," and we sometimes see it, with a sad fatality, subordinate to itself little by little, in spite of prejudices, in spite of long predominant feelings, in spite even of the most elementary logic, all the healthy parts of the mind on which it has seized. The fixed idea, like a perception or hallucinatory image, is affirmed at certain moments contrary to inward protestations which ought, it would seem, to suffice,

THE FEELING OF PRESENCE

if the feeling of reality is only the result of representative combinations, at least to neutralise the opposed illusion or perception.

3. NEGATIVE HALLUCINATIONS AND FEELING OF UNREALITY

We have just seen that the feeling of present reality is not *originally* the resultant of a complex structure of precise representations skilfully fitted together, since, on the one hand, it may be attached to an extremely poor psychic content, and, on the other, it is not necessarily accompanied by representative syntheses as complex as those presented by pseudo-hallucinations. And if it be objected that these latter are lacking in the character of reality precisely because, being contradicted at every moment by a more vivid sensation or antagonistic image, they have not reached a sufficiently high degree of synthesis, we shall observe that this neglects a certain number of cases wherein the action of this " antagonistic reducer," which intervenes to fetter the feeling of reality, is not strictly capable of being revealed, and inversely, that even in the case of perceptions or hallucinations of small content, the action of powerful reducers may show itself lacking in efficacy. But it does not matter, for we are going to recall a whole order of facts in which the *feeling* of the real is disjoined from the sensation itself : we may say at once that we are going to draw from them the conclusion that, if a certain state of mental de-synthesising, of dust-like mental dispersion, is almost always fatal to the conviction of reality, it is not the fact, however, that this conviction is *necessarily* bound up with that high degree of representative synthesis from which it is desired to make it result. Let us rapidly review a few facts.

As a counterpart to positive hallucinations it is fitting to place " negative hallucinations "—that is, abnormal gaps created in the field of perception. We do not wish to assimilate the examples on which we are going to base our case to hysterical anæsthesias in general, although they offer some analogy with those regional pseudo-anæsthesias the territory whereof remains the starting-point of certain reflexes normally associated with a sensation.[42] Boris Sidis writes : " Both positive and negative visual hallucinations of persons and things could be given by suggestion. If a person, rendered invisible to the subject, was placed in her path while walking, she ran directly into him, and tried to walk on, pushing by him and appearing entirely unconscious of his presence. She could not explain when questioned what had interfered with her progress. This negative hallucination did not extend to objects handled by the invisible person. They seemed to her as if suspended in mid-air, and she could give no explanation of this incongruous appearance."[43] However, the absence here of complete perception is not consecutive on the absence of sensation. The impression of the object is normally received by the patient's eye and goes to produce—save for perception—the majority of its ordinary psychological consequences. The subject is sincere—we may be sure—in affirming that she sees nothing, but an attentive examination of her associations of ideas causes the discovery therein of the influence of the sensation that she claims to be non-existent.[44] A sensation, then, may be received, introduced into the network of mental phenomena, even expressed in equivalents or prolonged in perfectly adapted actions, without for all that entering, even as an image, into the fully-lighted zone of perception. The explanations of facts of this kind may differ; they are even less favourable to, even if they do not absolutely contradict, the hypothesis of a mental determinism which from the very complexity of certain psychic syntheses causes the feeling and affirmation of an objective reality to result of necessity.

Other facts, ingeniously analysed by M. Pierre Janet, present the same difficulty; these are the cases of true perception accompanied by the feeling of unreality.[45] We may be allowed to borrow their recital from M. Janet himself. He groups them under the heading: " Loss of the function of the real." " It seems to me in fact necessary," he writes, " in order to sum up the preceding observations, to distinguish an operation, or, if it be preferred, a part of the psychological operations, which the classical descriptions do not mention separately, but which illness seems to have analysed. A mental operation, a memory, an act of attention or a ratiocination, seem to remain of the same nature whatever be their object, whether it be constituted by wholly imaginary representations or its object be formed by events wholly real, belonging to the world in which we dwell. Association of ideas, it is often said, is the same in dreams and in the experience of life. Is this always accepted affirmation really true? The observation of our clinical patients discloses a singular fact—namely, that their mental operations are not disturbed when it is a question of the imaginary, and exhibit disorder only when there is question of applying them to reality.

THE FEELING OF PRESENCE

" . . . In the same way as the functions are correct in the realm of the imaginary, they remain perfect when it is a question of future or past. . . . All the disturbances we have noted relate to the present and to the real; the emotions are vague, with adaptation to the present and to real circumstances. . . .

" The most accentuated disturbances are met with in voluntary action, in the authentic perception of present objects, in the perception of the real personality, because these are the operations in closest relation with the apprehension of the real."[46]

Here is an example of this suppression of the feeling of reality. And it will be noted that the disturbance affects the internal as much as the external perceptions. " An old woman, of 58, Gou . . ., admitted to the Salpétrière, had just been sent to the hospital because she had been suffering for two months past with an extraordinary delirium. She would not do any work, nor busy herself about anything whatsoever, but remained constantly on her chair groaning and complaining. ' It is no use doing anything,' she repeated, ' for everything is dead . . ., they have put me in a grave where there is nothing, where I am quite alone amid frightful darkness. . . . All around me is black, as black as ink ; . . . all is empty, no one exists any more, there is nothing alive around me, it is as if I were dead myself . . .' etc. As always, the usual examination of the senses and behaviour causes us the same astonishment ; no disturbance, even the slightest, of any sensibility can be discovered, the patient sees objects and colours quite clearly and behaves quite correctly. . . .

" The principal feelings observed in this case as in the former ones are that of absence of relief, of darkness, blackness, queerness, strangeness, disgust, the unseen, the false, the unfounded, dreams, remoteness, isolation, death. What is the feeling to which all the others are attached ? It has been said that it is the feeling of newness and strangeness. I think it is rather that of the unreal, that of absence of reality. . . . The patients continue to have sensation and perception of the external world, but they have lost the feeling of reality which is ordinarily inseparable from these perceptions."[47]

It is noteworthy that these sufferers are victims of, or, if you like, beneficiaries by the same insufficiency of realisation in their pathological phenomena themselves : in their hallucinations —which remain pseudo-hallucinations—and in their impulses —which hardly ever result in a real action. Moreover, these

" doubters " and " scrupulous " folk can be hypnotised only with difficulty; their hypnosis almost always remains partial. " Not only," concludes P. Janet, " have they no longer any apprehension of true reality, but neither do they arrive at the illusion of reality. This fact would be enough to prove, if it were necessary, that the trouble does not consist in an insufficient action of reality on the subject, but in an insufficiency of the mental operations which lead either to the perception of reality or to the illusion of that perception. We can connect together a large enough number of their psychological disturbances by supposing, contrary to the common opinion, that present reality demands a special complexity of the psychological operation, and that there is consequently a special function which may be called the *function of the real*. It is a *disturbance in the apprehension of the real by perception and action* which sums up the disturbances exhibited by our patients outside their manias and obsessions."[48]

And to what is this disturbance in the perception of reality due ? " M. Ribot explains this state by a disturbance in the emotions; but," concludes M. P. Janet,[49] " we think we have shown that it is a case of the debasement of perception either personal or external, and that this debasement is due especially to an *incapacity to synthesise the new impressions, whether they come from within or from without*."

The weakening of the sense of reality, then, would be the *consequence of an insufficiency of personal synthesis*. Does it not follow, contrary to what we have so far maintained, that the feeling of reality is, of itself, a resultant ? By no means; for it is absolutely true, and we have never dreamed of disputing it, that new impressions, entering into conflict with the previous content of the consciousness, may be not only weakened thereby, but even prevented from rising from those lower strata of our Ego which are labelled " the subconscious." As we shall see, a certain unity of the consciousness, momentary at least, is required for true perception; but this unity need not necessarily be that of a *complex* whose close co-ordination creates the conviction or illusion of reality, in the manner in which a group of " antecedents " gives rise to its " consequent." It must be said in any case that the efficacious degree of this synthesis is essentially variable and relative; and on this, *in practice*, everyone agrees. " The feeling of reality, of the mechanism of which we are almost completely ignorant, must be a relative phenomenon and depend on a certain degree of average activity to which the individual is accustomed. An idiot who has had a feeble mental activity all his life arrives none the less at a certain sense of reality which is good enough for him. It is very probable that if our patients had always had this same weakness of thought, they would not now perceive it and complain that they do not apprehend reality, that they find everything distant and dead."[50]

Let us remark also that this synthesis, the insufficiency of which carries with it the loss of the " function of the real," is—as M. P. Janet will be the first to agree—a thing very difficult to define. Does it consist merely in the co-ordination of the representative elements with each other ? But it seems indeed that, among psychasthenics afflicted with a constant or general impression of unreality, the associations formed between the " unreal " perceptions themselves, and then between these and other mental representations, are not so far removed from normal associations. This " synthesis " of M. P. Janet, then, is not a simple *passive resultant* of associated representations; it implies—with caution—either a special activity of the mind, a kind of *Auffassung* or a perceptive effort *sui generis*, or at least a collection of relations which connect the representative groups with the *tendencies* and *personal action*. So that the synthesis consists fundamentally in a harmonious attitude of the entire empirical self, both the cognitive and affective elements.

Our problem, therefore, necessarily embarks on a new phase which we shall attempt to pass through as rapidly as may be: the *affective* connexions of the judgement of reality and its relations with the consciousness of the Ego.

4. THE AFFECTIVE CONNEXIONS OF THE JUDGEMENT OF REALITY

(a) Belief and Interest.

It is a constant fact of experience that the human mind, as soon as it descends from the calm region of the speculative connexions of concepts to enter the region of existences, where the " judgement of reality " comes in question, is immediately involved in a close network of inferences which have none of the cold and disinterested impartiality of pure representations. To affirm an existence is at once to take up a position before it, not only by a hypothetical attitude, which gives no actual impulse to our activity, but by a practical one, of the same order as the existence which is affirmed. It thus involves the acceptance of the consequences of that existence upon our personal activity. And it will be realised that the presentiment or the clear foresight of the consequences may influence the " judgement of reality " which in logic imposes them. Nothing is more natural, then, than this commonplace statement: " We believe what we desire; we also very readily believe what we fear." The object desired or feared—doctrines or facts—affects our action too closely for us not to be tempted to take account of it as of a real object. Conviction, moreover, is almost always derived from a need. In the religious order, for example, how many purely intellectual conversions do we meet with ? From a strictly psychological standpoint, Starbuck[51] reduces the conversions he has studied among American Protestants to two types: the first is characterised by an intense desire to shake off the yoke of sin, the other by a feeling of " incompleteness " and an aspiration towards a larger, more luminous, life; it is evident that the religious form which furnished a nourishment to the tendencies of these converts, by bringing to the one class " escape from sin," to the other " spiritual illumination," must on this account take on in their eyes the appearance of the most startling reality.

(b) Belief and Will.

Would we not be right in generalising this bond which everyone observes between conviction or belief on the one hand, and emotion or feeling on the other, and expressing it somewhat as follows: the reality of an object for us is measured by its echo in the sphere of our tendencies; a totally indifferent object would be non-existent for us ? And such, moreover, is the conception which rallies to its support the principal representatives of the English and American schools of psychology.[52] The affirmation of objective realities depends for them on " belief "; but belief itself is the expression of a feeling or act of will. " It consists," said Hume in his day, " not in the peculiar nature or order of ideas, but in the manner of their conception, and in their feeling to the mind. I confess that it is impossible perfectly to explain this feeling or manner of conception. . . . [Belief] gives the ideas more weight and influence; makes them appear of greater importance; inforces them in the mind; and renders them the governing principle of our actions."[53] Locke had observed, before Hume, that the ultimate human criterion of the reality of an object represented resides in the pleasure or pain which that object provokes.[54]   Nearer our own time, as we have already seen, Bain holds the same point of view and expresses it still more precisely: " In its essential character, belief is a phase of our active nature—otherwise called the Will."[55]   And W. James is only developing the interior logic of this same point of view when he enunciates and explains the following series of propositions: Among the various " worlds of representations," he says, " man is compelled practically to elect some one to be for him the world of ultimate realities."[56]

" The mere fact of appearing as an object at all is not enough to constitute reality.   That may be metaphysical reality, reality for God: but what we need is practical reality, reality for ourselves; and to have that, an object must not only appear, but it must appear both *interesting* and *important* (295)."   " In the relative sense, then, the sense in which we contrast reality with simple unreality. . . ., *reality means simply relation to our emotional and active life.* . . .   In this sense, whatever excites and stimulates our interest is real (295)."   " Speaking generally, the more a conceived object excites us, the more reality it has (307)."   " Every exciting thought in the *natural* man carries credence with it.   *To conceive with passion is ' eo ipso ' to affirm* (308)."   " The *fons et origo* of all reality, whether from the absolute or the practical point of view, is thus subjective, is *ourselves*."   " Our own reality, that *sense of our own life*, which we at every moment possess, is the *ultimate of ultimates for our belief* (297)."   " The world of living realities, as contrasted with unrealities, is thus anchored in the Ego considered as an active and emotional term.   That is the hook from which the rest dangles. . . .   And as from a painted hook it has been said that one can only hang a painted chain, so conversely from a real hook only a real chain can properly be hung.   *Whatever things have intimate and continuous connexion with my life are things of whose reality I cannot doubt* (298)."   And why, indeed, do I not doubt of them ?   Because, stimulated by the agitation of my tendencies, I will the existence of these things by reason of that very will wherewith I will my life.

This is also the thought expressed in a very striking manner by J. Royce (*Religious Aspect of Psychology*, p. 304.   Quoted by James, 318, note): " The ultimate motive with the man of everyday life [for believing in the existence of an external world] is the *will to have an external world.* . . .   The popular assurance of an external world is the *firm determination to make one*, now and henceforth." James adds this remark, that though external *matter* is doubted commonly enough, *minds* external to our own are never doubted. Here " empty appearance " no longer suffices us, a psychic solipsism is too hideous a mockery of our wants (318 note)."

We believe, then, in the reality of an object, *because* we will and postulate that object. What difference, then, is there between belief and will ? From the strictly psychological standpoint, none at all. " All that the mind does is the same; it looks at the object and consents to its existence, espouses it, says : ' It shall be my reality ' . . . The rest is done by nature, which in some cases makes the objects' real which we think of in this manner, and in other cases does not." " *Will and belief, in short, meaning a certain relation between objects and the Self, are two names for one and the same psychological phenomenon* (321)."

(c) Insufficiency of Phenomenalist Empiricism.

We are here very near to the common root of the theories which connect the judgement of reality with " belief," and make this last an expression of feeling or of will.

In the terminology of the old psychologists, all being carries with it a twofold transcendental relation; it is true, that is, it is the object of an act of the intellect: and it is good, that is, it is an object striven after and a motive force of action. Let us now set this *being* face to face with a particular intelligence coupled with an activity; it will be reflected in the intelligence, and at the same time set the activity in motion. The problem is to know when and in what way the *reality* of the being represented will first impose itself on this intelligence. In other words: is being " realised " originally for the human mind in the order of *truth* or in that of *finality ?*

From the purely phenomenalist point of view of the English school, the data of the problem are reduced on the one hand to a group of associated *representations*—corresponding to the " truth " of the object—and on the other hand to a correlative assemblage of *motor reactions*—corresponding to the " goodness " of the object. But to try to draw from a simple operation of representations the *absolute affirmation* of an existence is, as the proverb puts it, to try to get blood out of a stone; in fact, the concept and the image are in themselves indifferent to the attribute of reality, and from the exclusively representative point of view, from that of purely formal definition, " reality,"

as Kant says, " contains nothing more than the possible."
One supposes therefore that the psychologists of whom we are
speaking, finding no bond with the existential judgement in the
domain of pure knowledge, reduced for them to combinations
of images, have been compelled to fall back upon the strivings
and the will. And to this path, if they are to remain faithful
to their phenomenalism to the end, only one issue remains
possible: the identification of the *belief in reality* with the
attribution of a *value in action* to certain mental images, that is
to say, a narrow and exclusive *pragmatism*.

But does this identification truly answer to our personal
experience ? And does not the extreme phenomenalism which
we have just outlined, by its very frankness, drive us logically
back on an attenuated and bastard phenomenalism, which
prudently refrains from casting too vivid a light on the
mechanism of " belief "? When we affirm an existence, our
affirmation goes—rightly or wrongly—beyond the order of
purely representative or motor phenomena; we do not establish
a simple possible relation of images and movements, but we
claim to reach an " absolute," to give ourselves " something "
which is not exactly either the pure representation which we
have of it, or the attitude which this last has provoked. An
illusion, a chimæra, if you like; but the birth of this illusion,
the development of this chimæra, have none the less to be
explained.

And yet, if the reality of an object is not affirmed solely in
the realm of will and of " ends," neither is it affirmed solely in
that of the understanding and of " representations." Belief,
then, can be neither strictly intellectualist nor exclusively
voluntarist; it implies the feeling of a representation, but it also
implies an active reaction.

Here, it seems to us, we have one of the weak points of
phenomenalist psychology; it has cut the stout cord connecting
truth with finality; therefore, with the reduced elements it
allows itself, it fails to reconstitute the synthesis of belief.
Pure representations do not suffice, that is well understood; it
is perfectly well realised that " belief " implies " affirmation "
and that " affirmation " implies " activity "; but as far as " activities " are concerned it is desired to recognise only the voluntary
and motor reactions called forth by the movable content of the
representations. Unfortunately, these reactions only affirm
their subjective reality to themselves and their connexion with
certain images. Where are we to affix to them that *affirmation*

of absolute reality, which all the same is itself not a phenomenon to be neglected ?

Indeed—as we shall see better further on—to seek in particular acts of will for the final basis of the affirmation of reality is to fail to recognise the single *activity* which can be the legitimate principle of all affirmation and " belief: "[57] we mean the *dynamism* of the mind, its " nature," as the Scholastics would have said. For the mind is not only a collection of associated images, nor is it only the inert and receptive metaphysical substratum of these images, it is an " active potentiality," a force polarised towards something after which it aspires; the " true " is for it not only an ornament, but still more strictly a " motive force." But we must not anticipate. Let us continue with the patient inventory of the manifold facts which experience imposes on us in this connection. Perhaps we shall at last fin'd a frame in which they can be inserted.

(d) Participation of the Life of the Emotions in the Affirmation of Reality.

We have seen that, in order that an object may seem real to us, it must have a *certain interest* in our eyes. Let us admit this proposition without quibbling and record this " condition " of our belief in reality.

To have a çertain interest—and thus, generally, to appear to us as real—every object must be related in some manner to *our empirical Ego*, that is to say, that co-ordinated collection of representations, feelings, and tendencies which creates in each of us his proper physiognomy. Let us record this again: for this new " condition," if it were not a corollary of the preceding, would none the less be found to be almost an observed fact.

Who is there who does not know that impression of strangeness and unreality which we experience in the presence of the most familiar objects, when a strong preoccupation has displaced the axis of our psychological personality for the moment ? Here we are experiencing in miniature a mental dissociation. Let us accentuate the phenomenon, allow the groups of representations to swarm in our fundamental system of consciousness; in the measure that their associations with the central nucleus are relaxed, they will lose their index of reality and even fall into the subconscious. Separation from the Ego is fatal to the representations, so long at least as they have not, by grouping themselves apart, constituted a second psychological Ego, which, in the same subject, *alternates* with the primitive Ego.

A third " condition " of this perception of the real is implied in the two preceding, and moreover seems to obtrude of itself—namely, that the representation of the object is something more than a cold reflection imposed on our cognitive faculties, that in fact it puts in motion at the same time *emotions and feelings*.

Every sensation is marked by an " affective tone "; this fact is complacently inscribed on laboratory diagrams, and to controvert it we must deny that the somatic variations recorded are the natural reactions of affective agitations. But the affective tone, the *Gefühlston*, not only accompanies the sensation; it is attached in some degree to every representation which arises in the consciousness; every image has some echo in the emotional sphere. *A priori*, it is not impossible that to the various intensities of the *Gefühlston* correspond different indices of reality, and that the impression of the unreality of a sensation comes from the lowering of its effective tone. This hypothesis may be allowed all the more readily in that we possess conscious sensations only as engaged in more complex perceptions. Now the remark has often been made that a perception is not a bare and adequate assimilation of a present object; it is based on the apprehension of a small number only of immediate sense-data, which themselves bring back to life a whole system of previously acquired impressions; this compenetration of present and past elements strengthens the main lines of the object and determines its identification. A perception—in a mind already organised by successive experiences—supposes, then, amongst other operations, the " recognition " of a goodly number of already experienced elements. And, therefore, a sensation which presents itself with a notably weakened " affective tone " may not be recognised, may fail to enter into the apperceptive system and thus remain outside the zone of the real. Or, again, it may happen—as in the case of Alexandrine, studied by M. Revault d'Allones[58]—or as in that of numerous psychasthenics, that a general weakening of certain fundamental emotional reactions brings on a universal diminution of the " affective tone " of the representations; the latter may then be correctly associated among themselves, and the perception will be sufficiently correct; but it will leave an impression of unreality in the patient, who instinctively compares his present perceptions with the analogous perceptions he has formerly experienced, and opposes the desolating weakness of the former to the emotional eddies which the latter provoked on earlier occasions.

A certain intensity of the " emotional tone " of a representation seems thus bound up with the feeling of the latter's *reality*. But is it allowable to transform the " cum hoc " into " propter hoc ": or, in more exact terms, may we suppose that the spontaneous judgement of reality, which, as we have seen, is not the resultant of a joining together of pure representations, is rather the result of certain consonances of the affective order ?

We must confess that this supposition entails inextricable difficulties.

Or again, as seems to be the case with the pragmatist phenomenalists, is belief in reality *identified* with such and such characteristic combinations of feelings and acts of will ? We have already rejected this claim.

But we may also consider the belief in reality as a *new* synthetic product, *resulting* originally from certain combinations of affective antecedents. To justify this affirmation we should have at least to anticipate, in the analysis of the human mind, the *fixed law*—a truly natural law—which connects these antecedents with their consequent; we should have to discover the increase of intensity and the relative measure of complexity which the affective accompaniment of a mental presentation must exhibit in order to invest it with the character of reality; and had we determined this, our reason would not then find in it what it wants, for it would still ask what fundamental relation can exist between such and such a precise proportion of affective intensity and the affirmation of a reality.

Experience, in fact, affords nothing which would enable us to suspect the existence of the law stated above. Many of those tiny sensations which fill up our days are perfectly perceived in spite of the low degree of their affective tone; the affective dulness which habit engenders may indeed be accentuated to the point of making these sensations fall below the threshold of the normal attention; but, so long as they emerge into consciousness, they are at once " realised." On the other hand, purely imaginary simple representations sometimes move us violently, without that commotion causing the feeling of their objectivity to arise in us. We may at least conclude from this that no strict proportion exists between the " affective tone " of a representation and the " real " character of its content. And then, how often does not a sensation little in harmony with our tendencies succeed, by the evidence of

" reality " which it impresses on us, in breaking the affective connexion with which it finds us provided and even in modifying the course of our feelings ?   Are we to say that this sensation has no consistency and reality, and only imposes itself finally by the original strength of its " affective tone "?   Is it not, on the contrary, its undoubted " reality " which permits it to impose itself *in spite of* its unfavourable " emotional " index ?

In this connexion it is important to note carefully that the *affective* adaptation required of a representation which is to justify its claim to reality is not strictly of the same nature as that kind of *logical* adaptation the necessity of which we have recognised above.   An image which refuses to be included in our rational syntheses either modifies these syntheses or is confined to the " unreal " world; on the other hand, a representation which runs counter to our tendencies, which clashes with our deepest desires, is not by that fact alone eliminated; its reality may subsist entire, in spite of the affective antagonism it has let loose.   The logical contradiction slays the *real*, the antipathy allows it to subsist or only affects it indirectly, sometimes even strengthens it.   The unity of consciousness necessary to the perception of an object will be more rigorous, then, in the order of representations than in that of tendencies.[59]

(e) Attention and Belief.

However, we must not lose sight of the *preparatory rôle* usually—if not always—played by the emotional elements in the perception of the real.   Let us delay a little over this.

The content of a representation, in order that it may become the subject of a judgement of reality, must evidently first penetrate in to the clear consciousness, to be " apperceived " by the knowing subject.   Whatever be the nature of this *apperception*, an object only enters into clear consciousness by soliciting the *attention*.   Attention is not properly speaking, as Kohn[60] would have it, itself the consciousness one has of an object, the entering of this object into the clear consciousness—in short, the simple phenomenon of cognition; it is rather, we think, the general disposition, whether spontaneous or provoked or voluntary, which permits the knowing subject to become and to remain conscious of his representation—in other words, it is the *whole attitude* which permits of the establishment and maintenance of the subjective conditions of our consciousness of an object. In this very wide sense every conscious object is in some degree an object of attention, and it may be said in all strictness with Pillsbury[61] that " attention is consciousness regarded from one aspect." Now if attention is not, for us, the conscious representation itself, but the subjective disposition which enables it to maintain itself, if only for a moment, before the mind, we can—and even must—seek the origin of this disposition in the " active nature " of the knowing subject, that is, either in the will, the feeling, or the elementary motor reactions. A representation will be placed, if merely for the fraction of a second, before the consciousness, only if the psycho-physiological conditions which permit this phenomenon be maintained for an equivalent time; a *momentary polarisation* is produced which corresponds to the notion of elementary attention. Let this still obscure psycho-physiological attention be accentuated and grow more precise in a definite tendency, an *emotion*, a *feeling*, and the representation which it accompanies will have a chance of being maintained longer in the field of consciousness; for an emotion or a feeling will not let themselves be displaced so rapidly, and communicate to the image they support something of their " momentum of inertia." This more intense attention, due to the awakening of the feeling, may be further strengthened by a *voluntary act ;* in whatever way this psychological fact be explained, the influence of the will on the maintenance of the representations has to be admitted.

We can therefore subscribe in a certain measure to all the theories which place either a motor element, or an inchoative emotion, or a feeling, or an elementary volition, in short a certain active reaction, at the origin of the phenomenon of attention; so far as is at present necessary, we may lean on Wundt, Münsterberg, and Stout as on Bain, Ribot, Horwicz, or Stumpf. For it is enough for us here—and it seems that on this point there is a fundamental agreement between the most opposite schools—that the state of attention implies, among its subjective conditions, the awakening of certain organic and psychological tendencies. Now, since perception presupposes attention, it is likely that the necessity of an " affective tone " for every representation which aspires to " realise " itself is often only *mediate* and corresponds to a condition of the attention much more than to a condition of the perception itself.

Moreover, attention is a *direct path* to full perception, to hallucination, or, more generally, to belief; it realises, according to Ribot's expression,[62] a " relative monoïdeism," or better, as

Stout shows, it brings about an at least momentary *unification* of the mind by the predominance of one mental group, or, if you will, by the constitution of an " apperceptive system." " Mental elements which share in the activity of one mental system are for the time being disabled from acting, either in any other systematic combination or independently. When we are engrossed in writing or speaking about some serious topic, it does not occur to us, unless we are inveterate punsters, to play upon the words we use. When we are interested in a game of billiards, the idea of the billiard balls does not set us thinking about the trade in ivory and African slavery."[63] But this " mental unity," realised to some degree in the phenomenon of attention, is also the *sole subjective condition* which we have seen accompanies *always* the true or false perception of the real. There is no occasion for surprise, then, that we can, with Ribot, range the intensities of attention in a progressive series whose limit is true hallucination or absolute belief; the narrower the " unity of mind," the more categorical becomes also the corresponding judgement of reality. The mental group, first of all a simple object of attention, may, when the latter is intensified, become pseudo-hallucinatory or be transformed into a fixed idea; from the fixed idea, an " abortive delirious idea,"[64] the distance is not great to true delirium, which ends by seizing upon and obstinately unifying the activity of the mind; and this unbalanced systematisation is betrayed in true hallucination and morbidly tenacious belief.

5. DIFFICULTY OF CO-ORDINATING THE ELEMENTS OF THE PROBLEM IF THE " JUDGEMENT OF REALITY " IS SECONDARY AND RESULTANT

The accentuation of the psychological conditions created by simple attention, then, causes the rise of the feeling of reality and belief.[65] Now these conditions are summed up in a *closer synthesis* of the elements which actually cover the field of consciousness. It is with just cause, then, that M. Pierre Janet connects the " function of the real " with the " power of synthesis " of the knowing subject. On the other hand, this synthesis appearing hardly possible save on the basis of certain emotional tendencies, at least inchoative, it seems that M. Ribot and the English psychologists are likewise right in emphasising the rôle of feeling, in the widest sense of the word, in the belief in reality.

And here we are once more faced by the elements formerly met with: a *certain unity of mind*, realised by the *co-ordination of the representations*, with the *concurrence of the feeling*. These elements, in a mind which is no longer virgin from every psychological impression, are necessary for a judgement of reality to emerge; they must therefore be taken into account in any attempt to explain that judgement. But to suppose that that judgement is *originally* and *of itself* the *resultant* of a *certain complexity* of the representative combinations and of a *certain intensity* of the feelings excited by them is to come up against all the difficulties we have pointed out repeatedly in the foregoing pages; the stable law which is postulated is arbitrary and cannot be grasped experimentally.

IV. INVERSION OF THE TERMS OF THE PROBLEM

1. REALISM IS PRIMARY AND CANNOT BE REDUCED TO MORE ELEMENTARY CONDITIONS

The problem, as we have stated it, seems insoluble; may not this be just because it is stated badly ? Let us try to transpose its terms; instead of asking how the real can arise from the unreal, affirmation from doubt, the objective from the subjective, let us see if it would not be simpler—and, in fact, more logical—to postulate the *real, affirmation* and the *objective* as a primary fact, and to enquire how this fact is disaggregated or mirrored in the *unreal, doubt* and the *subjective*. We shall thus come once more, with a certain number of modern psychologists and impelled by experience, to the very clear, but insufficiently analysed point of view of the old Thomist psychology.

W. James is our ally here : " there is hardly a common man who (if consulted) would not say that things come to us in the first instance as *ideas*, and that, if we take them for realities, it is because we *add something to them*—namely, the predicate of *having also real existence outside of our thought*." And this conception, James says, " has pervaded psychology from the earliest times," and is the tradition of " *Scholasticism, Kantism, and common sense*."[66] After making every reserve with regard to so blunt an affirmation, we readily subscribe to what follows: " There is no question " that there is a portion of truth in the " orthodox and popular account": " the logical distinction between the bare thought of an object and belief in the object's reality is often a chronological distinction as well. The having and the crediting of an idea do not always coalesce; for often we suppose and then believe. And we are quite conscious of the succession of the two mental acts. But these cases are none of them *primitive* cases; they only occur in minds long schooled to doubt by the contradictions of experience. *The primary impulse is to affirm immediately the reality of all that is conceived.*"[67] Those who think, with James, that it is doubt and not affirmation which requires to be justified, can, moreover, claim illustrious ancestors.[68] We will call to mind only one, who is mentioned by the American psychologist.

Proposition 17 of the second part of Spinoza's *Ethics* is formulated as follows: " Si humanum corpus affectum est modo, qui naturam corporis alicujus externi involvit, mens humana idem corpus externum *ut actu exsistens*, vel *ut sibi praesens* contemplabitur, donec corpus afficiatur affectu, qui ejusdem corporis exsistentiam vel praesentiam secludat."[69] And later, in the Scholium of Prop. 49: " Si enim mens praeter equum alatum nihil aliud perciperet, *eumdem sibi praesentem contemplaretur*, nec causam haberet ullam dubitandi de ejusdem exsistentia, nec ullam dissentiendi facultatem, *nisi* imaginatio equi alati juncta sit ideae, quae exsistentiam ejusdem equi tollit, vel quod percipit ideam equi alati, quam habet, esse inadaequatam, atque tum vel ejusdem equi exsistentiam necessario negabit, vel de eadem necessario dubitabit."[70] However it may be as to the more profound—and only partially true—principles on which Spinoza bases his remark, it remains that, for him, *every uncontradicted idea affirms the reality of its content*; doubt is secondary, it results from an " inadequacy," discovered in the idea and compelling us to disjoin from it— at least, hypothetically—the attribute of existence. Now this " inadequacy," as we shall repeat further on, is discovered only in a " multiplicity," which intervenes to destroy the coherence of the mind and to inhibit its proper act, the absolute affirmation of *being*.

This is exactly what we find expressed from a strictly psychological point of view in W. James: " An object which remains uncontradicted is *ipso facto* believed and posited as absolute reality."[71]

It is true that this fundamental and primitive tendency of the mind to " realise," to " objectivise," is soon enough disguised in man as a result of the growing complexity of the elements which influence perception. To recover the spontaneous attitude of the mind before a representation in all its simplicity, we must go right back to the awakening of each individual consciousness, analyse that formless phase of which Baldwin speaks, in which the conscious Ego has hardly begun to free itself from the mass of indistinctly externalised objects. " It must be with the new-born consciousness," Höffding writes, " as with dream-consciousness; all that presents itself is at first taken as current coin, and there is no reason to dispose the content of consciousness in two different spheres: on one side the world of the possible and of fancy, on the other that of reality and perception; we only discover this opposition, on the other hand, through a series of experiences which are in great part painful. We must often come into collision with reality until its limits grow evident to us."[72] " So far is it from being true," declares W. James, " that our first way of feeling things is the feeling of them as subjective or mental, that the exact opposite seems rather to be the truth. Our earliest, most instinctive, least developed kind of consciousness is the objective kind; and only as reflection becomes developed do we become aware of an inner world at all."[73] " It is surely subjectivity and interiority which are the notions *latest* acquired by the human mind."[74]

As A. Riehl says,[75] instead of starting from pure " subjectivity " to discover how we can pass to " objectivity," it would be better to base ourselves on that datum of experience, the *immediate* objectivity of sensation, and thereafter seek for the conditions on which that objectivity, assumed in the first place, resists or does not resist the control of the reason.

2. RISE OF DOUBT AND OF THE DEMAND FOR A SYNTHESIS OF REPRESENTATIONS AND AFFECTIONS

Our problem, thus transformed, brings us, therefore, face to face with the question: How do doubt and the distinction of perceptions from free representations arise ?

But this question no longer finds us unprepared, as the reverse question formerly did, for we have a *principle of solution* in one of the *fundamental laws of the mind*—namely, the impossibility of its accommodating itself to a logical contradiction and even of remaining wholly secure when faced by a possibility of contradiction. The contradiction which arises eliminates, or rather transposes, one of its two terms; the mere threat of a contradiction suspends the mind's natural movement of adhesion. Such is the very simple principle of negation, distinction, and doubt; it is traditional, and is again implied in the following theorem of W. James: " The whole distinction of real and unreal, the whole psychology of belief, disbelief, and doubt is thus grounded on two mental facts—first, that we are liable to think differently of the same [object]; and second, that when we have done so, we can choose which way of thinking to adhere to and which to disregard."[76]

The child, which first of all reacts to the content of each representation without distrust, soon learns to his cost that not every association is stable nor every sequence invariable. A characteristic—for example, the colour white—which crops out in the memory, associated with tactile images and a sweet taste, imposes itself at first without counterpoise in the child's mind and releases its activity; but soon the presumed object eludes attempts to grasp it, or at least appears tasteless; the primitive association is broken, or rather begins to rank itself on several planes. In this deception " *the first foundation of the opposition between the possible and the real is postulated*. It is only then that *free representations* begin to be clearly opposed to sensation and perception; they take on the character of a thing which possesses no direct practical value, and lose the tendency to movement which was associated with them, and with which their character of reality was so closely connected. The exuberant mobility of the beginning is henceforth interrupted. . . . A certain doubt, a certain inquietude, begins to be felt, the state is no longer so clear nor so homogeneous as at first."[77]

As experiences multiply and the mind grows more complicated, then, certain associations will meet with contradiction, and thus be eliminated from the region of reality; others will persist uncontradicted. The latter, as is natural, are more and more erected into " models " of future perceptions and " prototypes " of reality; for the intrusion of elements of memory into perception continues to increase, and we see what difficulty a discordant sensation has to overcome in order to get itself accepted at the cost of breaking through the established framework. The requirements of co-ordination and synthesis increase with the growing multiplicity of the psychological elements; however, this complex " synthesis " does not *create* the judgement of reality; it merely wards off the contradictions which would prevent the judgement being produced.

But the conflict of representations is not the only eliminating agent which operates in a mind already " complicated " by life. We have seen what part the affective elements play here : they may cause a representation already formed to be misunderstood, prevent an association from being constituted, cause the abortion of an image even before it rises into clear consciousness; in short, they may either virtually suppress a representation or relegate it to the unreal.

3. SECONDARY MODES OF EMERGENCE OF THE JUDGEMENT OF REALITY. THE WHOLE COMPLEX OF FACTS IS EXPLAINED BY ONE OF THE FUNDAMENTAL LAWS OF THE HUMAN MIND

On the contrary, it may happen—secondarily, no doubt, and on the basis of previous experiences—that the feelings play the inverse rôle and assume the preponderating, if not exclusive, influence in the *realisation* of an image or an idea too weak or too incoherent to impose itself alone. We must here recall— and we would underline this fact, susceptible of more than one application to the psychology of the mystics—the importance that feeling may have in mental associations. The study of the phenomena of " affective memory "[78] seems to us to have brought to light—as might moreover have been foreseen—the possibility of an emotional state disengaging itself up to a point from the representation which had provoked it and intervening as an independent term in the associational relations.[79] What happens, in fact ? That the perceptions whose reality causes us the least doubt are found quite regularly accompanied by a sum-total of emotive impressions, quite vague, and varying from one individual to another, but the totality of which takes on a certain recognisable physiognomy for each one. On the other hand, from the moment when the shock of the logical contradiction has caused the notions of the unreal and subjective to arise in our mind, we possess quite distinct conceptual elements which correspond to the notions of object and of reality. These last concepts have been able to contract a close association with the emotional complex which is accustomed to accompany our most undisputed perceptions. It may therefore easily happen that this emotional state, arising in purely accidental connection with any idea or representation, tends to invest the latter with the attribute of reality which it brings in its train; that the mind is deprived at that moment of the means of criticism, and the association made, on an affective basis, between the actual representation and the notion of reality will suffice to carry with it the corresponding judgement.

To sum up in a few words, we will allow that judgements of reality and unreality, objectivity and subjectivity, although *originally* bound up with other conditions of emergence, may appear *secondarily* as the result, in the understanding, either of purely representative associations or of associations with an emotional basis.

In the normal adult, perception or belief is never quite free from the secondary influences we have just pointed out. Does this mean, however, that the " primitive mode " cannot, strictly speaking, be discovered any longer ? Far from it. Let us leave aside pathological cases, to which we have already appealed —for example the case of unsystematised delirium and of incoherent hallucinations. There remains in daily life an infinity of more or less indifferent sensible impressions which seem to us real and objective, for the sole reason that they present themselves to us without shock or contradiction, this seeming objectivity being prompted much less, or even not at all, by their *positive* co-ordination in a speculative or emotional synthesis. In the mental structure, which we are rebuilding at every moment, many of the stones are in practice indifferent and interchangeable; it does not much matter to our mental synthesis whether such and such a detail be replaced by such another or not. And this, it seems to us, explains the presence of numerous hallucinatory elements in our complex perceptions; they rise into the consciousness without being strictly postulated by the synthesis that we are making: but they peacefully enjoy a normal place in the background; and this circumstance is enough to enable them to benefit by that " realising " tendency which is the mind's natural movement.

However, to look at the matter more closely, the *secondary* modes of realisation, pointed out on the preceding page, are themselves based on our fundamental tendency to " postulate as real," to " affirm " without distinction, all the content of representations which are not placed in doubt either affectively, if we may so say, or logically. The attribute of " reality," if nothing acts as an obstacle thereto, infallibly arrives at joining itself, in the judgement, to the object with which the simple play of representations has previously associated it. We might analyse this mental attitude more closely. But this is enough. Here, once again, the human mind is simply following its innate bent. . . .

V. VIEW OF THE GENERAL PSYCHOLOGY OF INTUITION AND AFFIRMATION. DEEP REASON OF THE LAWS TO WHICH APPEAL IS MADE

The point of view we have just indicated not only has the advantage of grouping the observed facts without postulating anything other than the primitive laws of the mind, it is also perfectly in harmony with the principles of more general psychology. Here we may be permitted to be brief and to hope that the reader will follow our outline.

The empirical feeling of presence, the perception of a spatialised reality, is a particular case of *intuition*—the only case, moreover, which we meet with in our ordinary experience.

Intuition—defined in a quite general manner—is the direct assimilation of a knowing faculty with its object. All knowledge is in some sort an assimilation; intuition is an immediate " information," without an objectively interposed intermediary; it is the only act by which the knowing faculty models itself, not on an abstract likeness of the object, but on the object itself; it is, if you will, the strict coincidence, the common line of contact of the knowing subject and the object, their intimate compenetration so far as that is possible without suppressing their respective individuality.

We may say that every knowing faculty is naturally intuitive, that is, that its proper movement, its act, proceeds of itself direct to its object. But there is intuition and intuition. If we parcel out the single and complete power of " knowing " into partial faculties, limited cognitive powers—and in human psychology we are compelled to resign ourselves to this division —the higher concept of intuition, which expresses the finished ideal of knowledge as such, must itself also, in order to be still applied to partial acts, undergo degradations and restrictions; shut up in contingent determinations, it will move in a series of diminished and analogous expressions of itself. A lower mode of knowledge cannot be *intuitive* by the same right as a more perfect knowledge.

At the foot of the ladder of knowledge we encounter *sensible intuition*. If we understand by this an exclusive operation of the sensibility, it implies only a very imperfect assimilation of subject and object. The subject, as sensing, and the object, as sensed, are quantitative and extended; they remain spatially exterior to each other. Then, since the term reached by the sensibility is not the *being in itself* of the things or the qualities of these things, but only the relative and phenomenal aspect of these qualities, that active assimilation, knowledge, will not here, properly speaking, bear on an *object* as object—which would make the " sense " a metaphysical faculty—but on something depending at the same time on the nature of object and subject. The Scholastics used to say that the being of a thing, the object properly so called, is only a " *sensibile per accidens* "—that is, it is reached by a faculty other than sense, but co-ordinated with the operations of sense. *Being, object, subject*, being notions totally foreign to sensibility, the sensible intuition will be—in the order of knowledge—nothing else than the actual coincidence of sense and external object in a " configuration " co-extensive with both. Thus sensible knowledge really brings the subject into contact with its object, " *terminatur ad objectum* "; this white rectangle over which my pen runs is, *from the cognitive point of view*, at once both the content of my sensation and the exterior of my sheet of paper; no intermediary is interposed. But since the " sense " left to itself only attains to this configuration of things, this model-ling, which is common to them and to it, its proper act will not change, whether there subsist an object in itself or not, real and distinct, on the external face of this modelling; the Scholastics long ago admitted that this modelling of the sensible faculty may persist after the external object has disappeared, or even, exceptionally, result from the equivalent action of other causes.

The sense brings the subject *in contact with a real thing*, but *does not of itself discern reality*. The criticism of the sense-datum and the true perception of the real spring from a higher faculty—the faculty of " being," the *intelligence*. Now the purely psychological exercise of this faculty in man offers a spectacle which at first sight is bewildering. The proximate matter on which the intellectual activity is exercised is con-stituted wholly by sense-data, by elements, therefore, essen-tially relative; on the other hand, the intellectual act is an absolute affirmation of something which surpasses the sensible phenomenon; but this something is affirmed only as a *function* of the sensible phenomenon, is only attained by the intelligence *in* this sensible phenomenon. The intellectual act, considered precisively and according to the present conditions of its exercise, is thus constructive, synthetic, but *not strictly intuitive* ; it rebuilds, on the internal face of the phenomenal model, the supra-phenomenal unity which is its external and objective support; in other words it finds again, in the sensible appearance, the absolute *being* of the object which subtends it.[80]

Such is the spontaneous reaction of the human intelligence on the sense-datum; the first movement of the intellect is an unconditioned affirmation of *being*, a *judgement of reality* in the unlimited sense of the word. In the still multiple unity of space and time, in which object and sense meet each other, the intelligence superposes, without restriction and without mistrust, the transcendental unity of being; once released by the phenomenal sign, it goes at once to the very end of its course and implicitly affirms, under the species of the partial data, this " Absolute," this " saturating unity," which is both its motive and its end. But it is with the intelligence as with the child whose consciousness is hardly yet awakened; it has to learn, in the school of successive disillusionments, the art of doubting and handling its adhesions. It has to learn that the affirmation of *being*, which expresses its interior movement, infinitely surpasses in import the fragment of reality attached to isolated sensible presentations.

We have shown how this education of the power of affirmation comes about; it rests wholly on these two fundamental laws of thought: the primitive and natural movement of the mind is to affirm being; this movement is stopped dead by logical contradiction and provisionally suspended by the foreseen possibility of contradiction.

If we wished to seek for the final reason of these laws, perhaps we should find the following: that the human intelligence is not merely a mirror passively reflecting the objects which pass within its field, but an activity directed in its deepest manifestations towards a well-defined term, the only term which can completely absorb it—Absolute Being, Absolute Truth and Goodness. The Absolute has set its mark on the basic tendency of our intelligence; moreover, this tendency constantly surpasses the particular acts of the intellect; the mind is driven by its internal dynamism from intellection to intellection, from object to object; but so long as it gravitates in the sphere of the finite, it attempts in vain to liken itself to its internal movement, to rest in the fulness of its act, to affirm *being*, by identity, purely and integrally. And this unevenness of levels of operation, this disproportion between the anticipatory tendency and the actual object, is the very condition of the *act of reasoning*, the stimulant of that ever-unsatisfied " curiosity " in which the old Scholastics justly saw the principle of all speculation.

The human mind, then, is a *faculty in quest of its intuition*—that is to say, of assimilation with Being, Being pure and simple, sovereignly *one*, without restriction, without distinction of essence and existence, of possible and real.[81]   But here below, in place of the *One*, it meets with the *manifold*, the *fragmentary*. Now, in the order of truth, the unreduced multiplicity of objects suspends affirmation and engenders doubt, just as, in the order of will, the unreduced multiplicity of ends engenders indifference and suspends action. Before a single object, whose at least potential finiteness and multiplicity there is nothing to indicate, the intelligence, as we have said, could only make an absolute affirmation of reality, in which the infinite " implicit " object and the particular " explicit " object were mingled; but when multiplicity appears, it has first of all to be reduced in order that its elements may be affirmed; and if the reduction of these various elements can be obtained only by co-ordination, these latter will share in the reality affirmed *only in the measure* in which they share in the unified totality of which they form part. The affirmation of reality, then, is nothing else than the expression of the fundamental tendency of the mind to unification in and with the Absolute; this affirmation would only have its full objective value by becoming a direct intuition of the Absolute; it keeps, however, a diminished and analogous value in its application to every object which sets the activity of the mind going and allows itself to be co-ordinated with the totality of objects already affirmed; objects are real in the manner and to the extent to which they converge towards the total unity of the mind, or rather, objects are unreal only in the manner and to the extent to which they diverge from it.

We have said above—and it is perhaps well to recall the fact here—that phenomenalism, misunderstanding the active nature of the mind and its transcendent " polarisation," fails to make the synthesis of " belief " in the real.   The Thomist psychology was better inspired in seeking the active element essential to this " belief " at the very basis of the mind.

It remains for us now, in order to complete our study, to attempt a few applications of the preceding remarks to the mystical experience.

SECOND PART
APPLICATIONS TO MYSTICAL KNOWLEDGE

I. THE ESSENTIAL AND ACCESSORY IN THE MYSTICAL STATES

To a superficial observer, the mystical state is a Proteus of manifold and fleeting forms, barely connected by some undecided note of pathological religiosity. Again, among the manifestations of this state, the too limited view of pamphleteers, physicians unversed in psychology, or unenlightened devotees has too often only been able to discern somatic phenomena, bizarre forms of piety, and the crudely marvellous. Among serious enquirers, thank God, an agreement seems to have been reached at the present day to distinguish carefully between the essential and the accessory in mysticism. And on the actual delimitation of this frontier, delicate task as it is, authors of the most varying tendencies are beginning to be almost in agreement.

/We may judge of this from the two or three examples that follow.

Père Poulain—in a very well documented book, which does not aim at the psychological criticism of mysticism—says of " mystical states " that " their real point of difference from the recollection of ordinary prayer is this: that in the mystic state, God is not satisfied merely to help us to think of him and to remind us of his presence; he gives us an *experimental intellectual knowledge of this presence*."[82] This is, in truth, the fundamental mystical phenomenon—the direct feeling of God's presence, or the *intuition of God as present*. The remainder—physical ecstasy, suspension of the senses, sensible or imaginary visions, interior words, levitations, miracles, clairvoyance, etc.—are pure accessories, which may or may not accompany the fundamental state, and the immediate causes of which may be diverse.

M. Boutroux makes the same judicious distinction: " The essential phenomenon of mysticism is what is called ecstasy—a state in which all communication with the external world is interrupted,[83] and the soul has the *feeling that it is in communication with an interior object which is God, the infinite Being*."[84]

This is also W. James's point of view. These phenomena, he writes—visions, verbal and graphic automatisms, levitation,

stigmatisation, the healing of disease, etc.—" these phenomena, which mystics have often presented (or are believed to
have presented), have no essential mystical significance, for
they occur with no consciousness of illumination whatever,
when they occur, as they often do, in persons of non-mystical
mind. *Consciousness of illumination* is for us the *essential mark*
of ' mystical ' states."[85]

It would be easy to multiply quotations, easy likewise, and
more instructive, but here too lengthy a process, to appeal to
the harmonious witness of the mystics themselves. We are
then compelled, in the rapid sketch of some mystical states
which we are going to make, to take as our centre of perspective
the culminating point of these states—that is, *the feeling of the
immediate presence of a Transcendent Being*.

II. INTERMEDIARIES BETWEEN ORDINARY KNOWLEDGE AND THE HIGHER MYSTICAL STATE. THEIR PSYCHOLOGICAL MECHANISM

Between this—specifically mystical—culminating point and
ordinary knowledge is found a scale of intermediate states,
very similar to many of the psychological phenomena already
noticed in these pages.

1. Sensible Visions

There are first of all sensible, corporeal visions, whose
psychological mechanism necessarily enters into the framework
either of sensation or of hallucination. Controversy can bear
only on the objective determining cause of these visions; for
whatever be their cause, the—mediate or immediate—action
of that cause reaches the sensible subject only by modification
of his peripheral organs or by direct modification of the central
organs which govern sensibility. St Thomas already admitted
that sensible visions might result either from the sensible
presence of a corresponding object or from an alteration of
the sensible faculties without the presence of that object.[86]
From the psychological standpoint no greater latitude can be
demanded.

These visions have their corresponding pendant, in mental
pathology, in purely morbid hallucinations. They recall still
more, perhaps, certain of those telepathic hallucinations recorded in Gurney, Myers, and Podmore's well-known collection *Phantasms of the Living*, for these latter often manifest a

sort of finality, or at least do not seem to arise so arbitrarily as the hallucinations of the sick. But we do not dwell on this first category of facts, for the feeling of presence which goes with them has nothing more mysterious about it in mystical sensible visions than in profane hallucinations or sensations.

2. IMAGINARY VISIONS

We would readily say the same of those imaginary visions in the course of which the mystic contemplates the clearly spatialised image of an object, a person, a natural or symbolic scene, but without believing in the actual reality of the objects represented. Many pious persons have been favoured with a very vivid panoramic view of the episodes of the Passion,[87] or again have perceived, in symbolic imagery, certain mysteries, such as the Holy Trinity, the blessedness of heaven, etc. Sometimes there is a kind of oscillation from the imaginary to the sensible vision. " Now and then," St Teresa writes, " it seemed to me that what I saw was an image; but most frequently it was not so. I thought that it was Christ himself, judging by the brightness in which he was pleased to show himself. Sometimes the vision was so indistinct that I thought it was an image, but still not like a picture however well painted. . . . If what I saw was an image, it was a living image; not a dead man, but the living Christ."[88] We beg the reader to refer to the case of the English painter which we have given above from Taine (see p. 66); there the pseudo-hallucination alternates with pure hallucination, just as in St Teresa's case just quoted sensible and direct vision alternates with imaginary vision.[89] The " Census of Hallucinations,"[90] and the " Phantasms of the Living,"[91] might again furnish us with many examples of pseudo-hallucinations very similar to the imaginative visions of the mystics. But it would be useless to dwell upon this comparison, for—whatever be their cause—the psychological mechanism of these imaginative visions presents nothing which fundamentally distinguishes them from pseudo-hallucinations with or without precise spatialisation of the image.

3. LAWS OF THE HALLUCINATORY SPATIALISATION OF A REPRESENTATION. SPATIALISED " INTELLECTUAL " VISIONS

However, imaginary visions and pseudo-hallucinations are not so much cases of real " presence " as of spatial localisation and exteriorisation of an interior representation, or, in other words, of *unreal presence*. From our point of view, their interest resides especially in a particular feature which they bring to light—namely, that a *very precise spatial localisation may accompany the most meagre and least detailed representations possible*. We shall convince ourselves of this by an examination of the two or three examples that follow.

First of all, here is a case of telepathic hallucination, in which we are concerned with the hallucinatory mechanism alone. " On the evening of October 22, I was going to bed as usual in the little turret of the château at Carqueiranne. . . . It was about eleven o'clock. . . . At the end of a certain time which I cannot definitely state, I felt myself awakened by something which was near me, leaning over me, as it were. I thought at first that someone had come to frighten me; I said several times: 'Who is there?' 'Who is there?' But there was no reply, no movement. It seemed to me that there was an absolutely black figure; but I could determine nothing as to its shape, save that there was a face looking at me. Then I began to be afraid, and, sitting on my bed, pushed away with my right arm the figure that seemed to be leaning over me. But I felt nothing, and the shape seemed to disappear. . . . I am sure that I was awake at the time."[92] This hallucination coincided with a death; if it had not been for this detail, one might have said that cases of this kind are almost commonplace. They show the association of an intense and clear feeling of presence with an image of extremely confused features; in the case which has just been quoted, it will be likewise noted that the " gaze " which the apparition fixed on the hallucinated person does not seem to correspond to a visual hallucinatory detail, but to an interpretation of an emotional state on that person's part.

W. James, in 1902, declared that he was embarrassed to explain the following case by means only of the laws enunciated in his *Principles of Psychology*. A Mr. P., completely blind from the age of two, often, while seated at his piano, experienced the impression that a certain person, whom he recognised as a deceased friend, entered the room by sliding under the door, crawled towards the sofa and there lay down. A word or movement on Mr. P.'s part caused the apparition to disappear; moreover, he attributed the whole phenomenon to his state of nervous fatigue, joined to the action of the strong tea he had a habit of taking. But one curious circumstance which struck Mr. P. was that he, reduced by his total blindness to the use of tactile, auditory, and olfacto-gustatory images alone, noticed the presence and size of the person of the phantom with all exactitude, without any appreciable participation of those slight impressions of touch and hearing which often suffice to warn a blind man of the presence of an object. " On cross-examining Mr. P.," W. James writes, " I could not make out that there was anything like visual imagination involved. . . . It seemed to be more like an intensely definite *conception* than anything else, a *conception* to which the feeling of *present reality* was attached."[93] This case, if we understand its elements properly, is an example of *more exclusively spatial hallucination* than the preceding ones. The sensorial elements, which constituted the phenomenal outline of the idea of the deceased friend, were awakened only in the state of vague images, just enough to furnish material for a concept, but without in isolation taking on that character of hallucination which would have related them to their respective *sensoria*. What seems, on the other hand, to have been hallucinatorily objectified is the *residual spatial image* of the deceased friend, an image which had formerly resulted from the association of tactile and auditory sensations; but already sufficiently individualised and detached from its origins not to be immediately resolved into its sensorial components. There was then, James considers, the association of an *idea* with the feeling of a spatial presence; but, according to us, this association is nothing else than the *hallucinatory* projection into surrounding space of the very vague *spatial image* which subtended this *idea*.

To dispute the possibility of this explanation, we should have to deny that a synthetic image, generalised or merely vague, can be projected in an hallucination, *as such ;* to require that it must be always previously reduced to a formally perceived juxtaposition of exact sensorial elements. Experience does not seem to support such a claim. Here is a phenomenon which we have often experienced; we will readily call it a " partial hallucination." In the dark, when we were perfectly awake, we have had the impression that there, in a definite direction, a very delicate and as yet undiscernible object was taking shape, then drawing nearer with growing precision as it diminished in size, like rays converging towards their centre, or again like an image under the microscope the more and more perfect focussing of which gradually strengthens and thins out the features. In general the object did not arrive at assuming a clear contour; the illusion vanished before the term of the movement. Now from the beginning the *localisa-*

tion of this very vague object was precise; soon we even had the impression that we could quite well mark out the region of space which it filled, while its content was hardly beginning to be differentiated. In hallucination or pseudo-hallucination, the spatial images of localisation, direction, and extent seem therefore capable of being dissociated, not from all material content, but from all material content which is *distinct* and which has previously passed through the examination of the five senses.[94] For we do not dream of denying that a *purely* spatial image, a strictly geometrical imagination—a form without matter— cannot be an object of our sensibility; but we mean, what is enough for our purpose, that the spatial image may intervene in certain psychological operations as a whole *sui generis*, without being forthwith reduced into its various sensorial components.

This *relative independence* of the spatial image comes out better still, perhaps, in the most " refined," the most " immaterial " pseudo-hallucinatory phenomenon with which we are acquainted—one which it seems must be pretty frequent. In complete darkness we feel suddenly there, by our side, at a well-determined place, the presence of " something." Of what ? We should be in great difficulty to say; we experience rather a kind of " potentiality " of hallucination, which is localised before being developed into an act. It would seem, then, that the *idea* or the *concept* can, at all its degrees of abstraction, be associated with a spatial localisation. This association may remain purely imaginary and fictitious; it may, by laying greater hold on the attention and canalising the feeling, become pseudo-hallucinatory; it may, lastly, rise, by suppression or extinction of all its antagonisms, to the tyranny of pure hallucination. We have seen in the first part of this article what fundamental laws govern the succession of these stages.

The case we have just described seems to us identical with several of those related in *Phantasms of the Living* by Gurney and his collaborators. Here is a specimen: " Quite early in the night I was awakened . . . I felt as if I had been aroused intentionally, and at first thought someone was breaking into the house. . . . I then turned on my side to go to sleep again, and immediately felt conscious of a presence in the room, and, singular to state, it was the consciousness not of a live person, but of a spiritual presence . . ." etc.[95] Here is another observation communicated to W. James by Flournoy. It is a case of a lady who practises " automatic writing." " I always have," she writes, " the feeling of a foreign presence, external to my body. It is sometimes so definitely characterised that I could point to its exact position. This impression of presence is impossible to describe. It varies in intensity and clearness according to the personality from whom the writing professes to come. If it is someone whom I love, I feel it immediately, before any writing has come. My heart seems to recognise it."[96]

" Such cases," continues W. James, " . . . seem sufficiently to prove the existence in our mental machinery of a *sense of present reality* more diffused and general than that which our special senses yield."[97] And this " sense " is again manifested, under a negative aspect, in that feeling of unreality which certain persons experience in spite of the correct exercise of their outward senses.

We confess that all the examples of " material presence without image " which are brought in support of the assertion—the principal groups whereof we have pointed out—seem to us capable of a simpler explanation. For this the three following laws suffice, of which our earlier analyses furnish the justification:

1. Every hallucination comprises these two elements among others: the introduction of a representation into surrounding space; and the taking of this localisation seriously, or, if you will, the absence of any reason for throwing doubt upon it. The former element is sufficient to bring about pseudo-hallucination; the second needs to be conjoined with it for the hallucination to be complete.

2. The introduction of the aforesaid representation into surrounding space is brought about by the uncontradicted association of this representation with a corresponding hallucinatory " spatial image."[98]

3. The representation associated with the hallucinatory spatial image may be either an *image* of any degree of clearness, or an idea of any degree of abstraction.

The expression " presence without images," taken in the strict sense of the words, is inexact. In fact, *every presence* supposes at least the minimum of images indispensable to the constitution both of the spatialised representation and of the spatialised idea itself, however abstract we suppose it to be. Moreover, the spatial presence, the localisation of an object, of itself implies a relation of situation between the image of this object and whatever image the subject has of himself; the perception of an object's presence always supposes a simultaneous perception of the empirical and spatialised Ego. So far, then, the phenomena of presence which we have analysed are necessarily accompanied by a *certain consciousness of the* empirical *Ego ;* but let us note that this necessary accompaniment belongs to a peculiarity of *spatial* intuition, and that its necessity cannot on this head alone be extended to intuition as such.

Mystical literature, which has shown us so many examples of imaginative visions, analogous to pseudo-hallucinations, offers also in quite large numbers cases of " presence without images." We will quote only two or three to illustrate our remarks.

After the death of Fr. Balthazar Alvarez, a pious person, Doña Ana Enriquez, " sensed " him several times *beside her.* One night, for example, " it happened that suddenly, without thinking of him, I found myself with him. I did not see him with my bodily eyes, but I felt him *near* me, on my right hand, affording me company which greatly consoled me."[99] Fr. Balthazar Alvarez himself relates in his Diary an apparition of the same kind: " Having forthwith entered into prayer, I felt that our Lord (the Lord, God) was *there* present, in such wise that I saw him neither with the eyes of the body nor with the imagination; none the less I felt and possessed him with more certainty and evidence than anything that can be seen or imagined."[100] The Ven. Fr. Luis de la Puente, the biographer of Fr. Balthazar Alvarez, relates his personal experience in these words: " I have experienced in prayer and at other times the presence of God in divers manners. Sometimes it seems that we see God present, not with the eyes of the body nor in a very bright light, nor merely by reasoning, but in a special way, in which the soul suddenly feels that He to whom she speaks, He who listens to her and hears her, *is before her.* . . . This knowledge is similar to that which one man has of another, when, as they converse together, the light goes out and he remains in darkness without seeing or hearing him or feeling any of his movements, and yet he knows him to be present and speaks to him as being present with him."[101] Facts of this kind are numerous, and that great mystic, St Teresa, likewise does not fail to afford them. Delacroix has analysed them in Appendix I of the book quoted above.[102]

In order not to prolong our enumeration beyond due limits, we will conclude it here by recalling the description which another mystical writer, Fr. Alvarez de Paz, gives of these " intellectual visions," as he calls them. " One perceives no representation of the face or the body, yet one knows with greater certainty than if one saw it with one's eyes that the person (Jesus Christ or the Blessed Virgin) is present on one's right hand or in one's heart. . . . It is as if, in darkness, one should feel at once that someone is at one's side, knowing that he has goodwill and not enmity towards you; while one remains absolutely ignorant whether it is a man or a woman, young or old, handsome or ugly, standing or seated."[103]

One might be tempted to compare cases of this kind with certain relations of the higher mystical states where they are depicted as an investiture, an envelopment, an absorption by the Divinity. But we must avoid taking too literally expressions which are often only a *metaphorical* transposition of experiences of quite another order.[104] However, it is possible that a spatial imagination of the divine presence may sometimes be thus described; the case would then in reality belong to the category which we have just been examining.

We have no desire to upset the received classification; but we may all the same be permitted to remark that certain so-called " intellectual " visions are not strictly such, and remain impregnated with spatial imagination. Considering them from outside, by their experimental characteristics alone, they might be attributed indifferently either to supernatural action or to the simple play of the hallucinatory mechanism which has been summarily set forth above. For, from the phenomenal point of view, they present no specifically mystical element, no element which *of itself* transcends ordinary psychology. In order to attribute a religious value to them, we are compelled, in consequence, to seek for indications outside the realm of psychology. All the more so inasmuch as the rôle of experimental psychology is to disclose the laws of connection of mental phenomena, but not to discover the ontological causes of those phenomena.

THE FEELING OF PRESENCE

III. INTUITION OF A TRANSCENDENT PRESENCE IN THE HIGHER MYSTICAL STATE. NATURE OF THIS INTUITION

1. THE PROBLEM

Psychology, then—provided that the question of metaphysical causation be shelved—may claim a certain competence in the examination of the lower mystical states or phenomena, of which we have so far been treating. These latter, in fact, so far as they can be known from outside, seem of the same nature as normal psychological manifestations, and are not completely irreducible to experimental determinism. But the question of competence becomes more delicate as soon as we begin to consider the higher and essential mystical state: for in this, it is not only the nature of the metaphysical agents, latent under these phenomena, but the *mystical fact itself*, which may well escape the grasp of psychological science. This latter is founded on the laws of generalisation of empirical data commonly observable: but if the essential mystical state comprehends descriptive elements heterogeneous to these common data, by what right, and in what measure, can these ordinary laws be applied to it ? *It would not then, in fact, adequately enter into the object of psychology.*

We must then, before making up our mind, study the data of this new problem more closely. A whole book would not suffice for this; we can only claim, in the few pages here at our disposal, to set forth a few reflections which will remain strictly within the general lines of this essay.

2. MYSTICAL INTUITION OUTSIDE CATHOLICISM

The higher mystical state presents—everywhere—as it were an *intuition of the divine*, or at least of the *transcendent*. To judge of it merely by the descriptions given and the claims put forward, this state, very definite among the Christian mystics, finds an analogy, if not an exact correspondence, outside Christianity and even apart from all religious belief. Here are a few examples.

(a) *Neoplatonism.*

Let us recall in a few words *Neoplatonist mysticism*, that complete type of philosophic mysticism. The *One*, higher than being or thought, does not suffer itself to be embraced by the forms of our intelligence; it is only given to the soul in immediate and solitary presence; all multiplicity hides it, and the soul has already lost it when it bends back on itself to become conscious of its own intuition.[105] To this intuition, at once obscure and luminous, the soul may rise by a strict philosophic and moral discipline.

(b) Yogism.

There is the same natural ascension up to ecstasy in *Hindu Yogism*. The general goal of the Hindu religion is, according to its followers, the emancipation of the mind by detachment from the affections, seductions, and distractions of the body and the earthly surroundings. This emancipation procures an increasing consciousness of the identity of the individual soul with the Atman, the universal mind.[106] To hasten the liberation of the mind and its reintegration into the divine Absolute is the special goal proposed by Yoga; the *yogin* aspires to nothing less than the realisation of this end during his present existence, to the attainment of the superhuman condition of *Samâdhi*. Now " Samâdhi lies potential in us all ";[107] it therefore suffices for the ascetic methodically to *disengage* this unitive state, which is the very basis of ourselves. Hence may be imagined the special methods in use in yogism; they are almost mechanical methods of bringing the mind back from dispersion among phenomena to a more and more complete concentration. According to the Swami Râma-Krishnânanda, quoted by Max Müller,[108] the *Yoga-Vidya*, whose end is " to effect union between the individual mind and the universal mind," is practised at the present day in three manners: " *Mantra-Yoga* consists in repeating a certain word again and again, particularly a word expressive of deity, and concentrating all one's thoughts on it. *Laya-Yoga* is the concentration of all our thoughts on a thing or the idea of a thing, so that we become almost one with it. Here again the ideal image of a god . . . is the best. . . . *Râja-Yoga* consists in controlling the breath so as to control the mind. It was observed that when fixing our attention suddenly on anything new we hold our breath; and it was supposed therefore that concentration of the mind would be sure to follow the holding back of the breath. . . . *Hatha-Yoga* is concerned with the general health of the body; and is supposed to produce concentration by certain portions of the body, by fixing the eyes on one point, particularly the tip of the nose," etc.

The more or less complete ecstasy which crowns the prolonged use of these means is a silence of the soul, freed from phenomenal knowledge of the world and the self, and thus placed face to face with its subsistent foundation, which is none other than the Universal Mind.

(c) Buddhism.

For the *Buddhist*—as opposed to the Vedantist—the highest state of contemplation is characterised rather by negative notes; it leads, not to positive union with the Spirit, but to *Nirvâna*. We will not, for lack of space and even more of ability, enter into the question of the real nature of Nirvâna; is it a complete lapse into non-being, or merely the vanishing of appearance ? " *Nirvâna*," Paul Carus writes, " is not annihilation. It is the annihilation of error only; and in this respect it reveals, to him who lives in *Nirvâna*, the higher life of true reality."[109] However this may be, what interests us here is that the true Buddhist mystic[110] claims to arrive, during his earthly life, at a state of high contemplation, in which all the phenomenal phantasmagoria of representations and desires is effaced like a lying shadow, to give place to a formless and undifferentiated immensity. How is this immensity to be defined ? We might as well see in it pure *not-being*—that absolutely black basis of the picture which is marked for the profane by the vain phosphorescences of phenomena—as *Absolute Reality*—that light of so uniform and blinding an intensity that it becomes undiscernible by us as soon as it ceases to be sifted and broken up by the screen of appearance or " illusion," by the veil of *Mâyâ*. It remains in any case true that the Buddhist desires to arrive, by gradual stages of mortification of his empirical personality, at an extraordinary psychological state, identical perhaps, save in its interpretation, with the ecstatic union of the Vedantist system.

(d) Musulman Mysticism. Sufism.

Musulman mysticism, derived both from Christianity and from Alexandrian Neoplatonism, only exceptionally shows a touch of pantheism; its avowed object is the " one and personal " God of Islam.[111]

The Musulman *Sufi* rises or believes that he rises, by the double path of moral purification and contemplation, to a certain intuition of God. The stages of this inward journey are variously indicated by the spiritual masters who have succeeded each other since the epoch of the Hegira. Dou'n-Noun († A.H. 245, A.D. 859), for example, distinguishes three degrees of mysticism: astonishment, proximity, and annihilation. Bestami († A.H. 261, A.D. 874) gives more degrees; the highest are proximity and annihilation; the Sufi must pass through personal annihilation to find God.[112] In the epistle of Kocheïri (A.H. 465, A.D. 1072), "a complete and systematic explanation of the Sufi doctrine," "the unitary belief" (the belief in monotheism), he says, "is the beginning, the finding of God the middle, and existence[113] the end. We attain existence only after having come forth from the place of finding; and God only exists [for the soul] after the vanishing of the flesh, for the flesh cannot subsist when the sultan of truth appears."[114] Before Kocheïri, Avicenna († A.H. 429, A.D. 1037), without professing to be himself a mystic, had set out in detail the "stations" of the Sufi. The latter, "after he has gone through the stages of aspiration and exercise," reaches raptures, "delicious but at first short," then progressively more frequent. "He looks turn by turn at God and his soul in a reciprocal motion; but at last his soul itself disappears from his sight; he sees only holiness alone, or if he still sees his soul, it is in so far as the latter sees God. . . . Having arrived at this point, he has realised union."[115] Later it is Al Gazali († A.H. 505, A.D. 1111) who makes himself the champion of intuitive mysticism. According to him there are two worlds, the visible and the invisible, and in man two corresponding kinds of knowledge, discursive sensible knowledge and mystical knowledge. "Let us suppose," Gazali explains, "that a man wishes to bring water into a hole hollowed out in the earth; he may bring it from external springs by means of canals; but if perhaps he has dug at the interior of the hole, let him take away the layers of earth, and he may chance to find a more abundant sheet of water, less liable to dry up. The heart is like this hole. Knowledge may be brought to it from outside by the channels of the senses; but let a man on the other hand shut up these channels by solitude and retreat, and dig at the bottom of his heart by cleansing it from all the cares of this world, and he will see spring up therein the knowledge which will wholly fill it."[116] Ecstasy, then, for Gazali, is the normal outcome of mysticism.

We may set out again, after Gazali, a number of testimonies which would show the importance of this culminating point of the mystical states in the constant tradition of Sufism; union with God, a state of joy and brightness wherein " the soul is isolated in the company of God " (Djîlâni, A.H. 561, A.D. 1165). Rational science seems pale indeed to the Sufi beside this mystical knowledge: " The knowledge of those who possess the truth results from divine revelation, and is not capable of contradiction " (Ibn Arabi, †A.H. 638, A.D. 1240).[117] It is " an immediate perception, as if one touched the objects with one's hand "[118] (Gazali). And the race of the Sufis is not extinct even to-day.

(e) Contemporary Profane or Pantheistic Mysticism.

Let us now seek among our Western contemporaries for some examples of states of enlightenment, of transcendent " presence," which remind us of the mystical union.

These states may occur *apart from any religious* influence and *interpretation*. Such was the case with a friend of W. James, who often experienced the feeling of a suprasensible presence. " There was not a mere consciousness of something there, but fused in the central happiness of it, a startling awareness of some ineffable good. Not vague either, not like the emotional effect of some poem, or scene, or blossom, or music, but the sure knowledge of the close presence of a sort of mighty person, and after it went, the memory persisted as the one perception of reality."[119] The subject of this " experience," a man of the keenest intellect as James bears witness, did not, however, interpret it as a divine manifestation.

There are numerous examples which might be ranked under the heading " *Cosmic Consciousness* "—a term invented by a Canadian psychiatrist, Dr. Bucke. " Cosmic Consciousness " is not a simple exaltation or expansion of ordinary consciousness, it is a new function recalling, in another order, the direct intuition which we have of our Ego; it is a " consciousness of the cosmos—that is, of the life and order of the universe. Along with the consciousness of the cosmos there occurs an intellectual enlightenment which alone would place the individual on a new plane of existence. . . . To this is added a state of moral exaltation, an indescribable feeling of elevation . . ., what may be called a sense of immortality, a consciousness of eternal life, not a conviction that he shall have this, but the consciousness that he has it already."[120]

A scientific man communicated the following to W. James:

" Between twenty and thirty I gradually became more and more agnostic and irreligious, yet I cannot say that I ever lost that ' indefinite consciousness ' which Herbert Spencer describes so well, of an Absolute Reality behind phenomena. For me this Reality was not the pure Unknowable of Spencer's philosophy, for although I had ceased my childish prayers to God, and never prayed to It in a formal manner, yet my more recent experience shows me to have been in a relation to It which was practically the same thing as prayer. . . . Whenever I had any trouble . . . or when I was depressed . . . I used to fall back for support upon this curious relation that I felt myself to be in to this fundamental cosmical It. It was on my side, or I was on Its side, however you please to term it, in the particular trouble, and it always strengthened me and seemed to give me endless vitality to feel its underlying and supporting presence. . . . Now, at the age of nearly 50, my power of getting into connection with it has entirely left me, and I have to confess that a great help has gone out of my life."[121]

The following case—allowing for the nervous condition of its hero, J. A. Symonds—borders on pathology. " Suddenly . . ., when my muscles were at rest, I felt the approach of the mood. . . . Irresistibly it took possession of my mind and will. . . . One reason why I disliked this kind of trance was that I could not describe it to myself. I cannot even now find words to render it intelligible. It consisted in a gradual but swiftly progressive effacement of space, time, sensation, and the multitudinous factors of experience which seem to qualify what we are pleased to call our Self. In proportion as these conditions of ordinary consciousness were subtracted, the sense of an underlying or essential consciousness acquired intensity. At last nothing remained but a pure, absolute, abstract Self. The universe became without form and void of content. But Self persisted, formidable in its vivid keenness, feeling the most poignant doubt about reality, ready, as it seemed, to find existence break as breaks a bubble round about it."[122]

To descend into the deeps of the " pure Ego " and free the " cosmic consciousness " from it, it is not necessary to wait patiently for a favourable crisis or to prepare oneself by a *rigorous ascesis ;* it is enough prudently to inhale an anæsthetic. Mr. Blood has written a book on the " Anæsthetic Revelation,"[123] and W. James knew " more than one person who is persuaded that in the nitrous oxide trance we have a genuine metaphysical revelation."[124] He himself, from experience, thought that he could infer, not the mystical reality, but the latent presence within us of forms of consciousness entirely different from the ordinary; " we may go through life without suspecting their existence."[125] There are believers in the " anæsthetic revelation," which is often a monistic revelation; for them the *other* appears absorbed into the *One*. " Into this pervading genius we pass, forgetting and forgotten, and thenceforth each is all, in God. There is no higher, no deeper, no *other*, than the life in which we are founded. The One remains, the Many change and pass; and each and every one of us is the One that remains."[126]

(f) Ecstasy of Contemporary Protestants.

Let us leave the natural " monistic revelation "—which offers so many analogies with the ecstasy of the Hindu mystics —and come to the " approved " Catholic mystics, passing first of all by some *Protestant* intermediaries.

From a clergyman: " I stood alone with Him who had made me. . . . I did not seek Him, but felt the perfect union of my spirit with His. The ordinary sense of things around me faded. For the moment nothing but an ineffable joy and exaltation remained. It is impossible fully to describe the experience. . . . The darkness [of the night] held a presence that was all the more felt because it was not seen. I could not any more have doubted that *He* was there than that I was. Indeed, I felt myself to be, if possible, the less real of the two. My highest faith in God and truest idea of him were then born in me. I have stood upon the Mount of Vision since, and felt the Eternal round about me."[127] J. Trevor, in his book *My Quest for God*,[128] insists on the value of this kind of mystical state: " These highest experiences that I have had of God's presence have been rare and brief—flashes of consciousness which have compelled me to exclaim with surprise, ' God is *here !*' . . . I have severely questioned the worth of these moments. . . . But I find that, after every questioning and test, they stand out to-day as the most real experiences of my life. . . . I was not seeking them. What I was seeking, with resolute determination, was to live more intensely my own life. . . . It was in the most real seasons that the Real Presence came, and I was aware that I was immersed in the infinite ocean of God."[129] Lastly, a case taken from Flournoy's collection; the narrator is a Swiss, of whom no other particulars are given: " I was in perfect health. . . . I felt neither fatigue, hunger, nor thirst, and my state of mind was equally healthy. . . . All at once I experienced a feeling of being raised above myself, I felt the presence of God . . . as if His goodness and His power were penetrating me altogether. . . . I think it well to add that in this ecstasy of mine God had neither form, colour, odour, nor taste; moreover, that the feeling of His presence was accompanied with no determinate localisation. It was rather as if my personality had been transformed by the presence of a *spiritual spirit*. But the more I seek words to express this intimate intercourse, the more I feel the impossibility of describing the thing by any of our usual images. At bottom, the expression most apt to render what I felt is this: God was present, though invisible; He fell under no one of my senses, yet my consciousness perceived Him."[130]

3. Mystical Intuition in the Great Orthodox Catholic Contemplatives. Its Descriptive Characters

Among the *orthodox Catholic mystics*, we will question only three or four of the most authoritative; and, again, we will consider only the essential features of their truly mystical states. In order to remove from this little work all pretensions of a documentary or bibliographical nature, and for convenience of reference, we will borrow our quotations from that kind of " florilegium " of mystical texts which Fr. Poulain has added as an appendix to the various chapters of his *Graces of Interior Prayer*.[131] Where necessary the contexts have been verified. We do not, however, by our quotations, claim to impose our opinions in their completeness on the learned author, for they depart widely from his.

The mystical states properly so called range themselves in various degrees, the number and nomenclature of which vary from author to author. Fr. Poulain, for example, distinguishes in ascending order the prayer of quiet, full union, ecstasy, and transforming union. But these states are, according to him,[132] only stages or varieties of a single fundamental phenomenon, the mystical *intuition*, the intellectual *perception* of the Divinity as *present*.

" God," says St Teresa, " *visits* the soul in a manner which prevents it doubting, when returning to itself, that He was

within it and that it dwelt in Him."[133]   " I knew someone who
was unaware of God being in all things by presence, power, and
essence, yet was firmly convinced of it by a divine favour of
this sort."[134]

Let us attempt to explain more precisely the manner of this
interior perception of God.

" When the most high God cometh unto the rational soul,
it is at times given her to see Him, and she seeth Him within
her, without any bodily form, and she seeth Him more clearly
than one mortal man can see another; for the eyes of the soul
behold a fulness, *spiritual not bodily*, about which I can say
nothing at all, for words and imagination fail me."[135]   This is
from B. Angela of Foligno.   " Nothing is seen in this prayer,"
says St Teresa again, " *even by the imagination*, that can be
called even imaginary vision. . . ."[136]

" When all the faculties of the soul are in union [in the full
union] . . . they can then do nothing whatever, because the
understanding is, *as it were, surprised*.   The will loves more
than the understanding knows, but the understanding does not
know that the will loves, nor what it is doing, *so as to be able
in any way to speak of it*.   As to the *memory*, the soul, I think,
has none then, nor any *power of thinking*; nor are the *senses*
awake, but rather as lost."[137]   " The difference between
union and trance is this, that the latter lasts longer and is more
visible outwardly."[138]   St John of the Cross also clearly indicates this suspension of the activity of the lower faculties in
mystical contemplation: " This interior wisdom, so simple,
general, and spiritual, enters not into an intellect entangled
and covered over by *any forms or images* subject to sense."[139]

Again, to attain to this contemplation, the necessary path is
detachment from the " sensible," abandonment of " discursiveness," and the gradual recollection of the soul in itself.
Let us listen to a Christianised echo of Neoplatonism in that
" *Mystical Theology* " of the pseudo-Dionysius which inspired
so many contemplatives and theoreticians of prayer: " But thou,
O dear Timothy, by thy persistent commerce with the mystic
visions, leave behind both sensible perceptions and intellectual
efforts, and all objects of sense and intelligence,[140] and all things
both not-being and being, and be raised aloft unknowingly
to the union, as far as it is attainable, with Him who is above
every essence and knowledge (ὑπὲρ πᾶσαν γνῶσιν).   For by the
resistless and absolute ecstasy in all purity, from thyself and
all, thou wilt be carried on high, to the superessential (ὑπερούσιον)

ray of the divine darkness, when thou hast cast away all and become free from all."[141]

Πρὸς τὴν τοῦ θείου σκότους ἀκτῖνα: the ray of the divine darkness ! To understand the mystical state we must be in a position to bring about, otherwise than by words, the synthesis of this antinomy which is hurled so boldly in our faces. The divine intuition is *as dark as it is luminous.* " If anyone when he has seen God understands what he has seen, it is never God that he has seen, but some one of those things of His which exist and are known."[142] " The knowledge [in infused contemplation]," writes St John of the Cross, " is general and obscure—the intellect being unable to conceive distinctly what it understands."[143] And the following passage from Tauler is instructive: " The spirit is transported high above all the faculties into a void of immense solitude whereof no mortal can adequately speak. It is the mysterious darkness wherein is concealed the limitless Good. To such an extent are we admitted and absorbed into something that is one, simple, divine, illimitable, that we seem no longer distinguishable from it. I speak not of the reality, but of the appearance, of the impression that is felt. In this unity, the feeling of multiplicity disappears. When, afterwards, these persons come to themselves again, they find themselves possessed of a distinct knowledge of things, more luminous and more perfect than that of others. . . . This obscurity is a light to which no created intelligence can arrive by its own nature. It is also a solitude, because this state is naturally unattainable."[144]

It would seem, indeed, that the mystic, wholly absorbed in his sublime vision, loses the feeling of human personality and at the time makes no conscious return to his acts. In fact there is often revealed a *relative unconsciousness* which is not the cessation of all intellectual activity, but the *supreme reduction—* momentary, moreover—*of the multiplicity of acts to unity,* and consequently of the perceived distinction of object and subject. " God then [when He raises it to the union]," writes St Teresa, in a passage which deserves to be quoted in its entirety, " deprives the soul of all its senses that He may the better imprint in it true wisdom; *it neither sees, hears, nor understands anything while this state lasts.* . . . But, you may ask, how can a person who is incapable of sight and hearing know these things—that it has been in God and God in it ? I reply that she [*does not see them at the time,* but *sees them clearly later, after she has returned to herself,* and knows them[145]], not by any vision, but

THE FEELING OF PRESENCE

by a certitude which remains in the heart and which God alone could give."[146]

When we read these passages from St John of the Cross or St Teresa on the divine darkness and the absence of reflex consciousness, it is fitting not to lose sight of the commentary which their context and other texts of the same writers supply to them.

We will permit ourselves here to quote a few lines of Fr. Alvarez de Paz, which explain—so far as it is possible—the kind of psychological activity which accompanies ecstasy. " God manifests Himself to the soul by an image that represents Him very perfectly. The sensible faculties neither receive it nor give it, *it is not composed of forms that are already in our possession*, but it is a *new infusion* made to the mind. . . . Thus furnished and strengthened by the highest help, the mind sees God. *It does not accomplish this by denying* or withdrawing anything from Him, as when we say: God is not limited nor finite. Neither is it by *affirming* something of Him, attributing it to Him, as when we say: God is good and wise. But it is by *regarding* the divine greatness without any admixture of anything else, in the tranquillity of a calm day. Certainly, O reader, when you see the light with the bodily eyes, you do not arrive thereat by a comparison of ideas. . . . You simply see the light. In the same way the soul, in this degree of contemplation, *affirms nothing, denies nothing, attributes nothing, avoids nothing*, but in complete repose she *sees* God. It will be said: This is astonishing, or rather unbelievable. . . . I admit that it is astonishing. The fact, however, is very certain."[147]

This analysis would be translated into the technical language of modern psychology by saying that higher mystical contemplation is neither a sense-perception nor an imaginative projection nor a discursive knowledge, but, strictly speaking, an *intellectual intuition*, one of those intuitions whose exact type we do not in our ordinary experience possess. Before seeking to provide ourselves with some idea of what this intuition may be in the case of the mystics, we must add two or three remarks of a purely descriptive character.

1. In its highest degree mystical contemplation does not appear precisely as an effacement of the personality before the more and more exclusive brightness of the divine presence, but rather as a *union* in which the personality, far from being annihilated, is *upraised* and *transformed*. " It is a complete

transformation into the Beloved . . . in the perfect union of love, wherein the soul becomes divine, and by participation, God, so far as it is possible in this life."[148] " The soul seems to be God rather than itself, and indeed is God by participation, though in reality preserving its own natural substance as distinct from God as it did before, although transformed in Him, as the window preserves its own substance distinct from that of the rays of the sun shining through it and making it light."[149]

2. We have hardly paid any attention to the *affective elements* of the mystical states. This is because they are of less importance from the special standpoint of this work. But it is clear that their intensity and varieties would in themselves offer a very interesting object of study. We do not, however, think that they can *by themselves* solve the question of a fundamental distinction between the mystical and the ordinary psychological states, always somatic on one side or another. For it seems that, if the highest contemplation, as " knowledge," is freed from all participation of sensible and imaginary representations, it none the less maintains an affective polarisation of the whole human composite, body and mind. At least, we nowhere find that ecstatic love dwells exclusively—like intuition properly so called—" in the summit of the spirit,"[150] and we believe that we recognise numerous indications to the contrary. But if mystical contemplation is exercised without admixture of any sensible image, how are we to explain the maintenance of a certain lower affectivity ? or, at least, in what sense is it to be interpreted ? This is a problem—doubtless not an insoluble one—upon which we will not here embark.

3. Contemplation or ecstasy, in the great Catholic mystics, far from dissuading them from *action, favours* it; it only withdraws a few minutes or hours from the active life to invest it afterwards with exceptional vigour and fulness. Much more— and it seems that this is the most perfect state to which the mystic can aspire on earth—the highest contemplation becomes *habitual*, and then, instead of suspending the lower activities, it *restores them to their normal functions*, thus releasing in the subject favoured with it, not a unity momentarily prejudicial to the outer life, but a kind of harmonious duplication, which maintains it in contact with God without taking from it the liberty of mind necessary to earthly occupations. St Teresa offers a good example of this mixed state.

4. We think it useless to insist on the *interpretation which*

the mystics themselves give of the nature of their state. They are unanimous in considering the mystical union properly so called as a grace of God, not only in the sense that God has allowed them by a special providence to benefit by an exceptional concourse of otherwise natural circumstances, but in the sense that a *direct divine intervention has produced in them a state absolutely unattainable by merely human means.* " As all the natural operations of the soul, which are under its control, depend upon the senses only, it follows that God is now working in a special manner in this state . . . that the soul is the recipient on which He bestows spiritual blessings by contemplation, the knowledge and the love of Himself together; that is, He gives it the loving knowledge without the instrumentality of its discursive acts, because it is no longer able to form them as before."[151]   In these few lines St John of the Cross supplies us with the two great " psychological " reasons which bring the mystics to attribute to their state an *immediate* divine origin—namely, the reality of an *essential presence*, " nullo interposito medio "; it is firstly their apparent *passivity* and personal insufficiency in the bringing about of these states; secondly, the *very mode of the knowledge* which is then communicated to them, a mode not only extraordinary but in contradiction, as it would seem, with a fundamental psychological law, the necessity of the *intellectio in phantasmate.* We will not speak here of the theological and moral reasons which perhaps come to the support of these psychological ones. The question of the *immediate causality* of the mystical states is then already, in part, for the mystics themselves, an affair of interpretation and reasoning; the witness of the interested parties cannot have the same value here as on the point of direct observation that *the fact* involved is that of *an " intellectual intuition,"* of an " *imageless vision* " of God.

And this disconcerting phenomenon is formally affirmed. Does it constitute a *phenomenon " sui generis," surpassing our psychological laws,* or rather *is its originality only illusory* and *does it permit itself to be included, on analysis, in our ordinary classifications of phenomena ?*

4. Discussion

(a) Preliminaries.

Let us first of all note—it is worth the trouble—that though it is an excellent thing, in studying mysticism, to extend one's enquiry over as wide a field as possible, yet it would, on the other hand, be very unscientific to affirm, on the ground of a certain number of apparent similarities, the fundamental identity of all the cases compared. We should severely condemn the levity of a psychologist who, after a summary comparison of profane or religious examples, such as those we have adduced, should infer, not indeed the identity of the causes at work—for that would too obviously exceed the competence of a merely empirical psychologist—but the identity of the *phenomenal content* of all similar states.

And this remark seems to us all the more justified in that, among the Christian mystics themselves, the various degrees of union—as we find them described—are not all equally capable or incapable of being reduced to a purely psychological scheme. Sometimes, when the sensible or imaginative element subsists in them, it might be asked whether contemplation indeed implies an " intellectual intuition," and if it has not to be reduced, psychologically speaking, to the form of an interpreted hallucination. Sometimes the " intellectual intuition " —if there is one—will be accompanied at least by a confused spatial image; the mystic will feel God, *beside* him, *around* him, or even in a vaguely determined *direction*; is this case clearly different, in its content, from that " hallucinatory spatial projection of a concept " whose purely " profane " possibility we have recognised above ? Lastly, in the higher degrees, the intuition, according to the description of the mystics, may be not only imageless but also *without any localisation*, and in this case the actual consciousness of the Ego either is conserved or seems suppressed; here, *if the letter of the documents is to be believed*, we shall be compelled to renounce the task of finding corresponding states in ordinary psychology; but is not the mystic under an illusion ? Then, the juxtaposition, in the same subject, of the state of union and the acts of the exterior life throws a new light on the fundamental mystical phenomenon. Let us, therefore, beware of being too ready to assimilate states that are perhaps very dissimilar.

b) Statement and Criticism of Certain Opinions of Psychologists.

And with the help of this reserve, let us now make *a rapid criticism of some opinions* which have been formulated as to the psychological nature of high contemplation. We shall take no account of those which do not reach even that degree of information and discernment which may be looked for in an honest article written for popular consumption; among those which are worth taking into account, we will choose only two or three of the more typical.

Firstly, that of J. H. Leuba.[152] It amounts in essence to this: during the trance, the content of the mystical consciousness becomes increasingly impoverished and rendered uniform; this movement is pursued not only to the extent of a very vague monoïdeism (this is Th. Ribot's thesis), but even to unconsciousness, which Leuba looks upon as a perfect absence of ideas (*aïdeism*). On returning to himself, the mystic *interprets* the series of his states; in spite of their affective continuity, he perceives a gap, " he senses a void; this void, this nothing, thus becoming an object of thought, assumes existence and becomes the Nothing which none the less *is*."[153] And how does this come about? As a result of some preconceived doctrine concerning the attributes of the Godhead; there is a subsequent identification of an artificial concept with an experience, of God with the metaphysical speculation and the Nothing that is experienced, if we may so put it. . . . Change the doctrine, and the same experience would lead to the Buddhist Nirvâna.

William James, after remarking that the mystical experience, though it may be authoritative for the subject favoured with it, offers no reasonable guarantee to unbelievers, professes none the less that the simple existence of this subjective experience breaks down the authority " of the non-mystical or rationalistic consciousness, based upon the understanding and the senses alone,[154] to represent the totality of possible modes of knowledge. Later,[155] he proposes an *hypothesis* which seems to him to express the *common nucleus* of the most diverse forms of mysticism, and to connect this latter with experimental psychology without cutting it off from the contact which it *perhaps* has with an ulterior reality. Our conscious self is in continuity with a *subconscious self* (the equivalent of Myers' " subliminal self "), which is not a degradation of the conscious Ego, but a profound region of still unexplored treasures in which both the intuitions of genius and the mystical intuitions are elaborated in silence. Ignorance of this subterranean working causes its effects to be attributed to a cause foreign to it—and herein, he thinks, *we are only partially wrong*, for the subconscious, which on one side emerges from the clear consciousness, is on the other side continuous with a vaster world which surpasses and constantly influences it. This transsubliminal Reality will, however, receive diverse determinations in the diverse systems of metaphysics. For a Christian this Reality will be God, whose grace, the source of light and lever of action, bases itself upon the human subconscious to put in motion as a consequence the higher faculties of intellect and will.[156]

Closely analogous, but more strictly psychological, if we grasp it properly, is the explanation of H. Delacroix. " The feeling of passivity which the mystics so strongly experience, and from which they infer the transcendental nature of their states and their relation to a higher activity, to divine action, is the ignorance of an interior working, of *subconscious activity*. . . . Since these states seem to be beyond all expectation, sudden and causeless; since they have no known reason or rule; since they surpass nature by the value of their content and their power of action, they must be related to a foreign cause. Nature cannot excel herself. Now the hypothesis of a subconscious activity sustained by certain natural dispositions and regulated by a directive mechanism exactly fulfils the rôle of this foreign cause and wholly explains this feeling of *passivity* and *exteriority*."[157]

The subconscious, moreover, " accounts for all those characteristics which the mystics attribute to their visions and interior locutions."[158] Lastly, " it is no more difficult to attach to it those great confused intuitions, magnificent and unexpected, which suddenly emerge, putting in the shade the ordinary consciousness of self and of things. The intuitiveness latent under distinct acts of meditation and the Christian life, the intuitiveness which is the foundation of the mystical spirit and which appears obscurely in the efforts which it makes to free itself from logical thought and voluntary effort, this innate aptitude to react on the world, on the whole action of the world on the soul, not by local, multiple, and precise reactions, but by a whole vast attitude, free themselves, when the work of preparation allows them to do so, without there being a due proportion between the natural riches thus set free and the effort which brings them to light."[159]

Delacroix, then, does not grant to the mystics that this

intuitiveness, with which he recognised that they were endowed, is the faculty of having one of those strictly intellectual intuitions, unknown to our ordinary psychology, but the absolute possibility of which Kant himself, in spite of his agnosticism, admits. The mystical intuitiveness would be only a sort of æstheticism, superior and refined, capable of being reduced to the refined conscious and subconscious play of our tendencies and representations of sensible origin. The " nihil in intellectu quod non prius fuerit in sensu " would not have to abdicate any portion of its empire, and mysticism would open no breach in the rigorously psychological determinism of mental facts.

We will mention again, on its psychological side, the theory set forth by E. Récéjac in his thesis *Essai sur les fondements de la connaissance mystique*.[160] The author summarises his view in a short note on p. 61 of that work: " This is, in truth, the interior working of mysticism: the Will aspiring after the Absolute, at the same time striving against the empirical consciousness and leaning symbolically upon it, seeking to do without even symbols, arriving at last at a state of unconsciousness in which only the desire any longer subsists together with an assurance of moral purity which is equivalent to the possession of the Absolute." The mystical states, then, would be stages of that ascensional movement which draws the *Will* towards the Absolute; this movement is kept in being and constantly guided by the *symbols* which consciousness affords; but the will, under penalty of being false to its inner law, at each moment *surpasses* this particular symbolism, which is, at the same time, a help and a hindrance to it. The mystic seeks progressively to set free the profound striving of the will from its phenomenal supports; it first of all uses symbolism while reducing it; then, at the summit of ecstasy, succeeds in suppressing it, and thus finds, in the silence of the phenomenal consciousness, the whole purity of the tendency, of the basic desire, which made the unity and motive principle of its ascension. The mystic then meets with nothing else, in his sublimest trances, than the very basis of his Ego, his deepest Activity, or, if you will, his Liberty; but he meets there, at the same time, " the Absolute, immanent in Liberty "—that is, if we rightly understand, the pure, direct, non-symbolic affirmation, lived rather than thought, of the Absolute.[161]

Do all these interpretations give us a " higher mystical state " which exactly corresponds to the descriptions of those persons who have experienced it ? We do not deny that, by a suitable combination of the purely psychological elements with which we are furnished, complex states can in imagination be constructed whose *exterior* resembles the original states requiring explanation; but besides the fact that this wholly hypothetical mental chemistry is almost entirely uncontrollable, it is not so certain that a well-authenticated contemplative would recognise, in the products cleverly elaborated in the psychologist's retort, an at all faithful image of the result of his personal *experiences*. The synthesis of an original state by means of some of its analytical elements is always a very risky proceeding, when it is—as here—incapable of verification by experiment.

Our mystic, in any case, would admire the ingenuity of the pious automata of M. Leuba, and would congratulate their author on the skill with which he is able—with the aid of a slight transposition, it is true—to reduce the most transcendent aspect of their models to the phenomenal machinery. For see! The content of the consciousness, during contemplation, is continually degraded and weakened . . . in the automaton, for in the case of St Teresa, for example, it is made uniform by becoming more exact and intensified. The automaton is little by little *exhausted*, arriving at the most poverty-stricken monoïdeism; a solution of elegant simplicity, for imagine the manifold machinery which would have been necessary to represent a monoïdeism by concentration, an idea which is enriched in potentialities while becoming simplified, and is only isolated by laying hold of the partial representations scattered around it. And then the automaton *falls asleep* in absolute absence of ideas; a stupefying imitation of ecstasy; I doubt whether St Teresa or St John of the Cross, however would have quite approved of this equivalence being established between complete absence of ideas, total inactivity of the mind, and the relative unconsciousness of the soul wholly fixed in the intuition of God. On awaking, the automaton *disserts* on the transcendent " Nothing " with which he labels his ecstatic swoon; the mystic disserts also, sometimes, but on a " Nothing " which was *never* for him a pure nothingness, or a divine " Negativity " which is only a higher affirmation, on a " Darkness " more consistent and enlightening than the glow-worms of phenomena. And we admire M. Leuba's automaton because he seems to us cleverly handled and *perhaps* capable of realisation; but please do not let us make him into a Christian mystic!

The interpretation of W. James and H. Delacroix more

scrupulously respects the data of direct observation furnished by the mystics themselves. In truth, to hold by the latter, and to interpret them from outside—as every non-mystic is obliged to do—we should not dare to claim that it is *impossible* to conceive, depending on purely psychological *antecedents*, a sum of *consequent* phenomena which present the majority of the descriptive characteristics of the mystical union. However, even without leaving the narrow domain of experiment, we should not be quite at ease as to the legitimacy of this hypothetical assimilation. For if it is true that the subconscious can, by its secret and hidden working, create an illusion of passivity in the mystic, if it is true that it can stealthily elaborate these visions of a higher æsthetic, whose suddenness and concentrated reality compel the impression of something superhuman and make people of religious temperament fall on both knees, it must not be forgotten that the subconscious could bring about these wonderful effects *only* by a *happier co-ordination* of the very elements which constitute the texture of our ordinary consciousness. *The psychological subconscious remains in close dependence on the data of the senses.* The bird's eye view of genius or the intuition of the artist, however intense and refined we suppose them to be, are never free from all sensible image or all spatial representation; they may *tend towards a strictly intellectual intuition*, but after the fashion of a mathematical variable which indefinitely approaches an inaccessible limit. Now the mystic claims to have reached this limit; he claims to have experienced the intuition of God *without any image or spatialisation*; and he not only puts forward his claim in the heat of poetical and hyperbolic descriptions, but maintains it energetically—the Christian mystic at least—even when he is trying to express himself with all the precision of a very objective analysis; nay, more, he maintains it as the expression, not of an evident *interpretation*, but of a directly experienced *fact*.

The alternative then presents itself either of respecting in their integrity the data of immediate observation furnished by the mystics, and then to go beyond Delacroix' point of view; or to go with Delacroix, and then resign ourselves to refusing a part of the said data.[162]

It may be thought that *both attitudes can be justified*, and that psychology alone does not perhaps suffice to choose between the alternatives. We would show in a few words that even a psychologist may admit *without arbitrariness* the *possibility* of a

I

non-spatial intuition in the mystic—that is, of a perception of presence which is only *analogous* to the feeling of presence studied in our first part and is not adequately explained by the laws which govern the latter.

(c) *The Conditions of any Legitimate Explanatory Hypothesis.*

The question we are now treating goes beyond the particular problem from which it arose. On what conditions does the scientific spirit, before a new phenomenon, *impose* the choice of such or such an explanatory hypothesis ?

Every hypothesis explaining the constitution or nature of a phenomenon is summed up in the equation provisionally established between this phenomenon—apparently original— and a sum-total of simpler phenomena whose laws of appearance and combination are known: the heat of a body, for example, will be treated as a sum of living molecular forces. It will happen that these partial, simpler phenomena offer a strict similarity with such and such an aspect of the complete phenomenon which requires explanation, and that, in addition, the combination of their individual conditions of production, according to a determined mode, causes the effective birth of the complete phenomenon. In this case the hypothesis is experimentally *verifiable*.

Sometimes the hypothesis will not be directly or completely verifiable, but we shall at least know with certainty that the effects of the phenomenon to be explained and those of its hypothetical substitutes are of the same order; the experienced similitude of the effects enables us to infer, hypothetically, the similarity of their phenomenal causes; such, for example, is the explanation of the movements of the machinery of the heavens, either by central forces or by tensions of the environment. The experimental synthesis of the phenomenon to be explained is not possible, but at least it would only suppose a quantitative amplification of the real combinations directly observed. The hypothesis in such a case is *scientifically justified* and does not involve the risk of any misunderstanding as to the true nature of the object to be explained.

It may also happen that not only is the hypothesis unverifiable, but that it has no other foundation than an *inexact analogy* between the hypothetical elements and the complete phenomenon they are judged to represent, so that, strictly speaking, this imperfectly known phenomenon may be considered either as a simple result of the combination of the said elements, or, on the other hand, as a new reality frankly surpassing them. Thus it is not *evidently* legitimate to reduce to the determinist scheme all man's external activity, even hypothetically; or to assimilate the vegetative life to a perfected physico-chemical mechanism. In this third case, in order that the adoption of an hypothesis may be free from arbitrariness, *other principles must enlighten the choice*. Suppose that this hypothesis is neither contradicted, nor suggested, nor imposed by a *neighbouring science*, it seems that concern for a wise economy of the means of explanation justifies the use of the following rule, admitted in theory, if not always practised, by the Scholastics: not to explain by the *greater* what can be sufficiently explained by the *less*; not to appeal to preternatural causes when physical causes suffice; or again, to withdraw from the domain of the experimental sciences only those phenomena which *manifestly* fall outside their scope.

Now the higher mystical state is not susceptible of an explanation which enters into the first or second of these categories; not only can it not be reproduced experimentally, but it is not at all certain that its proper manifestations are of the same order as the effects of the ordinary psychological activities. So M. Delacroix' hypothesis comes rather under the third category; it is based on partial analogies between mystical intuition and the synthetic product, which as a clever psychologist he mentally builds up by means of common data. But are these common data, however cleverly synthesised they may be supposed to be, of such a nature as to cause the *objective* birth of, I do not say the true mystical fact, but merely a state which has *all* the appearance of it ? What psychologist would venture to reply in the affirmative, since the hypothesis of M. Delacroix compels the correction and transposition, on a point of the highest importance, of what the Christian mystics constantly present as an immediate datum of mysticism ?

In reality, M. Delacroix has let himself be guided here by a methodological *a priori* principle, *which can often be justified*—I mean by the prejudice of making every phenomenon which does not obstinately refuse to do so bend to experimental determinism. Now he could only bring to pass this taming of phenomena by attenuating what we ourselves have been tempted to consider as characteristic of true mystical intuition —namely, the *strictly intellectual* nature of its content. But—he would no doubt reply—does not the scientific spirit require us at all costs to reduce *to acceptable terms* this exorbitant claim of the mystics to impose on our belief a form of intuition the mere possibility of which is not indicated by ordinary psychological experience? Well! let us be frank; in the absence of any indication on the part of the related sciences, and supposing that this " intuitiveness " to which the mystics lay claim were not in any way a prolongation of our psychological experience, we would say with M. Delacroix: scientifically, mystical intuition can only be a product of subconscious elaboration of ordinary psychological elements—a higher intuition, not, however, surpassing the plane of sensible forms and of categories —unless, by excess of " sublimation," it vanishes into total unconsciousness. . . . It would be arbitrary and injurious to erect it into an original and irreducible fact, totally heterogeneous from the common data of experience; such a proceeding would involve the destruction of the scientific spirit.

(d) Psychological Legitimacy of a Metempirical Hypothesis which Respects the Letter of the Mystical Documents.

In point of fact, we will show ourselves more ready to welcome the transcendent ambitions of the great contemplatives; for the two conditions, under which we would grant a presumption of competency to a particular science like psychology, are neither of them fully realised in relation to the higher mystical state. For this mystical state, by its metaphysical and religious pretensions, belongs in part to *philosophy* and *theology*; then secondly, in the characters which it bears, if it surpasses ordinary psychology, it *remains*, however, *favourable to certain indications with which it supplies us.*

Let us explain ourselves on these two points.

I. Every *metaphysical system* which admits the existence of a true Absolute, of an Absolute whose action is not wholly immerged in the determinism of our experimental laws, will also admit the possibility of this action inserting itself in the contingent series, and of thereby provoking certain reactions which the lower agents, left to themselves, would not have exercised. To deny this is to deny the fundamental contingency of our natural laws and to erect our experimental determinism itself into an intangible Absolute. *A priori*, then, we cannot say that it is impossible for the human mind with the aid of the interference of a higher influence to produce a phenomenon which it could not otherwise have produced; this impossibility would only exist if the mind, in order to raise itself to this new mode of activity, had to deny itself. . . . Metaphysics, then, opens out an *absolute possibility* of intellectual " intuition."

Theology, on the other hand, has no constraining tradition as to the nature of the mystical intuition. It would be said, in the language of the Scholastics, that although the highest degrees of contemplation are *certainly* supernatural (considered as *gratiae gratis datae* and not merely as meritorious acts), they may none the less not be supernatural *quoad se* in their constitutive elements, but only *quoad modum*, that is in the actual circumstances in which they are granted. And some authors have made use of the very appreciable latitude left by this distinction to formulate hypotheses on the nature of the mystical state; this state would not *of itself* surpass the limits of natural psychology, and *in this relation* would not differ *fundamentally* from non-Christian or purely " philosophical " ecstasy.[163] He who would adopt this position would evidently have no objection *of principle* to oppose to the analyses of M. Delacroix, so long at any rate as these latter, maintained on the ground of positive science, respect the problem of the ontological causalities really at work in ecstasy. This second problem is, from certain points of view, more delicate; we have not considered it in these pages.

However, if theology does not make great demands in this matter, it must be confessed that the *common opinion* of its most revered masters is rather unfavourable to the hypothesis of a mystical state *purely* psychological *quoad se*, or, if you will, *in the nature of its content*.

The question, then, remains open, or nearly so, on this side.

II. Are we going, then, to conclude that the scientific spirit and sincere concern for progress in psychology suggest, in regard to the mystical *fact* in itself, abstracting from its met-empirical *causes*, a position analogous to that of M. Delacroix ? Not yet, for psychology itself opens out a very clear vista on the possibility of another hypothesis, which offers the advantage of making use of the descriptions of those who were, in the matter under consideration, the only experimentalists, the mystics themselves, *as they stand*.

The human understanding—as psychological experience shows—is, through phenomenon, concept and discursiveness, perpetually chased from the moveable, manifold and deficient towards the Absolute, towards the One and the Infinite, that is, towards *Being pure and simple*. This *Being*, implied in the very finality of our mind, is then at the same time its source and its need, in the sense that all the movement of our mind is only a long pursuit of the always fleeting *intuition of this Being*. Now the fundamental tendency of a faculty is indeed—if the notion of finality is to retain any meaning—the sign, at the very least, of a certain latent potentiality in that faculty. On the other hand, the human understanding, shut up in the narrow circle of the sensible and quantitative datum, does not, in spite of all its efforts after synthesis and co-ordination, meet there its proper intuition. What are we to conclude from this, if not that our understanding—orientated in its most intimate foundation towards an " intellectual intuition," if such there be, that of pure Being—is not totally disproportioned to this kind of intuition, but that, on the other hand, the actual law of its exercise, imposing on it exclusively sensible " presentations," radically prevents it from making its acts equal this its deepest tendency? The antinomy of this fundamental attitude, this *desiderium naturale*,[164] and the insurmountable restrictions which *intellectio in phantasmate* opposes to it, can only be removed by the intervention of an external force, capable of putting aside these restrictions by *directly* presenting to the understanding its true object, Being. It is the final solution which the Christian religion proposes, by assigning as term to the action of man, aided by grace, the *very vision of God*.

Let us return to our mystics.

The mystical activity, so long as it does not escape our analyses, appears to the psychologist as a *unification* of the content of the consciousness, by organisation and negation of particular determinations. It is an intense converging of all the elements of the mind towards an *Absolute*, not only dialectically *posited* as an extrinsic principle of co-ordination of a multitude of finite forms, but apprehended more and more directly as the Unique Subsistent into which flows back the reality of all contingent substances. This preparatory task of co-ordination and intense unification allows us to follow its convergent lines far enough, and does not, *de jure*, escape the control of psychology; but the *actual point of convergence* escapes all profane examination. A new intuition ? Absence of ideas ? The proper power of the human intellect vanishes at the critical point where the last spatial support gives way. But does the mystic reach this critical point ? Does he not retain at least that minimum of spatial multiplicity strictly necessary to stuff

THE FEELING OF PRESENCE

out and objectivise a concept of Being, however subtle and refined it be ? If we take the descriptions of the Christian mystics literally, no. Then is all that splendid structure, raised during the preparatory phases of the state of union, to melt away into absolute unconsciousness? Yes, if the mind is left to its own forces[165]—and supposing also that on such an hypothesis it has been able to raise the " splendid structure " to a point so near the summit. No, if, as the mystics say, God then presents himself to the soul, and, setting it free from the limitations of natural knowledge, arouses in it, even though obscurely, *that intuition of Being which, wholly inaccessible as it is to the efforts of the intelligence alone, nevertheless prolongs its initial movement.*

So that, even in the supernatural surroundings of the highest degree of contemplation, we find, as a psychological factor of a *higher intuition*, which is hardly more than analogically a " presence," *the same fundamental activity of the mind,* " appetite for being," to which we have had to appeal previously in order to explain the affirmations of reality and of spatial presence. The mind, on its way towards its unity, had affirmed the partial realities in the measure in which their multiplicity, letting itself be reduced by synthesis, thus brought it nearer, in a closer and closer analogy, to the one and sole Being after which it strove. Will it then be unreasonable and " unscientific " to suppose that in the course of ecstasy the human mind touches for a moment the end which provokes and directs all its proceedings ? We judge that the hypothesis is *psychologically* acceptable. And this was of old the opinion of St Thomas Aquinas. We have hardly done more than interpret his doctrine.[166]

NOTES

[1] This study first appeared in the *Revue des questions scientifiques* (Louvain), vols. 64 and 65, years 1908-1909; then in an Italian translation, under the title *Dalla percezione sensibile all' intuizione mistica* (1 vol. in-18, 208 pp., Florence, 1913).

[2] W. James, *Principles of Psychology*, London, 1902, vol. ii, p. 322, n.

[3] *Id., Varieties of Religious Experience*, London, 1904, Lectures III, XVI, and XVII.

[4] H. Delacroix, *Études d'histoire et de psychologie du mysticisme, Les grands mystiques chrétiens*, Paris, 1908, App. i, pp. 427-50.

[5] Delacroix, *op. cit.,* p. 436.

[6] The " judgement of reality " may also be only a *conclusion*, and consequently have no relation to the object immediately perceived. But it is to be noted that the judgement of existence is itself necessarily based on the direct perception, present or past, of some other object whose existence implies that of the former. The *fact* of a thing's

existence cannot be concluded from *pure concepts*. Every " judgement of reality," therefore, in our thought supposes an *immediate* perception and *presence*.

[7] James Mill, *Analysis of the Phenomena of the Human Mind*, ed. by John Stuart Mill, 2nd ed., London, 1878, vol. i, pp. 344-45.

[8] Cf. *Note on Belief*, in James Mill, *op. cit.*, vol. i, p. 412.

[9] A. Bain, *The Emotions and the Will*, 3rd ed., p. 536.

[10] W. James, *Psychology*, vol. ii, p. 283.

[11] Brentano, *Psychologie vom empirischen Standpunkte*, I, Leipzig, 1874, p. 266.

[12] It would be superfluous to pile up bibliographical references on a matter that has become classical; materials for completing our account might be drawn from the most varied psychological surroundings, without overlooking recent works on the part played by instincts and acquired tendencies in the awakening and succession of representations.

[13] It matters little whether the word " assimilation " (Lewes, James) be preferred to the word " apperception," or whether, as has been done in recent years, the concept that is labelled by these names be itself severely criticised; some sort of " apperception," in one form or another, will always remain indispensable to the psychologist. E. Clarapède (*L'association des idées*, Paris, 1903, p. 377, n.), among others, remarks this, but from a point of view that we do not share.

[14] Before the English Associationists, this was the thesis of Berkeley; it is still that of Wundt and the greater number of contemporary psychologists.

[15] G. Störring, *Vorlesungen über Psychopathologie*, Leipzig, 1900, pp. 61-62.

[16] This characteristic had, moreover, long been emphasised—*e.g.*, by Berkeley, *Principles of Human Knowledge*, §§ 28, 29 (Berkeley's *Complete Works*, ed. A. C. Fraser, Oxford, 1901, vol. i, pp. 272-73).

[17] W. Wundt, *Grundzuge der physiologischen Psychologie*, 5. Aufl., I Bd., p. 346.

[18] J. Séglas, *Séméiologie des affections mentales*, in *Traité de pathologie mentale*, published by G. Ballet, Paris, 1903, p. 216.

[19] Weygandt-Roubinovitch, *Atlas-manuel de psychiâtrie*, Paris, 1904, p. 51.

[20] G. Störring, *op. cit.*, p. 71.

[21] Weygandt, *op. cit.*, p. 49.

[22] Störring, *op. cit.*, p. 326 ff.

[23] A. Pitres and E. Régis, *Les obsessions et les impulsions*, Paris, 1902, p. 135.

[24] *De l'intelligence*, 8th ed., Paris, 1897, t. i, pp. 90-91. Taine relates this fact after Brierre de Boismont.

[25] G. Stout, *Analytic Psychology*, London, 1902, vol. ii, p. 14.

[26] *Études d'histoire et de psychologie du mysticisme*, pp. 432-33.

[27] E. Kraepelin, *Psychiatrie*, Leipzig, 7. Aufl., 1903, I Bd., p. 134.

[28] Ampère, *Essai sur la philosophie des sciences*, Paris, t. i, Preface, p. xl., n.

[29] Kraepelin, *op. cit.*, I Bd., p. 138.

[30] And this logical strictness, it should be noted, is necessary. For to make the " judgement of reality " the conclusion of a reasoning

implicit or explicit is neither more nor less than to introduce into the lived psychology of each man the deceptive logical problem of the reality of external objects, and to suppose that he solves it *rationally* in the affirmative.

[31] See the study in this volume entitled *Empirical Science and Religious Psychology*.

[32] V. Raymond and P. Janet, *Névroses et Idées fixes*, t. ii (*Leçons cliniques du mardi*), Paris, 1898, p. 169.

[33] Wundt, *op. cit.*, III Bd., p. 576.

[34] Our classification of psychologists may be thought to be very rigid, and our discussion of their opinions on the present question lacking in detail. Several of them, in fact, in analysing judgements of reality, express their point of view only imperfectly, and we should not be greatly astonished if they recognise their own real opinion in the complete conception which we ourselves sum up later on, and which seems to us almost to reconcile the opposing tendencies of psychological " subjectivism " and " objectivism." If any objection or difficulty arises in the reader's mind, or if it seem to him that we are forcing doors already unlocked, we beg him, therefore, to await the second part of this article before deciding.

[35] *Theory of Vision*, § 59 (Berkeley's *Complete Works, ed. cit.*, vol. 8, pp. 154-55.)

[36] J. Séglas, *op. cit.*, p. 209.

[37] Kraepelin himself agrees here. Cf. *op. cit.*, i, p. 142. It results at least from this that, if, in order to take its place in an already occupied consciousness, the perception or hallucinatory representation must from the beginning meet with a certain amount of connivance from that consciousness, it is none the less not such connivance which suffices to imprint on it the character of reality. See also Séglas, *op. cit.*, vi, *Les idées délirantes*, in *Traité de pathologie mentale, supra cit.*, p. 222 ff.

[38] See, *e.g.*, Krafft-Ebing, *Traité clinique de psychiâtrie*, trans. Laurent, Paris, 1899, IV*e* partie, ch. i; *L'alcoolisme chronique et ses complications*. The greater number of the cases quoted contain, besides hallucinations resting on more or less systematised fundamental delirium, other hallucinations which appear to remain on the margin of this delirium or to contract but a very loose tie therewith.

[39] See, among others, Krafft-Ebing, *op. cit.*, pp. 76, 428-31.

[40] We can get some idea of this mental state from the description given by Havelock Ellis (cf. Jastrow, *The Subconscious*, London, 1906, p. 257 ff.), of a state of " kaleidoscopic " vision obtained under the action of a Mexican drug; a fairyland of " dissolving " pictures. . . . Let the faculty of control, which the experimenter still preserved, be suppressed, and there will remain a succession of hallucinatory images mingled haphazard with previously formed associations.

[41] Boris Sidis, *Psychopathological Researches*, New York, 1902, p. 187 ff.

[42] Cf., *e.g.*, A. Pitres, *Leçons cliniques sur l'hystèrie et l'hypnotisme*, Paris, 1901, t. i, Leçons VI to XIV.

[43] Boris Sidis, *op. cit.*, p. 43.

[44] Cf. *e.g.*, Boris Sidis, *op. cit.*, pp. 51, 56, 57, and elsewhere.

[45] These cases may be usefully compared with those of " insanity

of doubt," the *Grübelsucht* of the Germans. Cf. Kraepelin, *Psychiatrie*, . . . I Bd., 187, and II Bd., 773.

[46] Pierre Janet, *Les obsessions et la psychasthénie*, Paris, 1903, t. i, pp. 433, 434.

[47] Pierre Janet, *op. cit.*, t. i, p. 432.

[48] *Ibid.*, p. 438.

[49] P. Janet, *Névroses et idées fixes*, t. i, 2nd ed., Paris, 1904, p. 48.

[50] P. Janet, *Les obsessions*, t. i, Paris, 1903, pp. 439-440.

[51] E. D. Starbuck, *The Psychology of Religion*, 2nd ed., London, 1901, pp. 85 ff.

[52] It will not be forgotten that these words were written before the recent development of the psychology of the instincts and tendencies. [Added note.]

[53] Hume, *Inquiry concerning Human Understanding*, sect. v, part 2 (Hume's *Essays and Treatises*, new ed., Edinburgh, 1800, vol. i, pp. 51-52).

[54] Locke, *Essay concerning Human Understanding*, book iv, ch. 2, § 14 (*The Works of J. Locke*, 8th ed., London, vol. i, 1777, p. 134).

[55] James Mill, *Analysis of the Phenomena of the Human Mind*, edited by John Stuart Mill, 2nd ed., London, 1878, vol. i, p. 394 (note by A. Bain). *N.B.*—This whole note 107 (p. 393) of Bain should be read, as also the fine reply made thereto by J. Stuart Mill in the following note 108 (p. 402). It will be vividly grasped therefrom how much trouble is given to the phenomenalist empiricists by the fact of *belief in the real*.

[56] W. James, *Principles of Psychology*, London, 1902, vol. ii, p. 293. *N.B.*—The numbers inserted in the text of this essay after the quotations from W. James refer to the corresponding pages of this vol. ii.

[57] Always in the extended sense that English psychologists give to this word.

[58] Revault d'Allones, " Rôle des sensations internes dans les emotions et dans la perception de la durée," *Revue Philos.*, December, 1905, p. 592 ff.

[59] However, the same demand for unity would often be found if it were a question of the fundamental " natural " tendency, and not only of immediate and partial tendencies.

[60] *Zur Theorie der Aufmerksamkeit*, Halle, 1895. Cf. W. B. Pillsbury, *Attention*, London, 1908, p. 292.

[61] *Op. cit.*, p. 292. See also E. Dürr, *Die Lehre von der Aufmerksamkeit*, Leipzig, 1907, pp. 148-170.

[62] Th. Ribot, *Psychologie de l'attention*, 9th ed., Paris, 1905, p. 125.

[63] Pillsbury, *op. cit.*, p. 275.

[64] Th. Ribot, *op. cit.*, p. 135.

[65] James goes so far as to identify attention and belief. Cf. *Psychology*, ii, p. 322, n.

[66] W. James, *Psychology*, ii, p. 318.

[67] W. James, *op. cit.*, ii, pp. 318-19.

[68] And it is remarkable that they will find them among the philosophers who escaped most completely from the empiricist consequences of nominalism.

[69] B. de Spinoza, *Opera*, recognoverunt Van Vloten et Land, ed. altera, t. 8, Hagae Comitum, 1895, p. 89.

THE FEELING OF PRESENCE

70 Spinoza, *op. cit.*, p. 115.

71 W. James, *op. cit.*, ii, p. 289.

72 Höffding, *Esquisse d'une psychologie fondée sur l'expérience*, trans. Poitevin, Paris, 1900, p. 168.

73 W. James, *op. cit.*, ii, p. 32.

74 W. James, *op. cit.*, ii, p. 43.

75 *Der philosophische Kritizismus*, 1. Aufl., Leipzig, II Bd., 2, p. 64.

76 W. James, *op. cit.*, ii, p. 290. We remember the reservations made above on the pragmatist conception of the existential judgement in W. James.

77 Höffding, *op. cit.*, p. 171.

78 By this expression has been denoted the *reviviscence of an emotional state already experienced*, without reviviscence, at least proportionate, of the representative antecedents which had formerly evoked it.

79 Fouillée, in his *Psychologie des idées-forces*, attributes to the feeling an important rôle in the association of ideas. " The association of ideas presupposes that of the emotions, and beneath that of the emotions that of the impulses." " Ideas are not only connected by wholly mechanical and logical relations," but also " by a relation of adaptation to our feelings " (t. i, p. 221 ff.).

80 S Thomas Aquinas repeats to satiety that we can only know the " intelligible quiddities " " *in phantasmatibus*," " *convertendo nos ad phantasmata*." But the " *phantasma* " as such only as yet represents in the knowing subject the proximate *exigency* of a determined " quiddity " (*phantasma est intelligibile in potentia*), an exigency which must be satisfied, *actuated*, by the spontaneous activity of the intellect (*phantasma fit intelligibile in actu sub influxu intellectus agentis*).

81 This, with all the consequences which flow from it, is the authentic teaching of S Thomas (cf., *e.g.*, *Summa contra Gentiles*, lib. iii, cap. 37 ad 63). Chapters 37 to 40, 50 to 53 are particularly significant from the point of view under consideration. If their interpretation leaves any doubt in the mind, we would refer to the commentary of Francis of Ferrara (*S Thomae Aquin., Doct. ang., O.P., De veritate Cathol. fidei contra Gentiles, cum commentariis Fratris Francisci de Sylvestris, Ferrariensis*, Parisiis, 1643). We consider it superfluous to heap up references here, all the more as the dynamic nature of the intellection in the Thomist philosophy has been brilliantly brought to light in a recent book, to which we cannot do better than refer our readers: P. Rousselot, *L'intellectualisme de Saint Thomas*, Paris, 1908; 2nd ed., 1925.

82 A. Poulain, S.J., *The Graces of Interior Prayer*, trans. by Leonora L. Yorke-Smith, London, 1912, p. 64.

83 We would not identify the mystical state, even in its higher degree, with ecstasy defined in so restricted a sense. Several mystics claim to realise the mystical communication without breaking contact with the external world.

84 E. Boutroux, *La psychologie du mysticisme*, Paris, 1902, p. 6.

85 W. James, *Varieties*, p. 408, n. 2.

86 *Summa Theol.*, III, q. lxxvi, a. 8.

87 These visions are lacking in agreement with one another and bear the mark of the personal psychology of the mystic who experiences them. They are stimulants to piety, but not lessons in history. Cf. Poulain, *op. cit.*, p. 320.

[88] *Life of St Teresa, Written by Herself*, trans. Lewis, London, 5th ed., 1916, p. 250.

[89] In emphasising this analogy of " mechanism," we have no wish to *assimilate* the two cases from the point of view of their psychological content alone. We have just re-read the 28th chapter of St Teresa's *Autobiography*, and we must confess that the vision she there relates infinitely surpasses in richness of content all the analogous cases we have met with in the profane order. And again, we have nothing to judge it by save a few words of description.

[90] *Proceed. Soc. Psych. Res.*, vol. x.

[91] See the French abridgement: Gurney, Myers, and Podmore, *Les hallucinations télépathiques*, trans. Marillier, Paris, 4th ed., 1905.

[92] *Ann. des sc. Psych.*, 1891, No. 1, *Documents originaux*, p. 39.

[93] W. James, *Psychology*, ii, p. 324.

[94] We might support this conclusion by a careful examination of the successive phases of an hallucination in course of development.

[95] E. Gurney, etc., *Phantasms*, . . . i, 384, by W. James, *Varieties*, p. 62.

[96] W. James, *Varieties*, p. 62.

[97] *Op. cit.*, p. 63.

[98] It will be remembered that we mean by this any " geometrical " dfferentiation (localisation, direction, configuration) superposed on the indistinct and habitual representation which we have of surrounding space in general. However, neither imaginary space in general, nor the particular spatial image, could persist in our consciousness without a minimum residue of sensorial data.

[99] Ven. Luis de la Puente, *Vie du P. Balthazar Alvarez, S.J.*, Paris, 1873 (trans. Bouix), p. 601.

[100] *Ap.* de la Puente, *op. cit.*, p. 164.

[101] Ven. L. de la Puente, *Memoirs* (after Poulain, *op. cit.*, p. 100).

[102] *Études d'histoire et de psychologie du mysticisme*, p. 427 ff.

[103] *De Inquisitione Pacis*, lib. v, pars iii, cap. 12 (Alvarez de Paz, *Opera spiritualia*, t. iii, Moguntiae, 1619).

[104] If we were not pressed for space, this would be the moment to attempt a psychological criticism of the theory of the " spiritual senses " (see Poulain, *op. cit.*, ch. vi). On descending from the climax of ecstasy, the mystics, fettered by the narrowness of ordinary speech, are reduced, as soon as they desire to explain their transcendental experiences in detail, to make use of analogous terms borrowed from the current psychology; they themselves warn us against translating these symbolic formulas literally and materially. Inadequate as they are, however, they are not arbitrary; it would be interesting to make a closer study of the reasons that determine their choice.

[105] The following is a short statement of the Plotinian mysticism. God, the *One*, the *Good*, is beyond *Being*, for Being presupposes Essence; he is above *Intelligence*, for that implies the duality of Intelligent and Intelligible (*Enneads*, III, viii, 8; V, v, 6; VI, ix, 1, 2, etc.). God in himself, then, is inaccessible to our intelligence; we know him as something that moves us and surpasses all that is knowable; we know him after the fashion of inspired persons (ὥσπερ οἱ ἐνθουσιῶντες), who perceive that they bear within them something

THE FEELING OF PRESENCE

" greater " (ὅτι ἔχουσι μεῖζον ἐν ἑαυτοῖς. *Enn.* V, iii, 14, ed. Didot, Paris, 1896, p. 323), without for all that being able to define this something.

How does the ascent of the soul towards the *One* take place ? The first step to be attained is the contemplation of *Intelligible Beauty*, the pure Intelligible, and the necessary path to this is gradual purification. (κάθαρσις), or the renunciation of lower beauties. The soul will only see this intelligible Beauty by becoming conformed thereto, just as the eye only sees the sun if it takes on its luminous form. (Οὐ γὰρ ἂν πώποτε εἶδεν ὀφθαλμὸς ἥλιον, ἡλιοειδὴς μὴ γεγενημένος· οὐδὲ τὸ καλὸν ἂν ἴδοι ψυχὴ μὴ καλὴ γενομένη, *Enn.* I, vi, 9, Didot, p. 37). Thus the purified soul, ἡ ψυχὴ καθαρθεῖσα, finds again *in itself* the form of intelligible Beauty, the splendour whereof wholly com-penetrates it; it contemplates by becoming what it contemplates (Οὐ θεαταῖς μόνον ὑπάρχει γενέσθαι . . . ἀλλ' ἔχει τὸ ὀξέως ὁρῶν ἐν αὐτῷ τὸ ὁρώμενον. *Enn.*, V, viii, 10, Didot, p. 358; cf. *Enn.*, V, viii, 10 and 11, Didot, pp. 357-58).

But intellectual contemplation is not the supreme summit of the ascensions of the soul; above the Intelligible dwells the supreme *One*, the *Good*. How then can the soul raise itself above the Intelligible ? Arriving at the summit of the Intelligible, it is then, says Plotinus, borne beyond by the very flood that has brought it thus far (ἐξενεχθεὶς τῷ αὐτῷ τοῦ νοῦ οἷον κύματι. *Enn.*, VI, viii, 36, Didot, p. 503); for at the basis of all the movement of the intelligence was operating from the beginning the tendency, not purely and simply towards the Intelli-gible, but towards the *Good*, towards *Unity*, through the Intelligible; and now we see the soul cast, above all the forms of thought, face to face with the Good, with God. The latter, then, is not satisfied with appearing to the gaze of the soul which contemplates it, but wholly fills it (καὶ οὗτος οὐ κατ' ὄψιν φανείς, ἀλλὰ τὴν ψυχὴν ἐμπλήσας τοῦ θεωμένου, *Enn.*, VI, vii, 35, Didot, p. 502). This is *Union* (Μεταξὺ γὰρ οὐδέν, οὐδ' ἔτι δύο, ἀλλὰ ἓν ἄμφω. *Enn.*, VI, vii, 34, Didot, p. 501. See also *Enn.*, VI, ix, 10, Didot, p. 538, *et alibi*).

And what does the soul do in this supreme ecstasy of love ? Nothing, save to live in God; its operation, united to the divine operation, is, like the latter, beyond movement, beyond the sensible and animal life, beyond even the intelligence: οὐδὲ κινεῖται ἡ ψυχὴ . . . οὐδὲ ψυχὴ τοίνυν [ἔστί] . . . οὐδὲ νοῦς. Ὁμοιοῦσθπι γὰρ δεῖ· νοεῖ δὲ οὐδ' ἐκεῖνο, ὅτι οὐδὲ νοεῖ (*Enn.*, VI, vii, 35, Didot, p. 503). This is then *unconsciousness, in the enjoyment of the Good*. But until death has freed the soul from the prison of the body, this ecstatic union can only be transitory (*Enn.*, VI, ix, 10, Didot, p. 538).

Plotinus, according to his disciple Porphyry, enjoyed more than once during his life this unitive ecstasy, which he describes.

[106] " There is, in the Isa-Upanishad, a saying which enables us to penetrate exactly into the spirit of the doctrine : ' The man who under-stands that all creatures subsist only in God, and who is acquainted with the unity of being, has no sadness nor illusion.' " Chantepie de la Saussaye, *Man. d'hist. des religions*, French trans., Paris, 1904, ch. x, *Les Hindous. La religion védique et brahmanique*, p. 350.

" He who knows what Brahman is becomes identified with all being: the Gods themselves cannot hinder him " (*Upanishads*).

Quoted by Chantepie, *ibid.*, p. 351. In the doctrine of the *Vedânta*, the philosophical codification of the Vedic religion, *brahman* is identical with *atman*. (General bibliographical references concerning Hindu mysticism may be found at the end of this volume.)

[107] Swami Vivekananda, *Râja-Yoga*, London, 1896 (after W. James, *op. cit.*, p. 400).

[108] Max Müller, *The Life and Sayings of Râmakrishna*, new impression, London, 1910 (*Collected Works of Max Müller*, xv), pp. 8-9. J. C. Oman, *The Mystics, Ascetics, and Saints of India*, London, 1905, p. 172.

[109] Paul Carus, *Homilies of Science*, Chicago, 1892, p. 124. Note, however, that this " error " from which *nirvâna* liberates us is not only sensible phenomena, but also all affirmation and activity. Without doubt good, " right action," is a journeying to *nirvâna*, but good " is still an action, and it is necessary to raise oneself above all *karman* (above all action)." " Buddhism," writes Dr. E. Lehmann, " is by no means a ' cult of annihilation,' as some have called it. The negative character which definitely has the upper hand in this religion results from its being opposed to many positive dispositions and affirmations, not from its furnishing any theory of ' annihilation '" (Chantepie de la Saussaye, *op. cit.*, p. 383). On Buddhist " dogma," may be usefully consulted the works of M. L. de la Vallée-Poussin— *e.g.*, *Bouddhisme* (*Études sur l'histoire des religions*), Paris, 1909. (For a more extended general bibliography, see below, p. 208 ff.)

[110] We do not here speak of popular Buddhism.

[111] Such at least is the very well founded opinion of Baron Carra de Vaux (*Avicenne*, Paris, 1900; and *Gazali*, Paris, 1902). The pantheism of the Sufis has been greatly exaggerated; the destruction of this legend would result in lessening the importance of the supposed connection with Hindu religions. It would seem in any case that the Sufis of the first centuries of the Hegira must be distinguished from those of later ages. (More detailed remarks on Musulman mysticism will be found in a later essay in this volume.)

[112] Carra de Vaux, *Gazali*, p. 182.

[113] Probably " existence " directly perceived in God—or the " unitive life," as M. Carra de Vaux says (*op. cit.*, p. 187).

[114] *Op. cit.*, p. 186.

[115] *Op. cit.*, p. 197.

[116] *Op. cit.*, p. 205.

[117] *Op. cit.*, p. 267. Note that Ibn Arabi is a monist.

[118] A. Schmölders, *Essai sur les écoles philosophiques chez les Arabes et notamment sur la doctrine d'Algazzali*, Paris, 1842, p. 68. (Cf. James, *Varieties*, p. 405.)

[119] W. James, *Varieties*, p. 60.

[120] Dr. R. M. Bucke, *Cosmic Consciousness*, Philadelphia, 1901 (James, *op. cit.*, p. 398).

[121] James, *Varieties*, pp. 64-65.

[122] *Op. cit.*, p. 385.

[123] B. P. Blood, *The Anæsthetic Revelation and the Gist of Philosophy*, Amsterdam, N.Y., 1874.

[124] James, *op. cit.*, p. 387.

[125] *Op. cit.*, p. 388.

[126] *Op. cit.*, p. 389.

[127] *Op. cit.*, p. 66.

[128] London, 1897.

[129] James, *op. cit.*, p. 397.

[130] *Op. cit.*, pp. 67-68.

[131] 5th ed., Paris, 1906. English trans. by Leonora L. Yorke-Smith, second impression, London, 1912. The page numbers given in the subsequent references are taken from this translation.

[132] We would not put forward this thesis in so absolute a manner at least as far as the prayer of quiet is concerned.

[133] *Interior Castle*, v 1 (Poulain, 85).

[134] Poulain, 86.

[135] *Life*, ch. 52 (Poulain, 267).

[136] *Castle*, vi 1 (Poulain, 99).

[137] St Teresa, *Second Letter to Fr. Rodrigo Alvarez* (Poulain, p. 241).

[138] Poulain, p. 242.

[139] *Dark Night*, ii 17 (Poulain, 134).

[140] In the Neoplatonist sense, τὰ νοητά signifies the proper object of finite knowledge or γνῶσις.

[141] *De myst. theol.*, c. i (Poulain, 134).

[142] Pseudo-Dionysius, *Letter* i (Poulain, 121).

[143] *Living Flame*, iii 3, § 10 (Poulain, 121).

[144] *First Sermon for the Second Sunday after Epiphany* (Poulain, 272).

[145] We restore these few words, which are replaced by dots in Fr. Poulain's quotation.

[146] *Castle*, v 1 (Poulain, 241 and 99).

[147] *De inquisit. pacis*, v, 3rd art., ch. 14 (Poulain, 282).

[148] St John of the Cross, *Spir. Canticle*, xxii 1 (Poulain, 294).

[149] *Id., Ascent of Carmel*, ii 5 (Poulain, 294).

[150] Alvarez de Paz, *De inquisit. pacis*, v 3, 14 (Poulain, 282).

[151] St John of the Cross, *Living Flame*, iii 3, § 5 (Poulain, 148).

[152] J. H. Leuba, "Les tendances fondamentales des mystiques chrétiens," *Revue philos.*, Paris, 1902 (t. 54), pp. 1-36 and 441-487. From the point of view we are concerned with—in spite of their very different appreciations of the social value of mysticism—compare M. Leuba with M. Murisier (*Les maladies du sentiment religieux*, Paris, 1901, ch. i).

[153] *Op. cit.*, p. 481.

[154] James, *Varieties*, pp. 422-423.

[155] *Op. cit.*, p. 512 ff.

[156] Cf. an idea of the same kind in A. Godfernaux, "Psychologie du mysticisme," *Revue philos.*, Paris, 1902 (t. 54), p. 169, n. 1. According to this psychologist, who has, however, no authority in theology, " the point of application " of (actual) grace is " in the kenæsthesia," in the general sensibility, and not in the higher faculties.

[157] Delacroix, *Études sur l'histoire et la psychologie des grands mystiques chrétiens*, pp. 404-5.

[158] *Op. cit.*, p. 405.

[159] *Op. cit.*, p. 405.

[160] Paris, 1896.

[161] For an appreciation of this system, see p. 144 of this work, n. 165.

[162] We would remark that if anyone, under the label of the sub-

conscious, includes the faculty on the part of the intelligence of arriving in certain circumstances at a *metaphysical intuition*, completely free from sensible elements, we should have nothing to object *here*, since *we leave on one side the question of the transcendental cause and the religious value* of the states whose *psychological nature* we are seeking to describe. We would, however, observe that the label would not be well chosen.

[163] Fr. de Munnynck, O.P., in a few pages written with great subtlety of thought (*Praelectiones de Dei existentia*, Lovanii, 1904, pp. 25-31), attempts an interpretation of " mystical contemplation " in which he makes use of this distinction: " Putamus nos," he writes, " sed haec modeste prolata volumus, hanc supremam contemplationem esse *quoad se* naturalem." He thus satisfactorily accounts for that " mirus consensus paganorum et christianorum " in the description of the mystical state; there is a natural ecstasy which can be attained by psychological forces alone. But " haec dicta volumus pro philoso phicis ethnicis; atque etiam pro christianis quatenus eadem via ad eumdem perveniunt terminum. Verum multis in casibus haec contemplatio sanctorum, etsi, saltem partim, naturalis quoad suum esse, supernaturalis tamen videtur pronuntianda *quoad modum*, quo ad illam perveniunt." For ourselves, as we state below, we are ready to admit, basing ourselves on the descriptions of certain Catholic mystics, that they reach, at least in certain cases, a psychological state whose *actual content* is qualitatively different from that of natural or philosophic ecstasy. But perhaps at bottom our view is not so very different from that of Fr. de Munnynck, who adds in a last paragraph these suggestive words: " Praeterea considerandum est hanc contem plationem, naturalem quoad esse, veluti continuo progressu pertingere ad contemplationem vere supernaturalem quoad esse, a qua rigorose separari non potest. Porro auctores mystici, speciatim Germani, una simul proponunt quae certe sunt supernaturalia et quae naturalia esse possunt. . . ."

[164] St Thomas, *Summa contra Gentiles*, iii, c. 50. See also the neighbouring chapters.

[165] We are far from claiming that this *ecstatic unconsciousness*, in which is attained the supreme effort of purely natural mysticism (see what has been said above of *Neoplatonist mysticism*, and of *non Christian mystical systems* in general), is devoid of all moral and religious value. On the contrary, thanks to the efforts which have led to it and the " pacification " that accompanies it, it *may* realise with a certain fulness the " affective polarisation " of the psychological mechanism: this unconscious ecstasy may, therefore, be beneficial for its results, but it does not, at least directly, enrich the knowledge. Is it not to be met with also in *certain* Christian mystics or pseudo mystics ? Why not ?

We have pointed out above, without discussing it, a theory of M Récéjac. In reality it is a psychological and philosophical theory of *natural* mysticism: and as such, on condition of widening the meaning given in it to the word " will," we think it *in its main line* acceptable. Only let good care be taken as to the nature of the ultimate term to which it brings the contemplative. Can we conceive a *pure intuition* of the *fundamental tendency* of the Ego towards the

Absolute to survive alone ? It is indeed true that the whole pre-paratory work of concentration and purification on the part of the mystic tends to free this tendency more and more from the sensible matter in which it is submerged; but at the end, since by hypothesis all sensible matter disappears, how can the *tendency*—a pure form—remain perceptible unless a supra-sensible presentation intervenes and substitutes a new nourishment for it ? Natural ecstasy, produced thus, would be neither conscious nor luminous; it is a state of *unconsciousness* (the word does not frighten M. Récéjac), but of *polarised unconsciousness* if one may so put it.

[166] See Appendix, on *The Intuition of God in Christian Mysticism*.

SOME DISTINCTIVE FEATURES OF CHRISTIAN MYSTICISM

SUMMARY

FIRST PART

GENERAL PHENOMENOLOGY OF THE MYSTICAL LIFE

I. A WORD ON METHODOLOGY.

II. THE FORMAL UNITY OF THE PSYCHOLOGICAL LIFE.

III. ON THE MYSTIC WAY. THE STAGES OF THE SPIRITUAL LIFE.

(*a*) A General Problem.
(*b*) Ritual and Vocal Prayer.
(*c*) The Interior Life.

1. General remarks.
2. The habit of interior prayer.
3. Purity of morals.
4. Asceticism.
5. Interior crises.
6. Renunciation of the Ego.

(*d*) Contemplation.

1. Sensible contemplation.
2. Imaginative contemplation. Sensible and imaginative visions.
3. Intellectual contemplation.

A. In the profane order.
B. In the mystical order.

(*a*) On the threshold of ecstasy ?
(*b*) Somatic and psycho-physiological anomalies.
(*c*) The summit of contemplation; negative characteristics.

Neoplatonism.
Hindu mysticism.
Moslem mysticism.
Profane mysticism.
Medieval Christian mysticism.
Christian mysticism of the Renaissance.

STUDIES IN THE PSYCHOLOGY OF THE MYSTICS

SECOND PART

THE PROBLEM OF ECSTASY

I. FIRST INTERPRETATIVE SOLUTION: THE ABSENCE OF MULTIPLICITY IN ECSTASY IS ONLY APPARENT.

II. SECOND INTERPRETATIVE SOLUTION: THE NEGATIVITY OF ECSTASY IS COMPLETE UNCONSCIOUSNESS.

III. LITERAL SOLUTION: ECSTASY IS THE SYNTHESIS OF AN EMPIRICAL NEGATIVITY AND A TRANSCENDENT POSITIVITY.

THIRD PART

ONTOLOGY AND THEOLOGY OF CHRISTIAN MYSTICISM

I. THE INTEGRAL DATA OF THE PROBLEM.

II. SOME ESSENTIAL CHARACTERS OF CHRISTIAN MYSTICISM.

SOME DISTINCTIVE FEATURES OF CHRISTIAN MYSTICISM[1]

HOW are we to lay down the special characteristic of Christian mysticism ? We will confess at the start that the determination of the characters most proper to it, those which would define its " essence " properly speaking, its ontological reality, always supposes the solution of several preliminary questions, as to which it would perhaps be rash to seek to say the last word. Our attempt will be not so much to solve the problem as to criticise its data: but it will not be possible for this criticism to proceed without some selection among possible solutions.

The problem of the " essence " of Christian mysticism being an ontological one, its data cannot, it is clear, be restricted to those of pure psychology, the competence of which, as an empirical science, does not surpass the limits of " phenomena." However, we would gladly have confined our task to the sorting out of the purely descriptive characteristics, or, if you will, the special " phenomenology " of the mystical states, if that very phenomenology had not at a certain moment brought us to a standstill, for its perfection, before an eminently ontological choice. We shall remember, then, at the right moment, that we must write as a philosopher and theologian; but, in the meanwhile, since many readers—it is none too clear why— feel in the matter under consideration less distrust for the psychologist than for the metaphysician, we are going, as far as possible, to attack the matter from the standpoint of the empiricist and the clinical investigator; it will not be wholly our own fault if this rôle shows itself difficult to maintain.

FIRST PART

GENERAL PHENOMENOLOGY OF THE MYSTICAL LIFE

I. A WORD ON METHODOLOGY

To anyone who examines the mystical states of consciousness, even if only superficially (we suppose that their general features at least are known), it will speedily be evident not only that these states are exceedingly complex, but that they are in close and immediate relation with the various stages of human activity, individual and social; the mystic, in the perfectly concrete reality of his special states, does not lose his temperament, nor his physical weaknesses, nor his nerves, nor his intellectual or moral culture, nor his receptivity in regard to the influences which surround him—in a word, neither the physiology nor the psychology that are natural to him. In order to attain to a complete knowledge of any mystic, it is well, therefore, as a preliminary to outline his medical, psychological, and moral physiognomy; and this presupposes a close acquaintance with both the individual and his environment.

If this be the case—and who, to-day, will deny it, whatever be his " theory " of mysticism ?—the reason can be only the following: that the " mystical states," even in their higher degrees, so strongly marked with the stamp of the individuals who experience them, throw out deep roots into the region of the general psycho-physiological activities, continue these latter, prolong them in a fashion, and extend their scope, far from substituting for them wholly " new " and heterogeneous faculties hard to be understood.

On this principle, which is almost a truism, everyone can agree. But beware: for it implies certain consequences and makes certain demands.

The consequences may be summed up thus: between the fundamental modes of human psychological activity and the various mystical realisations—even up to, and including, by hypothesis, supernatural mysticism—there exist *analogies of form and communities of mechanism.*

And the demands, on their side, are summed up in this task, which is henceforth incumbent on all theoreticians of mysticism: *to disengage the profound continuity* (we do not say *identity*) of the mystical states, as it is claimed that they are conceived, with the fundamental modes and general forms of psychology.

The most fully Catholic of apologists—as well as the least mystical of anti-religious sectaries—must, if he would take up a stand concerning the problem we are considering, accept this consequence and face this task.

We will, then, begin our rapid attempt by a very brief enquiry into certain formal and quite general features which are disclosed in man's psychological activity. We shall then find out what becomes of these formal characteristics when they enclose a religious content. This consideration will bring us finally to the problem of ecstasy, or better, of higher mystical intuition, as it presents itself both within and outside of orthodox Catholicism.

II. THE FORMAL UNITY OF THE PSYCHOLOGICAL LIFE

There is no question here, the reader may be assured, of transcribing, on the pretext of an introduction to religious psychology, a summary of any one of those admirable scholastic treatises which painstakingly expose the mechanism of human activity, in order to give ourselves the somewhat artificial pleasure of contemplating the scattered pieces, arranged motionless under suitable labels in our conceptual pigeon-holes. We know too well for it to need stating at length that man, in the order of knowledge as well as in the order of tendency, is an activity at superimposed levels, and that to these different levels, connected and hierarchically arranged among themselves, correspond planes of concrete manifestations or " phenomena " likewise arranged in order, grouped according to well-defined laws: physico-chemical and organic activity, receptive and active sensibility, intellectual syntheses and will, reason and action. It is evident that we shall find once more in the mystic, even if it be under new conditions, the inter-action of these elements and the governance of these laws. But that is not what we wish to consider at present.

Man, " microcosm " that he is, plunges on his lower side into the narrowly quantitative physical world; some part of him, therefore, oscillates perpetually in the flux and reflux of those inferior causalities which we theoretically characterise by the extreme case of " equality of action and reaction." On this plane—if we neglect the qualitative reflection with which even the most modest of material activities is of necessity coloured—human reaction has rightly no other unity than the purely relative unity of quantity. But the human material is alive; let us go one plane higher; the living being reacts as a *whole*. And here already, thanks to the organic reaction common to him and to the plant and animal, man finds all his constitutive multiplicity unified and directed in each of his reactions on the outward environment; the human biological reaction, like that of every living being, superimposes on the lowest unity of pure physical quality, that simple element of a diversified multiplicity, a higher unity embracing that very diversification; the unity of a *type* to be maintained, that is, to be continually realised.

Let us go a step higher, and we shall see the unity in human activity become closer and the interior finality extend proportionately.

Upon the confused substratum of vegetative life and physical receptivity, a few lines grow luminous here and there, some interactions are, so to speak, stopped on their passage, as by a selective screen, and transposed into a new and more intimate modality, that of sensation. Sensation, in a very modest and quite relative fashion, brings about the first degree *of the unity of object and subject in a consciousness with a view to an action*; and let us note how this unity, better than unity of the biological type, escapes the essential multiplicity of quantity; it does so to such a degree that it is denied all quantitative character, not only by Descartes, but also by philosophers and psychologists so independent of Cartesianism as Renouvier and M. Bergson. For our part we think that sensation is really quantitative, that it is, if one may say so, a " bodily consciousness," but we admit at the same time that it constitutes, by the formal characters of unity which it presupposes and of the reaction that it liberates, a first emergence, on the basis of organic finality, of a superior, individual, and conscious finality. We would readily say, with M. Bergson, that sensation has no *raison d'être* unless it be a beginning of liberty; in fact, in the degree that sensation is more than pure quantity, the action for which it prepares its subject is more than merely mechanical.

Sensibility, then, affords us an active mode of unity on the part of the sensing subject, which enables us to foresee by analogy the higher manifestations of personal finality. But even without going beyond the sensorial stage, it is easy to see that this unity may be more or less strict. Sensation emerges from among a confusion of other psychological elements of which it is not independent; it will only develop its natural reactions to the degree in which the multiplicity wherein it is inserted suffers co-ordination with it. The unity of sensibility, therefore, as a function of a given representation, is sometimes more strict, sometimes less, like all unity of co-ordination. It will reach its maximum when the motive tendencies aroused by the associated representations happen to converge; when the emotional state, the totalised reflection of the organic reaction, promotes this convergence; when, lastly, the automatisms created by habit at the same time clear the way for the motive potentialities which are stimulated at the moment.

Now the unity of sensibility, if it may in its turn be the effect of a higher psychological unity, is firstly, and always, the condition, and in a way the measure thereof. It would be an illusion to seek to establish Unity—whatever it may be—at the apex of the mind, without an appropriated discipline of the imagination, a governance of the automatisms, a mastery of the affections, a choice among the sensations, and even a complaisant correspondence on the part of the dispositions of the body. The unification of the mind, by any method, requires the unification of the whole man, body and soul.

Let us mount a step higher still.

We have just recalled how, in the very bosom of his physical dependence on a material environment, there is established in man a stricter and stricter unity of co-ordination, in the first place an organic unity, afterwards a unity of sensibility. In fact, this latter unity, to which our inner experience bears witness, only touches our clear consciousness when inseparably inserted in a higher synthesis the characters of which do not respond to the law of quantitative interactions. That there is brought about in man an active synthesis, one which dominates and clothes the pure sensibility, the majority of philosophers have in all ages agreed, and the experimental psychology of recent years tends to give us better evidence of the fact; a few psychologists alone still deny it, held back by a narrow associationist empiricism. Let us consider, then, in this higher unity of the human mind, those general aspects which are of interest to us.

It manifests itself in wonderful fashion in that very characteristic internal proceeding the *judgement*, the immediate forerunner of action. What is it that we meet with here ?

Two aspects alone concern us, but they are fundamental.

First of all a " higher synthesis of the datum of sensibility," a synthesis brought about in conformity, not with the concrete and quantitative characters which the sense-data present, but with formal, abstract, non-quantitative characters, with a " modal type " which defines the very form of the judgement. We could show that this " modal type " of the judgements is identically the pure categorical form of our concepts, and that the non-quantitative unity under which it gathers together the sensible datum is always a symbolical approximation to and a more or less distant participation in the absolute Unity, that of Being.

The other aspect of the judgement which we must here consider is the " objective reference " which it always implies—that is to say, the transposition to the ontological order of the categorical synthesis effected in the concept; that is, once more, the affirmation of this synthesis as an element of the " real," of the order of " values," or, if it be preferred, of the order of " absolute finality," this being only Being considered as the natural term of possible action.

The judgement, then, unifies the sense-datum from two convergent points of view; the " speculative " standpoint of *Unity*, that is, of Being considered as the form of the datum, and the " practical " standpoint of *Finality*, that is, of Being considered as the last end—and consequently the prime mover—of action. These two points of view are manifested to the empirical consciousness as two progressive and correlative series, capable of indefinite extension, whose common limit is absolute Being; as two tendencies whose common term, which is betrayed in their convergence, is yet heterogeneous to each of them.

Let us from this deduce the ontological conditions of this convergent progression, and we shall meet with a conclusion explicitly formulated in Neoplatonism, and at least indicated in all the great metaphysical systems; namely, that the Absolute, Being pure and simple, beyond all determination, is at the same time the latent mover, the ideal form of unity and the last end of the strivings of the human soul; at the term of these latter, at their perhaps inaccessible point of convergence, the One and the Good are mingled in the *intuition of Being*; for only in this intuition, the limiting activity of every created mind, will the soul realise at once the supreme unity of speculation and the unmixed possession of love.

It has been necessary to sketch this metaphysical integration at least in outline, in order to characterise the very special " becoming " of the human soul. We see that it could not be adequately defined by characters immanent in the soul, for its most original feature is its transcendent relation, its " objective reference " to an *absolute Unity* and an *absolute End*, one, therefore, distinct from the soul. And here we encounter a very strange condition of human psychological phenomena; the type of their co-ordination is the very negation of their essential multiplicity, and their centre of gravity is above the plane of their movements. Is the human mind, restricted to spatial presentations and conceptual elaborations, to see the ideal

Unity which it untiringly pursues indefinitely flee before it? In any case, if left to itself, it will mimic it with increasing perfection in vain; it will never lay hold of it so as directly to assimilate it.

Of the immediate intuition of Being we must therefore lay it down that it *surpasses the limits of human psychology* and at the same time *commands its whole perspective*.

III. ON THE MYSTIC WAY. THE STAGES OF THE SPIRITUAL LIFE

(a) A GENERAL PROBLEM

There is, as several contemplatives have themselves remarked, a striking analogy between the formal framework of human psychology, outlined above, and the most characteristic stages of the mystical ascent towards God; if we grant to the progressive unity of the mind an ontological value and a final realisation, we shall be very near to reaching what the most diverse religious writers describe as a closer and closer union with the Divinity. So much is this the case that theoretical systems, like Plotinian Neoplatonism, Vedantism, Buddhism, if we limit our consideration to their main lines, may bear the labels " metaphysical " or "higher mystical" indifferently. Is not the pseudo-Dionysius the Areopagite, the inspirer of so many medieval mystics, a Plotinising philosopher to the very extent that he is a mystic? And did not his distant emulators of the thirteenth and fourteenth centuries, Eckhart, Tauler, Suso, Ruysbroeck, and their fellows, insert their most intimate experiences into the framework of a Plotinian scholasticism? Unquestionably. The question therefore necessarily arises as to whether mysticism is anything more than a sublime manner, carried out in the life of the mystic, of hypostatising the very form of our mind in order to project it into the ontological order.

Before attempting to reply to this question, we must endeavour to apprehend in greater detail the parallelism between the phenomenology of the religious life and the form of the psychological life, and to analyse to some extent the influence of a religious content on the psychological activity which surrounds it.

We will not embarrass ourselves with the thankless and deceptive task of attempting to give a nominal definition of " religion "; our enquiry may be limited to those very diverse phenomena which all agree in recognising as " religious." We would, moreover, emphasise the fact that we propose to consider solely the descriptive characteristics of these phenomena, abstracting provisionally from the problem of " grace."

(b) RITUAL AND VOCAL PRAYER

At the lowest step of the manifestations of religion which concern the personal life we meet with " ritual " and " vocal prayer." Here, the reader will say, we are a long way from mysticism ! But no; we are on the direct road thither. Ritual, in its wider sense, sacrifice, symbolic gestures, prostrations, any ceremonies whatsoever, " spoken prayer," to which we may add liturgical chant, and the Rosary, beside their several functions as vehicles of collective worship, have always held for the individual the admitted rôle of support for an interior movement. Now this interior movement itself—adoration, deprecation, repentance, amendment, and so on—what is it but an orientation of the individual relatively to a religious object, and hence an effort towards interior unification, an effort which is interfered with the less in proportion as the body is itself co-ordinated with it in external action ?

Ritual, in its origin, is not by right the mounting up of the mechanical functions to the mind in order to harden it, but the descent of the mind into the hostile mechanism so as to make an ally of the latter by pointing it to a higher end. Yes, it may be replied, but is not this procedure of the mind in encumbering itself with a mechanism, this eccentricity of a principle of unity sinking itself to begin with in a multiplicity, the very negation of that endeavour after union which is the business of mysticism ? Perhaps, if the body were a companion which we chose for ourselves; but not if the mind of man is compelled by its very nature to depend upon his body in its every action. The mind goes beyond the body only by first co-ordinating the latter with itself, whether by force or persuasion. Ritual and vocal prayer represent the method of persuasion.

Among the external actions which authors generally connect with ritual practices, some have a value principally symbolical, others bring about a disposition of the body which is, at least negatively, favourable to the soaring of internal devotion. In most cases, however, these two characteristics meet in juxtaposition, in diverse proportions. Consider, for example, a symbolic gesture, such as the oblation of the victim in the acrifices of old, or again, among Christians, the sign of the cross, he use of holy water, the wearing of liturgical vestments. t cannot be disputed that the frequent repetition of these acts weakens their positive symbolic value; the gesture of the acrificing priest of old must often have become mechanical, ust as the Christian's sign of the cross may sometimes descend o the level of a reflex movement, or the putting on of the sacerdotal vestments by the Catholic priest, in spite of the significative prayers which accompany it, may not always awake n his soul a very precise religious echo. Does this mechanisation, which is always possible, and even in a certain degree unavoidable, prevent ritual from developing an appreciable psychological efficacy? By no means; for, first of all, the at least generic religious significance of the outward symbol comes to life again at the slightest effort; and, secondly, the performing of the external rite is, each time it is repeated, an at least transitory orientation of the automatism in the direction of spiritual things, a simple and modest canalisation of the sense-life.

Other outward " rites " and practices contribute still more evidently to the unity of the spiritual life, since it is their express function to produce a bodily disposition favouring the acts of this higher life. Think of the kneelings, the prostrations, the motionlessness of the body during prayer, the choice of place and time for prayer, that pious " mechanisation " which, in accordance with one's own particular notions, one chooses to praise or to condemn, especially, perhaps, greatly to exaggerate, in the *Spiritual Exercises* of St Ignatius Loyola. All these practices are easily justifiable, not that they have in themselves, as material gestures, any religious value at all, but because they bring about in us, on the mechanical and sensible plane, a harmony that is prerequisite for the life of the spirit. This harmony will be all the fuller the less it is drawn to self-dispersion by the representations and feelings which arise from below.

What is true of " ritual " is true *a fortiori* of vocal prayer, which is, indeed, in the religious field the subtlest external symbol, and that which evokes its spiritual object most directly. In addition to this it offers the advantage of an easy and discreet regulation of the bodily mechanism.

Look at this good old woman telling her beads, on a winter evening, in the chimney corner. During the day her attention was dispersed over the small cares of her household, and confined to the limits of a modest village horizon. But see how now, her duties done, she sits down on her shaky chair, draws out her rosary, and after making a great sign of the cross, begins to mutter Hail Marys one after another in a slow rhythm. The monotony of these repetitions clothes the poor old woman with physical peace and recollection; and her soul, already directed on high, almost mechanically, by her habitual gesture of drawing out the rosary, immediately opens out with increasing serenity on unlimited perspectives, felt rather than analysed, which converge on God. Distraction may, perhaps, supervene from this direction or that; but thanks to the continual and monotonous rhythm of the recitation, the affective polarisation which it maintains or restores continually and gently brings her attention back in the direction of God. What does it matter, then, if the humble *orante* does not concern herself with living over again the exact meaning of the formula she is repeating ? This meaning will, in the very nature of things, return to her from time to time; but often she does better: she allows her soul to rise freely into a true contemplation, well-worn and obscure, uncomplicated, unsystematised, alternating with a return of the attention to the words she is muttering, but building up in the long run, on the mechanical basis they afford, a higher, purified, personal prayer.

If simple folk be told to make a quarter of an hour's mental prayer, the majority will not succeed; but if they be made to recite the rosary or litanies, or other unsubtilised devotional exercises, with recollection, there will arise of themselves, gently, unconsiously almost, on the concrete basis of the outward prayer, confused but captivating thoughts and affections, much more independent of the formulas recited than one would think. These latter, however, were a necessary first step to the interior devotion, and they often remain its indispensable support; they have brought about in the inferior automatism that adaptation, that *Einstellung*, which contemporary psychologists affirm as clearly as ever must necessarily concur with the operations of the mind.

From the personal standpoint, then, interior devotion, sustained by ritual and vocal prayer, may be considered as a first stage, a humble beginning, on the path of mystical union. It is the only stage which most people are capable of reaching, for their body and sense-life, necessarily tossed hither and thither at the call of material cares, distract and weigh down the mind; for them the concentration effected by external religious practices, even though it be not very strict, is eminently beneficial; it is so also in many cases, however, even for those who habitually live a more interior life; however severely they may have reformed their sense-operations and regulated their automatisms, they will from time to time feel that the guidance of it escapes from their hands, and will then return to the artifices of beginners. Without speaking here of " physical " preparation for ecstasy—almost wholly unknown to Christianity—we will merely remark that the greatest mystics, quite apart from the obligations or conventions of public worship, have made great use of external aids to devotion.[2]

This being so, we are quite ready to admit that ritual and vocal prayer, though a useful introduction to the mystical life, are in any case only its first rung and primary support.[3]

(c) THE INTERIOR LIFE

1. General Remarks.

Outward practices have no religious value save for the interior devotion which inspires them and is supported by them; they may create a favourable physical disposition, but they do not deeply touch the actual continuity of the psychological life. It is otherwise with interior prayer, which by mingling with the very source of our mental activity can wholly colour it and become a real principle of spiritual life.

A magnificent example of this " interior life " which is truly a continual prayer is afforded by the *Imitation of Christ*. This little book was beyond question actualised in the life of its author, and in any case remains the faithful reflection of many lives which have been spent in saintly wise in the exercise of the Christian religion.

The *Imitation*, whatever some superficial critics may have thought, is neither monotonous nor lifeless;[4] it is a poem of the soul, most varied and penetrating, through which pass in turn a surpassing and often humble joy, a confidence triumphant and suppliant, distress, doubt, disenchantment, gloomy sadness, repentance, desire and renunciation, the bold cry of love which soars and the weary appeal of a struggle that is going against one, tender affection and frozen austerity, enveloping suppleness and wounding rigidity, the limpidity of a pure heart and a gaze fixed on God, then the soiling mist which the subdued flesh exhales from below like a groan or a revenge—in short, the whole complicated and unforeseen, but infinitely restrained

play of our passions, emotions, desires, difficulties, acts of will
remorse, hopes. And yet, what unity of tone and tendency in
this very human variety! All the diverse ways of the most
undulating psychology lead in it to the same final end, God
Therein the soul is taken as it is: it sings, groans, sighs, smiles
is encouraged, steels itself, abandons itself with perfect natural
ness, sure in the last resort that every one of its movements
if loyally supported, tends towards God. And we may b
permitted to remark in passing that Protestant writers have no
always remarked sufficiently with what ease the " Servant," in
the *Imitation*, assimilates to his inner religion the specificall
Christian elements, bends himself to the " institutional prin
ciple," makes use of the sacraments, and even goes through th
smallest observances of the cloister. His soul does not fin
its balance disturbed or its flight impeded either by dogma, o
outward observance, or the monastic rule; all this diversit
of tradition is integrated to perfection in a spiritual life that
while multiform, is yet most truly " one."

We are less surprised, after this, at the exceptional favou
with which Christian folk, by a healthy instinct, have surrounde
this jewel of the piety of the cloister; for there is to be found i
it, in a most endearing realisation, the type of an interior lif
capable of being broadly practised even amid the surrounding
of the " world," of a spirituality as supple and mobile as th
soul's natural life, yet marked at the same time with that stam
of great unity and supernatural stability which is the specia
seal of the work of God.

But the interior ideal depicted in the *Imitation* could not b
definitely incorporated into the psychological life of the Chris
tian save at the cost of some effort. Let us consider a few o
the principal lines along which this effort must develop; an
see how admirably they lead, by a progressive unification, t
the highest states of contemplation; we will mention the habi
of interior prayer, purity of morals, the organisation of the sense
life by asceticism, detachment from the Ego.

2. *The Habit of Interior Prayer.*

The exercise of interior and personal prayer is one of th
most powerful means of psychological unification. Even i
conversations with our fellows, as soon as they pass the leve
of a commonplace and conventional exchange of civilities, i
not the whole of our personality stretched out towards, and, s

to say, " fixed " on, our interlocutor; whether it be to understand and sympathise with him, or on the other hand in self-defence, we live for the moment, willy-nilly, as a " function " of him. In prayer this orientation of the Ego towards an object capable of entering into relation with it is the very end that is pursued. Sometimes it is actualised at the first onset, and the soul, seconded by a well-regulated disposition of the senses, is directly installed at the very centre of the divine perspective. But more often it has to make use of a " method," whose function is merely to detail the partial attitudes which prepare for and constitute the complete attitude of prayer.

An example—we will choose one as classic as possible—will enable us to grasp this tactic of unification. The following is the directive " scheme " which St Ignatius Loyola, in his *Spiritual Exercises*,[5] sets before his retreatant in order to assist him in making an hour's mental prayer. Let us suppose that the prayer is to take place in the morning. On the preceding evening the retreatant considers in anticipation the general lines and the end pursued. Before going to sleep, he is invited to call a truce to all other preoccupations, and to concentrate his mind for a moment on the subject of his prayer; as far as is possible, he will hold to this thought until he falls asleep, and this course cannot fail already of deeply guiding his whole psychological activity towards the exercise of the morrow. His first voluntary preoccupation on awaking will be the approaching meditation; he will endeavour to create in himself a disposition of the affections suitable to the end proposed. Thus prepared subconsciously and affectively, and in possession of a plan for his reflections which is sufficiently considered to avoid gropings in the dark, he enters upon the exercise of prayer proper. If it be possible, he will have previously arranged the exterior circumstances in such a way as to assist his active recollection. He kneels, let us suppose, before his prie-Dieu, already cut off from the routine of exterior life both by the material isolation of the chosen spot and by the psychological isolation which has been practised since the previous evening. He pauses for an instant, thinks of what he is about to do, reminds himself with a most intense faith of the presence of God, kneels in adoration, implores the grace to concentrate on God and to attach his faculties and their operations to the divine will. He realises, if we may be permitted thus to recall the technique of psychology, the fundamental *Einstellung* and *Aufgabe*, the active general adaptation, which is to react on the whole of his prayer; a voluntary " polarisation " towards God.

His prayer, thus divided up, and so to speak provided with its situation, may now be diversified and particularised, in conformity with the more special end which the retreatant has proposed to himself. Beneath the gaze and constant attraction of God, who is present with him, thoughts organise themselves, affections are born and harmonised; even the imagination, expressly called upon to collaborate in the whole task, will to the best of its ability co-ordinate its creations therewith; memories will revive and future possibilities be outlined, arranging themselves in accordance with an order of values related to the Absolute; lastly desire will be awakened and eventual or immediate resolutions affirmed, always under the same dominating principle of unity. And St Ignatius earnestly adjures the person who is meditating to direct his efforts rather to depth than to breadth; to allow the work of impregnation and unification to be effected quietly, without insisting on making it embrace a large variety of matter; not to forget that intellectual assimilation must be brought about in the order of will and of action; and lastly, to respect the sovereign independence of grace.

In recalling this method, it is not our concern to defend it; all methods inspired by the normal activities of human psychology are of necessity coincident in their main lines. But what we wish the reader to grasp is the development of the power of unification by the exercise of a prayer which organises the soul, down to its very depths, under an absolute Ideal. The prayer, if it be frequently repeated, every morning for example, will accentuate its efforts and even end by marking all the activities of the Christian with a sort of " divine co-efficient "; the spiritual life, no doubt, remains at this stage a multiplicity, but it is already a multiplicity which is vivified and stabilised by a higher form of unity.

3. *Purity of Morals.*

Prayer restores or momentarily increases the speculative and affective unity of the moral life. By itself, moreover, it is a " moral action," since it tends above all to strengthen the orientation of the will towards the Good. We should do wrong however, to consider it as a magic wand, capable by its inherent virtue of bringing about the most startling metamorphoses

Were it not supported and prolonged by a very severe effort of moral purification, it would never suffice to establish the lasting unity of the interior life. Suffer the will, in the intervals of prayer, to turn back again to evil or the " less good," or merely to fall into inertia, and every fresh beginning of prayer will entail the renewal of an interior conflict. The progress of inward unification requires that the undulating curve of the psychological life of every day should constantly diminish its minima so as to rise by self-rectification to the level of the maxima realised in prayer. And it is evident that the condition of this progressive rising is the continual restoration and subsequent maintenance of that higher rectitude of action wherein purity of morals consists.

" Deliverance from sin," " conversion to good,"[6] will, then, on any hypothesis, remain the first and most indispensable step on that long journey which leads, through the stages of an increasingly perfect interior life, to the threshold of the mystical states; and " continual conversion from good to better " necessarily characterises this forward march to the very end. To wish to isolate prayer, asceticism, or mysticism from an efficacious concern for moral perfection would be meaningless. It is a matter for astonishment that several psychologists have failed to observe the clear line of demarcation made by this very high and normal preoccupation between true mysticism on the one hand, and its aberrations or counterfeits on the other.

4. *Asceticism.*

The habit of interior prayer does not, any more than constant purity of morals, subsist without asceticism—the methodical, persevering and, at times, painful organisation of the lower tendencies and the movements of the sensibility. Every personal systematisation whose dominant principle is " nature " —that is to say, in the most general sense, " created good "— breaks the complete equilibrium of prayer and holiness of life, by relaxing the subordination of our speculative and practical activities to our essential striving towards God.

War, therefore, must be proclaimed on the curiosity of the senses as soon as it becomes a solvent of the unity of the mind; war on over-keen passions, not only in so far as they are sources of sin, but in the measure in which their demands turn the soul aside, however little, from its effort after God; war on enjoyment and relaxing comfort; war, in a word, on everything that may loosen from below the ties of the interior life. In this war on nature, certainly, the difficulty is at times the transformation of the means into an end in itself, the putting of the emphasis on penance and the forgetting of the love which should prompt it, the oppressing of nature without upbuilding the spirit. But however it may be as to these unhelpful and often bizarre aberrations, it remains true that asceticism, by disciplining the sense-life and regulating its automatisms, is the indispensable condition for a life that is made one in God, a life of prayer.

But asceticism is not only a war which suppresses obstacles, it must also and even above all be a positive training of the lower activities to subdue themselves with perfect suppleness to the orders of the mind; for though they may become a fetter on the higher life of the soul, they remain nevertheless, normally, its preliminary condition, its support and an instrument of its efficacy. The Church, and the great Christian mystics with her, has always condemned that fanatical fakirism which is concerned rather with destroying than with regulating, which mutilates the body and damages the organic functions. And there is also a psychological fakirism, likewise unknown to the great contemplatives, which we refuse to rank in the ascending scale of the mystical activities; it consists in the blunting and dulling of the senses and the imagination, the dilution of the providential springs of human sensibility. Such an asceticism, though sometimes excusable, would not be according to God, for it is *of itself* impoverishing and deteriorating; God has not entrusted us with a harp that we may turn it into a monochord, but that we may draw from it complete harmonies to his glory. The great Christian mystics have, at least in practice, understood this rôle of the sense-life; with all of them it was and remained very rich, in the case of several it became exquisite; think of St Francis of Assisi, St Catherine of Siena and her namesake of Genoa, Blessed Henry Suso, St Teresa.[7] It is true that in Christianity the mystical ideal is inseparable from the ideal of the Gospels; and to say that suffices.

5. *Interior Crises.*

Asceticism, the effort it demands and the constant attention to moral purity which it presupposes, ordinarily bring in their train periods of lassitude, anguish, and internal crises. Writers have spoken of " negative mystical states ";[8] these are in fact, as it were, revenges, somersaults, of a temperament that has been too completely repressed, breakings down of an energy that has been stretched too taut. To one who envisages the individual religious life after the biological type, as an oscillatory rhythm, these " negative states " would represent phases of successive minima. This schematisation, however, seems to us very inexact; for though we readily admit that the determining causes of these states of " temptation," of " spiritual torpor," of " affective dryness," of darkness and scruples, are generally physiological, and that thus a certain rhythm can be established between them and the opposite states of dilatation and joy, we cannot in the periods of depression perceive serious indications of a recoil from the ascetic life; they are, on the contrary, periods of intense labour, of experience, of powerful and progressive organisation; the ascetic emerges from them with a more tempered and efficacious will, and more independent of those contingencies which influence the lower psychological life; and this, if we look at the matter more closely, amounts to saying that he comes out of them with his lower automatism reinforced in its useful parts, with habits of virtue which are more solidly anchored in the sense-life itself. The weakness of the flesh has served as a footstool for the spirit.

And always, amid the most diverse wanderings, it is the same great Unity which is being progressively realised.

6. *Renunciation of the Ego.*

We must here insist on an essential characteristic of the unity of the interior life in Christianity; the ideal type of this unity is superior to and transcends the Ego; for the principle of interior simplification is *love*, true love, whose swift arrow pierces without being stopped by the paper screen of the Ego, to fly to its true end, God.

Thus, in the history of Christian mysticism, the most abstract singers of Unity were at the same time the most fervent *Minnesänger*, singers of that divine love which causes self-love to be forgotten.

> *Verlass ich mich,*
> *So find ich dich,*
> *O überwesentliches Gut !*

So ends a most beautiful anonymous *Lied* of the thirteenth century.[9]

Relinque te et invenies me, says our Lord again in the *Imitation*. And such is the formula of the Christian tactic of reaching divine union which is unceasingly inculcated by ascetical writers: " You will find me in the degree in which you renounce yourself."

This " detachment from self," what does it mean ?

First of all, clearly, it is detachment from the lower and sensible Ego—that is, the habitual subordination of the fleshly to the spiritual point of view, the co-ordination of the lower multiplicity under a higher unity.

Again, it is detachment from the " vainglorious Ego," the dispersed and capricious Ego, the plaything of external circumstances, the slave of fluctuating opinion. The continuity of the inner life could not accommodate itself to so fluctuating a unity.

Above all, it is detachment from the " proud Ego." We must have a right understanding of this, for humility is rightly considered as one of the most characteristic notes of Christian asceticism and mysticism.

The " proud Ego " is that which sets itself up as the absolute end of personal action. In the midst of the everyday dispersion of an ordinary life, pride betrays itself only fragmentarily, in manifestations which cause a partial betrayal of its malice without displaying its radical monstrosity in its completeness. But let us suppose that the sense-life is unified and subjected, the life of thought concentrated and dominant; then there may be born explicitly in a man a perverse will to pursue his proper end to the exclusion of a higher end, the unity of his " Ego " isolated from a broader unity. Christianity, moreover, reprobates all this essential pride because it is the precise negation of the creature's natural dependence, in its being and its end, in relation to God. Metaphysics must likewise reprobate the meaningless claim to erect the finite and relative into an unconditioned and absolute. And psychology, without at all trespassing on the domain of the transcendental, will in its turn avow that the " proud Ego," turning the whole finality of its action back upon itself, arbitrarily restrains the becoming of the soul; the latter, indeed, must know no other limit to its fundamental striving than the possession of the unlimited Good and participation in the uncircumscribed Unity. The " proud Ego " displaces the natural polarity of the mind in a downward direction.

Metaphysics and psychology teach the same lesson of fundamental humility as does Christianity. We do not, therefore, claim that it is peculiar to the latter. It constitutes, however, one of those norms from which the Christian mystics, unlike some others, have never departed; for them the end of man is mingled with a higher end which subordinates the latter to itself by realising it; the " centre of gravity " of the religious life is situated beyond the innermost point of the soul, in God. This point of view, moreover, is only the expression of that law of love whose first commandment cannot fail to be " the free subordination of the self to God," " *Diliges Dominum Deum tuum ex toto corde tuo, et ex tota anima tua, et ex totis viribus tuis.*" And is Christian humility, even in its refinements, anything else than the detailed and lived acceptance of the law of love ? " *Nonne Deo subjecta erit anima mea ?*"[10]

We may here observe once more how all sincerely religious life prepares for the states of high contemplation. Christian humility, by preventing the Ego from becoming enamoured of itself to the exclusion of God, maintains in the soul *the only orientation compatible with the mystical states properly so called.* But we must not anticipate.

The religious forms which we have so far been considering, from ritual religion to the really interior life, inspired by the spirit of prayer, maintained by asceticism and guaranteed by humility, have been borrowed by us especially from the Christian religion, wherein all their riches are put to a very supple and harmonious use. They might also be considered, in greater isolation one from another, at the different stages of the religious development of mankind; in the material worship of primitive peoples or degenerate races; then in the more organised cults whose exterior surroundings hide too well, if they do not even extinguish, the spiritual nucleus; then once more in the great religions, more interior and closer to Christianity in spite of their profound differences therefrom. Such an inquiry, which we have not the space to undertake here, would usefully illustrate our subject, but is not indispensable thereto. We will pass directly, then, to the study of a form of prayer which is already exercised in a modest degree in the ordinary spiritual life, but finds its full blossoming in the mystical states properly so called. This form of prayer is *contemplation.*

(d) Contemplation

Contemplation, as commonly understood, is not intuition, since the name " contemplation " is also applied to an intellectual and imaginative activity. Might it be defined as an at least inchoative intuition ? Perhaps, in a way; yet it must be noted that sensible intuition, the only kind of which we normally have any experience, is not necessarily contemplation. This latter seems to require in addition a certain fixity, a more prolonged or intimate communion. We recollect a visit we once made to a famous place in company of a band of tourists, not very given to recollection, and some more meditative individuals who kept to themselves, the former, content to "see," were always impatient to go on, to the indignant despair of the latter, who would have preferred to " contemplate " at leisure. There can be no contemplation without sustained attention, at least for a few moments; now attention acts on the psychological elements after the fashion of the poles of a magnet, which gather up iron filings into magnetic shapes. Perhaps the characteristic of contemplation is rather a deep *orientation* of the human being *in* an intuition or *towards* an intuition ?

However this may be, there exist various kinds of contemplation.

1. *Sensible Contemplation.*

Firstly, there is a sensible contemplation, of which we will not speak, although many mystics have practised it and placed it at the service of their religious life. Surely the sun, the birds, which enraptured St Francis of Assisi, the tiny flower or the star-strewn heavens which threw St Ignatius Loyola into an ecstasy, were for these contemplatives only symbols wherein with their loving lucidity they discerned the magnificence of the Creator; the pole of their innermost being at such moments was not the sensible object itself.

2. *Imaginative Contemplation.*

SENSIBLE AND IMAGINATIVE VISIONS.—There is also an imaginative contemplation. All those who have dealt with the theory of prayer have commended it. Among Christians it generally consists in the sympathetic consideration of the mysteries of the life and death of Christ, carried as far as possible into the life of the contemplative.

A passage from a work long attributed to St Bonaventure[11] will show with what charming—some would say puerile—simplicity highly cultured minds and souls of virile temper have practised this exercise: " Let us come now to our Lord's return from exile. Lend a diligent attention thereto, for this meditation is extremely devout. Return then into Egypt, and there visit the child Jesus. Perhaps you will find him out-of-doors, with other children; on perceiving you he will come to meet you, for he is good and full of affability. You will kneel and kiss his feet, then take him into your arms and enjoy some rest in his company. Perhaps after this he will say to you: ' We have been permitted to return to our native land; we start tomorrow morning. You have come at an excellent moment; you can return with us.' Reply to him gladly that you are greatly rejoiced thereat and that you wish to follow him where-soever he goes. Continue to take your delight in his conver-sation after this fashion. Then he will take you to his mother, with tokens of great respect for her. Kneel before her and do her reverence, and the like to the old man Joseph, and stay with them." St Ignatius Loyola counsels an analogous practice for the contemplations of the second week of his *Exercises*.[12]

In spite of the esteem in which this pious exercise of affective imagination has always been held, and recognising with the pious Franciscan writer that " these apparent puerilities have a great value," " *quoniam ad majora transmittunt*," we think none the less that they are ill-adapted to certain temperaments, and that the most complete humility of heart is compatible with an absolute powerlessness for imaged realisation. On the other hand, among persons naturally disposed or trained to intensify a dominant representation to the detriment of its " antagonistic reducers," the effect may easily go beyond its end and the picture disclosed by contemplation may become pseudo-hallucinatory or even completely hallucinatory. This is the case, we think, in numerous—and, moreover, discordant—visions of the Passion and of other scenes in the life of our Lord and the Blessed Virgin, and again in those symbolic visions for which many mystics have had a liking.[13] The character of hallucina-tion—which, moreover, is only accidental, and depends on the nervous constitution of the subject much more than on an immediate intention of Providence—does not in such cases necessarily lessen the value of the visions for edification; it may even be strengthened thereby. For it is important not to confuse these two very different problems: those of the religious value and the psychological mechanism; an intention of Providence and even a special intervention of God may easily be conceived to exist in visions whose psychological mechanism enters in other respects into the categories of pure or psychical hallucination.[14]

Moreover, visions, of whatever nature—and the same might be said of all " somatic " marvels—do not express the essence of mysticism; they are only showy, secondary and often debateable episodes in it. They may be of assistance to the mystical life by the comfort and stimulus they bring to it; but the most eminent of those who have enjoyed them are unanimous in telling us, with St Paul: " *Aemulamini charismata meliora.*" There exists a higher contemplation, not directed towards any product of the sense-life, however noble, but in closer touch with the fundamental, intelligent, and loving tendency of the mind towards God.

3. *Intellectual Contemplation.*

Here we must go very carefully, so as not to be led astray by partial resemblances.

The interior movement of intellectual contemplation tends, by its very nature, towards the proper unity of the mind, and thus towards the simplification of its content.

Now there are two very different kinds of simplification of such content: a simplification which impoverishes, and a simplification which enriches.

(1) IMPOVERISHING SIMPLIFICATION.—Firstly, an impoverishing simplification. This is what we meet in clinics for mental diseases and insane asylums.

Take an hysterical patient, to whom, let us suppose, a religious *motif* is suggested in the hypnotic state. Even less: one of those ideogenic zones, which happens by good fortune, as in the case of Pitres' patient,[15] to be a " zone of ecstasy," is excited in a slight degree. The hands are joined, the body is composed, the eyes raised to heaven, the affective system takes on a religious direction, the words are full of devotion, the imagination is intensified to the point of hallucinatory visions of Christ or the Blessed Virgin. Will you then, by your procedure of suggestion, have evoked a transitory but deepseated alteration of the personality of the patient under a religious ideal ? And do you perhaps anticipate from this the construction of a therapeutic system of moral elevation ? Any physician with a little experience will smile at your optimism. For the moment your patient is under the influence of a religious suggestion, true; but this suggestion, instead of profoundly orientating the whole personality of your subject, has merely detracted from it and organised a few superficial elements which allowed themselves to be assimilated. You have brought about a momentary equilibrium, but only the poorest possible, by putting to sleep for a moment the true personality, a personality sometimes very depraved and as unmystical as can be. It is a relative unification, it is true, but it involves impoverishment.

There is the same impoverishment, to an even more lamentable degree, in the religious mimicry of some catatonics. We recall, for example, a very advanced case of *dementia praecox*, which we were able to observe in a clinic abroad; the patient was invited to kneel; with the delay and tergiversations to be expected from a catatonic, he at last fell on his knees, with hands joined, eyes closed, and an impressive air; then he prostrated himself to the earth, forehead to the ground, kissed the floor, and prolonged his prostration in a state of immobility. He might have been thought a contemplative abasing his nothingness before God in profound adoration. . . . But suddenly he was seen to creep forward, and glide completely under a bed which was in the room; no doubt his poor brain perceived in this absurd gesture the ulterior realisation of the impulse received. No doubt there was, in this succession of motor activities, a real and even tyrannical unity; but it escaped the influence of the whole personality. It was, once again, a simplification by impoverishment.

But we need not go to the asylums to look for our examples. Every hallucinatory or impulsive tendency, every fixed idea, bears with it an impoverishment when it results from the breaking up of the content of the consciousness. Even the state of scholarly distraction, when it is not brought about by the contemplation of an object worthy to lay hold of the whole soul, is a mark of a lack and a weakness; when transitory it may be useful, but if prolonged it would mean the ruin of the Ego and permanent loss of balance. To speak plainly, it seems to us that the over-mechanical processes employed by certain sects to procure ecstasy are no more calculated to enrich the personality. And we are not speaking now of the extravagances of shamans or dancing dervishes, but also of more sober proceedings. Imagine this young " Yogin," squatting on his mat, his head slightly bent, his eyes half closed. He is training to enter into communication with the Atman, the universal Spirit, by freeing himself from " phenomena "; to this end he must methodically efface the diversity of sensation and thought. And these are the instructions he has received: the " Vidya " Yoga is practised in four manners. " Mantra-Yoga consists in repeating a certain word again and again, particularly a word expressive of deity, and concentrating all one's thoughts on it. Laya-Yoga is the concentration of all our thoughts on a thing or the idea of a thing, so that we become almost one with it. Here again the ideal image of a god . . . is the best. Râja-Yoga consists in controlling the breath so as to control the mind. . . . It was supposed that concentration of the mind would be sure to follow the holding back of the breath. . . . Hatha-Yoga is concerned with the general health of the body; and is supposed to produce concentration by certain positions of the body, by fixing the eyes on one point . . ." etc.[16]

In our humble opinion, proceedings of this kind seem calculated rather to wipe out and efface the elements of the personality than to grasp them closely in a higher unity. At the most doubt may be permitted as to the two first forms of training; if in them the *word* or the *ideal image* which expresses the divinity be charged with that concentrated signification, remaining itself wholly in potentiality, which the whole of the personal experience may deposit in them, it may be conceived that they may on this ground serve as a luminous pole for an effort of interior unification, of true " concentration." It seems, unfortunately, that their significance for the Yogin remains in the last resort accessory, and that the result sought is the psychological simplification for its own sake, independent of its content. Perhaps M. Leuba's theory of monoïdeism, aïdeism and the " experience of Nothingness " might find some application here.

These proceedings of Yogism, however, even if they tend *of themselves* to procure a species of ecstasy that is somewhat negative, poor, and empty, are not necessarily *incompatible* with a richer ecstasy, the exact value whereof would depend on other simultaneous influences.

In the history of Christian mysticism do we not meet with cases of psychological Yogism or misunderstood quietism, wherein the states of simplification are merely negative, ineffectual and impoverished states ? We do not doubt it, although the concrete diagnosis must be very delicate to arrive at. They will especially be met with, no doubt, among those aspirants to mysticism who have in view not so much moral perfection as the rapid attainment of extraordinary states, and who, even when they think they have entered into states of union, do not display in their conduct that active and practical love which ought to possess them if their whole personality were truly impregnated with God. We here gain a glimpse of the psychological value of those moral criteria which the Catholic Church has always considered decisive in the estimation of extraordinary states;[17] the psychologist, with an end and a scale of values very different, will not be far from measuring with the same rule. The great mystics for their part were not ignorant, even apart from what they looked upon as illusions of demons, of certain natural falsifications of the higher states of prayer; witness the very fine remarks of St Teresa on the pretended prayer of quiet or the ecstasy of those good folk who devoutly prepare themselves for sleep or swooning.

(2) ENRICHING SIMPLIFICATION: *A. In the Profane Order.*— There exists, then, an impoverishing psychological simplification, which in certain of its characteristics is able to simulate another rich and full simplification. In what does this latter consist ?

A few examples borrowed from the profane order will help us to grasp it.

Let us suppose two visitors standing before " The Praying Youth " (*Der betende Knabe*), that wonderful Greek bronze in the Museum of Antique Sculpture at Berlin. One is a simple, uncultured amateur, the other an artist and an archæologist. Both are smitten with the beauty of the work, and are " contemplating " in that semi-numbness of mind which the beautiful induces. Perhaps, if we could obtain a snapshot of the sensations, feelings, representations, and formal judgements present at the moment in the clear consciousness of the two admirers, the negatives would seem very similar, and also both very incomplete. Yet what a difference in the inner and lived reality ! Under the superficial community of visual perception and æsthetic emotion, the ignorant amateur brings only a certain natural good taste, poor moreover in experience: the artist-archæologist may bring, in addition, the confused resultant, subconscious but very rich, of a treasure of accumulated impressions and incipient representations: it is an awakening of potentialities which pass into act only just enough to colour the artist's contemplation by recalling him to the dull and moderate feeling of his inward power of evocation. The same object apprehended by both parties with a dumb and simple admiration, is diversified by the depth and richness of the echoes whose awakening it prepares. The two contemplations, then, differ immensely in their potential symbolism and their latent dynamism.

Are you still able to recall the idea you first conceived of the " Siècle de Louis XIV " through the narrow and dry medium of a school-book ? Since then you have read Saint-Simon's *Mémoires* and the *Caractères* of La Bruyère, the Letters of Mme. de Sévigné and the *Oraisons funèbres* of Bossuet, the plays of Corneille, Racine, Molière, the satires of Boileau; you have entered deeply into the politics of the time, its intrigues, its wars, its finance, its economic life, its art, its rather florid religious dignity, its mystical experience and inexperience, and how much else ! And when you think now of the " Siècle de Louis XIV," even before any precise diversification crops out on the threshold of your consciousness, are you not quite aware that you think " infinitely more " and " quite otherwise " than in the old days with your unformed schoolboy's brain ?

To take a last example, which will bring us back to our mystics. Let us take one of those general notions which border at the same time on the speculative and the active life, such as that of moral Good. Few men totally lack all idea of morality; let us concern ourselves only with those who would give the same abstract definition of it. Let us see once more what an infinite diversity there is in the psychological treasure laid hold of by an identical concept. Peter, a worthy person, not given to scruples, and a mediocre thinker, will have hardly elaborated in speculation or in practice the notion in question; it remains outside his interior life, and appears to him only with that aureole of boredom which is attached to a solemn abstraction and a threat of constraint. Paul is a speculative moralist and a man of learning; when he thinks of moral Good, it is especially as a connected series of systems and a theory of proper names which move in his subconscious. John is an emotional person, a refined soul, all of a piece; to him moral Good is his whole interior life, with his enthusiasms, his generous illusions, his disinterestednesses, his refinements, his aspirations, his faith, his God; he has " lived " the abstract idea and it is an active force in him. James is a mature and wise man, whose rectitude tempered with finesse has found in the experiences of life a lesson of indulgence; moral Good represents to him an Absolute inged with a relative element, an ideal beloved in itself, but tolerated without too much contempt in its human deformations, an inflexible Law, accomplished with a smile and proclaimed with a moderation which conceals a grain of melancholy scepticism. With Peter, the idea of moral Good has remained, both speculatively and affectively, impoverished; with Paul, it is enriched especially with associations of knowledge; with John, it is charged with a power of life and action; with James, it lives also, but carries with it a kind of discreet reflection of disabused experiences. And all this varied accompaniment arises in potentiality as soon as the idea passes through conciousness.

B. In the Mystical Order : (a) On the Threshold of Ecstasy ?— On the lines of what precedes it seems less difficult to form a correct idea of what would in the religious domain be an intellectual contemplation, enriching and simplifying at the same time.

The contemplative—by a coincidence which for the moment we will not go into more deeply—fixes his inner gaze on an idea which is the purest expression of God, Absolute Unity. He thus supports his efforts on the most central line of the natural development of the mind. Moreover, thanks to the convergent and often prolonged exercise of vocal and mental prayer, of moral activity, asceticism, humility, he has connected, and connects more closely each day, with his idea of God all that is dearest and most intimate to him: God has become the keystone of the arch of his Ego, the point from which he views all his proceedings, the pregnant symbol, the assimilative force of all his experiences, the ideal of all his dreams, the centre of all his affections, the dominating principle of all his actions—in short, the centre of equilibrium and the vital impulse of his whole psychological being.

And when the contemplative, set free from the diversity of time and space, enters into prayer, the powerful co-ordination which he has prepared in himself by the whole course of his life awakes and is locked in the bosom of a growing recollection. Let us hear what is said on this point, not by the mystic alone, but even by a simple man of prayer: " Lord, thou art wholly hidden in the heart of each thing. . . . I beseech thee, turn my heart towards thee, into the interior of myself, into the depth of my soul, so that there, in the silence of creatures and the quieting of inordinate thoughts, I may remain with thee, unceasingly behold thy presence, love and worship thee, hear

thy voice, discover to thee the wretchedness of my exile an
find comfort in thee."[18]

God at the deepest point of the self : that is the fixed poir
towards which, after a few rapid oscillations, the soul of the tru
contemplative is clearly orientated; just as the magnetic needl
seeks the North. And the exercise which he then performs i
one of mighty possibilities from the psychological point (
view; under the urge of a powerful love he uplifts his idea (
God and holds it at the surface of his consciousness: tha
fascinating symbol which for him is not so much a concept a
an orientation of his whole being; and by the same effort h
keeps standing, in his subconscious self, the formidable edific
of a complete psychological life crystallised around the symbo
No artist's vision was ever of a more concentrated richness
more terrific in its power of evocation, or more violently tens
in its dynamism, than this simple and fixed gaze of the cor
templative on God.

Is this ecstasy ?[19]

Perhaps, in a strained sense, when the contemplation jus
described reaches a great intensity; but it is not yet the fu
union of the Christian mystics. What is still lacking ?

(b) Somatic and Psycho-physiological Anomalies.—Is it perhap
certain external and glaring details, which for a long time pas
have in the eyes of the populace and of not very far-seein
physicians summed up the essence of the mystical states: th
phenomena of real or merely imaginary levitation, catalepsy
suspension of the senses, not to speak of the sensible vision
which we have mentioned above ?

Here a remark of Suarez puts us quite at ease. He consider
it not only possible but probable that, among physically pre
disposed subjects, a very intense mental application or a violer
affective movement may suspend the exercise of the outwar
senses. And from this he concludes that it is not necessar
to explain the psycho-physiological characteristics of ecstas
by a grace distinct from that of " infused contemplation," fo
they are merely the natural consequence of this latter.[20]

This is very wise. And whatever may be the case as to th
natural or supernatural character of contemplation itself, w
can foresee that a state of such violent concentration will nc
remain without some echo on the body, on the actual exercis
of the senses. The commonplace phenomenon of attentio
already stretches the muscles engaged, spaces out the respira
tions, and moderates and lessens the pulse; more intens

attention interferes with or suppresses the perception of sensible objects which are not within its focus, and is often accompanied by slight contractions; here we have in normal psycho-physiology an anticipation of the phenomenon of ecstatic weakness, catalepsy, alienation of the senses, ligature of the inferior powers. The difference *under this head* between the mystical and the ordinary psychological states seems to us to be only a difference of degree. As for levitation—a purely accidental and secondary, and likewise very inconstant episode —described in the profane ecstasies of Iamblichus or the uncanny states of Hindu fakirs, as well as in the trances of spiritistic mediums, we confess that we have no definite ideas as to its nature and causes.[21]

Physical ecstasy, then, is in our eyes a feeble adaptation of our somatic mechanisms to the excessive central supertension of high intellectual contemplation. Many mystics stop short at this incomplete adaptation; others, like St Teresa, arrive, by a partial and harmonious self-duplication, at a much better physical adaptation, which restores them to social life without interrupting their contemplation.

Since the psycho-physiological concomitants have only an accidental and variable relation with the states of prayer, let us seek elsewhere for what differentiates contemplation, as described above, from mystical union properly so called.

(c) The Summit of Contemplation : Negative Characteristics.— It would suffice us, truth to tell, in order to connect the states of union which the mystics describe with contemplation, to continue to its extreme limit the progression which led us to contemplation itself. We have seen that it is a simplification of the Ego by the concentration of this latter under a transcendent unity. The limit towards which this process tends, then, may be characterised by the negative notes of pure intellectual unity: (1) total abandonment of " discursiveness " and of fragmentary conception by " composition and division "; (2) reduction to the state of subconscious potentiality of all mental " imagery," and representations of sensible origin, and at the same time total abandonment of the spatial form of intuition; (3) abandonment even of all consciousness of the fundamental dualism of Ego and non-Ego.

Let us, for the moment, seek the total or partial realisation of these negative notes in states which all agree in considering as the summit of mystical contemplation. We will choose only a few examples of them, for we cannot dream of displaying

the evidence fully in this short essay; and in order to prejudg
nothing as to the questions we shall examine later, we wi
make our choice indifferently within Christianity or outside i

Neoplatonism.—A tout seigneur tout honneur. The writing
of Plotinus are the first truly complete literary manifestatio
of high mysticism; and we may indeed affirm that in the We
at least they have directly or indirectly influenced all who hav
written on the theory of contemplation.

Mysticism, for Plotinus, is the crown of metaphysics; it i
metaphysics *lived to the end*, the ascent of the soul toward
Unity. In the very bosom of sensible beauty, the soul purifie
by asceticism (ἡ ψυχὴ καθαρθεῖσα, *Enn.* I vi 9) discovers i
itself the intelligible Beauty whose splendour wholly com
penetrates it. But the contemplation of the " intelligible "-
which also carries with it the distinction between *intelliger*
and *intellectum*—is not the supreme summit of its ascension
For the very movement which carries the soul towards th
intelligible bears it on further like an impetuous wave (ἐξενεχθει
τῷ αὐτῷ τοῦ νοῦ οἷον κύματι, *Enn.* VI vii 36). Whither, the
does it bear it? Towards absolute Unity, the Good, God, who
the soul attains in the supreme " Union "; this is no longe
strictly speaking, a contemplation, but a possession: καὶ οὗτο
οὐ κατ' ὄψιν φανείς, ἀλλὰ τὴν ψυχὴν ἐμπλήσας τοῦ θεωμένο
(*Enn.* VI vii 35). The duality of the soul and its object i
reduced: . . . οὐδ' ἔτι δυό ἀλλὰ ἓν ἄμφω (*Enn.* VI vii 34). Th
soul really lives the One, in immortality and unconsciousne
of itself: οὐδὲ κινεῖται ἡ ψυχή, . . . οὐδὲ ψυχὴ τοίνυν (it i
no longer, properly speaking, a ψυχή, a principle of sensibilit
. . . οὐδὲ νοῦς . . . (nor a νοῦς, a finite intelligence
'Ομοιοῦσθαι γὰρ δεῖ· νοεῖ δὲ οὐδ' ἐκεῖνο, ὅτι οὐδὲ νοε
(*Enn.* VI vii 35). Its whole task now is to assimilate itself t
the sovereign One: it does not even notice that it does not think.
Here we have the effacement of the Ego in the embrace of th
Good.

Hindu Mysticism.—Leaping over some centuries—we mu
be allowed this paradoxical phantasy, which is imposed by lac
of space—we meet, quite near our own times, with the Hind
mystic Râmakrishna (1833–1886), a very typical example of th
same fundamental process, free in his case from all touch c
Hellenism.

He was fascinated by the goddess Kâli, whom he looke
upon as the mother of himself and of all things. After som
time of devout service began a period of more and mor

frequent ecstatic visions. Urged by zeal for perfection and the desire to reach the divine Presence underlying the diversity of phenomena, he began for twelve years to practise ascetic exercises of unheard-of severity, thus progressively detaching himself from his body and his Ego. And his states of mystical union with the goddess developed likewise. One day, a Sannyâsin (Hindu ascetic), not being able to understand Râmakrishna's love for the goddess his " Mother," treated it as a pure superstition and laughed at it. Then " Râmakrishna made him understand that in the Absolute there is no Thou, nor I, nor God, nay, that it is beyond all speech or thought. As long, however, as there is the least grain of relativity left, the (so-called) Absolute is within thought and speech and within the limits of the mind, which mind is subservient to the universal mind and consciousness; and this omniscient universal consciousness was to him his Mother and God."[23]

Moslem Mysticism.—Let us go back to the twelfth century, and question a representative of Moslem (Persian) mysticism. Farîd-ed-Dîn-Attâr (born *circa* 1120) describes, in a book entitled *The Language of Birds*, the seven valleys passed through by the contemplative.

As a beginner he has already passed successively through " the Valley of Seeking " and Desire; through " the Valley of Love " which surpasses reason as fire pierces through smoke; through " the Valley of Knowledge " which discovers the sweetness of Being under the husk of sensible things; through " the Valley of Independence " of the soul which has reached self-sufficiency. It now enters the " Valley of Unity." " When the pilgrim has entered this valley, he is effaced in his own eyes like the ground which gives way beneath his feet. He must lose himself, for the sole Being is about to be revealed. He will remain dumb, for the Only Being will speak. The Part will become the Whole, or better still, there will no longer be either Whole or Part. . . . What has become of the Understanding ? It has remained on the threshold of the door, like a child born blind."—" He who has taken the Unity into his heart forgets all and is himself forgotten. When he is asked: Art thou or art thou not ? hast thou the fulness of Being or not ? art thou in the midst or on the margin ? art thou visible or hidden, mortal or immortal ? art thou this or that, or rather neither the one nor the other ? art thou thyself or art thou not ?—he will reply, I know nothing, I am ignorant of all this and of my very self. I am in love, but I know not with what; I am neither faithful nor unfaithful. What am I then? My very love I know not; I have my heart both full and empty of love." A last experience in the " Valley of Consternation," and the devout pilgrim enters into the last Valley, that of " Nakedness and Death." " When the sea of infinitude begins to roll its waves, how can the moveable images which are traced out on its surface subsist? These images are the world present and future. . . . He whose heart is plunged into this sea is lost there for ever and remains at rest. . . ." " Cast the mantle of Nothingness about thee and drink the chalice of annihilation, cover thy breast with the love of Nought and place on your head the turban of Not-being. Put thy foot in the stirrup of unconditional renunciation and urge thy mount decidedly towards the place where nought any longer is. . . . When thou hast heaped up thy whole inner man into total negation, then thou wilt be beyond good and evil: and when there is for thee no longer either good or evil, then alone wilt thou love in truth and be worthy of that deliverance which is the work of love." " I was a tiny drop lost in the ocean of mystery, and now I can no longer find even that tiny drop."[24]

Is there not, in these last passages from Attâr, a smack of Pantheism, a flavour, as it were, of Nirvâna? This problem does not particularly interest us here; we will, however, seize this occasion to emphasise the extreme prudence which is necessary in applying the label " pantheist " to descriptions of the mystical states which exaggerate an important characteristic of them without pretending to furnish an adequate definition of them *per genus et differentiam*. In any case, other Moslem authors, such as Avicenna (†1037), would escape this suspicion.[25] After detailing the successive " stations " of the Sufi, his exercises and raptures, this writer describes the highest degree as follows: " He (the Sufi) looks turn by turn at God and his soul as in a reciprocal motion; but at the end even his soul disappears from his sight; he sees no longer aught but Holiness itself, or if he still sees his soul, it is inasmuch as this latter sees God. . . . On arriving at this point, he has realised union."[26]

Profane Mysticism.—It may be interesting to compare with the religious raptures we have just recalled a purely profane type of " ecstasy." We take our example from the personal experiences of J. A. Symonds, whose nervous condition really bordered on the pathological. " Suddenly . . . I felt the approach of the mood. Irresistibly it took possession of my mind and will. . . . One reason why I disliked this kind of trance was that I could not describe it to myself. I cannot even now find words to render it intelligible. It consisted in a gradual but swiftly progressive obliteration of space, time, sensation, and the multitudinous factors of experience which seem to qualify what we are pleased to call our Self. In proportion as these conditions of ordinary consciousness were subtracted, the sense of an underlying or essential consciousness acquired intensity. At last nothing remained but a pure, absolute, abstract Self. The universe became without form and void of content. But Self persisted, formidable in its vivid keenness, feeling the most poignant doubt about reality, ready, as it seemed, to find existence break as breaks a bubble round about it."[27] This typical description is not an isolated one. Amiel's *Journal Intime*, for example, is a mine of similar observations.[28]

The reader will remark the analogy which subsists between the " pure Self " of Symonds and the indefinable Reality, the negativity ulterior to the Ego, of the mystics previously quoted. And we will add that many of the raptures of pious persons, Protestant or Catholic, strongly resemble this purely profane ecstasy, save for the subjective religious interpretation.

Medieval Christian Mysticism.—We will now rapidly continue our enquiry among the Christian mystics, and see what becomes of the negative characteristics of high contemplation in their case. The field of documentation is wider than ever here, and has been the object of manifold explorations; we will therefore, since we cannot embark on a very detailed criticism, content ourselves with recalling a few typical examples.[29]

We know how prolonged were the reverberations of Neoplatonism in the Middle Ages; philosophers and mystics were tributary to it in various ways and respects, from John Scotus Eriugena to Tauler and Ruysbroeck, by way of Bernard of Clairvaux, the Victorines, Albertus Magnus, Thomas Aquinas, Bonaventure, David of Augsburg, Eckhart—brilliant theoreticians, who were, moreover, no strangers to transcendental experiences—and through a whole pleiad of devout persons of either sex, given up to the practice of contemplation, but not disdaining at the proper time to dissert on the " loss of the soul in Unity." Beside St Augustine, one of the most potent intermediaries of this Neoplatonist influence on medieval thought and religious life was unquestionably the pseudo-Dionysius the Areopagite, whose works, *The Celestial Hierarchy*, and especially *The Divine Names* and *Mystical Theology*, present a Christian variation of Hellenist philosophy. The Plotinian accent peeps through from the very first words of the *Mystical Theology*: " Friend, tend with all thy might towards mystical contemplations. . . . Abandon the impressions of the senses and the acts of the understanding, all that is sensible and intelligible, what is and what is not, and without natural knowledge urge thyself, in the measure that shall be given thee, to union with That which is beyond all being and all gnosis."[30] Here we find once more, in Dionysian contemplation, the abandonment of discursiveness, of the concepts and forms of sensibility, which we have remarked elsewhere. And no medieval mystic denied this negative type of divine union.

It is also to be noted that mystical theory in the Middle Ages only transposed into life and practice the two procedures whereof speculative theology made use in order to define—analogically—the essence of God; they are already named by the pseudo-Denis, and are doubtless of earlier origin; they are the positive procedure, *via affirmationis*, καταφατική, which consists in affirming of God, as the cause of creatures, all the perfections of the latter, and the negative procedure, the *via negationis*, ἀποφατική, which consists in denying of the absolute and transcendent God the diverse and finite gamut of created perfections. The mystic, as distinct from the " pure speculative," carries out the negative procedure to the extent of effacing from his consciousness every determination, every diversification, not only that of quantity and quality, but also of Ego and non-Ego, of Being and not-Being. It would, however, be a mistake to see in this any pure negativity among the great Christian mystics; the *via affirmationis* was represented in their simplifying ascension—we have already seen that simplification and enrichment are not mutually exclusive—and it is prolonged even to the ultimate limit of their ecstasy. We shall have to return to this point later. For the moment let us notice, in the fundamental inspiration of Christian mysticism, in its principles so to speak, the share of the negative notes which we theoretically recognised at the higher limit of contemplation.

It would be superfluous for us to occupy ourselves now with bringing out these negative characteristics in detail, in the case of authors whose whole attitude clearly implies them, such as Eckhart, so " Plotinist " that he seemed—and in the eyes of many remains—pantheistic,[31] or Tauler, who eloquently depicts the " mysterious darkness " wherein the soul " is absorbed into something, one, simple, divine, unlimited," from which it is no longer able to " distinguish itself," so much " is the feeling of multiplicity effaced in this unity."[32]

Others, of a more simple and affective nature, such as Blessed Henry Suso, speak at bottom in no other fashion; replying, in his capacity of " spiritual father " to " his well-exercised daughter " (Elizabeth Stagel), the " servitor " (Henry Suso) explains to her the supreme rapture of a soul which is admitted to follow the Son of God " there where he is according to his pure Divinity . . . and to enjoy him in a spiritual manner . . . in time and eternity, as far as is possible, in a greater or less degree." Now where will the soul meet with " the place of the Son's pure divinity "? " In the resplendent light of the divine Unity." It is wholly plunged therein. " And in this dark ignorance, every diversity disappears, the mind loses all personal initiative. . . . And there is the highest end, the *where* without end (without delimitation) in which the spirituality of every spirit is extinguished; and to be lost in this state is the greatest felicity."[33]

With Ruysbroeck the Admirable, so personal in spite of his close relationship with the group of Suso and Tauler, the negative characteristics of the states of union are continually recalled. Let us merely quote a passage from the *Spieghel der ewigher salicheit* : " Here our reason must be put aside, like every distinct work; for our powers become simple in love, they are silent and bowed down in the presence of the Father. This revelation of the Father, in fact, raises the soul above reason, to an imageless nakedness. The soul there is simple, pure, and spotless, empty of all things, and it is in this state of absolute emptiness that the Father shows his divine brightness. To this brightness neither reason nor sense nor remark nor distinction may serve; all that must remain below; for the measureless brightness blinds the eyes of the reason and compels them to yield to the incomprehensible light."[34]

The same descriptive features are once more found outside the group of the German mystics; for example, in France, with Gerson. They are also found in English mysticism before the Reformation; the Dionysian influence, moreover, is not absent therefrom. Here is a short extract from a very original work, *The Cloud of Unknowing*. The mystical experience, it is there stated, consists in " a swift, piercing act, an act of direction, a naked intent of the will fastening itself upon God." In this God-directed impulse of love " there is taken away from the man all knowing or feeling of his own."[35]   Later we observe more or less clearly similar experiences among Protestants in England and elsewhere. For details we refer the reader to collections like those of James or Buber, or again to general works like those of Jones, Inge, Pratt, Beck, and others. German Protestant mysticism, impossible even to outline within the limits of this essay, would deserve a special study by itself. Read, *e.g.*, the study of E. Boutroux on J. Boehme, or again the chapters devoted to Protestant speculative mysticism by Windelband in his *History of Modern Philosophy*, or directly, if you have the necessary courage, a good edition of Boehme.[36]

Christian Mysticism of the Renaissance.—If we pass to the post-medieval Catholic mystics, on whom the influence of Plotinism was less direct, we again meet on all sides with the same negative characteristics of the mystical union. The quotations that might be made are infinite. Since the subject is here better known in its main lines, we limit ourselves to two characteristic and often-quoted passages from St Teresa.

" When all the faculties of the soul are in union (with God) . . . they can then do nothing whatever, because the understanding is as it were surprised. The will loves more than the understanding knows; but the understanding does not know that the will loves, nor what it is doing, so as to be able in any way to speak of it. As to the memory, the soul, I think, has none then, nor any power of thinking, nor are the senses awake, but rather as lost, so that the soul may be the more occupied with the object of its fruition; so it seems to me. They are lost but for a brief interval; it passes quickly away " (*Second Relation to Fr. Rodrigo Alvarez*).[37]

" Do not imagine that this state of prayer (of union) is, like the one preceding it (the prayer of quiet), a sort of drowsiness. I call it ' drowsiness ' because the soul seems to slumber, being neither quite asleep nor wholly awake. In the prayer of union the soul is asleep, fast asleep, as regards the world and itself; in fact, during the short time this state lasts it is deprived of all feeling whatever, being unable to think on any subject, even if it wished. No effort is needed here to suspend the thoughts: if the soul can love—it knows not how, nor whom it loves, nor what it desires. In fact, it has died entirely to this world, to live more truly than ever in God " (*Interior Castle, Fifth Mansions*, ch. 1).[38]

" Let us now speak of the sign which proves the prayer of union to have been genuine. As you have seen, God then deprives the soul of all its senses that he may the better imprint in it true wisdom; it neither sees, hears, nor understands anything while this state lasts. . . . God visits the soul in a manner which prevents its doubting, on returning to itself, that it dwelt in him and that he was within it. . . . But, you may ask, how can a person who is incapable of sight and hearing see or know these things? I do not say that she saw it at the time, but that she perceives it clearly afterwards, not by any vision but by a certitude which remains in the heart which God alone could give. . . . If we did not see it, how can we feel so sure of it? That I do not know: it is the work of the Almighty and I am certain that what I say is the fact" (*Ibid.*).[39]

And St John of the Cross explains why this high contemplation cannot be expressed: " If (the soul) could have a wish to speak of it, and find terms to describe it, it would always remain secret still. Because this interior wisdom is so simple, general and spiritual that it enters not into the understanding under any form or image subject to sense, as is sometimes the case, the imagination, therefore, and the senses—as it has not entered in by them, nor is modified by them—cannot account for it, nor form any conception of it, so as to speak in any degree correctly about it, though the soul be distinctly conscious that it feels and tastes this sweet and strange wisdom" (*Dark Night of the Soul*, Book II, ch. xvii).[40]

What has been written on this subject by St Teresa and St John of the Cross can be found with equal ease in St Francis de Sales, St Alphonsus Rodriguez, Blessed Mary of the Incarnation, Louis de Blois (Blosius), Frs. Balthazar Alvarez and Alvarez de Paz, even Mme. Guyon, if you will, and many others also.

A very delicate *psychological problem* is thus raised: the consensus of the testimonies we have educed is too unanimous to be rejected. It compels us to recognise the existence in certain subjects of a special psychological state, which generally results from a very close interior concentration, sustained by an intense affective movement, but which, on the other hand, no longer presents any trace of " discursiveness," spatial imagination, or reflex consciousness. And the disconcerting question arises: after images and concepts and the conscious ego have been abolished, what subsists of the intellectual life? Multiplicity will have disappeared, true, but to the advantage of what kind of unity?

This is the real *problem of ecstasy*.

SECOND PART

THE PROBLEM OF ECSTASY

Three kinds of solutions have been put forward.

I. FIRST INTERPRETATIVE SOLUTION: THE ABSENCE OF MULTIPLICITY IN ECSTASY IS ONLY APPARENT

The first solution lessens the negative characters of high contemplation, to the extent of reducing them to a psychological operation absolutely similar, save in its intensity, to ordinary contemplation.

In truth, the character which really causes difficulty is not so much the absence of reflex consciousness, or even the momentary abandonment of the discursive mode of knowledge. Have we not, in fact, in our non-religious experience, clear enough examples of this twofold " negativity "? Concentration of the attention on a difficult problem or a captivating object is capable of abolishing the actual apperception of the Ego. We do wrong to be surprised at the allusions made by the mystics to the " unconsciousness " of full union; this unconsciousness is merely forgetfulness of the Ego; and who, indeed, will claim that our psychological personality is continually present to us ? As for the suspension of " discursiveness "—that is to say, of the intellectual appreciation of objects by alternate analysis and synthesis, by successive " composition and division "—this seems indeed to be produced at times, if only for a moment, in æsthetic contemplation for example.

The third negative characteristic, on the other hand, which is universally testified to, is more disconcerting. The contemplative, when he recalls his ecstasy, is conscious of having lived through an absolutely simple state, devoid of all imagery, free from all objective multiplicity. Is this compatible with the fundamental psychological law which connects the exercise of the human intelligence, here on earth, with a sensible and spatial content, clothed with a higher form of unity by it alone ? How could the naked intelligence, an empty form, apart from a content which determines it, exercise as such any activity whatsoever ?

In fact, unless we admit a strictly intellectual intuition in our normal psychology, we cannot escape from the contradiction which is left by the descriptions of the mystics. But do these merit so entire, and so to speak so literal, a faith ?   Must we not correct the data which they afford ?

Firstly, let us suppose—it is at least the most convenient hypothesis—that the mystic is under an illusion as to the in-quantitative and formless character of his ecstatic intuition. Has he not confused the inquantitative with the vague ?   His intuition, when afterwards he analyses, and perhaps interprets, it, always includes, in sum, these three elements: (1) an intense attraction of the soul to the Absolute by love; (2) a notion of some kind concerning this Absolute; (3) the vague perception of a very immediate relation with this Absolute.

The first element is an affective state which may remain conscious, under the form of an aspiration still obscurely related to the Ego; the mystic would experience not so much " *his* love for God " as simply " *God* loved "; now this pre-dominance of one of the terms of the affective relation at the expense of the other is not outside the possibilities of normal psychology.

The second element would be merely a very refined concept of the Absolute, of God; if the mystic were a better analyst, he would discover subtle traces of representation in it; for example, a very attenuated semi-sensorial, semi-emotive symbolism, as when we translate our impressions of great, good, immense, high, terrible, motionless, and so on; or a symbolism purely verbal—that is to say, one which crops out discreetly in the consciousness, a vague image of a word such as God, Infinite, Goodness, Justice, Love, and so on.   The mystic, a prey to the violent transport of love, is not interested in this weak imagery, which is of less value for what it formally represents than for its implied dynamism: how is it astonishing that he does not observe it ?

As for the third element, the ineffable perception of a very immediate relation with the Absolute, is not this, unknown to the contemplative, the simple hallucinatory imagination of a spatial relation on the part of the subject with the ideal object he believes himself to apprehend ? a confused localisation of the Absolute placed in immediate connection with the very vague kinæsthetic perception of his own body retained by the mystic ? in appearance a transcendental intuition, but in fact an hallu-cinatory spatial presence, very indistinct as a representation, but intensely emotional ?

M. Delacroix,[41] who is, perhaps, among unbelieving psychologists, the most conscientious observer of and subtle theoriser concerning Catholic mysticism, finds himself logically forced to interpret thus the greater part of the testimony of the contemplatives. While he admits that ecstasy may sometimes end in unconsciousness (this is a second way of escape, which we will examine in a moment), it seems to him that it generally comports " the maintenance of a certain form of consciousness." This form of consciousness he interprets by comparing it with a series of states more accessible to observation than ecstasy itself, distinguishing it clearly from the debased states of mental pathology, comparing it with the highest æsthetic intuition, and finding for it a relationship with that higher apperception which comes to life in one " who contemplates life and pierces through appearances "; " the irrational perception of an essential will, scattered throughout all nature and repeated by her in numberless variations, as music scans the movements of the soul." But M. Delacroix does not recognise in it *intellectual intuition* properly so called; the " form of consciousness," which persists in the states of full union, would not, then, in his eyes, be anything other than an unusual intensification of ordinary contemplation; on careful examination one must of necessity discover in it imagery and spatiality—that is to say, extended multiplicity.

Since the testimony of the mystics as to their own inmost states cannot be checked, it is undoubtedly permissible to a psychologist to interpret it conformably to a theory which he judges to be the only one acceptable. Moreover, we do not claim in this matter to " refute " M. Delacroix; " refute " is an unpleasant word, which too often conceals an indecisive dialectic; we merely desire to put in a claim for the philosophic and psychological legitimacy of a point of view differing from his.

If we put aside the doubtful testimonies, there remain a very large number, especially in Christian mystical literature, which so expressly place the state of full union above all spatial or temporal intuition, above all multiplicity, that we still prefer to take them literally; we would not—since we have no theoretical objection to it—deface or weaken that clear line of demarcation which the mystical writers, the only persons with experience in the matter, unanimously trace between ordinary or " acquired " contemplation, even when it reaches a very high degree, and that of full union; we cannot deny that they have a very keen feeling of a radical difference, of the absence of any common measure. And when we come to analyse them more closely, after having protested the ineffable character of their intuition, they delimit it, haltingly but with remarkable unanimity, by characteristics which are the very negation of the mode of ordinary contemplation. It is useless to add further examples to those already quoted above, for conviction is imposed in this matter above all by the overwhelming uniformity of the witnesses. We think it, therefore, in accordance with scientific principles—if no higher principle is opposed to our doing so—to accept them as they stand in their *descriptive* and *concordant* parts.

Consequently, we will admit, until we are better informed, the absence of all quantitative and conceptual multiplicity in the explicit content of ecstasy.

II. SECOND INTERPRETATIVE SOLUTION: THE NEGATIVITY OF ECSTASY IS TOTAL UNCONSCIOUSNESS

But since human psychology is unacquainted with any purely intellectual intuition, does the absence of multiplicity, then, signify the cessation of activity? Is ecstasy unconsciousness, and not only momentary suspension of self-consciousness, but absolute unconsciousness? We will not dispute it: from the point of view of empirical psychology, there is no escape from the alternative: either multiplicity—as much reduced as you will—in the content of mystical contemplation, or a lapse into complete unconsciousness.

Many psychologists take their stand on the second alternative, and indeed they cannot be blamed for doing so if they confess that their attitude is dictated to them by a necessity of deduction, which in its turn is attached to what they claim to be axioms of methodology.[42] But why then, like Leuba do they attempt to discover—by induction—complete unconsciousness in the documents themselves? We will return to this point in a moment. Let us remark in the first place that there is unconsciousness and unconsciousness; there is the actual unconsciousness of syncope or deep sleep: there is the consecutive unconsciousness (amnesia) of the secondary states in epilepsy, hysteria, or hypnosis; and beyond these may be imagined another unconsciousness belonging more especially to ecstasy. Whatever the state of the case, the documents in the case of the mystics would only reveal to us directly consecutive unconsciousness, amnesia, relative to their moments of deep ecstasy; and there would be a free field for hypothesis concerning the kind of activity which is exercised during the ecstasy itself. Again, the descriptions of the best qualified mystics present, to anyone who reads them in their integrity, the very reverse of an amnesia of this kind.

Let us, however, benevolently suppose that ecstasy is marked by complete unconsciousness, entire inactivity of the intellect; it would, in any case, be necessary to distinguish it from sleep and syncope, by reason of its antecedents and its effects. Its antecedents carry with them, we will admit, a diminution of the field of the free consciousness, an invading monoïdeism which perhaps falls away into aïdeism, but they also imply a powerful organisation of the whole individuality, an affective polarisation and subconscious tension of the reproductive tendencies of the imagination. Is the internal edifice which is thus built up so completely dependent upon the conscious intellectual activity that on the cessation of this latter it must be dislocated and fall into fragments ? Doubtless, no; the very inertia inherent in the mechanism, when once overcome by the organising idea, becomes the collaborator of the latter and in case of need takes its place. Total *unconsciousness* might here be more rightly called a *subconsciousness*, not disintegrated, but gathered together and directed. It may be perceived if one will in the effects of the mystic union, a tonic of the life of the soul and a lever of moral action.[43] The only kind of unconsciousness admissible in the explanation of ecstasy (we speak of the ecstasy of the great mystics) would be, on any hypothesis, a " polarised unconsciousness," the religious value whereof might be very considerable.

III. LITERAL SOLUTION: ECSTASY IS THE SYNTHESIS OF AN EMPIRICAL NEGATIVITY AND A TRANSCENDENT POSITIVITY

But—and this is the essential question for a psychologist— do the documents fit in with the hypothesis of unconsciousness in ecstasy ? It is relatively easy to establish a theory explanatory of anything, if one arrogates to oneself a discretionary power in dealing with the data of the problem. We have already reminded ourselves that M. Delacroix, a very attentive reader, has not found any very serious indications of states of total unconsciousness in the mystics with whom he is familiar. It is true that he has consulted especially the Catholic mystics, and that while lacking faith he has not refused them the necessary minimum of intellectual sympathy. Is their *Nirvâna*, then, less negative than that of other heroes of asceticism or prayer ? Perhaps, indeed, after all, it is—at least speaking generally. However, since the consciousness of a Yogin or a Sufi is a hundred times less open to the penetration of us Westerns than that of a Christian ecstatic, we can rely on the image-bedecked and often excessive language of the former only with reserve. Moreover, it is not indispensable here to diagnose non-Christian mysticism. Let us be satisfied with observing the rarity of *clear* affirmations of the positive character of the transcendental experience therein. We are then justified in limiting our view, for the moment, to the Christian mystics; and we abstract from the others, not in contempt, but by reason of the complexity of the problems they raise.[44]

In Christianity the positive character of mystical intuition is affirmed on all hands, and that not as a dogmatic interpretation, but as an experience carried into life.

Is there any need to demonstrate this proposition ? As far as the great Spanish mystics, and the Catholic mystics of the Renaissance generally, are concerned, anyone who has read them to a sufficient extent is deeply astonished at hearing their ecstasies taxed with negativity and pure unconsciousness. We could understand the psychologist thinking that he had to " conclude " unconsciousness *a priori* ; but we admit to a deep embarrassment in qualifying the writer who in the descriptions of the mystics does not observe, beside the affirmation of negative characteristics, the if possible even clearer affirmation of the positive character of ecstasy. Turn, if you will, to the quotations which follow chapter xviii of Poulain's book, *Les grâces d'oraison* (10th ed., Paris, 1922; English ed., *The Graces of Interior Prayer*, London, 1912); better still, go back to the originals and read without prejudice. We think that you will come, like ourselves, to sum up these numerous testimonies—whether they be due to illusion on the part of the contemplatives themselves or not—by the following few lines of St Teresa: " In mystical theology, of which I spoke before, the understanding ceases from its acts, because God suspends it—as I shall explain by and by, if I can. . . . We must neither imagine nor think that we can of ourselves bring about this suspension. That is what I say must not be done; nor must we allow the understanding to cease from its acts; for in that case we shall be stupid and cold, and the result will be neither the one nor the other. For when our Lord suspends the understanding and makes it cease from its acts, he puts before it that which astonishes and occupies it; so that, without making any reflections, it shall comprehend in a moment more than we could comprehend in many years with all the efforts in the world " (*Life*, ch. xii).[45]

This comprehension is in the first place the actual mode of the intellectual union with God; an " immediate presence," a distinct " sight," a " touch," an " intuition," a " vision " clearer than that of the eyes of the body, a " widening of the intelligence," a " ray which pierces the night," an overpowering and absolutely new " brightness." . . . " Above the reason," writes Ruysbroeck, immediately after the words we have quoted above, " in the depth of the intelligence, the simple eye [of the contemplative soul] is always open, it contemplates and gazes at the light [=the Word] with a pure gaze, enlightened by the light itself, eye against eye, mirror against mirror, image against image " (*The Mirror of Eternal Salvation*, translation quoted, t. i, p. 141). This light, once more, is a supereminent knowledge of the mysteries of the essence of God, of his attributes and his unity, of his universal Fatherhood, of his creative activity, and above all of his unfathomable Trinity. . . . And this knowledge shows itself so radically different from ordinary knowledge, from the threefold standpoint of immediateness, mode and content, that the contemplative remains in the deepest stupefaction thereat. For in his case it is not amnesia which appears after the ecstasy any more than it was complete unconsciousness during it; the mystic remembers perfectly, but he does so through the belittling and dividing forms of the understanding, which once more oppress him; and, overcome thereby, he stammers out his ecstasy in human language. . . . He uses forced metaphors, embarks on a series of contradictions, and excuses himself for his inability to express the ineffable. Through these very stumblings of a sublime and blundering expression struggles the very vivid remembrance of a state which had nothing in common with an absolute " void " of consciousness. Some psychologists must have needed all the self-sufficiency of an unconscious prejudice, or at least all the levity which current prejudices explain, not to perceive this.

The only Catholic contemplatives who at first sight might seem to be describing a void ecstasy, a " lapse into nothingness," are the great German and Flemish mystics of the end of the Middle Ages. Their Dionysian terminology is " negative " in the extreme; under their pens God is much less Being (conceptual) than Nothingness (of finite determinations), and, consequently, union with God is above all characterised by a gamut of metaphysical attributes of non-Being: darkness, loss, cessation, forgetfulness, effacement, nakedness, unconsciousness, etc. . . . It would be childish of us to allow ourselves to be imposed upon by these expressions, which have their counterpart beside them. The ecstasy of the pseudo-Areopagite, of Eckhart, Suso, Tauler, Ruysbroeck, is neither more nor less negative than their metaphysics; now, who will claim—even apart from the protestation here made in detail by the texts—that these men, all of them positive believers, and the four last imbued with Scholasticism, had the slightest inclination to assimilate God with pure non-Being ?[46] Besides, one general remark is enough to avert from their contemplation all suspicion of " total unconsciousness "—namely, that with all of them it attains at its highest summit the immanent operations of the Trinity. If naked Unity can be confounded with Nothing, the relation that is perceived in Unity reveals positive Being in it. We cannot conceive how a " lacuna of consciousness " could carry with it a keen apprehension of the eternal generation of the Word or of the procession of the Holy Ghost.

Illusion or not, what our great Plotinising mystics *describe* is a positive ecstasy. " We can indeed know," writes Ruysbroeck, " that the bosom of the Father is our own basis and origin, and that our life and being find therein their life and principle. From this basis that is proper to us—that is to say, from the bosom of the Father, and from all that lives in him—shines forth an eternal brightness, the generation of the Son. And in this brightness, which is the Son, God sees himself openly, with all that lives in him. . . . All those who, above their created being, are raised to a contemplative life, are one with this divine brightness. They are that brightness itself, and they see, feel and discover, under this divine light, that according to their ideal or uncreated being, they are themselves this abyss of simplicity, the brightness whereof shines without means in divine modes. . . . Thus the contemplatives attain their eternal exemplar, after whose image they have been created, and they contemplate God in all things, without distinction, by a simple gaze, in the divine brightness."[47] We dare not flatter ourselves that all our readers will have completely grasped the meaning of this passage, though it is relatively clear for anyone who is familiar with the turn of mind and the terminology of these Scholastic mystical surroundings—but, at least, it does not seem to us that anyone ought to recognise in it the affirmation of a total cessation of intellectual operation in ecstasy. Moreover, one might find still more decisive passages; this one, in its discreet tenor, has the advantage of representing the medium tone and one of the general points of view of the mystical epoch with which we are concerned.

We will sum up the last few pages as follows: Two affirmations stand out from the descriptions of the Christian mystics, which according to them express data of immediate experience, yet data, on the other hand, constant and universal enough to escape the accusation of being purely subjective and individual illusion. They are:

1. The affirmation of negative characters which radically separate the ecstatic state from the normal or abnormal psychological states of ordinary life; the effacement of the empirical Ego, the leaving aside of imagery and spatiality, the absence of all enumerable multiplicity, that is to say, in a word, the cessation of conceptual thought. Ecstasy is *negative*.

2. On the other hand, the affirmation that this cessation of conceptual thought is not total unconsciousness, but rather an enlargement, an intensification or even a higher form of intellectual activity. Ecstasy is *positive*.

Now these two affirmations are contradictory on all imaginable hypotheses save one; namely, that the human intelligence is able, in certain conditions, to attain *an intuition which is proper to itself*, or, in other words, that the intelligence, instead of constructing its object analogically and approximately from materials borrowed from the sensibility, can sometimes attain that object by an *immediate assimilation*.

The great majority of psychologists recoil before this consequence, and prefer to expurgate the mystical documents from either the first or second of the above affirmations. Mysticism thus becomes once more the vassal of ordinary inductive psychology. Are they wrong? Their especial error, it seems to us, is that they too often hide—or, if it be preferred, there is hidden from them—the treatment they inflict on the sole basis for induction which is possible in this matter, namely, the texts. Were it not for that, we would willingly pardon their use of a process of methodology which is not so rare in the practice of the sciences, since theory—and therefore *a priori* arguments—influences in them in a large measure even the observation of facts; only this influence of a theoretical postulate, in the psychology of mysticism, is not subject to the check of experiment; it is purely *a priori,* for it consists in the *presumed* extension of empirical determinism, or at least of ordinary psychological causality, to the higher mystical states.

The psychologists of whom we are speaking have quite well observed, or foreseen, that the admission or rejection of a strictly intellectual intuition, such as that which the mystics claim to have experienced, is not a problem of pure phenomenology. Intuition means the immediate assimilation of an object and a knowing subject, according to the possibilities of their respective natures. Now, in the special case of the intelligence, this object can only be defined as an ontological absolute; it is Being. And in the immediate assimilation of Being, the distinction of phenomenon and noumenon being effaced, the special object of empirical science disappears with it. The phenomenon has become a " metaphysical object "; and if we admit the claim of the mystics, empirical psychology would then end, at the summit of the states of contemplation, in an intuitive theodicy, either pantheistic or rather theistic.

We cannot ourselves see in this consequence the slightest inconvenience; on the other hand, we find it quite natural that the sciences—psychology neither more nor less than biology or even physics—should not arrive, if we may be permitted the neologism, at " buckling " their explanations on the empirical plane; all, more or less directly, lead to God, the universal last End. We do not wish to confiscate mysticism for the advantage of religious apologetic; it would be quite superfluous to do so; but neither have we any reason for recoiling before a consequence the possibility of which we have elsewhere admitted. Our apriorism, open-minded enough not to exclude a transcendental experience, is as good as any other; and it permits us to respect the letter of the mystical writings.

Thus we see in what sense we were enabled to write, at the beginning of this article, that the phenomenology of mysticism itself brought us up before an ontological choice.

Psychology having thus attained the extreme limit of its competence, the moment has come to let the theologian and philosopher speak.

STUDIES IN THE PSYCHOLOGY OF THE MYSTICS

THIRD PART

ONTOLOGY AND THEOLOGY OF CHRISTIAN MYSTICISM

One preliminary remark.

Even supposing that a *purely psychological* (*phenomenal*) theory of the states of prayer could be perfected on all points, there would always remain room beside it for a theological interpretation of the nature and causes of these states. For without question God can act supernaturally in the human soul after an empirical manner capable of reduction to the classical forms of psychology. The doctrine of grace remains in any case untouched. We have elsewhere insisted on the distinction of points of view which is here imposed.[48]

Therefore, if we take the trouble to form an ontological and theological conception of the mystical states (one which is likewise in positive harmony with their positive phenomenology and with the indications of psychology) this is assuredly not in order to save the dogma of supernatural grace, which is in no wise threatened, but from a purely personal concern to come to grips as closely as possible with the " integral " truth.

Let us then, from this complete point of view, once more examine our problem on all sides to enumerate its data.

I. THE INTEGRAL DATA OF THE PROBLEM

1. First of all, as we have seen, the most authoritative witnesses of Catholic mysticism unanimously affirm the existence of a strictly intellectual intuition in the high states of contemplation, the object whereof is not the pantheistic Absolute, but the personal God of Christianity, the indivisible Trinity.

2. This intellectual intuition, in spite of its sovereign liberty, is very generally prepared for by a progressive " unification " of the complete psychological and moral life of the contemplative.

3. On the other hand, from the standpoint of purely profane psychology, the life of the mind in man consists entirely, with the fettering but necessary collaboration of the body and the sense-life, in an effort of *indefinite co-ordination*, whose limit is the possession of the absolute Good. This twofold effort represents the two aspects of the fundamental tendency of all intelligent nature to the immediate assimilation of Being in an

intuition. The radical finality of the human individual, then, is wholly directed towards the Absolute, although it only contrives to display itself here on earth in the plane of quantity. Being is never naturally presented to our intelligence apart from material symbolism, although the interior movement of our intelligence carries it beyond matter; and though even if we had the immediate, intellectual intuition of created " intelligibles," our radical capacity for embracing *being* would not be satisfied. All our psychology is contained in this natural inadequation of the fundamental tendency and the possible realisation.

4. Let us pass to the point of view of Catholic theology. The inadequation whereof we have just spoken is the connecting-link, the " stepping-stone," as Cardinal Dechamps said, of supernatural grace in human nature. We must not indeed forget that the bestowal of grace supposes an *aptitude* in the subject for its reception; a stone or a vegetable is of its nature inapt for this purpose. Now what is supernatural grace ? It is a help, a gratuitous gift of God, which is marked by its finality; it is essentially and directly ordained to the supernatural end of man—that is, the " beatific vision," the intuition of God in the other life. Grace renders our acts " meritorious " —that is to say, able to bring about the vision of God under given conditions; it establishes a real, ontological relation between our activity and our supernatural end.

Thus it will be seen how " nature " and " grace " suppose and complete each other. The Christian God is not really distinct from the philosophical Absolute. The intuition of the divine Being, which constitutes, in the natural order, for the mind left to its own powers, an ever-receding limit, an inaccessible ideal, becomes, in the order of grace, the real and efficaciously procured end. Truth to tell, the natural activity of the mind is already seized upon, orientated and constantly stimulated by the implicit desire—*desiderium naturale*, as St Thomas dares to call it[49]—for absolute Being; but this obscure desire hurls itself against the barriers of quantity and falls powerless; it grasps of Being only an image refracted in sense-perception, and all its effort has to be limited to refining a symbol. Let " Grace " supervene to compenetrate this effort, and the symbolic unity which it prepares in us will take on an ontological value; it will become an efficacious preparation, a real and internal title, to supreme unification in the intuition of God. Much more, it is a teaching of Catholic dogma that the very degree of charity—that is to say, in empirical language, the degree of unification of the interior man by love—is in a very real sense the measure of final beatitude, of the supernatural possession of God.

In sum, Grace completes and crowns Nature by transforming into an *end* properly so called what was only the superior and inaccessible *limit* of a radical tendency, or, if you prefer, by building up into *efficacious means of attaining an explicit end* psychological activities which by themselves were but the *impotent expression of a hidden tendency*. The unifying development of the psychological life in natural ascesis, and the intimate development of the religious life in supernatural *ascesis*, then, work in a parallel fashion, in conformity with a single ideal of unity; it may be said that they are identical save in *value*. And this gives the explanation of many analogies which might otherwise seem disconcerting.

But in what can this " supernatural value," this " lived title " to divine intuition, really consist ? One aspect of the problem alone concerns us here. It is quite evident that this " title " supplies for a natural insufficiency in us. What ? There is one which immediately comes to mind. The human mind cannot, any more than any other creature, have the smallest " right " to God; sovereign independence is a primordial attribute, if not of the pantheistic Absolute, at least of the true Absolute, transcendent in relation to the world. But the intuition of God supposes the intimate and immediate union of the divine Being with the human intelligence, the direct " information " of the latter by the former; and this kind of taking possession by created passivity of uncreated activity is only conceivable as the effect of a benevolent initiative, an active and absolutely free " presentation," on God's part. We foresee here at the crown of supernatural destiny a " complementary event," at the same time withdrawn from the natural exigency of the human mind and indispensable for the latter's integration into an " absolute unity," for making its indefinite progression " proceed to the limit." What, then, does supernatural grace bring about ? It gives, here below, for the future life, the certain pledge, the real title, of that benevolent initiative of a God who wills to communicate himself to saintly souls according to their capacity to receive him; it is, so to say, a " right " which God confers on them over himself, in the measure of their good works; or again, a proximate possibility of " seeing God " as soon as the veil of matter is torn away.

FEATURES OF CHRISTIAN MYSTICISM

Now the Christian mystics have believed that their ecstatic intuition afforded a foretaste, a pale and fugitive anticipation, of the face to face vision of eternity.

II. SOME ESSENTIAL CHARACTERS OF CHRISTIAN MYSTICISM

Here, then, if we are not mistaken, are the principal data which the mystical documents, general psychology and Catholic theology in turn supply to us; the agreement of these data is so evident that a few words will be enough to enable us to bring to light a few really distinctive characteristics of Christian mysticism.

1. The first and most fundamental of these characteristics resides in *supernatural grace,* which compenetrates the whole religious life of the Christian. Truth to tell, this is an ontological characteristic inaccessible to direct experience. In fact, from the empirical and external point of view, all the isolated religious manifestations—lower than the mystical states described as immediate union with God—seem identical from one religion to another; there is certainly a difference in their combination and harmonisation, but not in the psychological types to which they are individually reducible. On the contrary, from the interior, from the ontological standpoint, there is a radical difference between purely natural religious activity and that which grace—as is normally the case in Christianity—supernaturalises; it is, as we have seen, nothing less than a difference of value and finality.

When we say that grace is not the object of direct experience, we by no means claim that grace has no empirical object. Quite on the contrary, in the terms of Catholic doctrine, the supernatural elevation of acts which have become " meritorious " (*gratia elevans*) is not separated from a powerful aid (*gratia adjuvans*) lent by God to the effort of the human freewill in pursuit of moral Good. The " supernatural finality " then can betray itself, to the psychological experience, by the particularly strong and elevated orientation of a whole of acts. But as this whole may always, in the eyes of a psychologist, be explained also by purely empirical antecedents, it is a chimæra to wish to *demonstrate* the influence of grace by way of pure induction. The rôle of actual grace must already be admitted in order that its concrete traces in personal experience may be recognised.

The first distinctive characteristic of Christian mysticism, then, is principally theological.

2. The second distinctive mark of Christian mysticism is drawn from the states of union; it is at the same time phenomenological and ontological. Not everyone will admit its reality; for it is not forbidden even to Catholics to reduce the higher mystical states to a simple quantitative increase of normal psychological potentiality and ordinary supernatural grace, or, if you will, in theological language, to a pure intensification of the infused virtues communicated at baptism.

We consider, however, basing ourselves on the unanimous declarations of contemplatives—the sole witnesses of their inner experiences—that high contemplation implies a new element, qualitatively distinct from the normal psychological activities and from ordinary grace; we mean the active, non-symbolic presentation of God to the soul, with its psychological correlative: the *immediate intuition of God* by the soul.[50]

This literal interpretation of the texts alone furnishes a clear demarcation—and not merely a difference of degree—between the mystical states and ordinary contemplation. The hypothesis, moreover, does not seem exorbitant from the point of view of Catholic dogma, since the life of grace by which the mystic lives is an efficacious preparation for, and a title to, the vision of God; why should not God sometimes grant an anticipation of the other life, when the subject shows himself physically and morally susceptible of that anticipation? From the point of view of psychology even, the hypothesis does not seem so very strange; we have seen how the intuition of Being— the implicit ideal and latent regulator of all the mind's undertakings—is, so to speak, the centre of perspective of human psychology.

3. If the interpretation that has just been proposed be admitted, we possess the most decisive differential character— phenomenological and ontological, necessary and sufficient at the same time—of a definition of Christian and supernatural mysticism. It will not be useless, however, to complete it by some *secondary characters*, which are mostly only corollaries. Let us posit first of all that supernatural ecstasy possesses all the psychological efficacy of natural ecstasy.

It may be asked indeed, since the essential of ecstasy depends upon God's free initiative, what rôle the psychological unification brought about by asceticism still has in it. This rôle, we think we may affirm without boldness, is very important.

Let us not insist on the moral preparation which it seems in God's designs to require as a preliminary condition of his favours. There is another point of view, very often neglected —namely, that God, in ecstasy, communicates himself, not to a soul separated from a body, but to a " man," whose spiritual form has not ceased to be the very act of the body and the principle of sensibility. It may be imagined, then, that the repose of the ecstatic vision cannot fail to require a fitting adaptation of the lower functions; now is not the adaptation which will best favour for it the transcendent operation of the soul, a harmonious unification, analogically realising here in the lower parts in diversity the very type of unity which the summit of the organism enjoys? The whole man must be " prepared " for the divine communications by his natural dispositions or by the training of ascesis. And if God, by an exception of which his providence is not lavish, choose suddenly to ravish to himself a soul still in prey to exterior agitation, to the conflict of tendencies and the play of scattered impressions, it will never be without at the same time reducing that tumultuous diversity to harmony and silence.

However, God is not accustomed to do violence to our natural mechanism. The normal predisposition for mystical favours will always remain, with a privileged physical tempera- ment, the perseveringly progressive ascesis of recollected prayer and moral action.

4. The preceding remarks supply the key to a problem set us by the affirmations of the Christian mystics themselves. On the one hand they demand of the contemplative the assiduous practice of asceticism, renunciation, prayer; and they make of this not only a salutary exercise of moral perfection, but also, and especially, a prerequisite condition for the states of union. A superficial reader might believe that they profess, in these passages, to supply an efficacious method of training for ecstasy. On the other hand, they insist, with even greater energy, on the absolute powerlessness of the contemplative to attain to mystical union by his own strength; it is a free and gratuitous gift of God, a favour *independent of any law, withdrawn from human will* and consequently impossible to foresee.

The conciliation of these characteristics, so easy from the point of view of Christian mysticism, is doubtless also a differ- ential note thereof.

In fact, in profane or pantheistic, and, it would seem, in Buddhist mysticism, *ascesis* appears to be the necessary and sufficient condition of ecstasy. The texts of the Moslem mystics are less affirmative on this point; while the God of their ecstasies is transcendent Being, the true God, the processes of training seem to possess in their eyes, if not a proper and independent, at least an infallible efficacy. The Christian mystics, however, formally vindicate the sovereign liberty of the divine initiative; for them the *ascesis* constitutes a condition normally necessary for ecstasy, doubtless, but it is never a sufficient one.

5. If mystical activity in Christianity is informed by grace, and constitutes therefore, relatively to our supernatural destiny, either a superior stage or the imperfect and transitory anticipation of the term itself, we may deduce from this necessary finality a new characteristic—rather negative, but very important —of true mysticism: *its entire agreement with Christian dogma and morals*. A complete concordance, it is true, would constitute only a presumption of its supernatural value; but a real disharmony would evidently ruin on the very point of conflict all claim to a supernatural value. Such is the exact bearing of the " moral " and " ecclesiastical " criteria applied to the mystical states.

We now understand the point of view of the Catholic Church in the valuation of states of this kind. Doubtless she admits, in a general way, their possibility and even their existence. But how is she going to diagnose concrete cases ? Their mechanism does not interest her. Authorised guide of our ascent to God as she is, she is especially preoccupied with the relation of our proceedings to that supreme end; her appreciations and approvals have no other law. Were the mystical steps for a pious person a ladder of sanctity ? Do they conform to the Gospel ideal ? The Church will approve, convinced that every good and salutary effect was seconded by divine grace. But she does not claim either to solve the " how " of this influence, nor to side with the particular interpretations, the subtle teachings, the true or pretended revelations which the writings of an approved mystic may contain; all these are " guaranteed " only in the exact measure of their supernatural value, a measure very different from that of human curiosity. Again, in the terms of Benedict XIV's[51] formal declaration, and in agreement with the most assured principles of theology, the guarantee given by the Church to particular revelations cannot compel the belief of the individual Christian; it is only a datum, eminently worthy of respect, whereof Christian prudence requires us to take account. The most entire liberty, therefore, is here left to the Catholic psychologist; all that is asked of him is to avoid levity, and when he wishes to judge, to put all the weights in the scale.

6. In conclusion, we ought to reply to a question which has probably arisen in the minds of some of our readers. Where is that supernatural ecstasy, whose general features we have outlined, to be met with? Above all, doubtless, in the princes of orthodox Catholic mysticism; but do all the high ecstasies attributed to Catholic contemplatives answer to this type? It is very probable that they do not; and we see no inconvenience in admitting that many descriptions of pretended mystical states cover in reality only more or less high stages of ordinary contemplation. But it will readily be seen that an attempt at particular qualification will often meet with insurmountable difficulties.

Are there, outside Catholicism, among Christian dissidents, true supernatural ecstasies?

Since everyone agrees that they share, if they are in good faith, in the grace of Christ, there is nothing to prevent, in principle, their benefiting, on a personal title, by the highest mystical favours.

But contemplatives outside Christianity: Moslems, Brahmans, Buddhists—or even mere philosophers without any positive religion?

We will not speak of the shocking practices of numerous "professionals," who lower mysticism to the level of a very material game. We willingly recognise that there are others whose relations of their experiences or theoretical writings bear such a seal of honesty and spiritual elevation that it would be repugnant to us to deny to their ecstasies all religious value. But we must not forget either that simple natural contemplation—even if it should, by excess of concentration, finally lapse into total unconsciousness—may already present a very high religious efficacy, since it ameliorates the moral life and thus prepares the ways for supernatural grace.

No doubt; but does not Catholic theology teach that supernatural grace, whatever be the manner of its bestowal, is not refused to any soul of good will? Why deny, then, that God may manifest himself sometimes even more directly, even outside Christianity, to some devout ascetic, who seeks him haltingly, with humble and persevering energy, perhaps by means of proceedings of a touching and exotic quaintness?

STUDIES IN THE PSYCHOLOGY OF THE MYSTICS

Let us hope, dear reader, that it may be so, but as to this you are asking us much more than we can know.

NOTES

[1] This study first appeared in the *Revue de Philosophie* (Paris, 1912). The subject which the *Revue de Philosophie* did me the honour of confiding to me covers, in part, that of essays which I have published in other reviews. I have none the less attempted to make the present essay a complement to, rather than a replica of, my earlier articles.

[2] " Qui non assuescit orare vocaliter, vix assuescet orare mentaliter." Schram, *Institutiones theologiae mysticae*, 1777, i, § 47. " I have remarked again that during the period preceding her death, whatever might be her infirmities or the occupations that pressed on her, she never failed to recite her rosary."—Information from Avila, on St Teresa. (*Œuvres complètes de sainte Thérèse de Jésus*, traduction nouvelle, t. ii, Paris, 1907, p. 336).

[3] It goes without saying that this phrase must be read with its context, and we must not see in it any depreciation of the liturgy, still less of the frequentation of the sacraments. We merely say—and it is a truism—that " ritual and vocal prayer," considered in themselves, are a first degree in the scale of mystical activities. The contemplative, who is not constantly " patiens divina," will do *very well* to order his devotion in accordance with the " liturgical cycle "; he *must*, like every Christian, take part in the common prayer and the sacraments of the Church.

[4] " The scheme of that book (the *Imitation*) carried out would make the world the most wretched, useless, dreary, doting place of sojourn. There would be no manhood, no love, no tender ties of mother and child, no use of intellect, no trade or science—a set of selfish beings, crawling about, avoiding one another, and howling a perpetual *Miserere*."—W. M. Thackeray, *Letters*, p. 96 (quoted from Jones, *Mystical Religion*, p. 327).

[5] *Exercitia spiritualia S Ignatii de Loyola, cum versione literali ex autographo hispanico* (Brugis, 1883). See the annotations at the beginning, and the preambles to the First Exercise of the First Week.

[6] The psychology of conversion would show us the confused exercise of the same fundamental tendencies which direct and sustain the developed interior life. See, from the Protestant point of view, Starbuck, *The Psychology of Religion* (London, 1901), and the monographs. From the Catholic standpoint, monographs are numerous; as studies of the whole subject, see those of Frs. Huby, S.J., and Mainage, O.P., mentioned in the bibliographical list which follows this article.

[7] See *I Fioretti di S Francesco d'Assisi* (Traduction, introduction et notes, par A. Goffin, Paris, Collect. Science et Religion, Nos. 516-17), or *The Little Flowers of St Francis of Assisi*, edited by Dom Roger Hudleston, O.S.B., London, 1926.—F. von Hügel, *The Mystical Element of Religion as studied in St Catherine of Genoa and Her Friends*, 2 vols., London, 1908.—*Oeuvres mystiques du Bienheureux Suso*, traduction nouvelle, by P. Thiriot, O.P., Paris, 1899 (cf. *The Life of*

FEATURES OF CHRISTIAN MYSTICISM

Blessed Henry Suso, Written by Himself, translated by T. F. Knox, London, 1913). See especially, in ch. xxvi of the *Life,* the touching episode of Suso's search for his guilty and humiliated sister.—In the *Life of St Teresa,* and in her *Book of Foundations,* are abundant instances of her delicacy of soul. M. Pacheu (*L'expérience mystique et l'activité subconsciente,* Paris, 1911, p. 219) reminds us in extremely just terms that the asceticism of the mystics " does not mutilate in them the beauty of human nature; neither art, science, nor social duty is incompatible with it. B. John of Fiesole, Fra Angelico, before their brushes, are types of the artist-ascetic. SS Thomas, Bonaventure, in their professorial chairs, their philosophical folios, are examples of the ascetic eager for knowledge; and as for social activity, both St Catharine of Siena, St Catherine of Genoa, St Teresa, St Vincent de Paul, St Ignatius Loyola, and many others afford us examples so numerous and varied that we ask ourselves how a scholar can seriously imagine that there is an irreducible antagonism between the true mystic and his social duties, between his asceticism and the full development of his life and personality."

[8] G. Truc, *Les états mystiques négatifs* (La tiédeur, l'acedia, la sécheresse). *Revue philosophique,* 1912, No. 6.

[9] W. Preger, *Geschichte der deutschen Mystik im Mittelalter,* I Band, Leipzig, 1874, p. 291.

[10] Ps. lxi.

[11] *S Bonaventurae Opusculorum* tomus i, Parisiis, 1647. *Meditationes Vitae Christi,* ch. xiii, p. 361C.

[12] Compare also the contemplative exercise which St Ignatius calls " application of the senses."

[13] Supposing that these visions were really " externalised "; for, undoubtedly, in many cases, the authors have claimed only that they were describing their pains and more or less vivid imaginations. We find numerous examples of symbolical visions among devout folk at the end of the Middle Ages, in Germany and the Low Countries. See, *e.g.,* the Works of Zuster Hadewijk (van Mierlo, S.J., *Hadewijk,* Proza 2 vol., Leuvense Tekstuitgaven, Leuven, 1908-1910). On this subject may be read with much profit ch. xxi of Poulain, *Des grâces d'oraison,* 7th ed. (*The Graces of Interior Prayer,* 3rd ed.); the manifold "dangers of illusion "which visions and particular revelations present are there exposed by an abundant selection of historical examples.

[14] I have elsewhere explained this mechanism in detail. Cf. " On the Feeling of Presence in Mystics and Non-Mystics."

[15] A. Pitres, *Leçons cliniques sur l'hystérie et l'hypnotisme,* Paris, 1891, t. ii. Plates at end of volume.

[16] Max Müller, *Râmakrishna ; His Life and Sayings* (Collected Works of Max Müller, xv). New impression, London, 1910, pp. 8-9. After the Svâmin Râmakrishnânda, in the *Brahmavâdin.* See also J. C. Oman, *The Mystics, Ascetics, and Saints of India,* London, 1905, p. 172.

[17] See, among others, J. Zahn, *Einführung in die christliche Mystik,* Paderborn, 1908, especially IIIes Buch, II 2, §§ 40, 41, 42. Poulain, *The Graces of Interior Prayer,* London, 1912, ch. xxii. Cardinal Bona, *De discretione spirituum,* Romae, 1672.

[18] Leonardi Lessii, S.J., *De divinis nominibus.* Opusculum post-

humum. Adjectis precationibus ex operibus ejusdem auctoris, Lovanii, 1643. Precatio ad immensitatem Dei, pp. 53-54.

[19] The word " ecstasy," in the use given it outside mystical treatises, has, however, no precise meaning. Even psychologists who make ecstasy an object of special study use the word in an extremely wide acceptation. See, *e.g.*, Beck, *Die Ekstase*, Bad Sachsa, 1906.

[20] Suarez, *Tractatus de oratione et devotione*, lib. ii, cap. 19, § 30. (*Operum*, tomus xii, Venetiis, 1742, p. 115, col. 2.)

[21] Some of our friends, whose scruples we respect without here sharing them, show themselves astonished at this comparison. We think all the same that we ought to maintain it, as we are not able to see how Christian mysticism suffers from a community of negative and purely empirical notes with other mystical systems. If this article be read to the end, it will be seen, however, that in our eyes the similitude, even in the field of pure phenomenology, is only partial, and that the difference, on the other hand, in the field of " values " is profound.

[22] The references are taken from *Plotini Opera Omnia*, ed. Creuzer, 3 vol., Oxonii, 1835. According to Porphyry (in his *Life of Plotinus*, reproduced at the beginning of vol. i of the above edition, ch. xxiii, p. lxxvii), Plotinus had experience of complete ecstasy four times to his knowledge. Porphyry himself had an ecstasy at the age of sixty-eight.

[23] Max Müller, *op. cit.*, p. 48. The last lines of this quotation recall a doctrine dear to the Hindu religions: many of the aspects of Brahmanism and Buddhism have a very important mystical significance. See some remarks on this subject below, in our essay on " The Comparative Study of Mysticism."

[24] Farid uddin Attar, *Mantic Uttaïr* (The Language of Birds), translated by Garcin de Tassy, Paris, 1863. We quote and retranslate from the German of M. Buber (*Ekstatische Konfessionen*, Jena, 1909), pp. 25-28. At the moment of writing, I had not at hand Garcin de Tassy's translation; and on verifying it, it seems unnecessary to alter my version, which is sufficiently faithful, for the sole purpose of reproducing the exact words of the French translator. The prolix Attar sometimes has a pregnant formula: thus, describing the ecstatic annihilation of the soul in God, he says: " The shadow is lost in the sun: that is all " (*op. cit.*, trans. G. de Tassy, p. 236).

[25] Avicenna seems to have been a theoretician of Moslem mysticism rather than an experimenter. We may, however, suppose that he faithfully relates the experience of others. Moreover, the descriptions agree in essentials from one author to another. See later, in this volume, a study of " The Problem of Mystical Grace in Islam " (first centuries of the Hegira), after the recent works of M. Louis Massignon.

[26] Carra de Vaux, *Gazali*, Paris, 1902, p. 197. Cf. *id.*, *Avicenne*, Paris, 1900.

[27] Quoted from W. James, *The Varieties of Religious Experience*, London, 1904, p. 385.

[28] Amiel, *Fragments d'un Journal intime*, 2 vol., Paris, 1883.

[29] See, from the historical standpoint, the following general works: Pfeiffer, *Deutsche Mystiker des XIVen Jahrhunderts*, 2 vol., Leipzig, 1845, 1857; W. Preger, *Geschichte der deutschen Mystik im Mittelalter*,

FEATURES OF CHRISTIAN MYSTICISM

3 vol., Leipzig, 1874-1893; Denifle, *Archiv f. Literat. und Kirchengesch. des Mittelalters*, II, Berlin (*Meister Eckharts lateinische Schriften und die Grundanschauung seine Lehre*); H. Delacroix, *Essai sur le Mysticisme spéculatif en Allemagne au XIVe siècle*, Paris, 1900; W. R. Inge, *Christian Mysticism*, London, 1899 (Lecture IV, Christian Platonism and Speculative Mysticism in the West. *N.B.*—Partial lack of understanding of " Catholic devotion "); R. M. Jones, *Studies in Mystical Religion*, London, 1909 (ch. vii-xiv) (*N.B.*—Wesleyan (? Quaker) inspiration very marked, but careful for exactitude); R. A. Vaughan, *Hours with the Mystics*, 9th ed., London, s.d. (the Preface of the first edition is dated 1856).—(Since this note was written a dozen years ago, works relating to medieval mysticism have multiplied. We shall have occasion to quote some of them elsewhere. We mention here, among those of a more general character: Dom Cuthbert Butler, *Western Mysticism*, London, new edition, 1927 (analysis of the mystical teaching of St Augustine, St Gregory the Great, and St Bernard), and P. Pourrat, *La spiritualité chrétienne, Des origines au moyen âge*, vol. i, Paris, 1915; vol. ii, Paris, 1921; vol. iii, Paris, 1926. English translation, *Christian Spirituality*, vol. i, London, 1922; vol. ii, London, 1924; vol iii, London, 1927.)

[30] *De mystica theologia*, in *Opera S Dionysii Areopagitae*, edidit Cordier, S.J., Antverpiae, 1634, t. ii, p. 2.

[31] Denifle has very sharply defended the scholastic orthodoxy—in essentials—of Meister Eckhart. Cf. *op. sup. cit.*

[32] *Ioannis Thauleri opera omnia*. Latin translation by Surius, Coloniae, s.d. (Sermo I in Dominicam Iam post Octavam Epiphaniae), p. 94.

[33] *Oeuvres complètes du Bienheureux Henri Suso*, Trans. Père Thiriot, O.P., Paris, 1899, t. i, pp. 287-88.

[34] *Oeuvres de Ruysbroeck l'admirable*. Translation from the Flemish by the Benedictines of Saint-Paul de Wisques, vol. i, 2nd ed., Bruxelles, 1917, pp. 140-41. *N.B.*—The most characteristic and perfect work of the mystic of Brabant is the treatise entitled *The Adornment of the Spiritual Marriage* (translation quoted, t. iii; English translation by C. A. Wynschenk Dom, edited with an Introduction and Notes by Evelyn Underhill, London, 1916). For the whole of Ruysbroeck's works, translated into Latin, see Surius, *Ioannis Rusbrochi opera omnia*, Coloniae, 1552.

[35] Quoted from R. M. Jones, *Studies in Mystical Religion*, London, 1909, pp. 336-37.

[36] E. Boutroux, *Le philosophe allemand Jacob Boehme*, Paris, 1888. W. Windelband, *Die Geschichte der neueren Philosophie*, 3e Aufl., Leipzig, 1904, Ier Bd. Jakob Boehme, *Sämmtliche Werke*, 7 vol., ed. Scheibler, Leipzig, 1832-1860.

[37] *Oeuvres complètes de sainte Thérèse de Jésus*, traduction nouvelle, t. ii, Paris, 1907 (Relation IV), p. 296. *Life of St Teresa of Jesus*, trans. Lewis, 5th ed., London, 1916, p. 479.

[38] *Oeuvres*, ed. cit., t. vi, Paris, 1910 (*Château intérieur*, v, ch. 1), p. 129. *Interior Castle*, trans. Benedictines of Stanbrook, 3rd ed., London, 1921, p. 121.

[39] *Ibid.*, French edition, pp. 134-35; English edition, pp. 125-27.

[40] *Les oeuvres spirituelles du B. Père Jean de la Croix*. Traduction

207

STUDIES IN THE PSYCHOLOGY OF THE MYSTICS

du R. P. Cyprien, carme déchaussé, Paris, 1652, p. 316. *The Dark Night of the Soul*, 4th ed., London, 1916, p. 158.

[41] H. Delacroix, *Études d'histoire et de psychologie du mysticisme*, Paris, 1908, pp. 386 ff.

[42] This question of methodology is treated of in our first study, " Empirical Science and Religious Psychology."

[43] M. Murisier has been very unhappily moved, in his *Maladies du sentiment religieux* (Paris, 2nd ed., 1904), thus to place the " individual form " of the religious sentiment in radical opposition to its " social form." He might be suspected of having never frequented the " Fifth Mansions " of the *Interior Castle* of St Teresa, or even of not having considered that every moral value is, indirectly at least, a social value.

[44] The texts of several Moslem mystics, such as Bistâmi (874), or especially Hallâj (922), Kocheïri (1072), Gazali (1111), etc., . . . denote an ecstasy which is not purely negative, nor yet pantheistic. Can it be " supernatural " in the Christian sense of the word ? See on this question the study which we devote later in this book to the mysticism of Hallâj (*The Problem of Mystical Grace in Islam*).

[45] *Oeuvres complètes*, ed. cit., t. i, Paris, 1907, p. 160. *Life*, trans. Lewis, pp. 191-92.

[46] Inge (*Christian Mysticism*, Bampton Lectures, 1899, London, Lecture IV) greatly exaggerates the significance of the " negative road " (*via negationis*) in the medieval mystical writers.

[47] *L'ornement des noces spirituelles* (*Oeuvres de Ruysbroeck l'admirable*, translation quoted above, t. iii, pp. 215-16). Having to limit our quotations, we hesitate to choose between this fragment of Ruysbroeck and a long passage from the *Exemplar* of Suso (3rd part, ch. 6): there we should see the juxtaposition of negative expressions on the one side, and on the other the evident presupposition and even the formal affirmation of the positive character of the ecstasy.

[48] *Empirical Science and Religious Psychology*. See above.

[49] St Thomas Aquinas, *Summa contra Gentiles*, iii, cap. 50. (See the commentaries of Francisco de Sylvestris, of Ferrara.)

[50] As is shown by the very expressions we use, we only apply the hypothesis of an " immediate intuition of God " to the *higher* mystical states, which represent the complete perfection of infused contemplation. For more exact details, see, in this volume, the study entitled " On the Feeling of Presence in Mystics and Non-Mystics."

[51] Benedictus XIV, *De beatificatione et canonisatione servorum Dei*. Vermeersch, S.J., *Quaestiones morales*, Tomus prior, quaest. i, ch. ii: *De oratione*, pp. 64-109 (*De oratione extraordinaria seu de theologia mystica* : a sober and very wise explanation of the point of view of Catholic theology). Brugis, 1912.

BIBLIOGRAPHICAL NOTES

1. *Original Writings of the Mystics.*—We have quoted as footnotes only a very small number of these, and we cannot think of completing the list in this short bibliography.

For *Catholic mystical writings* a list (still very incomplete, in spite

FEATURES OF CHRISTIAN MYSTICISM

of its length) will be found in the treatise of A. Poulain, S.J., *Des grâces d'oraison*, 10th ed., Paris, 1922 (English translation, *The Graces of Interior Prayer*, second impression, London, 1912).

Fr. Scheuer, S.J., has lately published a 40-page supplement to Poulain's list (see *Notes bibliographiques sur la contemplation infuse*, 44 pages. Extrait de la *Revue d'ascétique et de mystique*, 1923-1924). Readers are referred to the same lists for an account of the principal (theoretical) *Treatises* of *Catholic theologians* on asceticism and mysticism.

We know of no general bibliography of *Protestant mystics*. On the theosophic mysticism of Weigel, Böhme, etc., see some references in our text. A fair number of useful references, relating especially to the dissenting sects, are to be met with in the work of Jones, mentioned below. See also the Protestant encyclopædias: *Encyclopédie des sciences religieuses* (Lichtenberger), Paris; *Realencyclopädie für protestantische Theologie und Kirche* (Herzog-Hauck), Leipzig; we must add *The Encyclopædia of Religion and Ethics* (now complete in 12 vols.), which makes use of the collaboration of some Catholic writers.

The sources for *Greek mystical philosophy* are classical. On Plotinus in particular we may mention two recent works, specially interesting from the standpoint of the comparison between Plotinism and Christian mysticism: R. Arnou, *Le désir de Dieu dans la philosophie de Plotin*, Paris, 1921, and W. R. Inge, *The Philosophy of Plotinus* (Gifford Lectures), London, 1918.

Profane mysticism, independent of all positive religion, does not, so far as I know, possess a systematic bibliography. Everyone knows some isolated names, such as Novalis, Amiel, Emerson. W. James, in his *Varieties of Religious Experience*, furnishes some data in this regard.

As for the bibliography of the *Eastern mystics*: Jews (to whom it is best to give a place apart), Moslems, Parsis, Hindus, Chinese Buddhists or Taoists, etc., it is too specialised to find place here, even in summarised form. A few references will be found in the notes scattered through the pages of this and the other articles in this volume. For a first examination the Encyclopædias, especially the interesting *Encyclopædia of Religion and Ethics*, will render good service.

2. *Hagiography.*—The lives of holy persons, if written with greater discernment and exactness, would be a precious source of information on mysticism. But in the greater number of existing biographies, how is the psychologist to assure himself of the strict historicity of the exceptional facts that are related? As far as the Catholic saints are concerned, the field is, as everyone knows, partially cleared, thanks to the monumental and severely critical work of the Bollandists, the *Acta Sanctorum*. There is also much to be gleaned from the bibliographical analyses of the *Analecta bollandiana* (Bruxelles).

3. The point of view from which we write might have allowed us to extend our bibliography to cover a number of works on asceticism, metaphysics, the criticism of knowledge, general psychology, the history of philosophy, psycho-pathology or nervous pathology. We have considered this display unnecessary, and will strictly confine the following references to the psychology of Christian mystics.

STUDIES IN THE PSYCHOLOGY OF THE MYSTICS

4. *Articles in Reviews.*—These are too numerous to be quoted here, save exceptionally. See, for the period 1890-1899, E. C. Richardson, *Index to Periodical Articles on Religion*, New York, 1907. Two Catholic reviews, published in French, treat specially of ascetic and mystical subjects: *La Vie spirituelle* (from October, 1919), in which we would particularly call attention to the articles of Frs. Garrigou-Lagrange, Joret, Noble, O.P.; and the *Revue d'ascétique et de mystique* (from January, 1920), which publishes every three months a systematic bibliography of recent works; see, in this latter, the articles of MM. de Guibert, L. de Grandmaison, Picard, and others. In various (Catholic) periodicals of theology and philosophy studies or chronicles relating to the Christian mystics may be met with—*e.g.*, *Revue des Sciences philosophiques et théologiques*, *Revue thomiste*, *Études*, *Revue de philosophie*, *Études franciscaines*, *Revue apologétique*, *Revue des questions scientifiques*, *Collationes Brugenses*, *Civiltà Cattolica*, *Month*, *Studies*, *Razon y Fe*, *Stimmen der Zeit*, etc. We would note also as *special* reviews of religious psychology, but mixed in their inspiration: *Zeitschrift für Religionspsychologie* (1907-1913), *Archiv für Religionspsychologie* (from 1914), *Journal of Religious Psychology*. Moreover, isolated articles in various reviews of theology, philosophy, psychology, the history of religions, and ethnology.

5. We pass over *obsolete and unusable works*; and among them we rank (whatever their date of publication) the writings of authors who will not see anything more in the facts of mysticism than a peculiarity of medical interest.

6. In the following list, we only attempt to indicate, without going into the categories already mentioned under Nos. 1-5, the *chief* works utilised in preparing this article. Some of them, it is true, have no very great intrinsic value; if they figure here, it is by reason of their long standing, because they formed part of the tiny group of very unequal works which inquirers into the psychology of the mystics found at their disposition a few years back. Since then enquiries in this field have been extended to such a degree that a more or less complete bibliography would be very difficult of compilation. In the hope that it may be of use to a few readers, we will intersperse, in our former list, marking them with an asterisk, a small number of the more notable memoirs or books of various tendencies which have appeared since 1912, when this article was first published; it goes without saying that mention of a book is not necessarily meant as a recommendation of it.

ACHELIS: *Die Ekstase*. Berlin, 1902.
*ARINTERO, J. (O.P.): *Cuestiones misticas*, 2nd ed., Salamanca, 1920.
AUGER, A.: *Étude sur les mystiques des Pays-Bas au moyen âge*. Brussels, 1892.
BECK, P.: *Die Ekstase. Ein Beitrag zur Psychologie und Völkerkunde*. Bad Sachsa, 1906.
BENEDICT XIV: *De beatificatione et canonisatione servorum Dei*. (In *Opera omnia*, Rome, 1767-1768.)
*BERGUER, M.: *Psychologie religieuse*. Geneva, 1914.
*BESSEMANS, DR.: *Die stigmatisatie in het licht der hedendaagsche biologie*. Antwerp, 1923.

FEATURES OF CHRISTIAN MYSTICISM

BESSMER, J. (S.J.): *Stigmatisation und Krankheitserscheinung.* Stimmen aus Maria Laach, 69. 1905.

BOIS, H.: *Quelques réflexions sur la psychologie des réveils.* Paris, 1906. *La valeur de l'expérience religieuse.* Paris, 1908.

BOSSUET: *Instruction sur les états d'oraison, . . . avec les actes de la condemnation des quiétistes.* Paris, 1697. *Instruction, . . .* etc. Second traité, publié par E. Levesque, Paris, 1897.

BOUTROUX, E.: *La psychologie du mysticisme.* Paris, 1902. *Science et religion dans la philosophie contemporaine.* Paris, 1908.

*BREMOND, H.: *Histoire littéraire du sentiment religieux en France depuis la fin des guerres de religion jusqu'à nos jours.* 6 vols. issued. Paris, 1916-1922.

BUBER, M.: *Ekstatische Konfessionen,* gesammelt von M. Buber. Jena, 1909 *(2nd ed., Leipzig, 1922).

Bulletin de la Société française de philosophie. Paris (January, 1906: meeting devoted to the " development of the mystical states of St Teresa." Observations of MM. Blondel, Boutroux, Darlu, Delacroix, and others).

*BUTLER, DOM CUTHBERT, O.S.B.: *Western Mysticism.* The Teaching of SS Augustine, Gregory, and Bernard on Contemplation. London, 1922. New edition with additional matter, 1927.

*COE, G. A.: *The Psychology of Religion.* Chicago, 1916.

DAVENPORT, P. M.: *Primitive Traits in Religious Revivals.* New York, 1906.

DE GRANDMAISON, L.: *L'élément mystique dans la religion.* Recherches de science religieuse, 1910. *La religion personnelle.* IV. *L'élan mystique. Études,* vol. 135, 1913.

DELACROIX, H.: *Essai sur le mysticisme spéculatif en Allemagne au XIVe siècle.* Paris, 1900. *Études d'histoire et de psychologie du mysticisme. Les grands mystiques chrétiens.* Paris, 1908.

DE LA GRASSERIE, R.: *De la psychologie des religions.* Paris, 1889.

*DE LA TAILLE, M.: *L'oraison contemplative.* Recherches de science religieuse, 10e année. (English translation, *Contemplative Prayer,* London, 1926.)

*DE MONTMORAND, M.: *Psychologie des mystiques catholiques orthodoxes.* Paris, 1920.

*DE MUNNYNCK, P. (O.P.): *Introduction générale à la psychologie religieuse.* Semaine d'ethnologie religieuse, 11e session. Louvain, 1913). Compte rendu, Paris, 1914.

DENIFLE, O. P.: *Meister Eckharts lateinische Schriften und die Grundanschauung seiner Lehre.* Archiv f. Litt. und Kirchengeschichte d Mittelalt. II.

Dictionnaire de la foi catholique (d'Alès). Paris. Various articles.

Dictionnaire de Théologie catholique (Vacant). Paris. Various articles.

*DUDON, P. (S.J.): *Le quiétiste espagnol Michel Molinos.* Paris, 1921.

DURKHEIM, E.: *De la définition des phénomènes religieux.* Année sociologique, ii. 1898.

*DYSON, W. H.: *Studies in Christian Mysticism.* London, 1913.

Encyclopædia of Religion and Ethics (Hastings) Edinburgh. Numerous articles concerning asceticism and mysticism in the various religious bodies.

STUDIES IN THE PSYCHOLOGY OF THE MYSTICS

Encyclopédie des sciences religieuses (Lichtenberger). Paris. Articles: "Prière," "Mysticisme," and others.

Encyclopédie théologique (Migne): *Dictionnaire d'ascétisme*. Paris, 1854. *Dictionnaire de mystique*. Paris, 1858.

*ETCHEGOYEN, G.: *L'amour divin: Essai sur les sources de Ste Thérèse*. Bordeaux, 1923.

*FABER, H.: *Das Wesen der Religionspsychologie*. Tübingen, 1913.

*FARGES, MGR. A.: *Les phénomènes mystiques distingués de leurs contrefaçons humaines et diaboliques*. Paris, 1920. (English translation, *Mystical Phenomena*. London, 1925.)

FLOURNOY, TH.: *Les principes de la psychologie religieuse*. Extrait des Archives de Psychologie, ii, 1902. *Une mystique moderne. Ibid.*, 1915.

GARBAN, Dr. L.: *Les déviations morbides du sentiment religieux à l'origine et au cours de la psychasthénie*. Paris, 1911.

*GEMELLI, DR. A. (O.F.M.): *L'origine subcosciente dei fatti mistici*. Florence, 1913.

*GIRGENSOHN: *Der seelische Aufbau des religiösen Erlebens. Eine religionspsychologische Untersuchung auf experimenteller Grundlage*. Leipzig, 1921.

GODFERNAUX, A.: *Le sentiment et la pensée*. 2nd ed. Paris, 1906.

GOIX, DR.: *La psychologie du jeûne mystique*. Revue de philosophie, 1909.

GÖRRES, J. J.: *Der christliche Mystik*. 5 vol. Regensburg, 1836.

*GRABMANN, MGR. M.: *Wesen und Grundlagen der katholischen Mystik*. Munich, 1922. *Die Lehre des hl. Thomas von Aquin von der scintilla animae in ihrer Bedeutung für die deutsche Mystik des Predigerordens*, Jahrb. f. Phil. und spek. Theol., XIV.

*HATHEYER, F. (S.J.): *Die Lehre des P. Suarez über Beschauung und Ekstase*. In F. Suarez Gedenkblätter, Innsbruck, 1917.

HÉBERT, M.: *Le divin. Expériences et hypothèses*. Paris, 1906.

*HEILER, FR.: *Das Gebet*. 2e Aufl. Munich, 1920. *Die Bedeutung der Mystik für die Weltreligionen*. Munich, 1919.

*HOCKING, W. E.: *The Meaning of God in Human Experience*. London, 1922.

*HODGSON, G. E.: *English Mystics*. London, 1922.

HÖFFDING, H.: *Religionsphilosophie* (IIIer Teil: Psychologische Religionsphilosophie). Leipzig, 1901. *Problèmes et méthode de la psychologie religieuse*. Rapport au VIe Congrès international de psychologie, Geneva, 1910.

*HOORNAERT, ROD.: *Ste Thérèse écrivain, son milieu, ses facultés, son oeuvre*. Paris, 1922.

*HOWLEY, J.: *Psychology and Mystical Experience*. London, 1920.

*HUBY, J.: *La Conversion*. Paris, 1919. *Foi et contemplation d'après S Thomas*. Recherches de science religieuse, 10e année.

IMBERT-GOURBEYRE, DR.: *La stigmatisation, l'extase divine et les miracles de Lourdes*. 2 vol. Paris, 1894.

INGE, W. R.: *Christian Mysticism* (Bampton Lectures). London, 1899. *Studies of English Mystics*. London, 1907.

JAMES, W.: *The Varieties of Religious Experience*. London, 1904.

JANET, PIERRE: *Une extatique*. Bulletin de l'Institut psychologique, Paris, 1901.

FEATURES OF CHRISTIAN MYSTICISM

JOLY, H.: *Psychologie des Saints.* 5th ed. Paris, 1898. (English translation, *The Psychology of the Saints*, third impression, London, 1919.)
JONES, R. M.: *Studies in Mystical Religion.* London, 1909.
*KREBS, E.: *Grundfragen der christlichen Mystik.* Freiburg i. B., 1921.
LAVRAND, DR.: *Hystérie et sainteté.* Paris, 1911.
LECLÈRE, A.: *La psychophysiologie des états mystiques.* Année psychologique, xvii, Paris, 1911.
LEHMANN, E.: *Mystik in Heidentum und Christentum.* Leipzig, 1908.
LELEU, L.: *La mystique chrétienne et sa psychologie générale.* Annales de philosophie chrétienne, 1906. *La mystique et ses attaches ontologiques. Ibid.,* 1907.
LEROY, E. BERNARD: *Interpretation psychologique des visions intellectuelles des mystiques chrétiens.* Revue de l'histoire des religions, 1907.
LEUBA, J. H.: *Les tendances fondamentales des mystiques chrétiens.* Revue philosophique, liv, 1902. *Psychologie des phénomènes religieux.* Rapport au Congrès VIe internationale de Psychologie, Geneva, 1910. *The Psychological Origin and the Nature of Religion.* London, 1909. **A Psychological Study of Religion.* New York, 1912.
*LONGPRÉ, E. (O.F.M.): *La théologie mystique de Saint Bonaventure.* Archivum franciscanum historicum (Quaracchi), xiv, 1921.
*LOUISMET, S. (O.S.B.): *Mysticism True and False.* 2nd ed. London, 1919.
*MAINAGE, TH. (O.P.): *La psychologie de la conversion.* Paris, 1915.
MENENDEZ Y PELAYO, M.: *Historia de los heterodoxos españoles.* 3 vols. Madrid, 1880.
*MESCHLER, M. (S.J.): *Ascese und Mystik.* Freiburg i. B., 1917.
MEYNARD, O. P.: *Traité de la vie intérieure . . . d'après l'esprit et les principes de S Thomas d'Aquin.* 2 vols. Paris, 1885.
MICHAËL, E. (S.J.): *Geschichte des deutschen Volkes,* IIIer Bd., *Deutsche Wissenschaft und Mystik während des dreizehnten Jahrhunderts,* Freiburg i. B., 1903.
MURISIER, M.: *Les maladies du sentiment religieux.* 2nd ed. Paris, 1903.
MYERS, F. W. H.: *Human Personality and its Survival of Bodily Death.* 2 vols. New York, 1904.
*OESTERREICH, T. K.: *Einführung in die Religionspsychologie.* Berlin, 1917.
PFEIFFER, F.: *Deutsche Mystiker des vierzehnten Jahrhunderts.* 2 vols. Leipzig, 1845-1857.
*PICARD, G.: *La saisie immédiate de Dieu dans les états mystiques.* Revue d'ascétique et de mystique, iv, 1923.
PICAVET, F.: *Essai d'une classification des mystiques.* Revue philosophique, 1912.
*PINARD DE LA BOULLAYE, H. (S.J.): Article: " L'expérience religieuse," in the *Dictionnaire de théologie catholique* (Vacant-Mangenot), 1912. *L'étude comparée des religions,* t. i. Paris, 1922
POIRET, PETRUS: *Bibliotheca mysticorum selecta.* Amsterdam, 1708.

STUDIES IN THE PSYCHOLOGY OF THE MYSTICS

POULAIN, A. (S.J.): *Des grâces d'oraison.* Traité de théologie mystique. 7th ed. Paris, 1909. *10th ed., with an Introduction by M. J. Bainvel. Paris, 1922. (English translation, *The Graces of Interior Prayer.* Second impression. London, 1912.)

*POURRAT, P.: *La spiritualité chrétienne. Des origines au moyen âge.* 2 vols. Paris, 1917 and 1921. (English translation, *Christian Spirituality.* 2 vols. London, 1922 and 1924.)

PRATT, J. B.: *The Psychology of Religious Belief.* New York, 1907. *The Religious Consciousness.* New York, 1921.

PREGER, W.: *Geschichte der deutschen Mystik im Mittelalter.* 3 vols. Leipzig, 1874-1893.

Realencyclopädie für protestantische Theologie und Kirche (Herzog-Hauck), Leipzig. Articles, " Gebet," " Mystische Theologie," and special notices of mystical writers.

RÉCÉJAC, E.: *Essai sur les fondements de la connaissance mystique.* Paris, 1896.

*REYPENS, L. (S.J.): *Le sommet de la contemplation mystique.* Revue d'ascétique et de mystique, iii and iv, 1922-1923.

RIBET, J.: *La mystique divine.* 3 vols. Paris, 1883.

RIBOT, TH.: *La psychologie des sentiments.* 3rd ed. Paris, 1899. *Psychologie de l'attention.* 9th ed. Paris, 1905. *La logique des sentiments.* Paris, 1905.

ROURE, L.: *En face du fait religieux.* Paris, 1908.

ROUSSELOT, PAUL: *Les mystiques espagnols.* 2nd ed. Paris, 1869.

ROUSSELOT, PIERRE: *Pour l'histoire du problème de l'amour au moyen âge.* Extrait des Beitrage zur Gesch. der Phil. des Mittelalters, vi, 1908.

*SAUDREAU, A.: *Les degrés de la vie spirituelle.* 5th ed. 2 vols. Paris, 1920. (English translation, *The Degrees of the Spiritual Life.* 2 vols. London, 1921.) *La vie d'union à Dieu, d'après les grands maîtres de la spiritualité.* 3rd ed. Paris, 1921. (English translation, *The Life of Union with God.* London, 1927.) *L'état mystique, sa nature, ses phases et les faits extraordinaires de la vie spirituelle.* 2nd ed. Paris, 1921. (English translation, *The Mystical State.* London, 1924.)

SCARAMELLI, G. B.: *Il direttorio mistico.* Venice, 1770. (English translation, *Directorium mysticum.* London.)

*SCHEUER, P. (S.J.): *Notes bibliographiques sur la contemplation infuse* (Supplement à la bibliographie de A. Poulain, *Des grâces d'oraison.*) Extrait de la Revue d'ascétique et de mystique, iv and v, 1923-1924.

SCHRAM, D.: *Institutiones theologiae mysticae.* 2 vols. Cologne, 1777.

SEGOND, J.: *La prière. Essai de psychologie religieuse.* Paris, 1911.

*SEISDEDOS SANZ, J.: *Principios fundamentales de la mistica.* 5 vols. Madrid-Barcelona, 1913-1917.

SHARPE, A.: *Mysticism, Its True Nature and Value.* London, 1910.

*SNEATH, E. HERSKEY: *At One with the Invisible : Studies in Mysticism.* London, 1921.

*SPURGEON, C. F. E.: *Mysticism in English Literature.* Cambridge, 1913.

STARBUCK, E. D.: *Psychology of Religion.* 2nd ed. London, 1901.

FEATURES OF CHRISTIAN MYSTICISM

*STREETER, B. H., and APPASAMY, A. J.: *The Sadhu. A Study in Mysticism and Practical Religion.* London, 1921.

SUAREZ: *Tractatus de oratione et devotione.* (*Operum*, t. xii. Venice, 1742.)

*TANQUEREY, A.: *Précis de théologie ascétique et mystique.* Paris, 1923.

*TAURO, G.: *Il silenzio e l'educazione dello spirito.* Rome, 1921.

THAMIRY, E.: *Le mysticisme de Saint François de Sales.* Arras, 1906.

THOMAS AQUINAS, ST: *De veritate catholicae fidei contra Gentiles,* cum commentariis Fratris Francisci de Sylvestris, Ferrariensis. Paris, 1643. *Summa Theologica* (*Opera omnia*, Rome, 1882).

THOROLD, A.: *Catholic Mysticism, illustrated from the Writings of Blessed Angela of Foligno.* London, 1900.

*THOULESS, R. H.: *An Introduction to the Psychology of Religion.* Cambridge, 1924.

*THURSTON, H. (S.J.): Various articles on the *extraordinary phenomena* exhibited by the mystics. See *Month*, vol. cxxxiii and ff.

*UNDERHILL, EVELYN (MRS. STUART MOORE): *The Essentials of Mysticism.* London, 1920. *The Life of the Spirit.* London, 1922. *Mysticism.* London, 1911.

VALLGORNERA, O. P.: *Mystica theologia divi Thomae.* Rome, 1665.

VAUGHAN, R. A.: *Hours with the Mystics.* 9th ed. London, s.d.

VERMEERSCH, A. (S.J.): *De oratione.* § II. *De oratione extraordinaria, seu de theologia mystica.* (In *Quaestiones morales*, t. i, Bruges, 1912.)

VON HÜGEL, F.: *The Mystical Element of Religion, as Studied in Saint Catherine of Genoa and her Friends.* 2 vols. London, 1908. *2nd ed. London, 1923. *Eternal Life*, Edinburgh. *Essays in the Philosophy of Religion.* 2 vols, London, 1926-27.

*WAFFELAERT, G. J. (MGR., BISHOP OF BRUGES): *L'union de l'âme aimante avec Dieu, ou guide de la perfection, d'après la doctrine du Bx. Ruusbroec.* Translated from Flemish by R. P. Hoornaert. Paris-Lille, 1906. Numerous memoirs on mystical theology in *Collationes Brugenses.*

*WATKIN, E. I.: *The Philosophy of Mysticism.* London, 1919.

*WILLIAMSON, B.: *Supernatural Mysticism.* London, 1920.

*WUNDERLE, G.: *Aufgabe und Methoden der modernen Religionspsychologie.* Eichstätt, 1915. *Einführung in die moderne Religionspsychologie.* Kempten, 1922.

ZAHN, J.: *Einführung in die christliche Mystik.* Paderborn, 1908. *5th ed. Paderborn, 1921.

PROFESSOR LEUBA AS A PSYCHOLOGIST OF
MYSTICISM

PROFESSOR LEUBA AS A PSYCHOLOGIST OF MYSTICISM

PROFESSOR LEUBA'S[1] tendencies in religious psychology have long been known. His recent book does not disclose any progress, or even movement, in them; to-day, as formerly, he is inspired by a scientific optimism which is perhaps too much of a stranger to the " spirit of subtlety."

The author says that he wishes to write as a *psychologist:* " The book is to be judged primarily as a psychological study of aspects of human nature conspicuous in mystical religion " (p. ix). Good; the fundamental tendencies of human nature indeed have their expression even in the mystical states, and remain subject to psychological investigation. So long, therefore, as Professor Leuba remains within the realm of psychological science, we will, as he desires, judge him as a psychologist; as soon as he goes outside this particular domain— as is only fair—he will render himself liable to be judged by other methods. Let us at once confess that our desire in all good faith to understand him finds itself at a loss even in his Preface; at the very moment when he is issuing a declaration of neutrality, or, if you like, of scientific objectivity, does he not announce, with an artlessness which does honour to his frankness, two chapters (XII and XIII) in which his atheistical doctrine openly crosses the frontiers of positive psychology ? (p. ix).

The methods adopted—and this also does not lack significance—are the " genetic method " and the " comparative method," the two favourites of the sociological school; our readers know well enough, from the uncertainties of the history of religions, to what an extent these methods, in themselves excellent, give scope for arbitrary judgements. " Mystical experiences in early societies, where they are simpler, and therefore more easily understood," will be followed up, we are told, " in their main modifications and complications " (pp. ix-x), until we understand the refined forms which they present in the great religions. There will be postulated— rather than demonstrated—a causal derivation through the ages, and, so to say, a continuity in growth, between the phenomena which the author chooses to call mystical. At the same time, thanks to accommodating abstractions, we are to try and discover the equivalent of these mystical phenomena even outside the religious field: " Such phenomena, for instance, as ecstatic trance and the impression of illumination become comprehensible only when they are considered under the diverse conditions in which they appear—*i.e.*, out of, as well as in, religious life " (p. x). Let us first of all, then, agree on a nominal definition of the word " mysticism," pliable enough not to restrict in advance the scope of our enquiry: " It will mean for us any experience taken by the experiencer to be a contact (not through the senses, but ' immediate,' ' intuitive ') or union of the self with a larger-than-self, be it called the World-Spirit, God, the Absolute, or otherwise " (p. 1).

We can foresee what the general theme of the book is to be; from one end to the other of the series of psycho-physiological states which certain analogies allow us to group together under the label " mysticism," the essential basis remains the same, in spite of varying accidental features, such as the greater or less degree of refinement in the processes by which it is obtained, the greater or less enlightenment in its intellectual interpretation, and again its psychological or moral value, which likewise is very unequal for the individual and for society. Under all these heads, it is willingly recognised, Christian mysticism, Catholic or Protestant, towers head and shoulders above the other forms of mysticism. Unfortunately, from the essential standpoint of objective truth, the heroic effort of our contemplatives to lay hold of the " divine " falls powerless to the ground; even the psychological and moral value of their states— a value quite relative—is less, in itself, than that of a life soberly guided by so-called " scientific " reality; Professor Leuba goes so far as to speak of a " failure " of their asceticism. His thesis allows him to express in most cases a sincere goodwill, an admiration mingled with pity, towards the mystics, while at the same time he seeks thoroughly to discredit mysticism.

Let us examine this more closely by pointing out some characteristic details in Professor Leuba's demonstration.

It is attached, at the very start, to a presupposition which is too simplified and in no wise self-evident—namely, that ecstasy, conceived of as a state of trance, is the centre of crystallisation of all mystical life. We will go with him step by step through his generalisations of the idea of religious trance.

Chapter II, entitled " Mystical Ecstasy as Produced by Physical Means," furnishes the author with his real base of operations. In uncivilised or half-civilised races, the more or less deep trance provoked by the use of stupefying agents is considered as a state of communication with the divinity; classical antiquity even was acquainted with orgiastic ecstasies; this is the most primitive and elementary " fact " of mysticism to urge itself on our attention. Now, Professor Leuba goes on, the gleam of real mysticism with which this savage trance is coloured has no transcendent element; it is explained in the most natural way in the world, by comparing it with the effects of psychological dissociation and exaltation brought about, independently of any religious content, by certain drugs—alcohol, mescal, hashish, ether, nitrous oxide, etc. These drugs, as may be demonstrated by experiment in the laboratory, reduce the organic sensibility, give rise to sensorial illusions and hallucinations, modify the emotional state by lessening the control of the reason, and create the stimulating but deceptive impression of a marvellously increased vitality. And so all is clear; since " the end of religion is the exaltation and perfection of vitality," the primitive must be quite ready to suspect a transcendental origin and a religious significance in what is really but the effect of a narcotic.

The lower degree of the mystical life, then, so far as its transcendent interpretation is concerned, is perfectly illusory. The author, solidly supported on this first conclusion, goes on to insist on hoisting himself thence to the following degrees, by the strength of his hands alone, without ever unfurling the wings of metaphysics or of religious faith. We see him, in the first place, at the intermediate degree of Yogism. " The omniscience and omnipotence claimed for the Yogin should be placed in parallel with the similar claims made by the users of drugs in religious ceremonies " (p. 44). In both cases the fundamental state of interior exaltation, followed by sleep or unconscious trance, is the same, although the means of invoking it—means at the same time psychological and mechanical—are unquestionably more refined in the case of the Yogin. In the latter there already appears an " illogical craving for moral perfection " (p. 44), which brings him into comparison with the Christian mystic. The latter, in spite of his evident superiority, in his turn only adorns more richly the primitive canvas, from which he does not free himself: " In later chapters we shall find that in some of its phases the mystical ecstatic trance brings to the Christian worshipper also hallucinations, incomparable sensuous delights, an impression of limitless power and freedom; and, in other phases, of complete relaxation and perfect peace. And the Christian mystic also thinks of these ecstatic experiences as divine union " (p. 36).

Let us halt a moment. Without having any taste for the pharmaceutical ecstasies and gyrations of the shamans and dervishes, we may find the explanation of the religious significance of these extravagances given by Professor Leuba a little rapid. But we let it pass, for we admit, as does he, that the adepts of so inferior a mysticism are mistaken as to the proximate cause of their states. And neither is it our business to come to the defence of Yogism, though we think that Professor Leuba's judgement in this case also is a little summary; when one has deducted from the Yogis the multitude of charlatans, of avaricious beggars and naïvely credulous professionals, there undoubtedly remains a minority of heroic ascetics and intelligent contemplatives whose ecstatic states present a problem; at least that problem which is presented in different conditions by the philosophic ecstasy of Plotinus. We are inclined to believe, for reasons which we cannot go into here, that natural (or philosophic) ecstasy, pushed to the extreme, ends in absolute unconsciousness, and thus draws all its speculative value from its phases of approach to this final point. In this matter we find ourselves materially in agreement with our author; none the less we must reproach him with introducing here (for the first time) that error of method which consists in solving problems by one's manner of presenting them. In fact, faced with the trance of primitive folk or Yogist ecstasy (and it is the same, at a later page, with Christian ecstasy), he considers in the long run but one hypothesis; that of more or less exceptional psychological states, experienced as *subjective* states, but receiving from outside a metaphysical or religious *causal* interpretation: the problem then reduces itself to knowing whether the psychological states experienced demand, exclude or tolerate (Professor Leuba too often forgets this third member of the alternative) an adventitious causal interpretation. There remains a second hypothesis, which is not *a priori* absurd—namely, that the experience of the mystic is itself *intrinsically* metaphysical or religious. When the psychologist disdains this hypothesis, he must at least tell us whether he does so by virtue of a methodological principle, or by reason of strictly experimental counter-indications. Professor Leuba owed us this enlightenment all the more in the present case, because, according to the most authentic Vedantist doctrine, the rites of concentration, which, from their nature, considering them by themselves, would cause a tendency towards monoïdeism and unconsciousness, are not absolutely indispensable for obtaining ecstasy, and in any case are not proportioned agents of it; Yogi ecstasy, rightly or wrongly, is defined generally as deliverance from phenomena and the intellectual intuition of a reality superior to all distinction of concepts. From one end of his book to the other, Professor Leuba, on the other hand, takes the negative characters of ecstasy in an absolute and exclusive sense; he systematically identifies the " unconsciousness," of which the mystics sometimes speak, with a " psychological void "; if this identification were a thesis which he went about to prove, we should understand him and readily listen to his reasons; but he presents it from the start, either as an immediate exegetical datum—in which he is deceived, and has read the documents badly—or as a presupposition which goes without saying—in which he very audaciously forestalls his conclusion.

Let us come to Christian mysticism.

The spirit in which Professor Leuba carries on his enquiry may be judged well enough from the following preamble: " The successive forms of religious mysticism may be regarded as expressions of a gigantic experiential movement aiming at securing in diverse ways an ever fuller satisfaction of fundamental wants (of human nature). Certain wants and methods conspicuous in the lower forms of mysticism disappear or are reduced to secondary position in the higher; other needs and other methods take their place. The passage from one form of mysticism to another is marked, furthermore, by changes in the conception of the power which is regarded as the cause of the experience " (p. 48). This preliminary statement, as we shall see, betrays a praiseworthy concern for impartiality shackled by the unconscious influence of enormous prejudices of methodology.

Chapter IV, historical and descriptive, will not detain us long.

We need not say that we who are Catholics will always be

shocked to see St John the Evangelist and the prophet Montanus, Jacob Boehme and Tauler or Suso, Richard Rolle or Walter Hilton and George Fox or the Quakers, St Teresa and Molinos or Madame Guyon, deliberately confounded in a uniform perspective. Not that we object to the comparative study of religious phenomena, but because we are not willing to accept as a prefatory axiom the fundamental equivalence of all claims to mysticism; after all, the experiences of a Boehme and those of a Blessed Henry Suso, those of a St John of the Cross and those of a Molinos, are perhaps separated by an abyss. That these names be brought side by side as objects of study, that their literary dependences be pointed out, that their likenesses be indicated, all this is excellent; but on condition that steps be taken to avoid giving the inexperienced reader the impression that they are identical cases; if there is identity, it must be formally demonstrated and clearly shown.

Professor Leuba chooses, as types of Christian mystics, Blessed Henry Suso, St Catherine of Genoa, Madame Guyon, St Teresa, and St Margaret Mary. We deeply regret that he did not add St John of the Cross to his list, for he would have thrown additional light on an essential point. We will not quarrel with his sources; they are sufficient for the schematic and not very detailed use which he has to make of them, excepting always in the case of St Margaret Mary. Moreover, it does not much matter; for the few deep misunderstandings into which—in good faith, we do not doubt—the American professor falls, have other causes than the relative poverty of his documents.

Even in the fairly objective notices dealing with Suso, St Catherine of Genoa, St Teresa and Madame Guyon, a false note is heard from time to time.

For example, speaking of the prosaic Don Marabotto, the director of St Catherine of Genoa during her later years, Professor Leuba (who could not have chosen a less convincing case) dares to write: " Is there not a significant discrepancy between the profession made by all the divine lovers that God and God alone is sufficient to them, and the bonds of close friendship and pure love most of them (!) seem unable to avoid with at least some one human being of the opposite sex?" (p. 70). Let us, in this last line, strike out the word " love," which is evidently going too far. As for friendship—calm, discreet, devoted, reasonable friendship, born of mutual esteem and always marked with respect—how should this natural virtue be in conflict with the divine love which, far from excluding it, surrounds, ennobles, and broadens it ? So narrow a puritanism from the author's pen is astonishing; does he know of any human friendships more pure and spiritual, more justified and honourable, than those which many saints and mystics who have remained in veneration in the Church allowed themselves ? Please let us not cast on them the suspect shadow of a Molinos or even of a Madame Guyon. And to put things in their proper light, we must not forget either that the "bonds of close friendship" which offend Professor Leuba were not usually more than the confidential relations of spiritual direction; this direction, given in the Church's name, is certainly not indiscreet; it was an immense benefit to the Catholic mystics, and preserved them from many extravagances, as Professor Leuba must be well aware.

To give another example: St Teresa's confession of her long hesitation in sacrificing "certain friendships, very innocent in themselves" (*Life*, ch. xxiv), provokes this remark: " One may well suspect an attachment to a person of the opposite sex, more profound than she admits, deeper perhaps than she knew " (p. 103). Is there the *faintest* indication on which to base such a conjecture ? If not, how are we to describe it ?

We may more easily excuse the author's scandalised astonishment before St Teresa's respectful familiarity with the divine Majesty (p. 107): the " liberty of the children of God " involves distinctions difficult for the outsider to appreciate. But here again are paltrinesses which we may be allowed to find in very bad taste: " Did St Teresa attain her ethical goal ?" Professor Leuba, a more severe censor even than the judges in her process of canonisation, thinks not, but that this saint, so delightful in her spontaneity, remained a very vain daughter of Eve; even worse: " On many occasions she speaks with obvious pride of her influence upon various persons " (p. 108); in the reform of the Carmelite order she withdrew herself from obedience " by dint of persistent secret diplomacy " (p. 109); in short, " The conviction of her greatness welled up more than once. . . . Her saintliness was shot through with an ambition and a pride that death alone could subdue " (p. 109). All this—to be moderate —proves one thing at least: that Professor Leuba, in spite of his application, has not reached that degree of psychological perspicacity and historical information needed in order to judge of certain exceptional beings. Even towards Madame Guyon, who is far from offering such guarantees of moral perfection as St Teresa, the American author's judgement seems to us unjust and unkind.

Moreover, whatever may be the case as to the very remarkable moral elevation which distinguishes the great contemplatives recognised by the Church, what should lead us to suppose that the mystical state must be a state of accomplished perfection, and not merely a means of perfection, so that we must speak of a *failure* wherever some common human weakness remains ? There are decidedly many aspects of Christian asceticism and piety which Professor Leuba misunderstands or completely ignores.

But his ignorance of or failure to comprehend Catholic devotion, joined with his strange incapacity to reconstitute the historical circumstances, reach their culminating point in the treatment inflicted on St Margaret Mary (pp. 109-114, *et alibi*). Many of his readers will be indignant at these odious pages; but let us put indignation aside; the professor of Bryn Mawr was, here more than elsewhere, incapable of proper understanding; we may, however, regret that he did not perceive this, and did not even feel that a minimum of reserve was imposed upon him, as a psychologist and a gentleman, before the unanimous admiration which is inspired in the Catholic world by the courage, humility, self-abandonment, and many other astonishing and heroic virtues of the poor Visitandine of clumsy bearing and deficient education; if he had thought of this, we would willingly believe that he would not have uttered the following condemnation, more odious even than absurd: " Intellectual inferiority, combined with a powerful sex-impulse, early awakened by religious symbolism and directed to Jesus, made of her a link between the great, accepted mystics and a class of mystics with whom the Church will have nothing to do " (p. 110).

Chapter V, " The Motivation of Christian Mysticism," repeats the contents of some former articles of the author (1902). The " fundamental tendencies " whose operation delivers up the deep secret of the mystical life are reduced by Professor Leuba to four groups:

1. " The tendencies to self-affirmation and the need for self-esteem " (p. 120). It would be more correct to say: The need to be worthy of esteem; but let us pass on.

2. " The need for moral support, for affection, and for peace in passivity and in activity " (p. 122). The mystical life

indeed answers to a need for a higher harmony, and it is based upon the interior consolation—austere and virile, in general, rather than sweet—of the soul's filial relationship with God.

3. The tendency to " the universalisation or socialisation of the individual will " (p. 127). Friends of the mystics, who have so many causes for complaint against Professor Leuba, will be grateful to him for having clearly proclaimed, since 1902, in quarters not used to such language, the essential transcendence of Christian asceticism and contemplation over egoistic individualism. In the case of our mystics, abstracting even from a formally apostolic intention (which is almost always present), the moral " values " sought after are *in themselves* universal; what is it they seek, indeed, but " the transformation of the earthly into a divine man—*i.e.*, the replacement of the egoistic individual will by the universal Will " (p. 131)? The great contemplatives do not aspire to enjoyment, even the enjoyment of ecstasy, as an end: " Whatever the mystics may say that seems to subordinate unselfish activity to the passive enjoyment of God is belied by specific passages, . . . by the general trend of their writings, and still more convincingly by their lives; all of them, so soon as unity was established in their consciousness, have spent themselves without stint in the service of their fellow-men. The delight of the ecstatic trance is for them, in final instance, God's way of encouraging them to greater effort towards saintliness, of clarifying their moral vision, and of making of them more useful instruments of divine action " (p. 128). How could the writer of this panegyric resolve to efface its principal trait by resuming, without even modifying his old thesis of " the erotomania of Christian mystics " ?

4. " The sexual impulse " is, in effect, the fourth group of " fundamental tendencies " obeyed by the mystics. " If the mystics profess disdain for the body and its pleasures, it is not because they are indifferent to sensuous delight as such, but because they see some incompatibility between the pleasures of the flesh and the soul's welfare. When they are not aware of the bodily origin of sensuous enjoyment, they give themselves up to it with great relish and complete abandonment " (p. 117).

Let us carefully understand Professor Leuba's thesis. The great mystics, according to him, directed to the most scrupulous chastity by their whole ascetic training, do not knowingly seek sensual pleasure;—in actual fact, however, in good faith and unconsciously, they pursue it and encounter it under more or less masked forms—but even then, while innocently tasting these sensuous delights of whose hidden origin they are ignorant, they relate them as means to a purely moral and religious end. Let us note again that, according to Professor Leuba, pleasure of the sexual order constitutes only a part of the total delight of ecstasy: " The mystic, in his search for divine love, . . . finds a variety of sensory pleasures—those of relaxation, and at times of general erethism, of bright visions, of anæsthesias, and, eclipsing all these, pleasures and pains of sexual origin, delightful beyond anything else known to them. That is already much, yet he gets a great deal beyond that, things more directly to his purpose. For the mystic's purpose is far from being attained when he has secured the pleasures just named. During the moments that precede the extinction of consciousness in the trance [?], and afterwards as long as its influence lasts, he enjoys also happiness. It is a happiness due to the satisfaction of fundamental tendencies and needs " (p. 154).

A rapid review hardly lends itself to the critical examination of so delicate a subject. We may be allowed to refer to the studies, still too conciliating, lately made by M. de Montmorand and Dr. G. Dumas; Professor Leuba, we do not know why, takes no account of the work of such writers, who yet are not " theologians." It will suffice for us to point out here two or three aspects of the question which the American author would have done well to touch upon at least superficially:

(a) *Mystical Symbolism.*—If a profound spring of lyricism wells up in the soul of the mystics, they are not all artists, and the particular symbolism which they use may not be to everyone's taste. At least, to speak only of the mystics approved by the Church, this symbolism, even when it borrows something from the poetry of profane love, seems quite tame as soon as it is studied in relation to current language, from which it borrows many a catachresis, or to the scriptural and patristic tradition, or the literary habits peculiar to certain times and places, or lastly to the contexts which determine the imaginative value and logical bearing of the words employed. It is truly an abuse to write: " Most people are familiar with the extravagant carnal imagery used by the mystics to describe their intense enjoyment of divine love " (p. 144). Our readers, most of whom are acquainted with the writings of the great Catholic mystics, can judge from this of Professor Leuba's scientific exactitude.

(b) *The Delights experienced in Ecstasy.*—Is the enjoyment of ecstasy, or of the moments when it is near at hand, in itself partly sexual ? Does the mystic unconsciously seek this sexual enjoyment, " give himself up to it with great relish and complete abandon," so that it may be described as one of the " motives of Christian mysticism " ? The few positive indications suspected by Professor Leuba in the confidences of the mystics are not only very meagre to serve as the justification of so vast and universal a thesis, but they are also all susceptible of an infinitely less pointed interpretation. Professor Leuba attempts to argue *a priori :* the mystic *must* be in a state of chronic sexual excitement, which will be reflected during the ecstatic trance or semi-trance; indeed, " is the flesh likely to remain unmoved when continence is combined with familiarity with a loved woman [he is referring to the affectionate and confidential relations between director and directed] and with indulgence in the imagery dear to the libertine ?" (p. 144) Once more, what juggling with facts ! When Professor Leuba has shown that real mystics lend themselves to " familiarity with a loved woman " and dream all day long of " the imagery dear to the libertine," he will justify our considering his objection. And then, what will he do with those mystics— and there is no lack of such—who contract no particular friendships, even of the noblest, and who, so far as we know, use no special symbolism of human love in their relations with God ? We are forced to ask, with increasing disquietude, what kind of an idea of the normal mystical life this professor of psychology, a reputed connoisseur in religious matters, can have formed.

But let us go so far as to suppose that unrecognised traces of " sexual pleasure " actually mingle with the intense " sensible consolations " which the mystic sometimes experiences: does he seek for and take pleasure in these sensible consolations with a kind of gluttony ? If Professor Leuba had attentively read St John of the Cross and other masters of the interior life, would he be ignorant that attachment to sensible consolation, or even to " spiritual " delight in prayer, is a radical obstacle to progress and a hindrance to the states of union ? For the true Christian mystic pleasure of any kind, and *a fortiori* bodily pleasure, is never a motive or an ideal, even a partial and pro-visional one; the mystic's aim is higher. Will it be said that he is under an illusion, and that he always yields in part to an instinctive taste for physical satisfactions ? By what right can this be affirmed ? Professor Leuba, in spite of what he seemed to grant elsewhere, is clearly haunted by the preposterous idea that the mystics aspire, not to a state of perfection, but to one of well-being, to a kind of hygienic equilibrium of body and spirit (see also p. 299).

(c) *The Affections in the Mystic and the Freudian Theory of Libido*.—We might indeed, with Freud, by a real abuse of terminology, raise the question of "erotomania" in the mystics, on ground less accessible both to proof and to refutation. If it be held that the *whole* affective sphere is fundamentally sexual, then obviously there is no movement of the soul in the order of social relations, or in those of æsthetics or religion, which ought not to be called in some degree sexual. But again we must understand one another; we are then calling "sexual" a kind of diffused hedonic capacity, the undifferentiated root whence spring those various more specialised tendencies which assure the satisfaction of our fundamental psycho-physiological needs; among these derived tendencies ranks in its due order the sexual appetite in the strict sense. Since Professor Leuba, without being "Freudian," judges it fitting to invoke here the theories of psychoanalysis as his allies (p. 203 ff.), we regret that he does not indicate more clearly their relation with his own conception of mystical erotomania, which itself supposes an already differentiated sexuality. For if he merely affirmed that the enjoyment of mysticism is neither more nor less sexual than the pleasure derived from appeasing hunger, or than the æsthetic rapture experienced before an artistic masterpiece, a great natural spectacle, or moral beauty, or again, neither more nor less so than the child's affection and respect for its parents, we might be surprised at so unusual and disputable a terminology, but we should do wrong to be too alarmed at what it signified: the honour of the mystics would be unstained. Unfortunately, Professor Leuba says more than this.

This is not the place to enter into a discussion of the Freudian theories of sex. As always, a kernel of truth is hidden under a mass of error; a commonplace truth enough, indeed, which we might formulate in these terms: In man a natural connexion and secondarily acquired associations exist between sexual activity and general sensibility or affectivity; consequently, every state of consciousness having an affective value may, under certain conditions, have indirect results in the sexual sphere.

For some centuries already the masters of Christian asceticism have drawn practical consequences from this truth; they point out the snares which an imaginative and sensible contemplation may offer to the imperfect, and the respectful reserve that must be maintained in the matter. Some of them, such as St John of the Cross, even note with extraordinary precision the indirect effects of the sexual order which may arise—though rarely—in the case of morbid or too sensitive beginners, from the noblest and most chaste flights of divine love. It goes without saying that to be willingly attached to such effects would not only mean the renunciation of the mystic ways, but would be sin. We may go further: According to the Spanish doctor, these " lateral reflections," which always contain an abnormal element, totally disappear in the higher states of prayer; and this disappearance is related to the effacement of the part played by images. Professor Leuba does not seem to have noticed that the psychological conditions required, according to the masters of Christian mysticism, for the ascent to the states of union exclude more and more, in the course of this " ascent," the risk of even an unperceived sexual disturbance. If we admit, therefore, in agreement with a safe tradition, that the " sexual instinct " may lead to snares for the mystics, on the other hand we really do not see how it can be one of the " motives of Christian mysticism."

In the foregoing pages we have been compelled to remark in Professor Leuba a lack of historical and psychological understanding of our Christian mystics, and then to criticise keenly on a very delicate point his analysis of the fundamental tendencies which motivate them. It is now the problem of *ecstasy* which is especially going to engage our attention, and that under three successive aspects: the place of ecstasy in the hierarchy of mystical states; the relation between the ecstatic trance and the nervous state; and lastly the intellectual content of ecstasy. We shall see reappearing here to the detriment of the Christian mystics the errors of interpretation which already manifested themselves in the introductory chapters.

Chapter VI, " The Methods of Christian Mysticism," contains two entirely erroneous affirmations—both very serious: (1) " The Degrees of Depth of the (ecstatic) Trance " correspond, in the view of the mystics, to so many " Degrees of Moral Perfection " (p. 172). That in a general way, without implying a strict proportion, the growth in union with God in prayer presupposes or procures increasing purity of heart, and that the state of " transforming union," especially, can hardly be imagined as existing in a soul which retains any voluntary attachment to sin, is indeed the view of the most authoritative writers. But that these authors evaluate personal sanctity according to the degree of " depth of the trance "—that is, according to the degree of psychophysiological ecstasy, or the degree of " alienation of the senses " or " sleep of the powers " —seems a disconcerting assertion to come from an author who claims to know the Christian mystics. (2) Perhaps the reader will be more astonished still at the free and easy way in which Professor Leuba allows himself to wipe out the characteristic phase of " deification " or " spiritual marriage " at the summit of the mystical union, during which the contemplative, without losing contact with God, resumes the use and perfect control of his natural faculties. According to the American psychologist, the descriptions of this last and lasting phase of the mystical life do not, like those of the foregoing phases, correspond to an original (perhaps illusory) subjective experience, but repose on a " confusion " committed afterwards, one which he chooses to call improbable.

This is to play fast and loose with the texts, which on this point agree so closely. Professor Leuba's vision is here falsified by a source of error which we have already remarked, and which belongs, so to speak, to his " personal equation "; in his " comparative and genetic " system, it is *necessary* that the ecstatic trance, crowned by complete unconsciousness, should be the culminating point of all mysticism.

What has reliable tradition to say ? If Catholic writers have at times exaggerated the religious significance of the psychosomatic phenomena of ecstasy, it is not necessary to possess exceptional learning to understand the extremely reserved attitude of the Church in this regard, and to know that the best tradition has never considered ecstasy, looked upon as trance, as the essential form or the summit of the mystical life; on the other hand, ecstasy, thus considered in its negative or even corporal aspects, is the price which the weakness of our nature has to pay for the wholly spiritual sublimity of divine union; the ecstatic trance, in itself, lends itself to many illusions—it may supervene at the lower stages of the mystical ascent, and tends to disappear at the summit. If Professor Leuba studies more closely particularly exact authors, such as Blessed John Ruysbroeck or St John of the Cross, he will recognise his mistake as to the value attributed to ecstasy as such in Catholic mysticism. We should even judge it probable that some contemplatives reach a very high degree of prayer by a continual and harmonious development, without any violent crisis and without " ecstatic trances " properly so called.

Professor Leuba, by attributing an exaggerated importance to what M. de Montmorand has called the " orchestration " of mysticism, constantly exposes himself to the subordination of the essential to the accessory. This displacement of values makes itself felt once more in the two chapters (VII and VIII) devoted to the parallelism between the observable expressions of the mystical life and the variations of the nervous state. No one will deny that there are certain correlations; the psychology of mysticism, under the action of God, remains a " human " psychology; and it is therefore not exempt from the natural dependence of the soul on the body. But must we speak of " neurosis " in this connexion ? We meet with mystics who are "neuropathic" constitutionally or as a result of various infirmities; there are others who show no appreciable neuropathological symptoms. The former did not become mystics because they were neuropaths; however, we readily admit that their nervous state cannot remain without influence on their affective life and on the psychosomatic aspect of their ecstasies. As for those mystics who enjoyed normal health, but knew the physical weakness of ecstasy, is it not natural that the exceptional mental concentration, in which their raptures culminated, should have had as a momentary effect inhibitions and dissociations in their lower psychism analogous to those observed in neuroses ? It is not these effects, frequent though they may be, that characterise true religious ecstasy, for they can be provoked by the most diverse causes. In the eyes of Catholic contemplatives, the essential kernel of the mystical state consists in transcendent union with God, which takes place in the centre of the soul; all the rest depends broadly on the physiological and psychological mechanism, which nature has not adapted in advance to the " flight of the soul "; some ruptures of equilibrium are to be expected therein—they are almost inevitable in a non-glorified body. Is that a reason for saying that the echoes of the transforming union in the lower psychism and even in the vegetal sphere are morbid ? that they are " hysterical and neurasthenic symptoms " (p. 191) ? These expressions, even when surrounded with reservations, seem to us very clumsy and positively open to criticism; for a particular symptom is only hysterical or neurasthenic in virtue of its insertion in a complete picture of hysteria or neurasthenia. Now Professor Leuba himself frankly recognises that on the whole, the symptoms of the great mystics " do not have the same significance as in the ordinary patients of the psychiatrist " (p. 201). In that case, was it worth insisting so strongly on the " hysteria " of St Teresa and St Catherine of Genoa ?[2]

At the stage we have now reached, Professor Leuba commences, in fact, to repeat himself more than he need. We are compelled to imitate him a little—as little as we can. Chapter IX, a comparative study of ecstasy, has above all the interest of a shelf of rare books; pictures of persons " in trance," showing more or less graduated transitions from religious to profane ecstasy. Look, the ingenious collector seems to say, they are all alike, they are all brothers; the difference between their ecstasies is reduced to " interpretation," which " transfigured the primary experience (the unconscious trance) and made of it a religious ecstasy " (p. 213).

Nothing can be easier than thus, by multiplying surface relationships, to draw up impressive series for the imagination. In the greater number of the cases related, there was indeed on the part of the subjects who lived through them a secondary religious interpretation of subjective states rather than an immediate experience of a religious content; in other cases, such as that of Mlle. Vé—Flournoy's " modern mystic "—a direct but very confused experience of the divine is formally affirmed, an experience whose illusory character was later on rightly recognised by Mlle. Vé herself; to this last case Professor Leuba evidently assimilates that of the great Christian mystics, who, by a like illusion, he thinks, projected their dogmatic interpretations in all good faith upon their subjective experiences, which are all the more devoid of significance as they tend more closely towards the annihilation of unconsciousness.

The American psychologist thus remains obstinately faithful to his old and even somewhat superannuated theory of an ecstasy which is devoid of ideas and totally empty. We quite grant that he is not bound to believe the mystics blindly when they affirm the transcendent origin of their states of prayer. Nevertheless, without passing the bounds of psychological criticism, it may be found that he very lightly throws overboard the very abundant descriptive literature of Catholic mysticism, which, apart from any polemical prejudice, contradicts on every page the hypothesis that ecstasy is a state of absolute unconsciousness. If our mystics describe obscure ecstasies, they do not describe them as empty; on the other hand, at the supreme summit of ecstasy, the radiant revelation of the Trinity in the light of the Word always comes, they repeat, to fill the souls of privileged contemplatives.

Professor Leuba's contempt for these testimonies, which he does not even examine, is dictated by that methodological prejudice which made him at an earlier stage misconceive the original character of the " spiritual marriage," which is none the less described, by the mystics who experienced it, as the crown of their mystical development. Once more we must repeat that Professor Leuba will perceive nothing essential in the facts of mysticism save ecstasy; and in ecstasy he will perceive nothing essential save " trance "—that is, an abnormal somatic state, accompanied by the shrinkage, and eventually the disappearance, of ordinary consciousness. So much the worse for the mystics if they think they can show that ecstasy is not essential to their higher forms of prayer, and if, in ecstasy, the element which they call mystical is not the trance itself—which is indifferent—but the awakening of a higher form of consciousness. Between the profane theoretician of mysticism and the chief group of his clients—we almost said of his victims—there is at least a radical terminological disagreement; and this involves a serious danger of lack of mutual understanding.

However, a ray of hope remains in this regard; in the sixth part of Chapter X, the author seems to desire to come to closer grips with the problem of the transcendental content of ecstasy. What, in the ecstatics, are the " roots of the conviction of ineffable revelation " (p. 263) ? The answer is deceptive. Once more he is satisfied, in accordance with his policy of successive glidings, to attach to the Christian mystical " revelation!" a chain of analogous cases, less and less susceptible of a transcendental interpretation, and even less and less susceptible of a natural interpretation surpassing the level of the most commonplace platitude; then, supposing the series homogeneous and continuous from all points of view—which, from the logical standpoint, is a violent step—he triumphantly concludes that the higher term can only represent a more complex modality, a " complication " of the lower term. This lower term, simple, clear and distinct, " scientific," in a word, would be represented, for example, by the effects of momentary exaltation produced by laughing gas: Sir Humphry Davy, whose introspection echoes that of other experimenters,

notes that " my emotions were enthusiastic and sublime ";
or, again, even less, they would be the " sublime and solemn
sensations " experienced by some neurasthenics (p. 266), such
as the congenial and grotesque " Jean " of Dr. Pierre Janet.

Et nunc reges erudimini : Professor Leuba lets fly this chain-
shot at the princes of mysticism—all the dialectic ballast of his
book: " We are now prepared to return to the problem as it
appears to the religious mystics. They affirm that, even
though they cannot formulate it adequately, divine knowledge
comes to them during their ecstasies. . . . (But) that belief in
an ineffable intellectual revelation cannot be accepted unless
its truth be demonstrated by something more objective than
the mystic's own conviction; for we have just found out that
the trance-experience is rich in phenomena able to produce
the illusion of transcendent revelation " (p. 270). Since the
witness of the mystic himself is deprived of power of conviction,
" the one remaining basis of proof is the behaviour of the subject
after the revelation. . . . But nothing that has happened to
the mystics with whom we are acquainted goes beyond altera-
tions and transformations referable to known natural causes,
physical and psychical " (p. 271). We must not object the
" clearness and certitude " (Chapter X) of the " ineffable
revelation," for that is an ordinary property of many states
of trance in which the question of an objective manifestation
does not even arise. As for the " sense of presence " (Chapter
XI), which can, as experience bears witness, be at the same
time clear and completely illusory, that in turn does not support
the thesis of a transcendental communication. Conclusion:
not only does simple psychology fail to show the value of the
supernatural claims of the contemplatives (if that is what
Professor Leuba wished to establish, he has given himself a
great deal of trouble to force an open door), but, positively,
psychology demonstrates " the illusory nature of the impression
of intellectual revelation in mystical trance " (p. 271).

Professor Leuba will forgive us for not being able to see this
positive demonstration in his pages. We can find only an
hypothesis, abundantly illustrated, it is true, but incomplete,
unverifiable and over-simple, as to the identity of the highest
Christian contemplation with the trance-states of uncivilised
peoples; one of those hypotheses which is proposed only from
lack of a better, so as not to give up all attempt at explanation.
Has Professor Leuba—it can hardly be believed—no better

opinion of it ? Does he fail to measure the distance which still separates, on the purely psychological plane, the meagre and inexact elements of explanation which he sets before us, from the singularly complex and comprehensive, living and life-giving realities which he seeks to elucidate ?

In any case, the audacity of several of his affirmations disconcerts our logic. And we come to ask ourselves if the real reasons for them are not much more distant, that is to say, to be clear, if the last two chapters (XII and XIII), offered us as the philosophical corollary of the volume, almost an accessory, do not perhaps, in fact, contain its premises. They teach us that the demonstrated emptiness of the mystical experience ruins the last atom of proof that might still support the belief in a personal God. And Professor Leuba, revealing the depth of his heart and mind, rejoices in the inevitable disaggregation of the " traditional faith," which he considers " mischievous " (p. 327 ff.). He beholds the perspective of a future of wholly earthly serenity, where a purified religion, which has become the simple cult of the ideal, will hold out a hand to science, in which it will at last recognise an ally: " Spiritual improvement may then be expected to rival in rapidity the improvement in matters of health and longevity which has taken place in consequence of the discovery and of the application of medical knowledge " (p. 332).

We regret this last phrase of Professor Leuba's, for his book, of which we have had to say some unpleasant things, seems to us none the less to deserve a better end than a sentence which we might think had been concocted by Bouvard and Pecuchet. We respect the writer's convictions, which are not our own, and his frankness, which we have imitated. But it seems clear to us—and we will make our peace on this point, if he will allow us—that it is not pure psychology which compels him to tax with illusion the transcendental intuition of the Christian mystics, as it is likewise not simple psychology, but above all a collection of theological presumptions, which makes us believers admit the possibility of such intuition. To continue the dispute, we should have to enter the domain of the general criticism of science; but that is another story.

STUDIES IN THE PSYCHOLOGY OF THE MYSTICS

NOTES

[1] *The Psychology of Religious Mysticism.* By James H. Leuba, Professor of Psychology at Bryn Mawr College, U.S.A. London, 1925.

[2] Mr. Leuba quotes at length the once celebrated and certainly remarkable monograph in which my learned and pious colleague of Louvain, the late Père Hahn, while calling attention to several physical indications of hysteria in St Teresa, showed also the complete absence of the corresponding psychological defects in the saint. With our present conception of hysteria this dissociation would be almost devoid of meaning, and Père Hahn would be the first, we believe, to condemn the unfortunate label under which he grouped the nervous affections described in his pages.

THE PROBLEM OF MYSTICAL GRACE IN ISLAM

THE PROBLEM OF MYSTICAL GRACE IN ISLAM[1]

ON the morning of March 26, 922/309, at Bagdad, al-Hosayn-ibn-Mansûr al-Hallâj, the "carder of con-sciences," the sublime and misunderstood "ecstatic," perished by the executioner's hand. Condemned on the advice of jurists of his own religion, and given over to capital punishment by the caliph al-Moqtadir, he had been taken the preceding evening from prison—where he had for many years undergone an honourable captivity—and dragged to the place of execution. "His hands and feet were cut off, after he had received five hundred lashes," relates his son Hamd (P. 9). He besmeared his face with his bleeding stumps, whether to hide his pallor or to perform the ritual ablutions for a last time in his own blood (P. 309, 453). " Then he was fastened to the cross, and I (his son Hamd) heard him conversing with God in ecstasy on the gibbet. . . . When evening fell, the caliph's messengers brought authority for him to be beheaded. But they said: It is too late, let us put it off till to-morrow. When the morning came, he was taken down from the gibbet and brought forward so that his head might be smitten off. And I heard him cry out and say in a very loud voice: What the ecstatic desires is the Sole One, alone with Him !—Then he recited this verse: (Kor. xlii 17): They who believe not in the last hour (the last Judgement) challenge its speedy coming; but they who believe are afraid because of it, and know it to be a Truth.—These were his last words. His neck was severed, then his body was enveloped in a mat, soaked with oil, and burnt. Afterwards his ashes were taken to the top of the Manarah (minaret) that the wind might scatter them " (P. 9-10).

In spite of the excommunications and the hate by which Hallâj was overwhelmed, the vision of this man of prayer, terribly mutilated, attesting from the height of his gibbet both his loving union with the Sole One, with God, and his faithful perseverance in the Koran, the Law of his people, this vision strangely fascinating, a vision of love and of blood, of liberty of the spirit and submission to the letter, of transcendence and wretchedness, has remained imprinted on the Moslem

241   Q

imagination, not only as a particularly tragic scene of martyrdom, but as the vivid expression and final act of a religious
drama, wholly interior and infinitely more moving, which was
played out and unfolded in the conscience of the tortured mystic.
More: the case of Hallâj grew, in Islam, to symbolise an
anguishing alternative which may—perhaps we may even say
must—present itself sooner or later, at least in a rudimentary
form, to every soul that seeks God in uprightness.

We would like to emphasise in a rapid outline the interesting
features for religious psychology and dogmatic theology which
are presented to us by the poignant destiny of " al-Hallâj, the
martyr-mystic of Islam."

I. HALLÂJ AND THE PRIMITIVE MYSTICAL TRADITION

Born about 858/244, of Iranian stock, at Madinat al Baydâ,
in the eastern provinces of the Abbasid Khalifate (to the north-
east of the Persian Gulf), Hallâj spent his childhood in Arab
surroundings, at Wâsit, nearer Bagdad. " At the age of
sixteen, . . . he left his family and went, as was the custom
for all novices, to act as a *servant* in the entourage of a sheikh
of Tostar in Ahwâz. It was in this capacity that he became
the disciple of Sahl-ibn-Abdallah, whose renown was increasing in all the neighbouring country " (P. 23).

Sahl al Tostarî (818/203-896/283) already marks a fairly
advanced stage along one of the lines of evolution of primitive
Islam. It is well known that there were soon constituted on
the common basis of the Koranic revelation theological and
juridical groups which were fairly divergent—hostile brethren,
all equally recognised by the mass of the " faithful." Tostarî,
while he was far from the rationalism of the Motazilites, and
a convinced adherent of the traditionalist (Sunnite) tendency—
" that faithful memory and fervent heart of the Moslem
community " (P. 28)—was yet not disposed towards that
sterile literalism and wholly external casuistry which some
upheld under colour of tradition. Respect for ritual and the
law were accompanied in him by a deep sense of the spiritual
life, understood as a life of progress towards moral perfection
and of the quest for God in contemplation.

Whence did the preoccupation with asceticism, in the highest
sense of the word, and even with mysticism, arise in Islam ?
" As against the pharisaical opinion of many *foqahâ*, which has

been accepted for sixty years past by a number of Arabic scholars," writes M. Massignon, " I have thought it necessary to recognise, with Margoliouth, that in the Koran there are the real seeds of a mysticism, seeds capable of an autonomous development, without fecundation from outside " (P. 480). Let us liberate these hidden seeds, the fine pearls of a true spirituality, which are not to be despised, however poor their setting may appear.

Besides ordinary believers, who serve the inaccessible and ineffable Creator outwardly in accordance with the prescriptions of the law, there are certain souls, says the Koran, to whom God—because " they please him "—communicates inwardly " his essential mystery," and causes an habitual grace of pacification of soul and of friendship with him to unfold itself in them on the root of the Faith. " The Koran even lets it be understood that, (in order to dispose himself) to taste this development of faith, (the believer must) give himself up wholly to a certain rule of life, submit to a course of training, exercise his will and render it docile, keep it in play in order immediately to obey the commandment (of God) as soon as he hears it: render to God a fervent worship " (P. 501). An invitation, hesitating though it be, to an ascesis which is not fulfilled by a few practices of the common service, but has for its formal end to render the soul docile to a prevenient and wholly personal grace.

" How can one arrive in practice at this state ? The Koran does not aim at teaching the paths for arriving thereat. It lays it down that only the *help of the (Holy) Spirit* . . . brings one thither; and it makes Mohammed say laconically that this mission of the Spirit to certain souls is a supernatural fact, a divine secret.—Say: ' The Spirit proceeds from God's Commandment ' (Kor. xvii 87) " (P. 502-503). The text mentions certain persons who benefited by this " help of the Spirit ": a purely external and prophetic help in the case of Adam, Moses, Mohammed; an interior and sanctifying help in that of Abraham, Job, al khidr (the companion of Moses), and in a quite special degree—we shall return to this later—in Jesus.

Thus the Koran, that code of an external and ritual religion, leaves at least a narrow path open to the irruption of the enlightening Spirit, which is of necessity a Spirit of love. Under the influence of this Spirit the meaning of certain verses of the Koran will be widened to the extent that the eyes of the faithful are opened; a Hallâj, for example, will read " *arcana verba*," with dizzy meanings, into this sentence, magnificent in its conciseness, which every believer could at least begin to understand: " Wherever you turn, you are face to face with God " (P. 588). Thus, again, the recitation of the Koran, or the minimum of ritual or ascetic practices required by the necessities of collective worship, might in the case of elect souls take on a new religious value and become the starting-point of an interior life—" metakoranic " or " suprakoranic," not " anti-koranic "—capable of being perfected to an indefinite degree.

In reality, from the very beginning of Islam, there shine out here and there some very pure gleams of an interior and disinterested religion. For example, that old *qâdî*, who had sacrificed his career for the sake of a scruple of equity, and who, tied to a sick-bed for the last thirty years of his life, was the admiration of all by reason of his amiable resignation. He refused all solace. To a visitor who expressed disgust at the nature of his malady, he replied: " Since God causes me to find it good, I find it good, for it comes from him " (E. 139).

In the course of the first century of the Hegira, groups of ascetics, moved by a feeling of penitence and devotion, were constituted at Kufa, Damascus, Bassorah, Mecca, and in the Yemen. . . . But in the second century the " mystic invasion " increased with incredible rapidity; and at the same time was organised an increasingly close-knit mystical doctrine, a doctrine that was likewise combated in an increasing degree by the extremists of juridical literalism.

This opposition already made itself felt in the case of the " patriarch of Islamic mysticism," Hasan Basrî (643/21-728/110). The principal reproaches levelled against his school by the Sunnite traditionalists do not lack significance: they concern " the importance of meditation in the religious life, and the reciprocal love which is to be desired between God and the soul " (E. 177). Under such complaints we catch a glimpse of the sharpening of the conflict of two irremediably divergent tendencies. Hasan seeks, beyond " the letter that killeth," " the spirit that giveth life." Not that he undervalued rite and observance: no one could be more scrupulously exact in their fulfilment; but " what he considers essential in an action is its intention " (E. 164). He stigmatises " the pharisaism of the lawyers, *toqahâ*, whose knowledge and works are void of all sincere intention " (E. 167). " Faith," he says, " is not a piece of finery to be put on or a fashion to be followed, it is what the heart reveres, and works confirm as true " (*ibid.*). This very vivid meaning of devotion, upheld by a kind of reserved tenderness towards God, inspires his eschatology: " If the faithful thought that they would not see God in the other life, their hearts would break with disappointment in this world " (E. 163).

We are here far above what we usually think of as " Mohammed's paradise." Here the spirit of servitude and the desire for reward give way before the allurement of God in himself. There is more. The rough asceticism preached by Hasan strives to realise here on earth the sanctity[2] of the Koranic " state of grace," that " reciprocal complacency of the soul and God." Delicacy of conscience, by the practice of tutiorism in morals, complete renouncement of perishable goods, continual attrition, fear of God and consequent attention to his Word, become so many means of offering oneself to the special gift of divine friendship, which by a wholly gratuitous grace comes to flower in the mystical state.

Let us listen to Hasan describing from within the ascensions of the contemplative: " From the moment when the dominant occupation of my beloved servant becomes that of remembering Me, I cause him to find his happiness and his joy in remembering Me, he desires Me and I desire him. And when he desires Me and I him, I raise the veils between Myself and him, and become a harmonious series of connecting-links before his eyes. Such men forget Me not when others forget Me " (E. 173-174).

The movement towards a more interior and deeper Koranic religion, so strongly seconded by Hasan, was continued in the school of Bassorah. Then, towards the end of the second century of the Hegira, Bagdad in its turn became " the meeting-place of many traditionalists and literary men sympathetic to mysticism " (E. 209). In the third century we can speak of a " school of Bagdad," and this brings us into immediate proximity with Hallâj. The parallel synthesis of dogmatic theology and of ascetic and mystical theology is regularly pursued there under the preponderating influence, first of *Mohâsibî*, later of *Jonayd*.

Since we cannot think, in this brief essay, of using the numerous technical details which M. Massignon supplies, we will be content with remarking two important characters in the normal development[3] of Musulman spirituality: (1) The persistence of an interior spirit, mystical but in no wise quietist;

(2) the birth of the consciousness of an interior crisis, long latent, which was to show itself in all its acuteness in the case of Hallâj.

Mohâsibî, born at Bassorah (781/865), died at Bagdad (857/243), is hardly known to us save by his teaching, in which " for the first time are combined with rare power, fervent respect for the most naïve traditions, the implacable search for an interior perfection of morals, and a scrupulous care for exact philosophical definition " (E. 212).

The ascetic system of Mohâsibî is at once penetrating and judicious, his theological teaching precise and certain. The rule of life he teaches is above all " to serve one only Master, God " (E. 221). Desiring to raise souls to a great height, he is careful to choose a very modest starting-point so as not to rebuff them at the beginning; for example, he begins " from the eschatology of the *Hashwiyah*, the bodily joys which the houris have in reserve, and then gently and insensibly he leads the reader to that solemn procession of the Saints towards the pure vision of the divine essence which alone gives perfect joy " (E. 223).

Now this calm and balanced soul, a friend of conciliation, experienced the first symptoms of the crisis whereof we have just spoken: " I discovered," he writes, " by the consensus of the Community, in the Book of God revealed to the Prophet, that the way of salvation is to hold fast to piety towards God, to the observance of canonical duties, scrupulous care as to lawful and unlawful things . . . —to act purely in all things for God and to take the Prophet for model. I then became preoccupied with learning what were the canonical duties, the canonical sanctions, the habits of the Prophet and strict observance, following the masters and the sources; but then I observed that there was agreement on certain points and disagreement on others. . . . My difficulties increased for lack of guides capable of conducting me, . . . and I feared that sudden death might surprise me in that state of distress in which the disagreement of the Community kept me " (E. 216-218).

Where does Mohâsibî look for the solution of his perplexity ? Not outside tradition, in an esoteric doctrine, selfishly reserved to a few adepts, and superimposed from without on the prescriptions of the Koran; but rather in sincere application to the discovery in these prescriptions themselves of the hidden heart of truth and the hidden flame of devotion which quickens

246

them, which are, as it were, the first echo of God's love in the soul. Indeed, he cries, " the origin of the love of the faithful for the acts of religion springs from the love of the Lord, for it is he who has given it birth. Indeed, it is he who has made himself known to them, who has led them to obey him, who has caused them to love him, without themselves counting for anything. And he has planted the germs of love for himself in the hearts of his lovers " (E. 218).

Interior worship will develop, through personal sanctity, under the breath of the Spirit, but without ever breaking its original tie with the letter of the inspired text nor with the outward observances which it prescribes. Those who are privileged by grace are thus made witnesses of God, benevolent counsellors of their brethren, spiritual physicians and inter-cessors for the Moslem community (cf. the text quoted by M. Massignon, E. 218-219).

This love of the Moslem community was pushed to the extent of the most active apostolic work by the founder of the (Sunnite) mystical school of Khorasan, *Ibn Karrâm* (A.H. 190-255), " one of the great thinkers of Musulman scholasticism " (E. 234). His disciples spread their preaching through the eastern provinces of the Caliphate, in Afghanistan, and even to India. Another precedent which may help us to understand the religious physiognomy of Hallâj.

Did space permit, we would gladly retrace here the rough historical outline of *Bistâmî* (†874/260), who died in the very year in which Hallâj began his career of asceticism. Later mystical writers have delighted to compare these two athletes of devotion, so similar in certain respects, but so different as a whole (cf. E. 254 ff.). Bistâmî is the type of violent mystical effort, tenacious, heroic, but too dependent on the " Self." In the mysticism of Hallâj, as we shall see later, the centre of gravity lies elsewhere.

Bistâmî " is the first to proclaim openly the end glimpsed and desired by his predecessors; . . . self-abandonment in face of the pure Unity of God. (His method of contemplation) ended in an attempt to confront the soul with the divine Essence, where the school of Ibn Arabî was to believe that it discovered its own monism, which is probably incorrect. . . ."—" In spite of an unheard-of keenness of intuition and stiffening of will, understanding, in Bistâmî, is vaster than love; what he unceasingly seeks is the abstract pursuit of an outward and impassible perception of the divine Essence, rendered naked in

247

its infinite humility—but without this moving spectacle enrapturing his heart to loving and transforming union. Hence those flashes of strange pride in his prayers. . . ." (E. 245-247).

Need we be surprised that this over-strained effort to reach God in his transcendence gives way before reaching its goal ? " Bistâmî states with bitterness that the very concept of this pure monotheistic evidence is only a deception. . . . To keep the intellect in simple contemplation, like a mirror exposed to the shining attributes of the divine Majesty, could only end in destroying the mystic's personality " (E. 248-249).

With *Tirmidhî* (†898/285), " the first Moslem mystic in whom appear the traces of an infiltration of Hellenistic philosophy " (E. 256), we already reach the immediate teachers of Hallâj, since Tirmidhî " prepares for the philosophico-gnostic compromise of Tostarî " (Sahl Tostarî: see above, p. 242). About the same time, " an independent writer, without personal affiliation to Sufism, but deeply influenced by the Sufis[4] of Kufa and Bagdad "—*Kharrâz* (899/286)—" brings a point of view more conformable to the requirements of Sunnite orthodoxy, of the vast syntheses of Tostarî and Tirmidhî, too closely allied as they were in certain directions to Imâmite gnosticism as well as to Hellenistic philosophy " (E. 270). He was connected with Jonayd and Ibn Atâ, one the principal " director," the other the friend of Hallâj. Let us note the bold clearness which the definition of the mystical state assumes with Kharrâz: " To be *annihilated* in God, he teaches, so as to *subsist* in him " (E. 271). " Ascetic mortification should end in a personal and positive transfiguration of the soul, transfigured by grace. And Kharrâz defines this final state as ' essential union,' of substance with substance " (E. 272). But the medal has its reverse: after the example of other mystics, " he shows himself indulgent towards . . . mental intoxication, the cult of ecstasy for its own sake " (E. 272). A point of view still too subjective: Hallâj will push the denial of self to a much further point.

" The doctrinal unification of the school of Bagdad will only be realised in practice by *Jonayd* (†A.H. 298), but it is seen in germ in the powerful synthesis boldly undertaken by Mohâsibî (†A.H. 243) " (E. 210). From the contemporaries of the Prophet to Hallâj, through Hasan, Basrî, Mohâsibî, and Jonayd, we thus see the unfolding of a continuous series of ascetics and mystics, more and more conscious of their teaching and their methods.

248

THE PROBLEM OF MYSTICAL GRACE IN ISLAM

" Jonayd," says M. Massignon (correcting on this point the more reserved appreciation which he put forward in *La Passion d'Al-Hallâj*), " constructed a complete theoretical sketch of the doctrine of Hallâj " (E. 277). But, if the basis is the same in essentials, the tone differs. To understand Jonayd, " we must make allowances, firstly, for his personal temperament—clever, prudent and timid, conscious of the danger of heterodoxy which is peculiar to mysticism; secondly, for his experienced wisdom—a director of conscience, who suspends his judgement and defers the question so long as experience does not seem to him decisive and crucial " (E. 275).

" So far as the mystical union is concerned, Jonayd is the first writer who embraced the problem in all its breadth, and stated it correctly; he has carefully marked out the threshold of that transcendent operation, that night of the will, whose anguish Bistâmî had foreseen and the experience whereof Hallâj was to undergo. Jonayd does not push his experimenting so far; he sets forth the data, leaving it to his hearers to come to their own conclusions by personal trial; thus, when the case of Hallâj came up, the school of Jonayd suffered schism. . . ." (E. 276).

But we must not anticipate. It is time to go back to the young novice, whom we left, training for a very austere asceticism, under the guidance of Sahl Tostarî.

After about two years, Hallâj left his first instructor to join the sufi Amrû al Makkî at Bagdad (*circa* A.H. 262). Eighteen months later, he married the daughter of another sufi, Jonayd's secretary; this marriage estranged him from al Makkî, and Hallâj went to take his place among the disciples of Jonayd himself, the eminent teacher of the sufi school of Bagdad, " the orthodox doctor, whom (at the present day) all the Musulman religious orders claim as their patriarch " (P. 34).

That Hallâj " took the robe of white wool, the sûf, from al Jonayd—this implied no initiation into a secret doctrine, nor any vow of following a special rule; it was an exterior sign of voluntary austerity—of a will fixed henceforth on living more apart from worldly agitations, and at the same time of remaining in all things strictly faithful to the tradition of the Prophet " (P. 26-27).

Jonayd professed " a strict and absolute mysticism " (P. 37). " The intelligence of Hallâj submitted for twenty years to the intense asceticism of this harsh teaching. He pushed to the extreme both physical and mental mortification at the same time " (P. 38). His rather wild, self-willed, and yet fervent character did not easily accommodate itself to half-measures. When he believed that he had had mystical experiences, and felt the inrush of God into his soul, he did not refrain from attributing to this inner light the same transcendent value as to the exterior Koranic revelation—and, more serious still, from saying so. His theory of internal sanctification already outlines itself, rising, in its ascensional movement, above " the consideration of all the *intermediaries*, rites, and virtues, to give place to the divine *realities* of worship, to immediate union with the divine essence " (P. 61, 52).

By this intrepidity in setting forth without reticence the doctrinal implications of the mystical effort, even to the last and extremest, Hallâj outran his teachers. A rupture became inevitable. Hard words were exchanged; and, if tradition is to be trusted, old Jonayd, confronted with the extremist attitude of his disciple, said: " As for me, Ibn Mansûr (a name of Hallâj), I see much presumption and lack of wisdom in your words " (P. 60).—" What a gibbet you will stain with your blood !" (P. 61, 52).

Detached from the sufi environment, Hallâj was enabled to give himself more freely to the inspirations of his zeal; for he was not the man to hide his light under a bushel. After two years of living in retirement at Tostar he undertook, about 899/286, a five years' preaching journey in Khorasan and Fars. In 903/291 he made his second pilgrimage to Mecca; then, still preaching and writing, he embarked for India and went as far as Eastern Turkestan, on the borders of China. The year 906/294 marked his third pilgrimage to Mecca, where he dwelt for two years. We now reach the decisive turning-point of his history.

" On his return from his third pilgrimage, he returned to Bagdad *much changed*," remarks his son Hamd (P. 114). This change, however, is but the last phase of a long development. " To the strict interior, ascetic and moral discipline of Sahl al Tostarî, is added, firstly, the traditional knowledge of the orthodox Sonnah, with the *ahl-al-hadith* sufis, then particularly devoted to the Prophet, as al Makkî, al Jonayd, and Ibn Atâ.—The mystical experiences of his inner life had led al Hallâj to select among the traditions of the Sonnah those which concern more particularly the life of renunciation and fervent humility; an overflowing faith had incited him to preach in public, to his Moslem brethren and even to idolaters—to the great as to the common people—those rules of life which he had found good in his own case. But so far, his personality does not contrast strongly with the silhouettes of other traditionalists with mystical tendencies; his freedom of conduct is not unique, even the use which he makes of Greek logical concepts is paralleled in the case of two others, al Tirmidhî and al Kharrâz. One thing, perhaps, begins to mark him off clearly from the others: the unusual number of folk who betake themselves to him as to a saviour—who write letters to him wherein they address him as ' he who succours,' ' he who gives to eat,' ' he who discerns,' ' he who is rapt in God.' And parallel with this movement of profound sympathy are the numerous miracles which are attributed to him " (P. 113-114).

It is at this point that he begins at Bagdad a preaching which sends its echo far and wide. The basis of it amounts to this— a statement which was bound deeply to shock the pure traditionalists: " At the term of sanctity, at the consummation of divine union, the saint is more than a prophet charged with the fulfilment of an external mission, delegated to see to the observance of a law; the saint, having perfectly united his will to that of God, comes in all things and through all things to interpret directly the essential will of God, shares in the divine nature, is ' transformed into God ' " (P. 115-116).

" O Guide of the wandering," he cried out publicly during his last pilgrimage to Mecca, " Glorious King, I know thee transcendent, above . . . all the concepts of those who have conceived thee ! O God, thou knowest that I am powerless to offer thee the thanksgiving which is thy meed. Come then into me to thank thyself, that is the true thanksgiving ! there is no other " (P. 116).

" I have become him that I love, and he that I love has become myself !

> " We are two spirits fused in a (single) body.
> Thus, to see me, is to see Him,
> And to see Him is to see us."
>
> (Hallâj, *Tawâsin*, p. 518.)

Such is the final discovery and the last message proclaimed by the vehement preaching of al Hallâj after 295/907. He cries out in his joy at having attained, at possessing " him who is at the basis of ecstasy " (P. 117).

This preaching overturned too many theological claims, too many ambitions and human susceptibilities covered with a religious pretext, too many timidities also, sincere or interested, not to arouse keen opposition. And this opposition was moreover complicated by more or less avowed political motives.

In spite of the numerous friendships in the capital which Hallâj enjoyed, even at the Caliph's court, his adversaries resolved to have him arrested. For this was needed the authority of a lawyer accredited to the tribunal of Bagdad. The advice of two lawyers of considerable note, Ibn Sorayj and Ibn Dâwoûd, was sought. The former abstained from giving an opinion. The latter—" chief of the sect for the zâhirite rite," whose theses were incompatible with the teaching of Hallâj—gave sentence of condemnation, and violently attacking the accused, concluded " that it was lawful to put him to death " (P. 164). This took place about A.H. 297-298.

The vizier ordered Hallâj to be apprehended; but he escaped and lay hid for some time at Sûs (in Ahwâz). Discovered and arrested in A.H. 301, he underwent a first trial at Bagdad and was put in the pillory, then detained for eight years in various prisons; but this did not prevent him continuing his apostolate to his visitors, who for a long time were allowed easy access to him. In 922/309 began a second trial, which ended with his condemnation to the cruellest punishment.

II. THE CHARGES MADE AGAINST HALLÂJ

Who was right from the standpoint of Musulman orthodoxy, Hallâj or his judges ? Is not the presumption of personal sanctity which a bird's-eye view of his ascetic career imposes in his favour vitiated by any contradictory fact, demonstrable from history ?

Thanks to M. Massignon, we have plenty of material to form a judgement on this point. The rôle of " devil's advocate," indeed, was played very actively by the prosecution in the course of the two trials at Bagdad; the conduct and sayings of the accused were scrutinised in every respect without showing him any favour. In looking through the principal charges that were laid against him, we shall be able to judge whether the prayer muttered by poor Hallâj during the sittings of the court ought to be understood as a retractation of his mystical claims or merely as a praiseworthy act of penance and humility: " Praise be to thee !" he said. " There is no

THE PROBLEM OF MYSTICAL GRACE IN ISLAM

God but thou! I have done evil, I have made evil use of myself. Pardon me, therefore—for there is none but thou that pardoneth sins!" (P. 251).[5]

Two groups of imputations must clearly be thrust aside. The first comprises a few bits of gossip rendered suspect by their origin and swarming with improbabilities; they go so far as to accuse Hallâj of trickery, and even of deceit on a large scale. The prosecution made no use of such evidently calumnious charges. The second group is composed of political accusations. Hallâj was accused of taking part in the social and political movement of the Qarmates—a kind of freemasonry, universalist in religion, but interpreting the Koranic revelation from a purely philosophic and pragmatic standpoint. At the time of Hallâj's arrest, the public crier, on the orders of the police, proclaimed: " Behold the Qarmate preacher!" Whether Hallâj was or was not for a moment favourable to the political aims of this body matters little from the point of view of religious orthodoxy; for, although he was akin to them by holding a rather broad conception of the vocation of non-Muslims to salvation, his religious teaching differed radically from the rationalist symbolism of these politicians. Moreover, the charge of Qarmatism was not upheld at the trial.

A more delicate imputation is that of magic and " public miracles." For the Orientals of this epoch, who were in frequent relation with India, where the fakir's tricks abounded, the frontiers of magic and miracle must have seemed somewhat ill-defined. It does not appear that anyone was complained of for astonishing the public by the exercise of white magic; rather it was an envied privilege to possess certain preternatural powers, " to have *djinn* at one's service."

Probably Hallâj did not think differently from his contemporaries on this subject. The following story, taken from one of his hearers, is of interest, both for the frank avowal of the witness and for the reply of the miracle-worker. " I was in admiration at what al Hallâj did, and I did not cease to search out and to follow the science of the sorcerer, and I performed *nîranjîyât* (tricks of white magic) in order to discover the nature of his performances. One day I came in to him, and after saluting him, sat down for a moment. Then he said to me: ' Tâhir, make no mistake; what you see and hear is done by other folk as well as by myself; do not think that it is a supernatural power or some trickery.'—And I could see that he was speaking the truth " (P. 135-136). M. Massignon interprets as follows: The public miracles of al Hallâj, according to him, " are not conjuring tricks of which he is the sole author, but real scenes, involving several persons, whose agreement is arranged by God alone; but the tone of the story suggests that he, Hallâj, plays the part of conductor in them by commanding the *djinn* " (*ibid.*; see also the decisive evidence of Ibn Atâ. P. 134).

If Hallâj had been content with performing wonders such as the fakirs produced, or even others still more surprising—with the supposed assistance of the *djinn*, or even with the personal conviction of a special assistance from God—no one, perhaps, would have taken offence at it. But he worked his " miracles " publicly, in support of the doctrine he preached. It was in this that the fault from which the traditionalists—even the sufis—could not absolve him consisted; for according to them the last " public " miracle was the revelation of the Koran (P. 137). If " private " miracles might in strictness be admitted, it was forbidden to divulge the " secret of divine Omnipotence," at the risk of " making vain the authority of the Prophet " (P. 138).

Here we see coming to light the fundamental charge, the sole charge during the process: by taking on the rôle of miracle-worker, the accused had superimposed on the doctrinal authority of the Prophet a new doctrinal authority, directly guaranteed by God. We shall see how all the accusations resolve themselves into one; and we shall then put our finger on the terrible and inevitable conflict which Hallâj had to face.

It is with this essential charge that the half-political, half-religious accusation which motivated the whole process begun against Hallâj is connected; of usurping the divine right of the Imâm, the sole authority competent to organise public preaching and to issue rules for worship; of infringing even the transcendent domain, which God cannot share with any mortal, be he imâm or prophet; and of thus setting himself up above all spiritual and temporal authority (P. 115, 138).

And it is once more the same offence, the same sincere or pretended fear of seeing the external framework of the Islamic religion perverted, that we feel peeping out through this other imputation, to which the majority of the traditionalists subscribe: they reproach Hallâj—himself a sincere traditionalist—with having set himself free from the legal observances, and with ruining their obligatory character in the eyes of the faithful;

they had in mind the official " profession of faith," canonical prayer, the prescribed alms, fasting, and especially the pilgrimage to Mecca.

In reality, a fatal misunderstanding grew up between the tendency represented by Hallâj and that to which the majority of the Musulman community more and more rallied. " At the beginning, Islamic religion did not, generally speaking, show itself so severely restricted to ritual literalism " (P. 773). The primitive tradition allowed of, if it did not impose, a more interior and personal moral and religious life, which gave to the rites themselves their inner signification and their fundamental efficacy. We have already said that an imposing line of theologians, ascetics, and mystics piously cultivated this delicate seed which Providence had enclosed in the very origins of Islam. But the élite of the " spirituals " counted for little in comparison with the mass of believers, who shut themselves up with ever-increasing jealousy in the letter and ritual; to such an extent that, at the present day, the expression " religious life in Islam " passes, with some appearance of justice, for a synonym of " mere outward exactness in ritual " (P. 772).

" Personally al Hallâj showed himself exceptionally strict in the observance of his obligatory duties. What has to be borne in mind, and what his enemies exploited against him, is that his teaching presented the canonical rites of Islamic religion as the external signs of a common rule of life, the temporary marks of a legal discipline;[6] to be practised merely as collective processes of asceticism, having in themselves no sacramental character, not conferring grace *ipso facto*, and destined to be broken off at the consummation of the mystical union, and in Paradise " (P. 784).

We thus see where the true stumbling-block lay for the more honest of the enemies of Hallâj. That an ascetic, following a lawful tradition, should set the personal practice of a more interior and perfect life beside the practice of the law might create misunderstandings and disagreements between him and the majority of his coreligionists, and even draw persecution down upon him. These results will be the fruit of fanatical intolerance, without being at all required by the fundamental principles of Islam. But when personal religion goes so far as mystical union, the case at once takes on a general aspect and becomes insoluble; for then it is claimed to introduce, beside and above the authority of the law, the more immediate authority of God present in the soul of the contemplative. The latter is withdrawn from the law by the author of the law himself; in the name of God who dwells in and transforms him, he can speak, command, and sovereignly ordain; rather, God speaks through his mouth. How, if the transcendent reality of the mystical state be admitted, can this consequence of it be denied? But how, on the other hand, can one fail to be terrified of a consequence which would submit to private, uncontrollable, and unforeseeable inspiration, the legal and traditional institution, political or religious, which follows on the Koran? For Hallâj makes no secret of it: while quite willing to remain submissive to constituted authority, it is indeed in virtue of a wholly interior authority that he claims the right to preach, to work " miracles," and to interpret the ritual law.

The prosecution of al Hallâj—whatever may have been the immediate bearings of any particular incident—thus comes down, in the last analysis, to the valuation of this *mystical union* of which he boasted. Did his claim constitute a blasphematory usurpation of the divine transcendence, or not? If it did, his condemnation to death would have warded off a danger and prevented prescription against official orthodoxy. But it was still necessary to discover what offence in the case of Hallâj was legally punishable.

" In Islam, to ' anathematise ' a Musulman, it is not enough to prove that he professes doctrinal errors. . . . As long as he remains a practising believer, and is found in the mosques amidst other believers, it is a very difficult matter to cut him off from the City " (P. 183). Thus theological excommunications on the ground of heresy generally remained inoperative, either because they were not pronounced by the unanimous agreement of the recognised sects, or because, having relation to a point of doctrine without social or political bearings, they offered nothing of which the " secular arm " could take hold. " To outlaw Hallâj it was necessary that the general opinion of the lawyers . . . should have brought this *kâfir* (heretic) to the notice of the Islamic community; and above all to prove to the State that al Hallâj had rendered himself guilty of *zandaqah*, and must be treated as a *zindiq* " (P. 186). For *zandaqah*, a particular kind of heresy, originally related to Manichæism, was considered as a crime against public safety.

This accusation of *zandaqah*, with which it was sought during the two trials to incriminate Hallâj, had regard to an important point of his doctrine: his theory of love of God. Islam, his accusers objected, demands faith towards God and worship of him; but love for God can be only metaphorical. For real love entails reciprocity; hence a proportion between God and man; hence negation of the divine transcendence. " To adore God by love alone is the crime of the Manichæans . . . these *Zanâdiqah* adore God by *physical* love, by the magnetic attraction of iron for iron, and their particles of light desire to rejoin, like a magnet, the Focus of light from which they came " (P. 161-162).

The enemies of Hallâj claimed to discover Manichæan emanationism in his mystical theory of divine love and transforming union. This is the complaint which was juridically embodied in the first sentence of condemnation, pronounced by Ibn Dâwoûd (see above, p. 252).

What was at stake in the process, then, was from the very beginning, and remained to the end, the mystical doctrine of union with God, either as regarded principally in its ritual and social consequences; or as perfidiously coupled with Manichæan impiety; or, lastly, as directly denounced for its own sake, as a usurpation of the divine nature. " Hallâj has preached that he was God," we are assured in the process of 301, and this is formally repeated in the process of 309 (P. 257).

Did Hallâj really deny the transcendence of God ? Did he, in the exaltation of ecstasy, equal himself with God ? Many of his coreligionists thought so, both in his own day and later.

We know what a high value is attached by Musulmans to the monotheist profession of faith, the *shahâdah : There is no God but God*. Now Hallâj prohibited his disciples from " wasting their time in reciting or meditating (superstitiously) on the *shahâdah* . . . a formula imperfect in itself, which God alone, by his enlightening grace, could make us utter . . . by leading us to be conscious of the mystery of his Unity, in the very operation of his action; by making us first of all deny our self in our heart, so as afterwards to affirm himself therein by his presence. Ecstasy shows us, moreover, that the *shahâdah* is only a preliminary veil; . . . like the Law, it falls to the ground when Grace comes to consummate the union " (P. 787).

Is there anything more in this than the affirmation of a transition of the discursive consciousness—analogical and negative—into positive and transforming intuition during the state of ecstasy ?

R

Later on, Musulman writers made Hallâj a forerunner of the monism of Ibn Arabî (P. 353). And mystical poets, themselves infected with monism—such as Jelâl-ed-dîn-Rûmî, or Attâr—inserted in beautiful verses, which dissimulate their real meaning, some famous words of the martyr of Bagdad.

M. Massignon clearly shows the baselessness of the charge of monism laid to his hero. The Hallagian theory of creation is in itself a sufficient proof of orthodoxy: God creates freely and has no need of his creation; " the divine unity is attested, in the void just as it is in the plenum," Hallâj proclaims against the emanationism of Rhazi the physician. His declarations çoncerning divine transcendence are frequent and formal. We will quote only a few lines, recorded as his by another mystic, al Qoshayrî: " (God) has bound the Whole to contingency, for transcendence is his own. . . . But he, praise be to him ! may he be exalted, can have neither an *above* which surpasses him, nor a *below* which lessens him, nor a *limit* which bounds him, nor a *near* which troubles him, nor a *behind* which reproaches him, nor an *in front* which bounds him, nor a *before* which makes him appear, nor an *after* which makes him disappear, nor an *all* which concentrates him, nor an *is* which enables him to be found, nor an *is not* which takes from him. There is no attribute to describe him, his act has no cause, his being has no limit. He remains far from the states of his creation, in him there is no mingling with his creation, his act permits of no amendment, he is withdrawn from them by his transcendence, as they are withdrawn from him in their contingence." (P. 638).

Hallâj is not a monist, either in intention or in fact. Are we to see a claim to identity with God in a few subtle—how subtle !—and moving plays upon words, on I and Thou, on an exchange of personal pronouns between God and the soul ? What contemplative could submit his diction to grammatical analysis ? The mystic is stammering of the ineffable. Here also the contexts are decisive and the protestations of Hallâj explicit.

All the same, there remains one loud, disturbing exclamation which legend has inextricably associated with his name. Was it ever in fact uttered ? Possibly. In a burst of foolish pride ? Very unlikely; all the more so as this phrase, when compared with other more technical declarations, seems to be only a flashing and paradoxical reaffirmation of the transforming union itself. "*Ana' al Haqq !* I am the Truth !" he cried. We cannot resist the pleasure of transcribing, in the guise of a commentary, this fragment from a " prose poem " by Kîlanî (†1166/561): " The mind of one of the Sages took flight one day, out of its nest in the tree of the body, and rose even to heaven, where it entered among the legions of Angels. But it was but a falcon among the falcons of this world, whose eyes are hooded by the hood. ' Man was created weak.'—Now this bird had seen nought in the heaven which he might pursue, when he suddenly saw the prey—' I have seen the Lord '— and his wonder grew greater as he heard his End say to him: ' Whithersoever thou turnest, thou wilt be face to face with God.' The falcon then came down to earth again, to hide that which he had caught, a treasure rarer on earth than is fire at the bottom of the sea:—but in vain did he turn the eye of his mind this way and that—he saw only the reflected rays of the divine splendour. Then he came back again, and he could not find in the two worlds any end save his Beloved ! Joy seized him, and he cried out, translating into speech the intoxication of his heart:' *Ana' al Haqq !* I am the Truth.' He caused his chant to resound in a fashion forbidden to creatures, he chirped with joy in the Orchard of Existence, and chirping such as this befits not the children of Adam. His voice uttered a song which delivered him over to death " (P. 411-412).

Perhaps Hallâj did not, even in the excess of his ecstasy, utter the words, " *Ana' al Haqq* "; it matters little; he uttered with full consciousness words equivalent thereto. Was it the sacrilegious boldness of the impious, who stretches out his hand to the holy ark to steal the hidden treasure, or the heroic sincerity of the " seer," who bears testimony to the indwelling of the divine Spirit, knowing the while that his confession is his death-warrant ?

Clearly one's judgement as to this alternative will depend on one's judgement as to the very possibility of a *mystical union.*

In what, then, according to Hallâj, does the higher mystical state consist ?

The poetical descriptions which he gives us, both in verse and in prose—ardent or severe in their extravagance—have their equivalents in most similar works of high mysticism. Every mystic, far or near, aspires to an " immediate union " in which is to be effaced—we will not say the personality of the contemplative, but the *opposition* between that personality and the divine essence. The opposition, moreover, may be reduced either by the final annihilation of the Ego, flowing back into the Absolute (pantheistic natural mysticism), or by super-eminent transformation of the Ego into God (supernaturalist mysticism).

Let us hear Hallâj breathing forth his inflamed " desire " for perfect union:

" Between me and thee (loiters) an ' it is I ' (which) torments me. . . .

" Oh, take away, of thy goodness, this ' it is I ' from between us !" (P. 252).

And this is the desired " term ":

" Is it I ?   Is it thou ?   That would be one essence within Essence. . . .

" Far from thee, far from thee, be (the design) of affirming ' two !'

" There is a Selfness of thine (which dwells) in my nothing-ness, henceforth, for ever . . . " (P. 524).

How is this to be understood ? The difficulty, we must admit, is not peculiar to the mysticism of Hallâj. The best thing we can do is to note the subtle definitions and sharp distinctions which our mystic himself draws, when he speaks as a theologian:

" My present statute (*hokm*) is that a veil separates me from my own Ego. This veil for me precedes the vision (*kashf*); for, when the moment of the vision draws nigh, the attributes of qualification[7] are annihilated. ' I ' am then separated from my Ego; ' I ' is only the subject of the verb, not my Ego; my real ' I ' is no longer myself. I am a metaphor (*tajâwoz*) [of God transported into man], not a generic relationship (*tajânos*) [of God with man]—an appearance (*zohoûr*) [of God], not an infusion (*holoûl*) in a material receptacle. . . . My present arising is not a simple return to pre-eternity,[8] it is a reality imperceptible to the senses and beyond the reach of analogies.

" Angels and men have knowledge of this; not that they know what is the reality of this qualification,[9] but by the teachings about it which they have received, according to the capacity of each. ' Each knows the source at which he must quench his thirst ' (Kor. ii 57).

" One drinks a drug, the other imbibes the pure water; one sees only (any) human silhouette, the other sees but the Sole One, and his gaze is obscured by the qualification;[10] one wanders among the beds of the dried-up streams of research, the other is drowned in the oceans of reflection; all are outside reality, all set before themselves an end and take the wrong road.[11]

THE PROBLEM OF MYSTICAL GRACE IN ISLAM

" The familiar friends of God (on the other hand) are those who ask their way *of him*; they are annihilated, and it is he who organises their glory. They humiliate themselves, and he shows them (to the others) as guide-posts. They give themselves up to the search for the wanderers, abase their own glory, and it is they of whom the graces of God himself take hold, it is they whom he ravishes to their attribute by his own qualifications.[12]

" O wonder ! Thou sayest that they have ' arrived ' ? They are separated. Thou sayest that they are ' seers '? They are absent (rapt out of their senses). Their external features (*ashkâl*) remain apparent in them and for them, and their interior states (*ahwâl*) remain hidden in them (and from them) " (P. 521-523).

This difficult passage, vibrant in its intellectuality,[13] restrained in its power, sober in its sublimity, reminds one of Ruysbroeck the Admirable; more of him, we think, than of Plotinus.[14]

But let us listen once more to M. Massignon, whose synthetic interpretation of the texts of Hallâj borrows so exceptional an authority from his long and fervent relationship therewith. We shall not be reproached, we believe, for the length of this quotation:

" (Hallâj) proves in himself . . . that there is a supreme degree of God's presence in his creatures, which can be realised and consummated in man, without division or confusion. He declares that the mode in which this mystical union operates is transcendent, above that which is created and all of which man is worthy; a free gift of the Uncreated, . . . above all created return. He limits himself to attempting to make this union visible by means of symbols which he knows to be inadequate, but which he does his best to make coherent. In insisting upon the preliminary transformation of the purified creature, not only in his soul by the infused virtues, but in his body, penetrated and renewed by the active and sensible irradiation, *tajallî*, of grace. The carnal *nafs* of man— that slave dependent on his body—is transformed into *Roûh*, which gains the mastery over, upraises, and transfigures the body. And by always recalling that this is a gratuitous operation of divine love, due to a supernatural initiative, transcending the natural order; and realising a pre-eternal vocation, nay, more, a participation in the primordial love of God for God, the continual exchange of a proof of love ineffably conceived, between ' thee and me.'

" The ' thee and me,' the voice of love itself, in which is reciprocally conceived the real intimacy of lover and beloved, by the essential exchange of speech, in perfect equality, this is the distinctive note of the mystical poems of al Hallâj—a familiar exchange of pure, immaterial, burning endearments. God has spoken; man replies to him. Thus in the very depth of this weak and divided humanity, in this heart which, having heard and recognised it, bows to the dust, a new divine intonation is born, which mounts to the lips, more ' mine ' than myself, which replies to him: the ray received in the mirror has aroused a flame therein.

" In the long and sometimes tragic story of mystical vocations in Islam, such superhuman accents are found neither before nor afterwards; accents wherein the whole passion of love lies prostrate before the personal presence of its God, with veneration and filial abandonment. They are, in al Hallâj, the fruits of a life freed from all things by renunciations and sufferings, constantly renewed in God by prayer for the souls of others, and crowned by the passion for the unity of the Islamic community, carried so far as to the desire (which was granted) of dying anathema for its salvation. Others, after him, will no longer find this equilibrium; they will content themselves too often, after their conversion, with the isolated and sterile exercise of a single power of the soul, either a ' moyen court ' of strengthening the resolutions they have taken at the beginning, or an ' immanent sign ' letting loose a concentration of thought, or a material ' image of meditation ' provoking the recall of ecstasy. For Sohrawardî of Aleppo, Attâr, and even Ibn Arabî, the more and more crystallised and abstract conception of a perfect and pure Idea is dominant, the God of the occasionalist philosophers like Descartes and Malebranche. For Ghazzâli, it is rather the more and more categorical imperative of a sovereign commandment, the God of the determinist moralists like Asharî or Kant. For the majority of the other mystics, such as Ibn al Fârid, Jalâl Rûmi, Shâbistârî, and Nâbolosî, it is the appearance of a face of Beauty, in which the fascinated God reveals himself; the God of the æstheticians such as Leonardo da Vinci. And they do not find Him again through it.

" The love-dialogues of the later mystical poets are mere echoes beside the Hallagian cries of ecstasy " (P. 529-532).

THE PROBLEM OF MYSTICAL GRACE IN ISLAM

III. THE "METACORANIC" TENDENCIES OF HALLA-GIAN MOHAMMEDANISM

One conclusion seems to us to impose itself at once, which limits the field of the interpretations which can be put upon the "case of Hallâj." His mysticism is certainly not founded upon gross and anthropomorphic illusion; neither has it any resemblance to pantheistic and nature-mysticism; it openly claims to surpass the boldest ascensions of the human reason, and even to surpass them by the whole distance by which the humble effacement of the creature, who allows himself to be invaded and upraised by divine grace, surpasses the titanic but powerless effort of the creature who pre-sumptuously leans upon his own powers. Neither does Hallâj's good faith admit of any doubt; his life and death bear witness to the sincerity of his utterances.

But all this is not enough to guarantee the *objective reality* of his union with God. Nor even to compel anyone to affirm in this particular case its *possibility*. All the more so as a really serious preliminary question is raised not only in the Christian but in the Musulman mind. It is this: the bestowal of such exceptional favours, especially when they are publicly invoked, seems of necessity to imply an at least general divine approval of the religious attitude of the recipient; what exactly would be the bearing of this divine approval on the hypothesis that the mystical states of Hallâj were indeed what he believed them to be?

Perhaps it will not be thought superfluous in us to remark, firstly, that an *individual* religious attitude cannot be valued solely by its more or less imperfect contingent dress; its latent potentialities are at least as important, if not more so; to judge of it we must observe whither it points, must see if its normal movement tends or not to eliminate accidental dross and to fill up passing gaps. If it does so, why should not God, *in this degree*, encourage and sanction it?

We have already brought out the greater number of the tendencies characteristic of Hallâj's Mohammedanism. At the risk of repeating ourselves a little, we will take up in order those which were sufficiently proper to him to borrow some authority from the personal privileges which he claimed. In an environment in which the divine inspiration of the Koran was not even a matter of discussion, Hallâj needed not to employ particular revelations or miracles in favour of the Musulman religion as such, but only in favour of a particular manner of understanding and practising that religion.

What is especially striking in the teaching of Hallâj is his constant concern with *interior religion*, in spirit and in truth.

Hallâj not only declared himself hostile to all superstition, even tolerated (as was at that time a certain magical usage of the letters of the Koran), but he desired that the " legal " worship should be quickened by the intention of the heart. "The Truth," he used to insist, " has established two kinds of religious duties; those which concern *intermediary* things (rites), and those which concern *realities*. . . . Now the duties regarding realities imply a knowledge which comes down from God and returns to him; while the duties towards intermediary things imply a knowledge which, coming down from that which is not he, only allows of rejoining him by being raised above itself, to its annihilation " (P. 277). This must not be understood in the sense that " faith without works " suffices for salvation; the believer who dies in a state of grave sin, having kept the faith, does not escape damnation: " He is a hypocrite and an adorer of Satan " (P. 673) repeats Hallâj after Hasan Basrî. But there are other grave sins beside the violation of legal observances, there are works of devotion other than exterior works.

Asceticism of the heart is necessary for real inward religion; and the first step of this asceticism is sincere conversion: " Conversion goes before wisdom " (P. 667). Only then commences the steep ascent of the mystical ladder. Listen to an Arab theologian, an adversary of Hallâj, summing up his doctrine on this point: " He who disposes his body in obedience to ritual requirements, occupies his heart with works of piety, endures deprivation of pleasure, and possesses his soul while refusing it its desires—is thus raised to the station of *those who are near* (to God). . . . Thenceforward he does not cease gently to descend the degrees of distance, until his nature is purified of what is earthly. And then, if no bond with fleshly things remains in him any more—then there descends into him that Spirit of God whereof was born Jesus, the Son of Mary. Then he becomes him whom all things obey, he no longer wishes for aught save what puts into execution the commandment of God " (P. 515).

And the interior motive of this search after perfect union of the human with the divine will ?

Hallâj wished to know of only one: love.[15]

Love, according to him, is the true secret of our relation with God and the mainspring of all religious life.

Love considered in God himself, in the first place. We might think we were listening to an echo of " Deus caritas est " in the magnificent passage wherein God is represented, before the creation, as " Love in Solitude "—in the solitude of his infinite Essence: moved by pure generosity, this self-sufficient Love, " essence of the divine Essence," became creative Love (P. 604-607).

To the uncreated Love ought to correspond love on the part of his creature. This return of love sums up the whole of the mystical teaching of Hallâj, as we already know. The true lovers of God seek him, the Sole One, in detachment from all things and from themselves; they seek him even here on earth, even to ecstasy, if it shall please him to raise them thereto; they seek him in their future reward, which is none other than himself. The love of the true contemplative is disinterested; in the intoxication of union it is not happiness which he desires, but God: " At the base of all ecstasy, as of all action, he desires to see only *him for whom he is bound, him who casts him into ecstasy*—God, who, from ecstasy to ecstasy, ceases not to draw him nearer to himself " (P. 496).

A most chaste, disinterested love, which sees God alone in the gift received—but all the same without disdaining the gift, by an exaggeration in which pride would have a share, when that gift is God himself. A certain excess of " pure love " would be tantamount to forgetting the essential indigence of the creature; that would be the crime of Satan (according to the Koranic legend); on the lips of the condemned archangel, Hallâj places these words, which mark the summit of pride: " I serve him now more purely: . . . formerly I served him for my dowry (for my own advantage), but now I serve him for his " (P. 681-682).

The humble and fervent service of God, for his own sake, leads to the final and definitive union of Paradise. According to Hallâj, there are two kinds of elect souls: the *ordinary run* of believers, who have faithfully carried out the prescriptions of the natural law, and who enjoy only the delights of the recovered Paradise of Adam; and the beloved, the " privileged souls," to whom, beside the accidental delights of the former, falls " the unique and supernatural privilege of the beatific vision (*ro' yah*) " (P. 694). At every epoch, among the members of the Islamic community, these privileged souls, " humble, faithful, pleasing to and beloved of God " (P. 749), are to be met with.

However, far as Hallâj carried his esteem and care for inward religion, it is always with the perfectly clear intention of maintaining it on the basis of the Koranic revelation and within the traditional framework of Islam. His state of soul is at the same time simple and complex. He does not wish to destroy the law; and when he dares to build up on its basis a higher perfection, he considers himself authorised to do so by the very limitations with which Mohammed surrounded the mission of Prophet and Lawgiver. In fact, "the divine right of commanding (claimed by the Prophet) is reduced to the instructions which he knew that he had received together with the Koran, according to the *hadith*—I have received commandment to make war on men until they openly declare: *There is no God but God*; when they declare this, their blood and their goods become sacred in my sight, save in case of crime, and their judgement belongs to God alone.—Hearts are not to be searched, but only those sanctions to be brought to mind which are incurred by the outward and social traces of sin: adultery (not impure desire), deceit (not lying), detraction (not envy), and so on" (P. 721). Save for the monotheistic profession of faith—supposedly sincere—the Koranic religion does not legislate for the external forum; it is social and ritual; it leaves the " interior " to the rule of natural faith and to the wholly personal invitations of grace.

An " extrinsicist " and an " intrinsicist " principle. On the one hand, outward revelation, visible authority, tradition, rite; on the other, interior sanctity, and in the long run direct and personal revelation. Hallâj thought himself bound by both principles at once, by the letter and the spirit, by the law and by grace. But he clearly subordinates the first to the second.

This superposition of two religious planes implied, in his case as in that of some other Musulman mystics, a very curious consequence; the *universal* character of their prayer for the salvation of men. The divine mission of the " prophets," as such, is limited in space: Mohammed is not qualified to intercede in favour of Jews or Christians—to whom the Koranic law is not addressed; the latter, confined to the plane of outward religion, must remain particularist. But on the higher plane, where the barriers of the Law fall, souls are united; for the Spirit bloweth where it listeth. In principle, salvation by holiness is offered wherever the true God is revealed; interior religion cannot be other than universalist. Hallâj, in his "ecstatic prayers," will pray first of all, it is true, for the Islamic community; with the accents evoked by the impassioned attachment of St. Paul for his "brethren" in Israel; but his apostolic intention will afterwards extend to all mankind, even to infidels and idolaters (P. 758).

The apostolic spirit, universalism: these features belong to the religion of Hallâj so far as, going beyond the specifically Koranic level of exterior grace, it is based on confidence in *the initiative of a more excellent grace*, calling men to friendship with God. This grace, when access is given to it, becomes an insatiable need of sanctity; "When the Truth has laid hold of a heart," he preached at the door of a mosque, "it empties it of all that is not Itself" (P. 125). All sanctification, every mystic gift, is the work of this "prevenient grace": "I call thee," Hallâj repeats in beautiful verses, "it is thou who callest me to thee! How should I have addressed thee: 'It is thou,' if thou hadst not addressed me 'It is I'?" (P. 519, 78*).

To the peculiarities, already very significant, which we have just enumerated, must be added one which cannot leave us Christians indifferent; we mean the part allotted to *Our Lord Jesus Christ* in the mystical theology of Hallâj.

We know what a strange and exceptional brilliance adorns the brows of Jesus and his holy Mother even in the pages of the Koran—a sweet light, sifted and refracted by the interposition of many errors, but, in spite of everything, a light which has emanated from the person of the Word Incarnate. It seems that it was by favour of this pure ray, mercifully wandering in the darkness, that Hallâj, aided herein by the progressive effort of the many ascetics his predecessors, was able to approach still closer to Jesus. We drew attention above to this culminating point of the mysticism of Hallâj, remarked upon by an adversary: "When there no longer remains any carnal affection (in the ascetic), then there descends upon him that Spirit of God, of which was born Jesus, son of Mary. . . ." (P. 515). The super-eminent type of union with God, whether in the beatific vision or in the mystical union, is that union which Jesus realised in his Manhood. We should not forget, moreover, that this union of Jesus with God, described as the most sublime which can be realised in a creature, was never, in the eyes of Hallâj, an "hypostatic union" (P. 515, note 1).

In what did he make it consist ? In a very close relation to the creative *fiat*. " Moqâtil-ibn-Solaymân had observed that this description of the creative act[16] intervened (eight times) in the Koran, solely ' on the subject of Jesus and the Resurrection.' Al Hallâj seems equally to have noticed this relation. In any case, he lays it down as a principle that the only aspect whereby the divine action directs itself to the transforming union with man is: not the *lâhoût*, creative omnipotence, that sovereign predestination, whose decrees are always inaccessible and likewise terrible, whose majesty had terrified Bistâmi, and whose knowledge had fascinated Satan; nor the *roûh* whose universal activity, everywhere manifest and everywhere adorable, can only be grasped if God himself explains it; but that intelligible essential word, which is at the basis of every commandment of the divine law—that *fiat* capable of being grasped and chosen which is the principle of every created thing. The mystical union of al Hallâj comes to pass, therefore, after the very type of that which the Koran attributes to Jesus, by union with the *Kon !* the divine *fiat*, obtained by means of an increasingly close and fervent adhesion of the understanding to the commandments of God which the will loves in the first place. And the result of this permanent acceptance of the divine *fiat* is the coming into the mystic's soul of the divine Spirit, which ' issues from the commandment of my Lord,' and makes thenceforward, of each of the acts of that man, truly divine acts " (P. 520-521).

This explicitly mystical doctrine is only the specialised expression of a more general theory of interior sanctity after the imitation of Jesus; a theory merely outlined, and not developed, in the Koran; for it is connected with the supernatural realm of grace, on which Mohammed throws a few furtive lights, without claiming the right to legislate thereon.

According to Koranic theology, indeed, two great happenings open and close the cycle of creation: the Covenant, the divine election of a universal order of predestination, a , kind of anticipated Judgement, preceding the effective creation; then, at the end of time, the general Judgement. At the Covenant, God proposes to the adoration of the Angels *humanity* as such, according to its complete predestination—that is to say, up to deified humanity inclusively. Now, according to Hallâj, interpreting the Koran, the " form (of deified humanity), assumed by the divine word anterior to all creation . . . is figured, at the Covenant, by Adam, and personified, at the

Judgement, by Jesus " (P. 601). Adam, we may say, was only the prefigurement of a universal essence (of humanity, with all its " obediential power "), Jesus is its realised ideal, its absolutely perfect personification.

This is why, after the general resurrection, at the supreme assizes of humanity, Jesus will return to earth in his capacity of Judge; or rather—for it is God alone who, in the last analysis, judges—the enlightening presence of Jesus, the complete type of the sanctity predestined for man, will have only to " shine forth " in order itself to become, by the evidence of contrast or likeness, the judgement that is awarded on souls; " God," says Hallâj, " will reunite the sanctified spirits, when Jesus returns to earth. There will be a throne placed for him on earth, and a throne placed for him in heaven. God, who has written a book containing the definitive Prayer, Tithes, Fasting, and Pilgrimage, will give him back this book by the hands of the Herald of the Angels, saying: ' Shine forth, in the Name of the eternal King!' " (P. 684-685).

Thus then—as we must note here—the choice of Jesus as universal Judge, according to Hallâj and several theologians who preceded him, is exclusively due to the permanent proximity of God, to his mystical holiness. The respective missions of the Prophet and the Saint are clearly distinguished (with a distinction which likewise has its roots in the Koran itself): " The prophets are warners, charged to make known the Law in decisive fashion, by proclaiming its authority over those for whom God destines it. The Koran clearly indicates that this eminent mission with which they are invested does not guarantee them against private failings, since it relates the weaknesses of some of them, nor even against the rebukes of God, whose open reprimands are directed against them, notably Mohammed " (P. 736).

But evidently the prophetic function, which does not include personal holiness, does not exclude it either. Soon enough the ascetics sought, in the examples of the great prophets—Abraham, Moses, Mohammed—the elements of a ladder of sanctity—that is to say, of a method of ascent towards the vision of God (cf. P. 741). In the eyes of Hallâj, however, the prophets are not, properly speaking, " types of increasing sanctification," but "simple prefigurements of the vision, more and more transparent " (P. 742). Mohammed himself, the latest comer among the prophets, did not attain to full union. " By a special grace,[17] he was suspended at the extreme horizon of the created; and his gaze, detached for a moment from creatures, . . . plunged directly into an immense, incomprehensible Essence, which he was obliged to confess himself incapable of worthily praising. This simple and negative vision finally purified his faith . . . (but) without uniting him to God, since his mission was to preach the *Madloûl*, the Judge who isolates divinity from creatures, not the Spirit which unites humanity with God " (after Hallâj, P. 743-744).

In the field of action of the unifying Spirit—that is to say, in the domain of interior sanctity—Jesus possesses, then, a universal and absolute pre-eminence. Not as legislator, but —better than that—as the one chosen by d.vine predilection and as an incomparable exemplar. Thus, before the time of Hallâj, " Mohâsibî, Jonayd, and their school meditated on the example of Jesus, ' the imâm of ascetics,' . . . and affirmed the necessity (in order to have access like him to sanctity), of an increasing abnegation, even to death."

But, to the extent that interior sanctity carries the day as compared with legal sanctity—which it presupposes among those who are subject to the Law—the " saint " as such excels the " prophet," Jesus Mohammed. This exaltation of Jesus, so bitterly combated by the schools attached to the prerogatives of external Islam, was professed even outside the immediate circle of Hallâj. Before him, for example, Tirmidhî (see above, p. 251) had opposed to Mohammed, " the seal of the prophets," Jesus, " the seal of the saints " (P. 753). After Hallâj, the same subordination of the providential rôles was formally taught, among others, by Ibn Arabî (1240/638), who distinguishes the " seal of the prophetical office " from the " seal of sanctity," and divides the " seal of sanctity " into the " seal of absolute sanctity " (Jesus) and the " seal of Mohammedan sanctity " (the Mahdi).

By the imitators of this sanctity, says Hallâj, the Islamic community is " quickened "; it " would perish of thirst without these divine springs " which are " the saints of God, by whom the earth is enlightened, for they are . . . the brightnesses of God, the places of his attestations . . . " (P. 754). This doctrine later became complicated, and led to deviation: with our mystic it still retains all its clearness.

If it be thought that Hallâj suffered the final punishment in order to testify to the prerogatives of " inner sanctity " understood as we have just explained it, a high symbolical value will be found in that prayer which an ancient legend attributes to

THE PROBLEM OF MYSTICAL GRACE IN ISLAM

him: " O God, accustom my heart to submit itself to thee, cut off from my mind all that is not of thee, teach me thy supreme Name, grant me what thou permittest and take from me what thou forbiddest, give me that of which none hath care, by the truth of (*the revelation made to Mohammed*), and cause me to die a martyr (*of the mission given to Jesus*) " (P. 420).[18]

IV. THE INTERIOR CONFLICT

The revelation of Mohammed, the mission of Jesus; the extrinsicism of the Koranic law, the intrinsicism of Grace; to these two poles of his religious life, Hallâj clung passionately. But how difficult was their combination in practice !

What did Hallâj claim ? Not, as has been charged against him, to correct or even to revive the Koran, which he believed to be a divine revelation—but to check, in accordance with the illuminations of his mystical life, the *human tradition* that issues from the Koran; in short, to interpret this latter in such a manner as to put it in harmony with the imprescriptible requirements of interior religion. Neither more nor less. Of necessity he had to come up against—not the Prophet directly, but the legitimate social successors of the Prophet, represented by the consensus of doctors, jurists, and constituted authorities; not the Koranic law, but the successive interpretation of that law in the bosom of the visible community. Now, does not the same Koranic revelation, which opens to him the freedom of the inner life and suggests to him docility to grace, tie him to historic Islam and to the framework of tradition which alone holds it together ?

In the measure that his dogmatic and mystical theology matured, the alternative seemed to him more distressing, because more inevitable. In the collection of his " ecstatic prayers," certain texts " show him, in the fulness of ecstatic union, becoming conscious, with anguish, of the conflict of the Islamic law with the mystical graces " (P. 758).

In reality the conflict went beyond the person of Hallâj. For he " was the representative *par excellence*, and his case of conscience the typical case, of the intellectual and moral crisis which the traditionalist milieu, that faithful memory and fervent heart of the Islamic community, was at that moment undergoing " (P. 28). A poignant symbol, which will always be comprehended with a sympathetic instinct by many sincere souls, more or less conscious of the same interior struggle.

" Since the last adherents of the sect founded by al Hallâj have disappeared since the fifth (eleventh) century," asks M. Massignon, " since the matter of his condemnation has been settled since 309/922, how does it come about that the ' Hallâj question ' is even to-day presented, before the consciences of Moslems, in individual cases, in its full keenness ? How does it happen that the matter has not yet been ' pigeon-holed,' as in the case of so many other heresiarchs who were more or less cruelly put to death ? We are here faced with a most unexpected phenomenon of history; the tenacious survival, in the Musulman memory, of a strong moral personality, distorted in vain by the coalition of the political power and the chiefs of religion, and honoured as a source of poetry, as a type of beauty and love by popular legend and scholarly literature " (P. 357-358).

The case of Hallâj remains presented to the Musulman conscience as the striking expression of a religious antinomy inherent in Islam.

The Koran had opened the crisis in its own day. It did not solve it, and could not solve it. Why this powerlessness ? Because the religious and social institution which it established is devoid of a living doctrinal authority, with power over the internal forum—and of " sacraments " in the proper sense, rites conferring grace. To reserve, above the Law, an intangible domain of interior Grace, where the divine spirit bloweth as it listeth, was, on the part of Mohammed, an act of religious sincerity—which we ought to be able to appreciate—but also, humanly speaking, a grave oversight. In the religion whereof he constituted himself the spokesman, he introduced a dangerous dualism, which sooner or later was bound to be a source of hesitations and conflicts.

In fact, in spite of the general belief in the divine inspiration of the Koran, the Islamic community, like every earthly society, had to encounter the dangers incurred by the traditional elaboration of the primitive data and the contingent exercise of a visible authority. We say the dangers, for tradition, to the extent that it went beyond the teaching of the Prophet, presented only a human value, and the visible authority, even while legitimate and necessary, was not infallible; both, left by Mohammed outside the permanent effusion of the Spirit, remained subject to deviation. Therefore, by what right could either be opposed to the immediate imperatives promulgated in the souls of the " saints," the

THE PROBLEM OF MYSTICAL GRACE IN ISLAM

" friends of God " ? There were, indeed, in Musulman dogma, attempts at reconciliation; they failed before the crude fact of the irremediable divergences in doctrinal interpretation and the all-too-human vicissitudes in the transmission or exercise of power. To the antinomy of personal inspiration and the exterior law, there is in Islam no *objective and universal* solution.

Do we not find this essential failing admitted in the very attitude of the majority of the sufis ? As soon as they saw themselves persecuted by the lawyers and the constituted authorities, many of them took refuge in the specious distinction between public and external religion and private and esoteric religion. This regrettable but excusable duplicity was a kind of compromise which deceived no one. They laboured to justify it theoretically: " The reality of sufism," they said, " has a twofold aspect: the external (objective) one of ambiguity, and the internal (subjective) one of sanctification " (related by al Baghdâdî, P. 362). For " to divulge the secret of divine Omnipotence is an impiety " (P. 370, 362, etc.). In the eyes of certain sufis, whose fleeting subtleties had nothing heroic about them, this " impiety " was above all an " imprudence "; but the very doctrine of mystical esotericism, so widespread in Islam, rests on a more serious principle, which might be defended in quite good faith; we mean on the at least confused consciousness that the mixture of interior with legal religion would dislocate the historic framework of Islam. To discover the " secret of the King " was perhaps not blameworthy; to reveal it was to sin against the Community of believers.

This conflict between the two principles—extrinsicist and intrinsicist—of the religious life must have been very deep, for the great theologian of Islam, al Ghâzali (1111/505) attempted in vain to solve it. Like the sufis contemporary with Hallâj, he reproaches the latter not with a doctrinal error, still less with trickery, but with over-boldness in having published private revelations; " in having disclosed an esoteric truth " (P. 370). In the end, he dares blame neither the martyr nor his judges: "Al Hallâj," he said, " was in the right, but those who condemned him did well." " This," remarks M. Massignon, " is the unhealthy theory of the two truths, too often employed in Islam with regard to sanctity " (P. 371).

Perhaps this " unhealthy " thesis reveals, here, not so much a mental perversion as an unsolvable difficulty of conscience. For an upright, sane, and austerely sensible character, such as

Hallâj, the crisis of conscience was a daily anguish and torment; until at last there opened before his eyes, with growing clearness, the perspective of a personal solution—the only possible solution; not a doctrinal and objective solution, for the antinomy subsisted after him, but a *subjective and heroic* solution.

There was brought to him, unknown to him, by his mystical doctrine of suffering, a proof of love. Outlined by Jonayd, this " science of suffering " blossomed fully in Ibn Atâ and Hallâj. " When God loves his servant, said the former, he tries him; and when he loves him more, he lays hold of him, leaving him neither goods nor child " (P. 618).—And the second, choosing trial for his lot upon earth, cries out: " Suffering is himself—while happiness comes *from* him " (P. 622). Hallâj knows that the love of God is a consuming fire which allows nothing of self-love to subsist; to this exacting flame he wishes to give himself up without reserve, even to annihilation and death—the dawn of the final union. He thus habituated himself to include the complete sacrifice of himself in the providential line of his mystical degrees.

At the same time was increased in him the feeling of soul-crisis which wrought in the best among his companions in religion. On the one side, has devotion to the Islamic community exalted him so far as to make him cry out in public his desire to " die anathema for the salvation of all " (P. 758). On the other hand, he could not stifle the voice of the Beloved, the Sole One, which filled his soul, and claimed from him a public testimony of love. A possible conciliation of the homage which he owed to God, the source of legal authority, with the absolute docility claimed by the Spirit of God, whose incomparable presence he felt, seems to have clearly appeared to him during the last years of his life: To obey the Spirit and to proclaim the gift of God, even to an at least apparent breach of the external law; at the same time, to obey the external law, by voluntarily submitting to its supreme sanctions, as a striking reparation offered to the Islamic community.

These were not for him vain speculations; he really saw the horizon darken, " he foresaw his eventual punishment; and, faithful to his doctrine of sanctification by suffering, he conceives and manifests the desire therefor, in increasing degree; not only so as to be united to God in death, but also from respect and recognition for his law; he demands to die, immolated thereby in sacrifice, like the legal victims, . . . thus making his respect for the Islamic community the decisive proof of that love which he bears towards all Musulman souls; happy to die by the hand of those whom he desires to save."

" Folk go in pilgrimage," (he sings, in a verse which tradition attributes to him)—" as for me, I go on pilgrimage towards the Friend who dwells within me."

" They bring lambs for sacrifice—as for me, I bring my veins and my blood " (P. 278).

Once more, alluding to his bold preaching, he said: " All contingent creatures utter only the contingent; if therefore I speak according to the absolute, they will forbid me, they will accuse me of capital sins, and will seek to have me put to death. But for that they are excused; and for all that they shall do to me they shall have their recompense " (P. 761).

On the day of his last torture, " arriving before the gallows, he prays thus: ' . . . Behold these folk thy worshippers; they have met together to slay me, out of zeal for thee, in order to please thee; pardon them ! If thou hadst revealed to them what thou hast revealed to me, and hadst hidden from me what thou hast hidden from them, I should not be suffering the trial that I am suffering ' (P. 763). Placed on the cross, Hallâj felt himself gripped by the anguish of abandonment; but, at the supreme moment, he utters the triumphant cry, his own solution—fearsome pride or magnificent love: ' What does the ecstatic desire ? the solitude of the Sole One, alone with Himself !' " (P. 764).

These sublime and disconcerting traits, the common nucleus of many traditions going back to his contemporaries, are perfectly authentic. " There is no question here," remarks M. Massignon, " of legends embellished at a later date; it is the direct impression produced on his immediate disciples by his martyrdom, that which made them think and which they dared not publish at once " (P. 764).

Legend, however, very soon lays hold of so exceptional a life, and one crowned by so dramatic an end. It throws into relief, often in a moving fashion, the lasting significance of the punishment of Hallâj; for example, in that supposed apostrophe of Jonayd to his former disciple: " Thou hast made a breach in Islam,[19] which only thy head can fill."

In conclusion, we would bring out another trait, confirmed by legend. Ought there not to be some resemblance between the divine Passion of Christ and the tragic Passion of him who wished to die " a martyr for the (mystical) mission of Jesus " ? For it is " by meditating on the example of the Koranic Christ that Hallâj had defined the sanctity [for which he died] as a permanent union with the divine *fiat* " (P. 769). The generation which had known him seized on and noted the resemblance; the generations that followed added to it. If the Hallâj of Musulman legend were compared, not without occasional indiscretion, to the divine Crucified, it is because the Hallâj of history really bore—without knowing the whole cost—some of the stigmata of the suffering Christ. M. Massignon, with patient and pious erudition, has brought them to light once more: " Through the disjointed lineaments of this biography, traced, thanks to the unconscious curiosity of the annalists, to the blind passion of adversaries or partisans, rise the elements of a real conformity, a configuration with Christ. This typical effigy of the Koranic Jesus coined by legendary history—this ideal symbol of martyrdom conformed to the Christology of Sufism—al Hallâj is animated for the observer like a strangely living image of the real Christ, as we know him " (P. 771).

V. CONCLUSIONS

Let us place ourselves definitely this time at the point of view of Catholic theology.

For the Christian, who knows, from the Holy Scriptures, from Tradition, and also, up to a certain point, from inner experience, something of the divine charity of our Saviour, it would be hard to imagine that an even distant appeal to Jesus could be repulsed by him, or that an imperfect but sincere homage to him could remain without response. What really took place in the consciousness of Hallâj ? That is the secret of God, which no historian or psychologist will ever penetrate with certainty. None the less, to the extent that it is permissible from external indications to conjecture invisible realities—*ex fructibus dignoscetis*—it seems that the " martyr-mystic of Islam," by his heroic fidelity in embracing that partial truth which filtered down to him, must have drawn upon himself the merciful predilection of that Jesus who is not only the human masterpiece of divine grace, as Hallâj believed, but " the Author and Finisher " of that grace.

Moreover, from the point of view of theology, what concerns us is not so much the historic *reality* as the very *possibility* of the graces with which Hallâj, a sincere Musulman, believed himself favoured.

That God can grant particular revelations and mystical gifts, even in a very eminent degree, to " negative infidels," who are kept outside the visible body of the Church by " invincible ignorance," is not a matter of doubt, according to the commonly received teaching. And we are speaking of graces super-natural in the strict sense. Already St Thomas, fearing to render the " universal vocation to salvation " an illusion, admitted the hypothesis of a means of approach to the faith, not only " *ex auditu*," which is the normal way, but by a personal and miraculous revelation.

Hallâj, then, *could* receive real mystical favours and find in them the elements of an " act of strict faith," the first step towards supernatural justification—" *initium salutis.*"

Must we suppose that the light of this act of faith disclosed to him the entire error of the religion of Islam ? By no means. If it seems certain that an act of supernatural faith contains the virtual and implicit rectification of all religious error, these implicit consequences do not necessarily become fully conscious to the believer. The domain of " implicit faith " may remain very wide with a sincere believer. What is true, on the other hand, is that the act of faith, an adhesion to the strict super-natural, would be incompatible with the profession of a religious doctrine which formally excluded the supernatural; but this is not the case with the Musulman religion as Hallâj under-stood it.

However, the religious attitude of the mystic of Bagdad is more complex. Two special features in it merit our attention: (1) Hallâj invokes his mystical graces (and, to a subsidiary degree, certain " miracles," real or supposed) *in support of his preaching*; (2) the mystical union is considered by Hallâj as the episodical crowning *of a more fundamental state* of close " friendship " with God, of " sanctity " founded on habitual grace. The problem of faith and justification is posed in his case, before the arrival of the miraculous revelations.

The apologetic use to which Hallâj deliberately put his mystical gifts ought, assuredly, to render them suspect to us, if he had sought in them a divine attestation in favour of Mohammedanism, in opposition to Christianity. But the case is perhaps otherwise, if, outside a comparison of which neither himself nor his hearers could have dreamed, the teaching of the mystical thaumaturgist was concerned only with safeguarding, before a more and more material and terrestrial Islam, the rights of an interior life, a life wholly of moral sincerity and love of God. God could, it seems, sanction this preaching, the effect whereof was to keep open, in the very edifice founded on the Koran, a door towards supernatural faith, and consequently to safeguard the individual possibility of salvation for Musulmans of good will. Undoubtedly, God could always force the doors, and save by miracle. But the ordinary conduct of Providence is to borrow in a large measure, for its higher action, the path of natural causalities. God, who acts gently and knows how to draw good even out of evil, does not, if one may so say, practise the policy of the worse, nor stage-tricks; if he has truly permitted that there should subsist in the Koran and in a notable part of Musulman tradition germs of a higher truth and props for the interior action of grace, the preaching and example of Hallâj take on a very clear meaning.

This last consideration brings us to a second aspect which we point out in the religious life of al Hallâj. Independently of all mystical revelation, he could find, in the teachings of the Koran, which he believed to be inspired by God, much more than the minimum content required for an act of " strict faith." We recall the essential articles of the Hallagian creed: A unique and transcendent God, the generous rewarder; a supernatural destiny, surpassing the " paradise of Adam," and extending even to an immediate possession of the divine Essence; a destiny rendered possible only by the initiative of a quite special grace, a grace of benevolent love, infinitely superior to the Mohammedan idea of grace; lastly, the knowledge and veneration of Jesus, as a model of sanctity, the perfect type of union with God and Prince of the spiritual kingdom of Grace. These dogmatic data, Hallâj borrows from the Koranic tradition; but whence did the Koran itself derive the first outlines of them, except from Jewish and Christian tradition ? An error as to the authentic intermediary of the revelation does not render faith in God the revealer impossible. Before the revealed truth—partial, doubtless, but already very enlightening—which the Prophet of his race transmitted to him, what did Hallâj need in order to make an act of supernatural faith ? Nothing save the illuminating, wholly interior motion, which should put his soul in perfect consonance with the supernatural truth revealed; the " grace of faith," which God does not refuse to any upright soul to whom the object of faith is proposed.

Perhaps other cases, more difficult than that of Hallâj, more difficult than that of Islamism in general, might be resolved on the same principles.

A last remark is suggested to us by certain very real preoccupations of present-day Catholic life, where zeal for mission work among infidels appeals more and more to the help of a " science of missions."

Although M. Massignon scrupulously confines himself to the domain of Oriental philology and religious history, his studies of Musulman mysticism, by opening out unexpected and very general perspectives on the ways and means of supernatural Providence, suggest—discreetly, and between the lines —a possible improvement in our methods of apostolate in relation to those great organised religions, such as Mohammedanism (why, *mutatis mutandis*, should we not add Hinduism and Buddhism ?) which so far seem hermetically sealed against Christian influence. Would it not be worth the trouble to seek, more attentively than ever, with exact science and wholly evangelic charity, for the " stepping-stones " which God has probably provided by his grace in these vast religious milieux ? So that a Musulman (or Hindu) of good faith, invited to enter the true home of the common Father, should not have the impression that he is being called upon to deny his race and traditions and to dwell in a strange house ? How many barriers would fall of themselves, if he could foresee in the Christian faith not a harsh rupture with the past, but the unfolding, the higher comprehension, the unhoped-for arrival of all the good that his ancestors obscurely desired.

Would it be overbold to suppose that M. Massignon—since he recalls, in his dedication, the holy memory of Fr. Charles de Foucauld, the hermit of the Sahara, apostle and victim of the Bedouins—has more than once, while writing so many learned pages, given thought to the actual problems of the apostolate, which those pages impose so strongly on our attention, though no formal mention of them is made ?

NOTES

[1] After the data, almost all unpublished, supplied by M. Louis Massignon, in the following publications: (1) *La passion d'al Hosayn-ibn-Mansoûr al Hallâj, martyr mystique de l'Islam*, 2 vols. of xxxi +942 + 105 pages (continuous pagination), Paris, Geuthner, 1922. This work is indicated by the letter " P." (2) *Essai sur les origines du lexique technique de la mystique musulmane*, 1 vol. of 302 pages +104 pages of Arabic text, Paris, Geuthner, 1922; this work, a precious complement to the preceding, is indicated by the letter " E." See also: Al-Hallâj. *Kitab al Tawâsin*, Paris, Geuthner, 1913, and *Quatre textes inédits relatifs à al-Hallâj*, Paris, Geuthner, 1914. M. Massignon announces the forthcoming publication of the " poetic

Diwan " of al-Hallâj. Since the present writer is not an Arabic scholar—which will dispense him from complicating the printer's task by the use of diacritical marks and other phonetic symbols—he can only suspect what immense labour M. Massignon has undertaken in unravelling the story of Hallâj. Others more competent than myself —*e.g.*, Père Lammens, in the *Recherches de science religieuse*, or Mr. Nicholson, in the article " Hallâj " in the *Encyclopædia of Religion and Ethics*, have rendered homage to the exceptional merit of this Orientalist, who, during long sojourns in the East—at Constantinople, in Mesopotamia, Syria, Palestine, Egypt—succeeded not only in tapping the least accessible MS. sources, but (a more difficult task, it would seem) in penetrating the depths of the Arab soul, and even sympathetically grasping the rhythm of its life.

² This caused indignation in the Imâmites, earthly sanctity seeming to them the " aristocratic privilege " of the *imâms* of the line of Ali, and not the effect of an actual grace of God freely choosing its beneficiaries (E. 173, P. 157).

³ M. Massignon also points out the deviations, sometimes very grave, which the mystical tendency in some cases underwent: illusions and excesses condemned by the most authoritative of the " spirituals," and particularly by those who represent, so to speak, the mystical ascendancy of Hallâj.

⁴ We use this word *sufism* in a generic sense, to indicate, among Musulmans, every public profession of asceticism or mysticism, individual or social.

⁵ In truth, this is only a formula of contrition, which is found elsewhere in almost identical form, and is derived from that which the Koran attributes to Jonah (P. 251, note 1; 76*).

⁶ " The rites of worship are not the essentials of religion, but its means; they are instruments which God gives us in order to reach realities " (after Hallâj, P. 772).

⁷ That is to say, the attributes which define the natural " Ego."

⁸ That is to say, if we understand rightly: is not only an intuitive return to my essence, as it existed from eternity in the designs of the Creator, who " predetermined " it to me. . . .

⁹ The mystery of this operation (note of M. Massignon).

¹⁰ By the attributes according to which he still seeks to express God, the Ineffable, the Separate.

¹¹ *All:* because, in a more or less refined manner, they still refer the vision, in which mystical union consists, to a natural operation of the created mind: imagination, abstraction, definition. . . . In the true mystical state, man is, according to the pseudo-Areopagite's expression, " *patiens divina*," undergoing the initiatives of grace.

¹² The equivalent of the " transforming union " of the Christian mystics.

¹³ " There is no Arab mystic whose language of love is at the same time more ardent and more chaste than that of al-Hallâj; no transposition of the symbols of profane love troubles its flight " (P. 117).

¹⁴ A friend, who knows the work of Ruysbroeck thoroughly, confirms our impression, and is good enough to point out to us, among other texts which have the same note as those of Hallâj, a " remarkable equivalent " in the *Book of the Twelve Béguines* of the Flemish mystic (French edition of David, pp. 141-42).

[15] We must understand love in its greatest, and, so to say, most intellectual, aspect; for Hallâj shows himself unceasingly hostile to all dubious sentimentality and to every more or less sensual deviation.

[16] In which the Koran distinguishes: the eternal *decree* of divine Omnipotence; the effective *commandment* or *fiat*; the *becoming* created.

[17] In the course of the visions related in the Koran.

[18] In the parentheses we replace the symbolic initials of suras 42 and 19 of the Koran by the traditional signification which they here bear, according to M. Massignon (P. 420, notes 1 and 2).

[19] By violating the secret of Sufi esotericism.

REFLECTIONS ON THE COMPARATIVE STUDY OF MYSTICISM

PREAMBLE.

1. A Problem.
2. An Obstacle to be Avoided.
3. The Elementary Factors of Mysticism.

I. DOCTRINAL ELEMENTS.

1. The Lower Forms of Metaphysics.
2. The Inevitable Problems of Metaphysics.
3. Dualistic and Pessimist Systems.
4. Pantheistic Monism.
5. Monotheism and the Possibility of a Supernatural Mysticism.

II. PSYCHOLOGICAL ELEMENTS.

III. CONFRONTATION OF DOCTRINE AND EXPERIENCE.

1. The Physical Trance.
2. Buddhist Negativism.
3. The Yoga of Patanjali.
4. Difference of Psychological Attitude between Eastern and Western Mystics.
5. Musulman Asceticism and Mysticism.
6. Christian Asceticism and Mysticism.

CONCLUSIONS.

NOTES.

REFLECTIONS ON THE COMPARATIVE STUDY
OF MYSTICISM[1]

PREAMBLE

1. A PROBLEM

W HETHER we like it or not, the facts of Mysticism are very largely included to-day in the field of investigation of men of science, particularly of psychologists who profess to regard their phenomenal aspect only, abstraction being made of any metaphysical or theological " value " they may have. We shall deliberately place ourselves in the following remarks on Comparative Mysticism at the point of view of these investigators—that is to say, we shall quote systems of metaphysics and theology solely *ad narrandum*, as psychological factors only, without pronouncing on their truth. This limitation of the field of investigation adopted on methodic grounds is not, in our opinion, the most natural or the surest way of approaching the subject; but it is the only one in which the majority of *mysticologues*, so divided by their philosophic opinions and beliefs, have the faintest chance of meeting in the common recognition of evidence.

The comparative psychology of mysticism, treated as a positive science, encounters the same perils as the comparative study of religious phenomena in general. In both cases there is great difficulty in not inadvertently substituting subjective appreciation for objective description, judgements of value for judgements of fact. This difficulty lies in wait for psychology from the moment when the choice of a nominal definition of religion or of mysticism compels it to delimit the field of its investigations. It pursues it throughout the observation of facts and the criticism of documents. It becomes still more urgent when, in accordance with the habitual method of the positive sciences, it seeks to pass from the static and classificatory to the genetic and causal point of view.

We point out elsewhere what general reservations are called for in the application to religious psychology of the methods of empirical science.[2] Here we confine ourselves to a narrower field, and, starting with a few commonplace data within the reach of every educated person and independent of all particular credal connection, seek only to bring to light a small number of principles, which, on any hypothesis, govern the working out of a comparative mysticism.

The phenomena usually called mystical offer, over a long period of time and in the most diverse surroundings, analogies with and dissemblances from one another which are equally noteworthy. If an attempt is to be made to construct a comparative psychology of mysticism, both resemblances and differences must be observed without prejudice, classified with exactitude, and, so far as is possible, receive a coherent and synthetic explanation. Our task will be, not to give this explanation in detail, but to bring to light the primary conditions implied in its possibility.

2. An Obstacle to be Avoided

" Mysticism "—what does it mean ?

The difficulty of finding for the words " religion " and " Mysticism " a definition *per genus et differentiam*, which pays full regard to the current usage of these words, has often been emphasised. And this is surely no matter for astonishment, since current speech is based upon outward analogies which do not of necessity cover homogeneous realities; the majority of the words in a dictionary possess, besides their proper and basic meanings, a gamut of derived meanings, complicated again by purely metaphorical significations.

From this remark, worthy of M. de la Palisse, we immediately draw an equally evident consequence. In order to define the basic reality expressed in the various senses of a word, no more fallacious and anti-psychological method can be imagined than to wish at any cost to extract the unambiguous residue left by the word's usual significations, after the differences have been eliminated—somewhat as one extracts the highest common factor of several numbers. Try, for example, by such a process to determine the common reality or physical affinity latent in a " phonema " as common as the noun " dog," which may mean either a quadruped, a shark, a constellation, or an article of furniture, and heaven knows what else. It is clear that the various acceptations of the word are connected by a very lax law of analogy, not by one of univocality.

Is it not the same with the word " mystic "?

COMPARATIVE STUDY OF MYSTICISM

An attempt is being made, let us suppose, to define the essential basis of mysticism. Nothing, in the eyes of some psychologists, could be more simple. Under the label " mysticism," taken in the widest sense that language allows, will be ranged in a descending series—Christian ecstasy, the yogi *Samâdhi*, the orgiastic exaltation of ancient paganism, the ritual trance evoked among certain savage races by frantic dances or the use of stupefying agents, sometimes even the cataleptic crises and the so-called religious hallucinations of hysterical subjects; since all these are " mystic " by definition, the lowest term of the series ought to include in itself the essential kernel of the mystical state; and it is this kernel which will be met with, under accidental varieties, in the other terms. If we stick close by our initial sophistry to the end, we arrive, not without some astonishment, at these extraordinary propositions, which anyone may have read in some book or other published in recent years : that Christ, considered as a " mystic," differs only in degree and manner from a delirious megalomaniac; or again, that the raptures of a St Teresa are to be found in germ in the visions of the hashish-smoker, or the religious intoxication of the animist medicine man, and so on.

It is clear that we cannot allow ourselves to be thus fettered at our starting-point by narrow and logically intolerable prejudices; confusion between a simple law of analogy and a law of univocality can no more be admitted in religious psychology than in the other sciences.

We must be on our guard, therefore, against supposing that the attribution of the word " mystical " to various groups of facts is a peremptory indication of the presence in them of a single, specifically " mystical " reality.

On the other hand, we willingly recognise at once that the homonymies of ordinary speech constitute a problem to this extent, that they indicate at least an analogy, a partial similarity between the homonymous objects. They may therefore be used to delimit provisionally the scope of a comparative science. Provisionally, I say, for a comparative science can only be *definitely* based on " homologies," not on " analogies."

STUDIES IN THE PSYCHOLOGY OF THE MYSTICS

3. The Elementary Factors of Mysticism

Whatever the rigorous scientific definition of the word " religion " may be, it will not be disputed that the religious attitude always includes in some degree the theoretical and practical recognition of a personal relation to a more or less transcendent and doctrinally defined object; every religious attitude is, therefore, in a certain sense, a religious experience; at least the experimental living of a doctrine. Hence we may designate as " mystical," in a given environment, a religious experience which is esteemed as superior to the normal: more direct, more intimate or more rare.

This summary idea, which we shall define a little more closely as we proceed, is enough for us at the start, for it already enables us to discern in all mysticism three fundamental elements.

(1) A religious *doctrine*—rational or revealed—which is always, in the last analysis, a metempirical doctrine, relative to the Absolute or to the relations of the universe to the Absolute.

(2) Certain psychological *facts* of actual experience, that are relatively rare or even entirely exceptional, and susceptible of a religious interpretation.

(3) A *synthesis* of the two foregoing elements—that is, an interpretation, arbitrary or necessary, mediate or immediate, of the psychological facts as a function of the doctrine. Thanks to this interpretation, the bare psychological fact becomes a " mystical fact " properly so called, a privileged portion of religious experience.

We do not lay it down *a priori* that the doctrinal significance of the facts, which is required for the threshold of mysticism to be passed, must be always mediate or immediate, or even sometimes one, sometimes the other. How, indeed, are we to know in advance whether the idea of a transcendental experience which carries its doctrinal content in itself is necessarily a chimera ? Or again, whether a doctrine which imposes itself on our belief, independently of any mystical revelation, cannot permit us to attribute *a priori* a mystical value to certain interior facts whose empirical characters, taken by themselves, do not radically distinguish them from commonplace psychological facts ? Or lastly, how can we know whether the juxtaposition of a metaphysical or religious doctrine with an extraordinary experience, cannot sometimes of itself, by virtue of the light they mutually shed on each other, guarantee at the same time both the psychological expression of the former and the transcendental significance of the latter ?

On the threshold of a comparative mysticism, it is convenient to leave these questions open.

Now that we possess a collection of *elementary factors* essential to all mysticism (whatever the real value of the latter may be), it is enough to attempt to combine them in various ways in order to compile the catalogue of the possible forms of mysticism both speculative and practical.

Let us examine these factors separately.

I. DOCTRINAL ELEMENTS

First, *the doctrinal factors* which can govern a mysticism. After having considered them as metaphysical doctrines, we will introduce the hypothesis of a supernatural revelation.

Metaphysics is by right, like truth itself, unique. But in fact the metaphysical systems hatched in the course of history are as manifold as are the chances of error on the part of human reason; they range themselves in greater or less proximity to that ideal, a unique metaphysic.

1. THE LOWER FORMS OF METAPHYSICS

Among the forms of metaphysics so arranged, some are inferior, the first stammerings of a thought which has not yet freed its internal unity from the plurality of the senses. Such, for example, is animism, which introduces behind the world of outward experience an unsubdued multiplicity of metempirical objects, an innumerable crowd of " souls."

A rudimentary mysticism may already be built up on such poor data as these. With the mysterious objects of his cultus the medicine man, the sorcerer, the ignorant devotee will associate the mystery of certain subjective states that are strange to his immature experience; dreams of sacred content; delirium provoked by narcotics; trances following on different physical manœuvres; hysterical ecstasies brought on by music or perfumes; chronic or temporary states of insanity, and so on. The inexplicable psychological state which is thus experienced is mingled with the unexplained objective occurrence that is encountered.

We will not tarry over this infantile and artificial mysticism, in which the bond between the doctrine and the lived fact is too weak to constitute a true experience. Truth to tell, there will be discovered on close examination, at the basis of even the grossest religious practices, a very confused and distant orientation towards an order of phenomena much nearer to real mysticism; animism is, perhaps, only the first clumsy attempt at a metaphysic of the Absolute. But we must refrain in this place from an analysis which would be both too delicate and too lengthy.

2. THE INEVITABLE PROBLEMS OF METAPHYSICS

More directly instructive will be the consideration of the higher forms of metaphysics, those which attain to the stating of the problem of the Absolute in all its fulness. However little we may dwell on this consideration, it will show us the close connection of speculative philosophy with religion in general, and with mysticism.

Michelangelo, in the great fresco in the Sixtine Chapel, shows us the first man rising slowly from the ground, attracted by the creative finger stretched out towards him. Adam's gaze, opening for the first time on the real world, remains fixed on the Divine Majesty hovering above the abyss. This panel symbolises in admirable fashion the awakening of the human intelligence to the notion of an Absolute distinct from itself. Man is conscious of his ego, at once infinite and limited; around this ego, further than eye can reach, he perceives the throbbing, far-spreading *universe*; but, above the ego and the universe, his thought obstinately seeks the *Absolute*. Soon a poignant problem arises: between these three terms, the ego, the universe, and the Absolute, there exist inevitable relations of primary interest: for these relations are, for man, at the same time the profound source of his potentialities of action in the physical order, and in the moral order the law governing his attitude and the key that unlocks his destiny.

What are these relations?

All the great metaphysical systems have attempted to define them. Let us for a moment put ourselves to school with them, and we shall see " natural " mysticism outline itself in its exact perspective.

Two relations specially interest us, for they are at the basis of all religion and all mysticism: (1) The relation of the universe to the Absolute, (2) the relation of the conscious ego to the Absolute. We will consider these two groups of relations simultaneously, for they can be separated only with difficulty.

The " universe "—that is to say all that is not formally either the conscious ego or the Absolute—offers a strange spectacle to the eyes of the metaphysician; it is changing, but without being a pure variability; it is manifold, without being a pure multiplicity; it manifests the attributes both of being and of not-being at once; it *is* not, but *becomes*. What does this mean ?

3. Dualistic and Pessimist Systems

Let us first of all listen to the echo of the dualistic systems of antiquity.

The universe, they say, is the expression of the conflict of two equally eternal principles: Being, Good, the positive principle; Non-being, Evil, the negative principle. The universe, considered as such, is essentially evil, because all its determinations are negations of being.

Here may be seen the root of a principle of destructive asceticism and negative mysticism, which was to characterise the attitude of a whole class of athletes of the spiritual life. We will call it the *Manichæan* principle, for it was first of all under the impulse of the Persian gnostic Mânî or Manes, who called himself the Paraclete (middle of third century), that this principle arose to contaminate the world of Western Christianity.

The radical dualism and the pessimistic cosmology professed by Manes were largely inspired by the ancient Iranian religion, which still survives to-day among the handful of Parsis. In the primitive teaching of Zoroaster (Spitama Zarathustra) an attenuated dualism is allied with monotheism; the transcendent supreme Being, Ahura-Mazda, creates the universe in accordance with two opposing principles, two *spirits*, at once: the " good spirit," the principle of reality, and the " evil spirit," the principle of non-reality; these are the two creators which a relatively modern terminology personifies under the names Ormazd and Ahriman. This teaching might be called a " cosmological " pessimism. All the same, Zoroaster's Mazdeism is not a radical pessimism; the two principles whose conflict is declared to be necessary to the physical equilibrium of creation have not the same claim to represent the supreme Being; the final triumph belongs to the Good. On the other hand, the destiny of individuals is prepared here on earth by renouncing the works of the " evil spirit," and, strange to say, it even owes its final completion to the malevolence of this destructive principle, which, in its blind fury against life, finally severs the bonds which hold the body to the soul; and thus opens to the latter the gates of an eternal life far above the attacks of evil.[3]

In short, the moral preparation for and the accomplishment of human destiny are to be defined, in Mazdeism, not so much as a positive perfecting as the stages in and completion of a process of deliverance.

Without its being necessary to delve further into this primitive conception it is easy to see its relationships to other more radical and consequently still less optimistic forms of Mazdean dualism, as likewise with the Manichæan dogma which declares nature to be originally and essentially evil.

Let us keep in mind this *pessimistic* strain in theo-cosmological dualism, for we shall see it appear once more in a different context.

So long as we maintain the transcendence of a " good " Creator, the " universe," vitiated from its origin though it be by the evil principle, keeps for its own some elements of reality and of goodness. On the other hand, as soon as the Creator loses the attributes of transcendence to become the immanent reality of all things—as happened in Hindu theology—the " universe," with its aspect of multiplicity, is reduced to the sum-total of the *limiting modes* of this fundamental reality; now what limits or restricts the Real, or Being, is the Unreal, Not-being; and it is likewise " what ought not to be," Evil; the " universe," then, will be evil and illusory at once. An Occidental involuntarily thinks at this point of the famous thesis of Parmenides—namely, his distinction between the sole *Being* and manifold *Appearances*; but as the summary formulas of the Eleatic system do not seem to have nourished any mystic, we do better to confine ourselves to the East, where the consideration of cosmological pessimism brings us to within a step of Buddhism.

We shall have made this step if, abstracting from all metaphysical problems whatever concerns reality in itself or the Absolute, we limit our view to the proximate conditions of our destiny—that is, to the ego and the universe as they are presented to us. However it may be as regards some state beyond life or more generally some condition beyond phenomena, our present lot, proclaims the Buddha, is that " there still remain birth, old age, death, sorrow, lamentation, misery, grief, and despair, for the extinction of which, in the present life, I am prescribing. . . . Accordingly . . . bear always in mind what it is that I have not elucidated, and what it is that I have elucidated. . . . Misery . . . have I elucidated; the origin of misery . . . the cessation of misery . . . and the path leading to the cessation of misery. . . . And why have I elucidated this ? Because . . . this does profit, has to do with the fundamentals of religion, and tends to aversion, absence of passion, cessation, quiescence, knowledge, supreme wisdom, and Nirvâna."[4]

Now the origin of misery is vain desire nourished by ignorance; ignorance of the inconsistent nature of the phenomena which constitute the ego and the universe; the extinction of misery, then, will consist in the suppression of desire, thanks to an intellectual and moral asceticism, founded on a just appreciation of the non-reality of appearances.

The Buddhist doctrine is not a cosmological dualism; neither is it a monism; it is a practical agnosticism. It may be compared with Manichæan dualism, since it rests on a pessimistic conception of the world. But it must be added that this pessimism is corrected by the affirmation of the illusory character of phenomena, and by the indication of an infallible method of freeing oneself therefrom. And then the Buddhist ideal, though negative, is not negatory; if it defines nothing beyond the deliverance, it does not thereby seem to exclude a positive transcendental destiny in its content. Unless we pay attention to this transcendental, at least hypothetical escape, the rich development of the Buddhist schools of mysticism becomes incomprehensible.[5]

Let us now cross with the fundamental principle of Buddhism the experience of Western critical idealism, and we shall obtain something akin to the system of Schopenhauer. With this last, who glories in it, the pessimistic element is still more relied upon. According to his famous formula, the universe, evil and miserable, is nothing else than the representation of it which I form for myself: " *die Welt ist meine Vorstellung*." Now, this representation is the result of my empirical will, my " will to live "; the will to live, then, which causes this representation, is the evil which has to be extirpated, so that there no longer remains either " will, or representation, or universe."

But will this be nothingness, then ? Unquestionably; it will be the renunciation of all man holds as real. With the serenity which the saints discover in the total sacrifice of their will, we must know how to look in the face " that nothingness which we fear as children fear the dark. That is better than deceiving our terror, as the Hindus do, with myths and meaningless words, such as reabsorption in Brahma, or, again, the Buddhist Nirvâna. We, on the other hand, go boldly to the end; for those whom will still actuates, what remains after the total suppression of Will is in effect nothingness. But, on the contrary, for those who have converted and abolished will, it is our present world, this so real world with all its suns and Milky Ways, which is nothingness."[6] Let us destroy this nothingness of appearance, without asking ourselves whether it hides Being from our eyes; the negation of negation is of value for its own sake; we must have passed beyond it to know whether it admits of a beyond.

In Manichæan pessimism, and still more in Buddhist pessimism or its modern idealistic revivals, we have, then, the doctrinal principle of a purely negative mysticism, a mysticism of simple liberation; objects, representations, actions, all that is limited, multiple—it is this that is the sole Evil, the obstacle, the not-being; and if by chance there exists an absolute order of Being and of Good, all this is once more the impenetrable veil which hides it from our eyes; since the nothingness is a cause of sorrow, let us deny it; since the veil is impenetrable, let us tear it away.

4. Pantheistic Monism

We have just met with a pessimistic, dualist or agnostic solution to the problem of the relations of the world and the ego with the Absolute—the most imperfect of all, for it renounces the final problems. We turn now to another, more profound and bolder, which likewise offers itself under naïve as well as critical forms: the pantheist solution. Here Being is no longer held in check by an equally primordial Non-Being; the primacy belongs to Absolute Being, and it is Being which postulates Non-Being. Only, unlike the theistic systems, with which we shall be concerned at a later stage, pantheistic metaphysics establishes a necessary and mutual bond between Being and Not-Being; in other words, it refuses to recognise the sovereign liberty of the creative Act.

We do not claim here to do more than give a rapid glance over the possible types of theory. If we would seek for their historical filiations, and not merely arrange them in logical order, it is in the East once more that we meet with the earliest clearly Monistic conceptions.

After the ancient Vedas, the Upanishads constitute the inexhaustible reservoir of philosophical, religious, and mystical traditions among the Hindus, organised later into systems by a series of commentators.[7] " The Upanishads," M. de la Vallée Poussin writes, " are the source whence springs the eternally fresh and abundant stream of idealist mysticism; all the philosophers, orthodox and heterodox, drink thereat, from the heretic Sakyamuni (the Buddha) to Samkara, the great monistic doctor of the Middle Ages (ninth century), to Râmânuja, devotee and theist (eleventh century), to the semi - Christian Rammohun Roy (nineteenth century)."[8] Now the mysticism latent in the Upanishads, though capable of receiving, even in India, a theistic interpretation, none the less shows a special affinity with idealistic monism. It finds its widest and most authoritative expression in the commentaries of Samkara on the Brahma-Sutras.[9]

The essential basis of this philosophy is summed up in a few classical formulas. " The fundamental idea of Vêdânta . . . is the identity of Brahman and of the soul, which means that Brahman, that is, the eternal principle of all being, the power which creates, preserves, and reabsorbs into itself all worlds, is identical with the Âtman—the *ego* or soul."[10] Evidently this Âtman, identical with Brahman, is not the individual soul considered as individual, but the profound, transindividual reality of the latter: the universal Soul. The sole and universal Reality, then, is the Âtman, which is Brahman or absolute non-duality.

Experience, it will be replied, sets before me unquestionably the multiplicity of objects. True, but that multiplicity has no real existence, it is only apparent, an illusion, Mâyâ[11]; it is, in my mind, the veil of the Absolute, the manifold refraction of the One. My destiny, if I do not resign myself to gravitate in the endless becoming of ignorance, is, therefore, to extirpate in myself the illusory multiplicity of objects and acts, and to retire within the Âtman, the absolute Unity that I am. Shall I then know the Âtman ? Yes and no; I shall not know it objectively, for that would mean the continued maintenance of the duality of subject and object; but I shall have become the Âtman, and the Âtman is its own light; I shall have become Brahman, and beyond that there is nothing.

Summary as they are, these few lines define one kind of

mysticism. By destroying the illusion of phenomena, and reducing in myself the multiplicity of representations and of acts, I wholly blot out the universe and the limitations of my *ego*; but by so doing I conquer myself, I become what I am, the Absolute. A mysticism negative in its psychological processes (and in this it does not differ from Buddhism), but positive in the fundamental orientation of its development.

Perhaps our last proposition a little exaggerates—that is the drawback of systematising abridgements—the equivalence between Buddhist renunciation and the negative side of the mysticism of the Vêdânta[12]. The "universe," for Samkara, is not so radically bad: is it even pure phantasmagoria ? Mâyâ, "mother of forms," is illusion, but is it illusion only ? In the hierarchy of " manifestations " or " forms," does not Brahma to some extent express his sovereign perfection, by coining it, so to speak, outside himself ?[13]

It is at least true, however, that Western pantheistic monism, more than Indian monism, throws the emphasis on the *positive* analogical relation which connects finite forms with the Absolute, of which they are the imperfect expression. While the mysticism inspired by Hindu monism seems to demand exclusively a turning within oneself, sacrificing the universe and leaving it to vanish away in its nothingness, Western pantheistic mysticism never in its boldest introversions makes a complete renunciation of the idea of an ascent towards God by the ladder of created things; renunciation is higher integration rather than simple detachment. Perhaps, from the speculative point of view, the opposing characteristics we meet with here may be reduced to two differentiations of an identical basis; in any case, we think they correspond at the least to profound differences of subjective attitude; a proof that monistic mysticism of the European type, which attributes a positive value to the degrees of being and to the movement which causes us to ascend them, will more easily than Hindu monism take on the appearance of a naturalistic, æsthetic or moral system.

Let us give a rapid glance at a few classical expressions of Western pantheism.

The most complete type of it in antiquity (in the third century A.D.) is afforded us by the philosophy of Plotinus, that general attempt to realise between God and the world a compromise formerly impossible between transcendence and immanence.[14] The teaching of the *Enneads* was to have the most widespread repercussions in speculative mysticism. Indeed, the influence of Alexandrian philosophy was infiltrated even into India, and there affected the medieval commentators on the Vêdânta; allied with Christian elements, it spread in the Musulman world, where the deepest doctrines of Sufism include an orientalised touch of Plotinism; lastly, by the intermediary particularly of the Greek monks and of the pseudo-Dionysius the Areopagite, as also of St Augustine, it was christianised, invaded the Western world, and there became one of the primary literary sources of all theoretical mysticism.

We may perhaps permit ourselves to sum up briefly the main lines of the mysticism of Plotinus. It had been prepared for a long time previously, in the history of Greek philosophy, by the monism of the Eleatics, the idealistic finalism of Plato, and the earlier Alexandrian speculations that preceded it. All these elements from the past were grouped by it into a highly systematised conception of emanation.

God, the One, the sovereign Principle, casts out his rays like a single sun to the very confines of non-being; he thus eternally creates the world, which he compenetrates without ceasing to be its ruler. This is the πρόοδος, or emanation, which does not exclude immanence. But the things themselves, divine fragments scattered in the infinite, bear within them each in its own degree a homesickness for Being, a desire for the ἐπιστροφή, the return to unity, to absolute Good (ἔοδος).

Now on the concentric circles of creation, half-way between the pure Ideas and matter, travels the human soul, itself likewise a divine emanation, constantly attracted towards the Centre by love, the immortal Ἔρως. Spirit as it is, it is conscious that it is, by its own innermost being, in relation with something which surpasses it, and if love predominates in it over its centrifugal tendencies, it begins to be concentrated. In the dispersion of the senses by which it is affected it first of all apprehends intelligible beauty, the principle of proportion and unity, which raises the sensible to resemblance with the Ideas; by contemplation it is purified and unified, for to contemplate is to become what is contemplated. Thus the soul passes into the region of sensible beauty, then that of concepts and of the Ideas; ceasing to operate as ψυχή, as the lower soul, it becomes wholly νοῦς, Intelligence. Does it stop here? It feels itself still relative and manifold; now the inner guide in its ascent, the divine Ἔρως, cannot rest save in the absolute Good, which is perfect Unity. The soul, therefore, completes its concentration, by refining its object, until it contemplates Being at the very summit of the intelligible world. Is it now at its goal? No: the intelligible still involves duality between the intellect and the thing apprehended by the intellect; Being is still the duality of existence and essence. Love soars a last time, and this time the soul, at the end of its course, realises " union," ἕνωσις; it is lost in the Ineffable, it flows back unconsciously into the absolute Unity, where there is no longer ψυχή or νοῦς, but only the One alone: Μεταξὺ γὰρ οὐδὲν, οὐδ' ἔτι δύο, ἀλλὰ ἓν ἄμφω.[15]

According to Porphyry, his disciple, Plotinus several times enjoyed this ecstasy, the theory of which he had constructed. At the point of death he told his friend, the physician Eustochius: " I was only waiting for thee that I might strive to restore the divine element in myself to the divine principle which dwells in all things."

In Plotinian mysticism, then, created perfections serve as an indispensable ladder by which the soul may rise step by step towards God: what matter if, on the last step, the foot spurns the ladder which is no longer of any service?

Western pantheism, affirming the necessity of creative emanation, in order to pass through the sieve of increasingly exigent philosophical criticism, took on the strict form of immanence. An Absolute, indeed, obliged by nature to create anything whatever *outside itself*, would not be a real Absolute; if creation is necessary, it must remain *within* the Absolute, immanent in the Creator whose infinite potentiality it particularises. And therefore it must be said correlatively, from the point of view of the created world, that the Absolute is its immanent cause—that is, it is the sole Principle latent in all things and the term, real or ideal, of the universal process of becoming. God and the world, logically inseparable, become ontologically equivalent as *natura naturans* and *natura naturata*.

Whether this immanent pantheism takes the realist form which we find given it by Giordano Bruno or a Spinoza, or else, as among the transcendentalists who succeeded Kant, an idealist form, it leads in either case to a mysticism, or better, it is already considered in itself a theoretical mysticism. In pantheistic immanence, indeed, metaphysics wholly absorbs religion, and all the normal psychological activities take on a higher religious dignity.

For example, when Spinoza defines our moral end, not only,

in negative terms, by the liberty gained over the " confusion " of " inadequate ideas " and the constraint of the " passions," but positively as the " intellectual love of God," identical with the love which God bears in us to himself and to all things,[16] does it not seem that from the very excess of rationalism a mysticism is born ? In spite of their geometrical arrangement, the theorems, corollaries and scholia of the fifth book of the *Ethics* take on a religious savour; what is it that they translate, at bottom, if not the progressive coincidence of our fragmentary intellectual activity with the creative action ?

When Fichte discovers, at the beginning of all consciousness, the " pure *Ego* " or the Spirit, opposing to itself and within itself a non-*Ego* (the universe) in order that it may progressively know itself therein and conquer itself by gaining the mastery over the latter, he raises the human intelligence, in which this proceeding takes place, to the dignity of an Absolute which creates itself. His metaphysical system is therefore, in essentials, a mysticism—a mysticism of " becoming God."

Mystical also is the philosophy of Schelling. The Absolute, the abysmal Identity, wherein the contrasts of Real and Ideal are wiped out, is revealed by a twofold process of becoming— Nature striving towards Spirit, and Spirit striving towards a supreme intuition wherein it will complete the identification of itself with Nature, or in other words will realise itself objectively in its own sight, as an Absolute. The idea of Schelling's metaphysic coincides with the bold dream of certain mystics: *eritis sicut dii.*

Lastly, in Hegel himself, in spite of his so plainly marked element of rationalism, may be recognised a mysticism of " becoming divine "—a becoming which is at the same time begun and completed in the rational progression developed by the *Logic.* What, indeed, is the " dialectic processus " but the rhythmic ascension of the Absolute Reason, affirming itself more and more explicitly, through the repeated oppositions of Being and Not-Being, as " Absolute Idea "—at the same time absolute Truth and absolute Good ? The Hegelian panlogism makes the internal cycle of subsisting Thought display itself in us: can mysticism be bolder than this ? It makes us think not so much of *eritis sicut dii* as of *dii estis.*

We have purposely confined ourselves in this sketch to recalling the properly so-called speculative theses of the pan- theist philosophies, for we wished to know in what sense metaphysics as such can invest the ordinary operations, of our understanding with a mystical significance. In fact, a Schelling and a Fichte were led by logical deduction from their premises to develop further the religious aspects of their rationalist systems; this evolution is manifested, still very guardedly, in the " second philosophy " of Fichte; less soberly in the " theosophic period " of Schelling or among such disciples as Baader. Immanentist pantheism here betrays a queer tendency to go beyond its proper boundaries, and to judge itself finally from a point of view which is essentially that of a transcendental religion pushed to the degree of a metarational mysticism.

But we cannot undertake historical comparisons which would call for too many details and distinctions. Neglecting the more or less confused attempts of modern pantheism to break the fetter of immanence, we shall once more conclude that the monistic systems are essentially mystical, since they integrate all the operations of the human spirit into a veritable " becoming divine." But the mysticism they inspire is purely natural, without anything to remind us of the Christian notion of " grace "; fundamentally rationalist as they are, they overlook the distinction of nature and supernature; for them nature is supernatural, or, what comes to the same thing, supernature is natural; and if the creature tends efficaciously towards ἕνωσις, towards intuition of the Absolute, it does so solely by the development of its native potentialities.

5. Monotheism and the Possibility of a Supernatural Mysticism

Let us now consider a third possible solution to the problem of the relations between the universe, the *ego*, and the Absolute: theism, in its completed philosophical form, monotheism.

God is strictly transcendent, without any common measure with that which is not himself. He possesses in himself plenitude of Being, without any direct or indirect admixture of Not-Being. The universe, on its side, is essentially a " becoming " proceeding from God and arranged by stages between two extreme and inaccessible limits, pure Being and pure Not-Being; it is a " becoming " external to God, but appointed, moved and directed continually by the divine action. Unquestionably finite things have not in this system, as they have in pantheism, the value of an Absolute that creates itself, but for all that they are not, as in the pessimistic dualist systems,

Evil or Nothingness; they are free creations of love, and possess, each in its own degree, a positive internal value, measured by their proximate or remote participation in the perfection of the divine Being itself: in their ordered totality they are the most expressive image of God which can be realised outside of him, since by the mediation of created intelligences and wills they tend indefinitely to reproduce the divine Ideal from which they emanate, and since nothing resembles more closely the actual infinity of that Ideal than the indefinite progress which makes one tend towards it.

We see how theist metaphysic also will be consummated by a mysticism, and even by a mysticism which will not lack analogy with that of Neoplatonism.

On the closed and impenetrable cycle of the immanent operations of the Divinity creation is grafted, so to speak, as an epicycle. At the origin of this epicycle, the powerful flood of divine action surges up constantly, but freely, and overspreads as far as the lowest degrees of existence, setting down in its passage the descending hierarchy of those deep principles of activity which constitute the innermost element of things, their internal finality, or in scholastic language their " nature." Now it is through these active natures that the flood ascends back to God; *omnia intendunt assimilari Deo*, says St Thomas: every material being tends to the perfection of its species; the entire physical world, by its regular co-ordination, tends towards vital unity; the vital unity, through its comprehensive interiority, foretells and prepares for consciousness; the lower unconsciousness, sensibility, reflects the unconscious world and brings it to the threshold of the idea; lastly, the intelligence recognises the intelligible in the sense-datum, and to its own " becoming " discovers no other end save God himself. The close of the epicycle is the same as its starting-point.

This last phase of the return of things to their first principle, by which we mean the ascent of the intelligence to God, is truly a mystical phase. In what sense are we to understand this ?

All becoming has a *law*, and inscribed in that law an *end*. What is the law, the term of this special becoming which God creates and fosters in the depth of the human soul ? We experience at every moment that our profound becoming is developed in two series of operations, which may be likened to a twofold mathematical progression: one in the order of intelligence, the other in that of will. Let us examine the essential characters of the intellectual series, and we shall see that its proper law is to tend indefinitely towards the assimilation of Being as a known object, towards Absolute Truth. Let us examine the characters of the voluntary series, and we shall find in it a similar law—the indefinite tendency to the possession of Being as absolute Good. But the complete possession of Absolute Being by a created intelligence could only be the immediate intellectual assimilation, the intuition of such Being. The two series, pushed to their limits, therefore, converge on a common term—the direct vision of God. But this term, even more than a mathematical limit, is heterogeneous to the progression which tends towards it; for our soul, itself a created thing, is by nature restricted to move only in the created plan, where Absolute Being is concealed behind the effects of its creative action; the direct vision would suppose an initiative on the part of God expanding our intelligence and revealing himself without intermediary.

This paradoxical conclusion of the metaphysics of theism separates it widely from Alexandrian emanationism. The intellectual creature would be incapable as such of realising the supreme ideal to which its becoming seems to be directed; in the finite intelligence, the radical (or, as the Scholastics say, the " obediential ") power would be vaster than the end that could be realised, the deepest desire would surpass the natural possibilities. The natural end of man would thus be something short of that absolute maximum of perfection which he is, strictly speaking, capable of attaining.

Such a conclusion would be paradoxical, even shocking, if it did not confusedly open new horizons which the ancient philosophers never suspected—the horizons of " grace " and supernature. Let us, indeed, suppose human nature, no longer left to its own powers, but raised above them by " grace," that is to say by the initiative of a transcendent God who communicates himself over and above his created gifts; then we see the fall of the supreme barriers which are opposed to the becoming of the soul. What is it, in the last resort, that erects these barriers before her, if it be not the sovereign and inaccessible independence of the Creator, over whom his creature cannot of itself have any right, any hold ? But is it a chimerical supposition that God, of his ineffable benevolence, may condescend to lend himself, so to say, to the soul's aspirations, and the direct vision, the inaccessible term of the natural ascent of every created intelligence, become the real term of a supernatural ascent ? There is nothing to suggest that there is any absurdity in this. Nay, rather, Catholic dogma, which was and is the most fruitful and purest source of Western mysticism, places in an immediate, fully satisfying and beatifying communication with God the supernatural crown of man's destiny. Who is to prove that there is any impossibility in a certain anticipation of that final gift in this present life ?

The theist metaphysic, unlike the pantheist metaphysical systems (we are not speaking of the " dualistic " systems, which are incomplete metaphysics), therefore reserves a place, at least negatively possible, for the supernatural order, and consequently for a supernatural mysticism. This latter gains support from natural mysticism in the same way as the general order of grace is raised on that of nature. The last word in this matter belongs not to reason, which admits its incompetence: we enter upon the domain of revealed theology.

A comparative study of mysticism cannot make a complete inventory of its doctrinal factors without lending an ear to the theologians. These latter are foreclosed *a priori* by pantheistic rationalism. But from the monotheistic point of view they have always the right, if not to demand credence, at least to have their solutions officially noted, since the supernatural explanation may, failing proof to the contrary, claim a hypothetical value of truth.

We have now come to the end of our rapid enquiry into the relations between Metaphysics and Mysticism. We have met in the course of it, as the respective crowns of various speculative philosophies, three principal types of mystical theories:

(1) A *negative mysticism*, a mysticism of simple liberation, the logical issue of the dualistic cosmologies and of philosophic pessimism.

(2) A *positive pantheistic mysticism*, a mysticism of a " divine becoming " immanent in the soul.

(3) A *theistic mysticism*, *likewise positive*: the mysticism of " objective " striving towards God by means of knowledge and love. Strictly speaking, this mysticism might be developed either on the natural plane, where the possession of God remains indirect, or on the supernatural plane, where the beatifying possession of God, by intuition of his essence, marks the supreme summit.

II. PSYCHOLOGICAL ELEMENTS

We are only at the half-way house of our study; for mysticism does not only consist in the doctrinal affirmation of the higher perspectives which open themselves to the becoming of the soul: it is the living of a doctrine, it is an experience. We must now consider it under this second aspect—that is, in its relations with psychology—and distinguish those amongst the subjective states which are capable of receiving a mystical signification.

If the natural becoming of the soul betrays, in the eyes of the metaphysician, an absolute Ideal, the concrete exercise of this becoming appears to the psychologist conformable with empirical and inductive laws, of which we would call to mind only the most fundamental.

Our psychological life is wholly governed, in the speculative order, by two great laws, which are the immediate consequences of the duality of the constituent principles of the human composite: the first of these laws, the law of *passivity*, binds us to matter, compelling us to receive every datum of our knowledge under the form of a sensible *multiplicity*; the second law, the law of activity or of *spontaneity*, expresses a prerogative of the mind—namely, the reduction of the sensible multiplicity to a higher *unity*. Two absolutely parallel laws regulate the field of action in us; our activity is only realised in the concrete multiplicity of acts, but secondly, the multiplicity of our actions tends to be effaced in the formal unity of will which orders them to a single final end.

Now it depends on ourselves, to a great extent, to make unification predominate over dispersion, mind over matter, in our personal psychology. It will be foreseen how this effort of unification, if it be inspired by a moral and religious ideal, will be an ascesis, imposing suppressions and rectifications, and may become a truly mystical activity.

Without delaying over the practical methods of unification which must evidently, in virtue of the laws we have enunciated, affect alike both body and soul, we will here make two important remarks:

(1) The maximum of internal unification realisable in man, in virtue of psychological laws alone, is bound up with the scope of the sense-life, that is to say, is a unity of co-ordination, conscious and subconscious; in the clear consciousness there always subsists a certain degree of sensible and spatial multiplicity. Supposing, however, that the effort displayed in

reducing the multiplicity passes beyond the goal and urges on the soul to that critical point where all spatiality gives way and every image is effaced, then the intelligence, having become a pure tendency and a form without substance, will doze in unconsciousness, while the will, for lack of an explicit end to pursue, will grow torpid in complete inactivity. It seems that this sometimes does happen. We must not say that the spiritual " *ego* " becomes in such an event luminous to itself as essence or " liberty "; this would entail a failure to recognise its substantial union with the body. Whatever some philosophers may have thought, human psychology has no knowledge of a purely intellectual intuition of the *ego*; our mind only knows itself by reflection on the operations which it performs jointly with the body. An interior unification which effaced all multiplicity of sense-impressions would thus, psychologically speaking, be equivalent to a lapse into unconsciousness.

But there is unconsciousness and unconsciousness, just as there is unification and unification; and this leads us to the formulation of a second remark.

(2) The kind of interior unification which corresponds to our normal psychological condition is a powerful integration of all the elements of consciousness—representations, acts of will, feelings, tendencies. This integration operates by means of a long interior working, as much moral as rational. It must embrace wholly and in one act, both clear consciousness and the subconscious; the integration, in fact, will be all the more rigid, as there are attached to a content of the clear consciousness, which is at the time more simple and more collected, richer and better organised potentialities in the subconscious. We could show, if we had the time to do so, that the psychological condition of integration we have just referred to is that which combines most clearly our incurably discursive intellectual activity with the intuitive mode of knowledge, as it is also that which gives our action its maximum of unity and power. It is true that an excessive effort of integration may lead to the exhaustion of unconsciousness, and that unconsciousness by itself is lacking in all psychological and religious value: but at least the powerful organisation which has preceded always lies in the subconscious, ready to rise at the first summons and to mark all further activity with its stamp.

Unhappily the interior unification, in man, is not always an integration; there also exists a form of interior unification which impoverishes him. This is an apparent unification, a

U

superficial simplification, by means of the doubling or dissociation of the consciousness, by a morbid repulsion, short of the luminous zone of apperception, of a still unassimilated mass of psychological elements. In this state a lapse into total unconsciousness is common and without compensation.

An example will make the contrast between these two states of simplification of the consciousness perfectly evident.

Let us compare—the parallel would be very unfitting if it were not to eventuate in a contrast—a St Teresa with some hysterical subject, both, let us suppose, falling into an ecstatic trance on hearing the word " God." Let us suppose also—a simple hypothesis—that the rapture is in both cases purely natural; would the two states be psychologically equivalent ? For St Teresa, the idea of God represents an ideal which holds her in every fibre of her being; for long years past God has been the centre of all her thoughts and affections, the motive power of all her actions, the term of her every hope; little by little, her conscious and unconscious life has become, so to speak, crystallised around the axis of divine love; the idea of God, in the consciousness of a St Teresa, has become a prodigiously condensed symbol, charged with all the potentialities of an infinitely rich and deep religious experience. But what is this same idea of God for the poor hysteric who has fallen into a swoon ? Hardly more than a word, a vague idea, coloured with a few perhaps very commonplace sentiments; an unsubstantial little group of dummies, which for a moment holds the stage of consciousness, while in the wings of the subconscious images and feelings are crowded together and heaped up haphazard, or are organised for the service of unspiritualised instincts. When a Saint, languishing with love, sighs " O God !" there is not a single atom in him which is not associated with the supplication; is it thus with the patients of psychiatric clinics ? Should the Saint, like the invalid, finally glide into the sleep of unconsciousness, must we say that this sleep, wherein the vibration of their subconsciousness is continued, makes them equal the one to the other ? To insist at all on this point would be superfluous.

Psychology, from its limited point of view, then, distinguishes *healthy* and *morbid* forms of mysticism: does it take us further ? Perhaps. It shows us, in the conscious and subconscious organisation of the ego, the combined play of fundamental instincts, data borrowed from the external world, emotions, feelings and habits, concepts and acts of will; in short, a synthesis of activities and psychic contents, restricted at the base by the necessary concurrence of the body and of matter, but unfolding towards the summit under the ideal type of abstract unity and of the unconditioned end. Now in following the ascending development of this synthesis the psychologist marks with almost mathematical exactitude a twofold progress towards two successive *limits*; something like the twofold progression made by an inscribed polygon which at the same time tends, by the multiplication of its sides, to the shape of the circle, and by the indefinite enlargement of the inscribing circle, towards that unrepresentable thing, a circumference with an infinite radius. In like manner our psychological activity, by unifying the various sense-data more and more closely, seeks to recover in them and by their means the unity of the ego: we may say that it tends towards the essential unity of the ego; but it tends towards this intuition of the ego according to a higher formal unity, which includes and surpasses the unity of the particular ego and even the unity of every limited object; we may say that it tends towards the *absolute perfection of unity*, that is, in reality, towards the intellectual possession of infinite Being.

The psychological analysis of our mental syntheses thus obtains for us the *notion* of a twofold passage to the term; but it does not, for all that, teach us that this twofold passage is *possible*. By trying to push the unification in ourselves of the sense-data to the extreme, shall we end by coming to the pure subsistence of the ego ? And by reducing the ego, and all things, to absolute unity, shall we meet with the divine Presence ?

To such questions as these, psychological science has no answer: its analytic methods confine it to a world where spatial quantity reigns. On arriving at the boundaries of its domain, it limits itself to pointing out to us with a wide gesture the infinite beyond, and leaves us to other guides—the metaphysicians and theologians.

We have already seen these latter mark out for us *a priori* the main lines of a theoretical mysticism; let us give them a second hearing, in order to confront their respective theories with the psychological possibilities guaranteed by experience, as well as with the " metapsychological " possibilities which experience does not authorise us to exclude, and even suggests for consideration as hypotheses.

STUDIES IN THE PSYCHOLOGY OF THE MYSTICS

III. CONFRONTATION OF DOCTRINE AND EXPERIENCE

All mystical *doctrines*, as we have seen, call for the reduction of interior multiplicity, either to the end of securing pure deliverance, or with more positive transcendental views. Let us now see, with the help of a few typical examples, how the fundamental processus of psychological unification may become the appropriate instrument of the most diverse mystical *realisations*.

1. THE PHYSICAL TRANCE

Is it fitting to call mystical those states of trance which are induced exclusively or chiefly by material means?

Travellers have described the savage rites practised in certain religious ceremonies of the Tungus tribes of Northern Asia. The "shaman," the priest or medicine man, the mediator between the people who surround him and the fearsome hierarchy of "spirits," undertakes to mimic, with a growing exaltation, by rhythmic recitatives, by cries, and above all, by rapid and violent movements, the ascent (which he is supposed to perform) of the various degrees of the heavens. All this sacred agitation soon brings him to a kind of auto-hypnotic "second state" which goes on increasing as his capers about the circle of awed bystanders become more unrestrained. Last of all, the scaling of the "highest heaven" and the arrival in the presence of the "supreme spirit" mark the culminating point of this dramatic trance; the "shaman" falls to the ground exhausted; then a few murmured sounds, a few slight contractions, and he lies completely motionless, surrounded by the religious silence of the assembly as by a shroud.[17]

Considered in themselves, proceedings of this kind, even if less extravagant, would not seem to be of a kind to procure a true integration of consciousness beneath a higher ideal; they dissociate and impoverish without compensation. Without compensation, we say; in fact, the subconsciousness which they liberate and stimulate, not having been first organised by an intellectual and moral ascesis, affords nothing which could supply the lack of the normal consciousness. As in the case of clinical patients, the psychological account is liquidated. Indeed, the trance-states of the "shamans"—and the same may be said of the pretended ecstasies evoked by narcotics—only receive the qualification "religious" or "mystical" by virtue of an extrinsic interpretation, of very little value in itself, and, ni any case, in no wise demanded by the interior characterisation of the states experienced. On closer knowledge they will appear, on the contrary, to be out of all proportion with a higher end of any kind. Mental disaggregation—to be tolerated perhaps in a certain degree, and transitorily, as the price of higher experiences—cannot be ranked, for its own sake, in the ascending line of religious progress which is crowned by mysticism.

2. BUDDHIST NEGATIVISM

Let us ascend a step higher in the hierarchy of mysticism. We next encounter the pessimistic systems, dualist or agnostic.

Evidently, the psychological ascesis which would satisfy the demands of a radically pessimist doctrine must procure a gradual effacement of conscious multiplicity carried so far as to abolish the universe in the *ego*, and even to bring about the loss of the individual *ego* in total unconsciousness. But let us take care here: according to the principles of the most definitely pessimistic philosophies, the unconsciousness that is sought in drunkenness, or stupefied exhaustion, or suicide, does not constitute a real triumph over illusory and evil multiplicity; for a state of unconsciousness that is purely accidental allows the twofold root of evil and illusion—namely, ignorance and desire—to subsist within the individual, either in this life or in future existences.

We should be mistaken, for example, if we likened the Buddhistic liberation to physical sleep or to death; it is essentially an interior simplification, obtained by setting oneself on the right path and by effacing desire. The problem of final annihilation by voluntary death could only legitimately present itself to ascetics who had attained to perfect psychological indifference; and then it would have lost all interest for them. Moreover, this problem received the attention of the casuists of primitive Buddhism; for reasons which are, it is true, a little obscure, and principally of the social order, they maintain the absolute interdiction of suicide promulgated by the Buddha.[18]

We may go further. An agnostic and negativist attitude, in no way sustained by any positive hope, is repugnant to human nature. Buddhism itself, in its later development, especially among the followers of the " Greater Vehicle," did not hesitate to assign more encouraging mystical ends; assimilating itself in this respect to Brahmanism, it glimpses, behind the illusory figure of this universe, the ineffable splendour of an ultra-phenomenal reality.

Even so, however, the way of access thereto remains exclusively a *via negationis*. This is how, in the Buddhist school of the Yogâcâras, one becomes an *arhat* or saint (it is question of a sanctity of humble degree, inferior to that of the great " enlightened ones," the " future Buddhas " or *bodhisattvas*). The aspirant to arhatship, we are told, passes to *bodhi* (illumination) by way of *samâdhi* (mental concentration, up to ecstasy inclusive), which leads to *samatha* (complete lulling of desire): " At the moment when ecstasy begins, the *bhikshu* (or mendicant monk), still plunged in a universe which acts upon him, but arming himself with energy and attention, reacts against the afflux which comes from without, to affect his intelligence and sensibility; although he has ideas and sensations, they no longer awake in him appetite or repulsion. This is the first *dhyana* (stage of contemplation): desires are at an end; intellectual operations still subsist, as well as joy and well-being. Soon thought is absorbed into itself, discursive thought is suppressed; joy and well-being still remain (second *dhyana*). Joy is a strong emotion which imposes itself on the consciousness and masters the mind. As the ecstasy develops this very positive feeling weakens, and soon well-being alone is felt (third *dhyana*). After this one arrives at a neutral state, in which the mind is alien both to the sensation of suffering and that of joy (fourth *dhyana*).

" The saint, now free, lives in a world which has nothing more in common with the world of forms and phenomena; he opens out immeasurably into infinite space, into infinite consciousness, into a state of mind in which nothing exists any longer, into the absolute: lastly, a supreme *attainment*, for which the words consciousness and unconsciousness are equally inadequate. . . . The process is complete. Beginning from distinct and consequently erroneous notions, the mind comes at last to the suppression of every notion, and is arrested in itself."[19]

3. The Yoga of Patanjali

These practices and experiences of Buddhist mysticism bear a singular resemblance, on their psychological side, to the practices and experiences of the yogis who derive from the orthodox Hinduist tradition—we are not now speaking, as will be evident, of the numerous yogis or fakirs who, though they bear this label, are hardly more than vulgar mountebanks or professionals in a quite unspiritual ascetic sport.[20]

The ecstatic proceedings of Yoga seem, in their essentials, to date from the very origins of Vedic religion;[21] developed in the bosom of Brahmanism, they were adapted to the dissidents. " There is in India hardly a single philosophical or religious doctrine which is not, at least on occasion, associated with some aspect of Yoga."[22] The heresy of the Buddha, as we have just seen, is no exception to this.

But the discipline of Yoga is best known from the classification of it afforded by the Yoga-sutras of Patanjali;[23] therein it is surrounded by speculations borrowed from the Samkhya, that pluralist, sensualist and pessimist system which is the one, among the six Brahmanic *darsanas*, which has most points of contact with Buddhism.

In spite of scattered allusions to the divinity, conceived of as the supreme Spirit (Isvara), the mysticism of Yoga emphasises above all else the liberation of the soul: not only deliverance from all pain, but the complete effacement of phenomena, and the return of the " seer " or the " soul " (*purusha*) to the naked reality of its own substance. " The Yoga, say the Sutras, is the suppression of the functions of consciousness; then will be attained the seer's subsistence in its own nature."[24] Having arrived at this term, the contemplative will truly have made his soul's conquest over error and evil; he will be plunged into the profound peace of formless ecstasy, of the " *samâdhi* emptied of all seed " (*nirvîja samâdhi*).[25]

But so far this is only a qualification of ecstasy. Does not the state of *samâdhi* afford any positive significance to the yogi ?

M. L. Massignon, comparing the mysticism of Islam with that of Patanjali, shrewdly notes that the latter " does not lead to any conclusion, it foresees as its term only a negative state obtained by very frequent intermissions of thought, which purge consciousness of all images; it is the intuitive destruction of all idolatry, the integral experimentation of asceticism up to the point of ecstasy, the mortification of the flesh, the extinction of images, the perfect detachment of will. . . . Hindu mysticism ended, among the disciples of Patanjali, in a demonstration *ab intra* of the emptiness of polytheism."[26] The temple is purified and cleared of idols; that is a great deal, but no echo resounds in its empty immensity.

It is likely, however, that, for the disciple of Patanjali even more than for the Buddhist mystic, renunciation is sustained by a positive, immense and indefinite hope; not necessarily the hope of the " preternatural powers " promised to the perfect yogi (they, in the eyes of the real mystic, are an effect, and a secondary one, rather than an end in themselves), but the hope that the complete stripping of the soul will realise, beyond the plane of phenomenal existence, the effective attainment of an absolute Good, whatever it be. The theoretical indetermination in which this Good is left allows the Yogist system to adapt itself, with perfect suppleness, to diverse metaphysical doctrines; it definitely puts aside only polytheism, as well as an anthropomorphic monism.

We cannot tarry to describe the particular methods of Yoga; methods based chiefly on meditation and contemplation, in Râja-Yoga; more exclusively psycho-physiological in Hatha-Yoga. Both kinds of methods tend equally (though with unequal risk of mental dissociation) to the progressive effacement of diversified and distinct thought, leaving the pure activity of the mind to subsist alone.

In the Vêdânta system, this pure activity of the mind is, according to the monistic idealist interpretation of Samkara, the âtman that is identical with Brahman. To turn inwardly back on the naked subsistence of the *ego* is, in this very subsistence, to touch the Absolute. " The Yogi, whose understanding is perfect, contemplates all things as if remaining in himself . . . and thus, by the eye of knowledge . . . he perceives . . . that everything is Âtma. . . . He (the Yogi) enters, with all beings (in so far as they are no longer distinguished from himself) into the Essence that penetrates all (and which is Âtma). . . . He is the supreme Brahma, who is eternal, free, alone . . . unceasingly filled with Blessedness, without duality. . . ."[27]

Apart from the metaphysical interpretation, which has become quite positive, the ascent of the Vedantist mystic, who rises, by meditation on the symbolic syllable OM, to supreme identity with Brahma, does not differ materially from the negative ecstasy procured by the Yoga of Patanjali. On both sides, it seems, the psychological experience lived by the contemplative passes through the two phases of mental concentration and unconsciousness described by M. Oltramare, according to the *Sarvadarsanasangraha*: " It is in two successive phases that the Yogi saps by anticipation the basis of further existences and effaces the impressions that determine the present existence. In the first it is *conscious*, samprajnâta-yoga; thought, then, is exclusively attentive to its proper object, and all the modifications of the Citta (the thinking principle) are suspended in the degree that they depend on exterior things; the fruits it gains under this form are either visible—the cessation of suffering—or invisible—immediate perception of Being which is the object of the meditation, that is, of Isvara or of purusha. The second period of Yoga is that in which it is *unconscious*, asamprajnâta: the thinking organ is resolved into its cause, prakriti; the feeling of personality is lost; the subject who is meditating, the object on which his thought dwells, the act of meditation itself, make but one thing. The Yoga is now said to be *without support* . . . the meditation having no further need of a vehicle or symbol."[28] This is the moment when the monistic mystic thinks to meet the Absolute in the naked substance of the ego.

4. DIFFERENCE OF PSYCHOLOGICAL ATTITUDE BETWEEN EASTERN AND WESTERN MYSTICS

Even from the mere psychological point of view, all has not been said when we utter the words " concentration " and " unconsciousness," " monoïdeism " and " aïdeism "; concentration, as we noted above, denotes an impoverishing simplification, a morbid division of personality, as well as a fruitful integration; and unconsciousness may be either complete inertia of consciousness or merely the cessation of empirical consciousness.

The danger of confusing in practice these two kinds of simplification and of unconsciousness, though it threatens all mystics, whatever their metaphysical or religious filiation, is the more imminent in pessimistic systems because in these the doctrine itself is an accomplice of the error of its followers.

Now all the Eastern religions seem to be tainted with pessimism to some degree; for them the created world, even when conceived of as the upspringing manifestation of an immanent Absolute, remains, in relation to the soul, rather an obstacle than an instrument; the Oriental mystic aspires to such a degree to detach himself from finite objects that in his capacity of mystic he hardly thinks of ordering them positively to the highest ends of religion. Thus, in the immense Hinduist group, or among those related to Hinduism, strictly æsthetic and moral considerations, even where they influence social life and ordinary religious practice, are not incorporated in the technique of higher mysticism.

In this there is for the latter a cause of weakness. Eminently " acosmic," negativist and quietist as it is, it leads to the illusion of thinking that the diversity is reduced in us as soon as it is banished from the field of the clear consciousness; and, on the other hand, although it gives itself over to the subconscious, it does not trouble to organise it under a harmonious ideal; it ignores constructive ascesis; and thus it fails to keep the underhand play of the psychological automatism under proper control, and does not give efficacious protection against the surprises of the unconscious. Must we see in this one of the reasons for the extreme frequency of apparently hypnotic or mediumistic phenomena, the natural results of states of mental dissociation, among Eastern mystics ? Far from claiming that all Eastern mysticism is necessarily condemned to such deviations, we are yet inclined to think that it is more exposed to them than other systems by reason of its theoretical views and its methods.

The general tendency of Western mysticism is very different. Alexandrian Neoplatonism (which none the less bequeathed to Christian mysticism a number of paradoxically negative formulas) already gave to the sympathetic contemplation of the Beautiful and the continued pursuit of moral Good a privileged part in the ascent of the soul towards God; the love which leads the soul back to the absolute Good is made up of the flowing together, in it and through it, of all the love dispersed throughout creation. Here comes to pass, in the psychological order, something analogous to what Hegelian dialectic seeks to realise in the logical order; in the course of the " dialectic processsus," the opposition of theses and antitheses is not purely and simply effaced, as by the passing of a sponge over it, before the synthetic term; it is reduced, in each synthetic term, by integration and sublimation. A mysticism that is lived, inspired by the Neoplatonist doctrine, would, therefore, in spite of a greater use of negative ascesis, run much less risk than Yogi mysticism of finding at the end of its course a sterile vacuity of consciousness (in whatever manner, moreover, the nature of Plotinian ecstasy is to be explained).

As for the modern systems of Pantheism (leaving Schopenhauer apart) we all know the important place that æsthetics and morals, or even the active sciences, hold in them. According to these systems, it is by the ladder of creatures, not only that man progresses upwards to his destiny, but that the Absolute itself is incessantly realising its own perfection.

When the divine value of the creation is exaggerated to this pitch, mystical contemplation, carried to its greatest height, far from being the triumph of negation, ought logically to coincide with a certain fulness of rational consciousness of the *ego* and the universe. Need we add that in fact modern Western pantheism, by reason of the very excess of its rationalism, shows itself powerless to arouse mystical vocations ?

5. MUSULMAN ASCETICISM AND MYSTICISM

It remains for us to consider, from the psychological point of view, the theistic metaphysic and the forms of mysticism it has inspired. Only the three great monotheistic religions concern us, Judaism, Islam, and Christianity. We will not speak of the first, remarkable for the " paramystical " rather than " mystical " phenomenon of prophecy.[29] The two last, especially the Christian religion, possess, as everyone knows, a mystical literature of the first rank, as regards both quality and quantity.

Although Christian mysticism preceded Musulman mysticism in chronological order, and even in a certain degree influenced it, it is the mysticism of Islam, and more particularly Sufism, that will first engage our attention.

It will not be forgotten that Islam derives both from East and West. The history of Sufism shows direct or indirect borrowings, not only from Hebræo-Christianity, but from Neoplatonist Hellenism and even Hindu Yogism; the Mohammedan Bîrûnî (†1048), in translating the Yoga-sutras of Patanjali, drew attention to their analogies with Sufi practice. However, according to some particularly competent scholars, these extrinsic meta-koranic influences were either superficial or late; " it is from the constant recitation, meditation and practice of the Koran that Islamic mysticism proceeds in its origin and development."[30] This mysticism, then, was in its primitive state monotheist in inspiration, and very rigorously so; it is right to interpret from this point of view the psychological processes employed, long anterior to any monistic contamination, in the Musulman schools of mysticism.

Now from the monotheistic standpoint the basic reality of the mystical states cannot consist solely in the soul's turning back on itself, as if the soul's withdrawal into its own substance possessed a religious value of itself. A monotheist, to be consistent, can only conceive of the mystical union in two ways:

either, within the limits of natural religion and without any direct experience of a transcendental order, as the higher intensive degree of a positive ascesis, making the mystic tend, by means of creatures seen " *sub specie æternitatis*," towards the more and more perfect knowledge and love of God the Creator, the final end of all things; *or* as the unforeseen arrival, in a soul which puts no obstacles in the way, of an extrinsic, transcendental gift, which in the last resort is none other than God himself communicating himself to his creature.

In either case, whether it is a question of *realising* a sublime, but purely " natural " and still mediate, union of the soul with God, or of preparing oneself for a " supernatural "[31] union in which all the efficacious initiative is on the side of God who gives himself, the psychological methods, so far as they depend on human industry, must be identical; that which in the first case was the actual goal becomes in the second case a condition *sine qua non* for supernatural participation in the divine bounty, necessary indeed, but not sufficient. Indeed, a soul that is still dispersed, and in conflict with the will of God, either because it makes an incorrect use of creatures or because it refuses to hand itself over completely to the infinite love which solicits it, is not ripe for the mystical union; God only gives himself to the soul that is disembarrassed and submissive; his omnipotence may, it is true, instantaneously transform, unify and bring into subjection an unprepared soul; but that, according to the mystics, is not the ordinary procedure of Providence. Monotheistic mysticism, both natural and supernatural, normally demands a moral ascesis, a rectification of the desires and the will, crowned by a complete abandonment of self and of all things to the transcendent Being, sovereign Lord and sovereign Good.

Now in fact, and however it may be explained, there is no moral perfecting or ascesis without suppression, without renunciation, without suffering. For the monotheist believer, therefore, the ways of access to the mystical state will resemble in more than one respect the proceedings of the negative mystical systems; on both sides there is much talk of " annihilation "; but all the same, in Monotheism, the mystical annihilation is in reality only the cessation of a squandering of energy: suffering itself becomes joy, for it marks the conquest—we might almost say the salvage—of the fragments of true happiness which are imperilled by capricious and divergent desires. We would not deny that in individuals monotheist ascesis remains subject to accidental deviations: that is inevitable; but all the same, it is, if properly understood, neither pessimist nor quietist; it does not devastate the soul to make it a wilderness, but transforms it, at the cost of heroic and ceaseless toil, into one of those " mystical gardens " sung of by the Persian poets, in which the perfumed flowers and the trees bending beneath their weight ot fruit offer themselves to the imminent arrival of the Beloved.

With the best of the Musulman contemplatives, this arrival is counted on with a firm confidence, which from the beginning sustains and directs the ascetic effort. The interior attitude of the Sufi differs notably from that of the Yogi formed in the school of Patanjali: " On arrival at the threshold of liberation from the flesh, the consciousness of the Musulman mystic [who believes in the revelation of a transcendent God] can no longer neglect the sovereignly real object, the superabundant Truth which his thought reflects; it is compelled to be on fire therewith, so as to be either transfigured or destroyed in it."[32]

Destroyed in it ? Unquestionably; the presumptuous Sufi, who wishes to force the threshold of grace by the intrinsic value of the ascetic effort, who saps all the natural props of the ego without finding the support of the divine arm in their place, must of necessity, after a phase of increasing exaltation of his inmost being, fall into a state of annihilation and unconsciousness which deceives his supreme ambition. Is this the bitter deception which M. Massignon notes in the case of the rough and imperious ascetic Bistâmî (†874) ? " To maintain one's intellect in simple contemplation, like a mirror exposed to the shining attributes of the divine majesty, would only end in the destruction of the mystic's personality."[33]

It is distressing, certainly, when one is at last, as one thinks, laying hold of God, to undergo physical collapse, grasping only an empty ego. The pessimist, who asks for nothing beyond unconsciousness, escapes this disillusionment, as does the disciple of Yoga, who is more concerned with defining the path than the goal; as does likewise the monist, who sees by anticipation, in a return to the pure emptiness of the ego, a direct communication with the immanent Absolute. To experience the deception of a Bistâmî one must be not only a monotheist in belief but also a bold theologian and an ascetic of no ordinary kind.

The Sufis, doubtless, attained only rarely the high summits where such a crisis presents itself. The majority avoided that crisis, either by limiting themselves wisely to an impoverished mysticism, sometimes even deviating towards a " mediumism " with no longer any specifically mystical element in it,[34] or by adopting as their own, in spite of Koranic monotheism, the monist interpretations favoured by Ibn Arabî (†1240). Others, on the contrary, like Hallâj (†922), and Ghazzâli (†1111), remained faithful to the monotheistic mystical ideal, understood in all its breadth and purity. For these latter it is the divine spark which alone can kindle the fire of ecstasy; at the culminating point of the mystical state, by the munificence of the transcendent God, the supernatural transformation of the soul in him, the immediate union of the understanding and will with him, is truly realised.

> " Thy spirit is mixed with my spirit, even as
> Wine is mixed with pure water.
> So, when aught touches Thee, it touches me.
> Lo, *Thou* art *I*, in all things ([35])."

And again, in more didactic language:

> " The states of soul whence arises divine ecstasy, it is wholly God who calls them forth,
> " Although the wisdom of the greatest be powerless to understand it !
> " Ecstasy is a stimulus, a gaze (of God) which increases by blazing in the consciousness.
> " When God thus comes to dwell in the consciousness, the latter, its keenness redoubled,
> " Permits the seer to observe three distinct phases:
> " That wherein the consciousness, still external to the essence of the ecstasy, remains a wondering onlooker;
> " That wherein the ligature of the apex of the consciousness is in operation;
> " And lastly (that wherein) it turns towards him who considers its annihilations, out of reach of the observer([36])."

The desire belongs to man; but the spirit bloweth where it listeth. In the ecstatic union, the initiative belongs to God. This doctrine was to persist later on among the Persian mystics themselves, whose delicious poems, however, are no longer of very pure monotheist orthodoxy. Turn, for example, to the words of Jâmî (1492), in the Prologue to " Salâmân and Absâl."

" In the name of God, the merciful, the compassionate !
. . . . All that can be said of beauty and of love has its origin in thee, in thee alone, and none other than thee is at the same

time Lover and Beloved. O thou before whom human beauty is but a veil, thou hast hidden thy face behind a curtain. Thou givest this curtain a reflection of thine own beauty, towards which the heart doth aspire as a bride still hidden in the nuptial chamber. . . . How long wilt thou remain dallying behind this curtain, while poor mankind is aflame with love for the image reflected thereon ? It is time for thee to raise the curtain that hides thee, and to show thy face to us, free from every veil. (It is time) for thee to make me lose consciousness of myself by contemplating thy charms, to make me free from the distinction of good and evil, that thus I may become thy lover, aflame with love for thee, my eyes fixed on thee, forgetful of all else. O thou who dost reveal thyself in the various aspects of truth, it is thou alone that actest in creatures . . . it is thou, the subtle philosopher hidden under the rags of humanity. In thy sanctuary there is no room for duality. . . . Deliver me, I conjure thee, from duality and give me unity, bestow on me a place in the stations of unity; and then, having made my escape from duality, I shall cry out, like that Kurd: Is it I that am here, O God, or is it thou ? If it be I indeed, whence doth this knowledge and power soar up in me ? And if it be thou, whence comes this powerlessness, this weakness ?"[37]

To reply to the mystic call of God it is necessary, according to Jâmî, " to escape from duality "—neither more nor less than in the Hindu Advaita—and to that end to plunge oneself into the current of consciousness, deep and undifferentiated, on which distinct phenomena float like straws. Jelâl eddîn Rûmî (†1273) will describe for us, in imaginative strophes, " the beginning of the enlightenment of the Adept's senses by the light which sees all mysteries ":

" When one sense in its progress throws off (its) bonds, (all) the remaining senses become changed.

" When one sense sees things which are not perceptible to the outer sensitive faculties, the hidden and mysterious are made manifest to all senses.

" When one sheep of the flock springs over a brook, then all successively spring over the same side.

" Drive the sheep of your senses to pasture. . . .

" Every sense of yours will be an apostle to the senses, and will draw (all) the senses to paradise.

" Senses will commune with your senses without literal expression, tongue or figurative expression.

" For this literal expression is open to interpretations, and this doubt is the source of figurative constructions.

" (But) that truth which is (conveyed) by actual vision is not susceptible to any interpretation.

" When every sense is the slave of your (spiritual) sense the celestial spheres cannot escape you.

* * * * * *

" The expression is like a nest, and the meaning is a bird; the body is a channel, and the soul is the flowing water. . . .

" Although you do not see the flowing water by means of breaks (in it), what are these sticks and straws every now and again upon it ?

" Your sticks and straws are the different forms of thought: every now and again virgin forms come on.

" The face of the water, the stream of the rational soul, in its movements, is not without sightly or unsightly sticks and straws.

" Shells on the face of this flowing water rush from the fruits of the Mystic Garden.

" Seek the kernels of the shells *within* the water, because the water comes from the garden to the channel.

" If you do not see the flowing of the water of life, look at this floating along of plants in the stream.

" When the water becomes fuller in its flow, the shells, the images, pass along it more rapidly.

" When this stream gets to flow extremely rapidly, no care (or trouble about anything) rests in the minds of the adepts.

" When (the stream) has become extremely full and rapid, then there is no room in it for anything but the water."[38]

Now let us not forget that, for Jelâl, " the soul is the flowing water "; when the giddy dance of floating appearances has vanished from the Sufi's eyes, the latter, plunging into the depths of his ego, will there gather the precious almond from the fruits of the " mystic garden."

We can easily perceive beneath these metaphors the common method of the positive mysticisms: concentration of the soul, simplification of its speculative content,[39] beneath the urge of a single love, sustained by the firm hope of a correspondence on God's part.

COMPARATIVE STUDY OF MYSTICISM

6. Christian Asceticism and Mysticism

I. Christian mysticism, *considered as a monotheistic mysticism*, ought to exhibit more than one trait in common with Musulman mysticism. Like the latter, it imposes an ascesis of detachment, without for all that limiting its ideal to the negative state of interior deprivation; on the contrary, in Christianity more than in any other religion, the idea of ascetic deprivation includes the whole series of renunciations required by the high integration of a soul which, by disciplining its desires and under the influence of prevenient grace, has arrived at the possession of itself in order, peace and unity, the conditions which are required for the divine visitation.

Let us suppose that this divine visitation is not refused to the contemplative. Then, possessing himself in God, he virtually possesses the created world; he has ceased to be its slave; he is spiritually its master, considering it from the height of the creative Wisdom and loving it by very means of the creative Love; he perceives the true beauty of things, which appear to him transfigured, worthy henceforth of being offered in homage—and not only as a holocaust—to the infinite Beauty; he becomes once more, in a certain fashion, what man was in the state of primitive integrity, the " priest of the sensible creation."

In spite of considerable differences of character and education, knowledge and sagacity; in spite, at times, of unfortunate if unconscious prejudices, or of unwise ascetic practices performed in good faith, the fundamental attitude of the Christian mystic to the things that surround him must always, in the last resort, be that which is expressed in the hymn of triumph so frequently repeated in the Bible: *Cæli enarrant gloriam Dei* (Ps. xviii), *Benedicite omnia opera Domini Domino* (Dan. iii). That exquisite feeling of nature and universal brotherhood, possessed in so high a degree by St Francis of Assisi, is not at all exceptional with our great mystics; the strictest of them suffer their mask of austerity to be pierced by that sincere and serene goodwill which they draw from the conformity of their wills with the fatherly Will, of which it is written: *Nihil odisti, Domine, eorum quæ fecisti.*

The aspect of the Christian conception of mysticism which we are here emphasising has a special interest for psychologists, since it enables them, from the character of the ideal that is striven for, to appreciate the healthy and positive nature of the preparatory ascesis.

STUDIES IN THE PSYCHOLOGY OF THE MYSTICS

Let us at once admit that, at the moment of ecstasy, the psychological and moral results of the ascetic preparation fade, or are even effaced, in the eyes of the mystic, before the divine Presence which lays hold on him. How can we be surprised, or why should we be scandalised, that the contemplative soul, dazzled and captivated, has at these moments no longer any eye for created things nor any tendency to turn back on itself? More surprising is it that it is sometimes able to raise itself even above the ecstasy, and to recover self-consciousness and the free use of its faculties without interrupting its ineffable union with infinite Being. It is worth noting; in the opinion of the mystics, this return to a harmonious equilibrium of the soul's powers, which take up their ordinary functions in the warm light of the divine presence which has become habitual, is the highest summit of the contemplative states on earth, the condition most nearly approaching to that of the angels, who, even in the exercise of their ministry regarding creatures, retain the permanent face-to-face vision of the Creator.

Christian mysticism, considered solely as a monotheistic mystical system, and abstracting from its specifically Christian elements, thus presents three clearly defined degrees.

1. A high degree of integration of the *ego* and its objective content, under the mastery of the idea of a personal God, Creator and final End. This is an ascending phase, which already covers the whole field of so-called " natural " mysticism.

2. The transcendent revelation of God to the soul which is thus prepared for it. This revelation is able to suspend all activity in the soul except the pure contemplation of God. Frequent as it is, the suspension or " ligature " of the powers does not appear to be an inevitable phase of the mystical state.

3. Without any interruption of the higher contemplation, a kind of readjustment of the soul's faculties, which resume their contact with creatures, by means of the ordinary processes of knowledge and action, but this time under the immediate and perceptible influence of God present and acting in the soul. This " theopathic " state may become permanent.

The first of these three degrees falls within the domain of ordinary psychology. The other two belong to the " hypothetical " prolongation of psychology referred to above; their reality cannot be scientifically checked, for they depend upon an exclusively personal and wholly incommunicable experience; their very possibility is only known through the testimony of the persons who believe that they have experienced them.

COMPARATIVE STUDY OF MYSTICISM

II. Christian mysticism is not merely a monotheistic mystical system; it is constantly *inspired by the teachings of revealed dogma*. There exists among infidel psychologists an unhappy tendency to overlook the by no means accidental influence of dogma on the interior life of contemplatives. This hiatus in information may easily carry with it grave errors of interpretation. How, for example, can the inner dispositions of a Catholic mystic (or *mutatis mutandis*, of any Christian mystic) be understood, if it be not kept in mind that his religious activity is illuminated by an extremely clear-cut Christological doctrine, drinks abundantly from the sacramental sources of grace, and has the social framework of a Church for its environment? Let us mention two or three of those more specially theological elements which will more clearly outline, reinforce and complete the summary sketch of Christian mysticism we have presented above.

In spite of some excessively abstruse formulas which have passed from the pseudo-Denis into the literary tradition of Western mysticism, the devotion of the Christian contemplative always has its vital centre in the person of the incarnate Word, the universal Redeemer and Mediator.

We see first of all how, in this perspective, suffering undergoes a new meaning. A redemption delivers from slavery; the belief (also existing in the Jewish and even the Musulman religions) in an " original fall " of the human race and in the many disasters occasioned thereby, in a certain degree darkens Christian ascesis and might seem even to approximate it to the pessimistic systems; the task of interior edification for it, in fact, is not only the joyous unfolding of a nature capable of infinite progress, but also and to as great an extent the restoration and reconstitution of a vitiated nature; it requires salutary destructions; it progresses by struggle and is accompanied by suffering; since the original fall of man, interior peace in perfect temperance—that psychological ideal of human asceticism—can be on earth nothing more than an armed peace, maintained at the cost of continual and active mortification. To speak of " Christian pessimism " in this connection would be going too far; the end of the penitent Christian is not, like that of the pessimist, the annihilation of a radically evil nature, but the gaining of the mastery over a rebel nature. It is true all the same that in Christianity suffering—" good suffering "—remains one of the most indispensable instruments of moral perfection; better, suffering is, so to speak, divinised.

Christian dogma, centred so rigorously about the person and saving mission of the incarnate Word, could not inspire a life of devotion, much less a mysticism, from which the co-operation of the affections in the work of redemption was absent; a partaking of the sufferings of Christ, since Christ willed to redeem the world by suffering; the " foolishness of the Cross," since Christ himself made of this " foolishness " supreme wisdom and the highest proof of love. Christian ascesis, then, will of set purpose be crucifying, far beyond the requirements of simple temperance; not through any morbid impulse, but through a spontaneous and generous movement of correspondence with the crucified love of which Jesus gave the incomparable example. It is clear that suffering, undergone through love, with an heroic disinterestedness, with an intention of universal reparation, like that of Christ, has nothing paltry or disparaging about it; it is a tonic to the soul, habituating it to the air of the heights.

We must add that Christian asceticism, thus understood (and the Catholic Church has never understood it otherwise), is not directly ordered to the attainment of mystical states. It has as its end the perfection of supernatural charity. At the same time, however, it makes the soul apt to receive mystical gifts, if God be pleased to confer them. To reverse this order of values is to distort the Christian conception.

Let us here note an instructive difference between the Christian and the Moslem.

The former finds in his religion not only a rule of monotheistic belief and a code of outward behaviour, but, even for his interior life, to whatever perfection he is ambitious of bringing it, a divinely authorised direction and an unfailingly abundant nourishment; participation in the sacraments throws open to him whenever he will the never-failing sources of supernatural grace. The divine response to his personal effort of purification is, therefore, constantly assured by the means of salvation offered by the Church to all her children. Without piercing the darkness of ordinary faith, he can know that he is united to God, and therefore in possession of all that constitutes the supernatural reality and intrinsic value of the mystical communications themselves; if these latter are granted to him in addition, he will rejoice as at receiving a magnificent bounty, without recognising in himself any claim upon them, however distant.

The Moslem, on the contrary, so far as his strictly supernatural life is concerned, is referred solely to the invitations of the Spirit of God, speaking without intermediary to the centre of his soul; the Koran, which turns a timid glance to the gate of the inner temple, abstains from entering therein; it institutes neither a living magisterium nor sacraments as efficacious signs of grace. Hence the Musulman believer who is not wholly satisfied by the practice of natural religion and the legal demands of Islam, but dreams of a more direct and interior union with God, finds himself directed almost of necessity towards the mystic ways, outside of which he can expect no providential response to his unlimited desire for perfection. Mysticism, with its experimental perception of God's action in the soul, has in his eyes after a fashion the value of a " necessary means," such as it cannot have in Christianity.

Hence, it seems to us, are to be explained certain characteristic features which stand out in Musulman mysticism from the beginning; not only the expectant desire for extraordinary states, but the formal search for them; the organisation of progressive methods for obtaining them; the conviction of a certain proportion (at least " ex congruo ") between such methods and the success anticipated; and, lastly, the formation of veritable schools of aspirants to ecstasy.[40] So direct an orientation of asceticism to mysticism evidently increases the risk of harmful deviation; the mystical goal, although it does not exclude the moral goal, may easily, more or less, mask this latter, or even take its place. An experience of many centuries in the most varied surroundings has shown that it is dangerous to exaggerate the rôle of human initiative in mysticism.

Christianity, or at least Christianity as controlled by the Church, knows of methods and schools for the attainment of spiritual perfection, but not, properly speaking, of schools or methods for procuring the mystical states, far less of procuring ecstasy.

Nor is this all. If we would grasp the physiognomy of the Christian and especially of the Catholic mystic exactly, we must remember that the latter, as a member of a Church which carries on the authority of Jesus down to himself, will of necessity give to his devotion a social character. Grafted into the mystical body of the Church, living by the sacraments, sharing in common prayer, penetrated by that mysterious solidarity in grace which is taught him by the dogma of the " communion of saints," associated in duty and in love with the work of redemption, by which he himself benefits, and thus happily having it made impossible for him to love God without loving Christ, and souls in Christ, he will, at the same time, look upon it as monstrous to present himself before the face of the heavenly Father apart from mankind his brethren, and to seek only selfish delights in prayer. It can easily be shown, also, that in every age the most authentic Christian mysticism has impelled souls to the exercise of charity and the apostolate.[41]

It would be easy to amplify these considerations and to corroborate them more fully. For example, what unlimited horizons are opened up for us on the authentic ideal of Christian ascesis by the dogmas of the " resurrection of the body," and of the " everlasting Kingdom of Christ "! For these dogmas signify that the mixed activities of the human composite and the objects of these activities include elements of goodness worthy, even before the judgement-seat of God, of a share in the building up of the " blessed city," the " new heavens," and " new earth," where Christ in glory is to reign without end. The most heroic detachment, the most impassioned love of the cross, thus easily ally themselves with a wide and fruitful sympathy for a world wherein nothing is really worthy of hate save sin. Of this harmonious fusion of contrasting feelings, in which the divine and human elements mutually support each other, the great Catholic mystics furnish incomparable examples.

To insist on this point seems unnecessary. In short, Christian asceticism, the indispensable training for any Christian mysticism, has absolutely nothing in common with an apathetic negativism, nor a sanctimonious quietism, nor a transcendentalist egoism, nor a destructive nihilism; it is hostile neither to nature, nor to action, nor to human society, nor to science nor art, nor to material progress; on the contrary, it desires, after Christ's example, to restore all things here on earth to their true and original splendour, by directly attacking sin, the sole cause of every stain, in the human soul where it is rooted.

Believer or unbeliever, the psychologist of mysticism must not forget that Christian mystics habitually live on these thoughts, and find in them an efficacious shield against impoverishment and weakness, those obstacles to a wrongly directed attempt at interior unification.

III. Moreover, we repeat, if the idea of a real communication with God in states of prayer be once admitted, the purely psychological and human excellences of these states are of merely secondary importance; the true and decisive justification of the mystical state is then God himself attesting his presence in the soul.

How are we to understand this transcendental presence and action, which the Christian mystics habitually affirm ?

We shall consider this matter more than once in other Essays.* And we shall not exhaust the question—far from it; for the elements of a reply that was at the same time both certain and detailed would need to be gathered along the whole course of a journey that would take its way firstly from the origins of Christianity to the first organisation of monasticism in Egypt and the Near East; then, passing through Hippo and progressing by way of the early Middle Ages,[42] would encounter in the West two particularly brilliant stages: one at the very climax of scholastic thought, the other, a little later, in the German-Netherlandic mystical groups of the fourteenth century—to reach at last the great classics of the Latin Renaissance, who inaugurate the modern period.

Instead of undertaking this immense détour—which is, within the limits of a short discussion, quite impracticable— let us take a side-track, go two steps hence[43] to the forest of Soignes, and knock at the door of the Priory of Groenendael, where that excellent man Blessed John Ruysbroeck will permit us, with the best grace in the world, to question him as to the secrets of contemplation. In the case of no mystic, save St John of the Cross, has a deeper theology sprung so directly from inner experience. In the doctrine which he will set before us, the point of view, the form, the shades, the subdivisions, will retain an element of their provenance, but the essential basis, it seems to us, is that of all Christian mysticism. For beneath all its various expressions there is but one Christian mysticism.

Ruysbroeck[44] divides the whole of the spiritual life into three stages, all three passed through under the influence of grace: an initial stage, more exterior and nearer to purely psychological possibilities; secondly, a strictly interior stage, intrinsically supernatural, which does not yet, however, as far as its psychological " mode " is concerned, transcend the type of operation proper to created intelligences; thirdly, a stage which is transcendent, " superessential " as he calls it, and which we shall describe more closely later.

The first stage consists in a unifying ascesis, an organising

* In a second volume not yet published.

of the realm of the soul, by the methodical practice of the Christian virtues and an undivided attachment to God without thought of reward. Towards the end of this stage the soul ardently desires to know God as he is in himself, *ut est in natura suæ divinitatis*;[45] but the understanding, while desiring to lose itself in the deep abysses of the Godhead, recognises that God is the Incomprehensible.

The second stage, marked by the meeting with Christ in the centre of the soul, is summed up in a word dear to all German-Netherlandic mysticism: *introversion*. This is a folding up, a concentration, of the soul, which, retiring from the vain self-dispersion of " acts," seeks to get hold of herself in her " intimate triple unity "—that is, in the unity which she possesses (*a*) as the principle of her sensitive-rational faculties, (*b*) as the centre of the active emanation of her higher powers (intellectual memory, intelligence, and will), (*c*) as a pure essence. Of this last unity, the motionless depth of our being, Ruysbroeck justly remarks that it surpasses the comprehension of our intelligence (at least, of our intelligence in operation as a particular faculty): (*quæ*) *nostra excedit quidem intelligentiæ captum, et tamen in nobis essentialiter inest.*[46]

But, it will be asked, has such a return on itself by the soul, granting its possibility, a religious value ? None, if the soul has nothing to offer us save its own limited reality. But the problem changes its aspect if the non-ego contains more than itself—that is, if it subsists only through the essential and active inhabitation of God.

For we must remember that created things, and therefore also the human soul, exist and operate in virtue of a total and immediate dependence on the Divine Being.

According to Ruysbroeck's forceful phrase, weakened in Surius' translation, the very essence of our soul is suspended in God, hangs on God: *dat wesen der sielen hanct in Gode*. The penetration of the essence of the soul, then, is truly to find God at the actual point of insertion of creative action in ourselves. And to apprehend the interior unity, whether by our spiritual faculties (unity of the Spirit) or of our mixed faculties (unity of the " soul " or the " heart ") is again to meet God— less immediately it is true—in the primitive expansions of his creative activity in us. Briefly, to rejoin, by introversion, our internal unity is, to the extent of our success in doing so, to give to our explicit and personal activity the form of the Divine Unity, not, doubtless, as it exists in itself, but as it is constantly

impressed on the depth of our nature. On this natural immanence of God in us is superimposed a supernatural immanence.
In theological language, grace, the communication of the
Divine life, far from destroying in us nature, adapts itself to it,
perfects and elevates it. In the supernatural order of grace
God, in a new manner, clothes our triple natural unity: our
essence by sanctifying grace; our higher faculties by infused
virtues and gifts; our mixed activities by the attraction of moral
virtues and extrinsic helps.[47] In order to explain properly this
more excellent insertion in us of the Divine action, it would be
necessary to make a close study not only of Ruysbroeck's conception of human psychology, but also and chiefly of his very
profound theological theory of the natural and supernatural
habitation in man of the Holy Trinity.[48] Our purpose in these
lines is merely a summary indication of the notion and object
of mystical introversion. Whatever be the detailed theological
interpretation of this process, we can see—and at this point
this is sufficient for us—that a soul capable of remounting
internally to the deeper and deeper sources of her supernatural
activity will be able to follow God in her most intimate depth,
by his traces so to speak—the traces of his ordinary or extraordinary infused gifts.

Ruysbroeck evidently presupposes in all men the psychological
faculty of withdrawing by stages from the multiplicity of
action to more distant forms of consciousness where this multiplicity becomes reabsorbed. If this return to a partial or total
vacuity of spirit were effected according to the " natural " mode
of our faculties outside any influence of grace, it would procure
a barren repose (analogous to the quietist ecstasies of Easterns):
it would establish the soul in a state of ambiguous receptivity
which would be very dangerous: witness the illusions of the
" false mystics."[49]

On the contrary, if this interior concentration or introversion
is practised under the influence of supernatural charity, that
is, under the stimulus of the Holy Spirit, the uncreated Love
who draws with him our faculties in his eternal return to the
Divine Essence, the disturbing ambiguity attaching to a purely
natural introversion disappears; for, now, the movement of
introversion is orientated by God and towards God; there is no
deviation to be feared; the static moments of unity experienced
in our centre are no longer empty and deceiving, for they are
the stages of the passing of a plenitude of Divine Love carrying
the soul beyond even its own essential indigence.

The direction of the supernatural inversion is clear; under the shock of an infinitely exacting love, introversion does not immobilise itself in the contemplation even of the gifts of grace (which are the highest created lights in us), but it throws the blinded intelligence on to the edge of the mysterious abyss where our essence perpetually emanates from the Holy Trinity. " Then," says Ruysbroeck, " the spirit plunges into the love of fruition: then, supernaturally and without intermediary, a meeting and a union in which we find our highest beatitude occur. . . . It is from this unity (with God) that all natural and supernatural gifts flow forth: nevertheless, the loving spirit (now) rests in that unity above all gifts; for at this point nothing remains but God and the spirit united with him without intermediary." This union prepared in a negative sense by the intelligence, which removed one after another all the screens between God and the soul, is only positively consummated by the will united to the Divine Spirit. By this degree of " fruitive possession," Ruysbroeck does not yet mean a direct vision of God; it is, properly speaking, an immediate seizing of God by a love weaned from any positive intellectual determination, but sustained by the supernatural movement of the Holy Spirit. It must be added that at the various stages of her interior unification the soul finds herself in the proximate dispositions to receive, besides the essential mystical gift, the most exceptional pledges of the Creator's munificence: flashing and irresistible "divine touches," "infused ideas" elevating the mind to the angelic mode of knowledge, or other gifts of the order of "gratiæ gratis datæ." This superfluity of gifts is at least very frequent during the mystical stage of which we are speaking.

We need not then be surprised to find Ruysbroeck indicating from the beginning of the second stage ecstasies and ravishments, sensible or imaginative visions, interior locutions, intellectual revelations, etc.; he does not fail to remind us, moreover, how hard it is to distinguish this accidental accompaniment of the mystical state from natural or diabolical delusions.

The second degree of the " spiritual life " brings the soul already so near to God that one might hesitate to admit the possibility of a still more immediate union here below. It should, however, be noted that if at the height of introversion the intelligence penetrates into God without obstacle, it is still supported on the created plane, still operates " in creato lumine,"[50] even at the moment at which, abandoning itself to love, it turns its gaze from every created object, however noble, and, by a sort of sublime renunciation, approaches the " great darkness," where nothing subsists but a divine life, an " eternal life." Introversion which has brought the soul to the very threshold of this " eternal life "—" ostium vitæ æternæ "[51]— cannot introduce her to that life.

Yet the soaring of the mystic sometimes, according to the testimony of those who have experienced it most completely, reaches still higher. Ruysbroeck calls this third stage " superessential " (or also " supernatural " in the strictest sense of the word). This stage is so eminent that he finds it necessary to underline the literal meaning and to insist on the profound seriousness of his witness to it. " I conjure all those who may take cognisance of the facts here recorded, to be good enough, if they do not understand them through lack of experience of the state of spiritual fruitive union, not to take offence and to permit things to be what they are: for I shall advance nothing which is not true."[52] At this stage the mystical possession of God is no longer only an ecstasy of love, but also the direct vision of God " without intermediary or difference "; the medium of this vision is no other than the " uncreated light," the Word communicating himself directly to the soul: and the supreme object of the vision is the Most Holy Trinity revealed in the Word. If the higher points of the second stage already surpassed the level of our human concepts, this third stage is absolutely " ineffable and divine ": " in Dei lumine et modo quodam divino agitur." Without abolishing the distinction between the Creator and the creature (a supposition as absurd as it is blasphemous), this stage is entirely developed in the bosom of God; it is to the radiant day of the Beatific Vision as the pale promise of dawn is to the noon-day sun: this comparison, used by Ruysbroeck himself, occurs frequently in the pages of the great mystics.[53] Few contemplatives could claim to have reached this summit. In order to understand the relations of Ruysbroeck's system to other " mystical ladders," we must remember that the passage from the second to the third degree with him corresponds to the entrance into the " Divine Cloud " of the pseudo-Areopagite. In this " abyss of obscurity " (" caliginis abyssus ")[54], which stretches beyond the essence of the soul, some favoured ones are privileged to see already in this life " the light of the Son of God " mounting like the dawn: " Isthic enim lux quædam incomprehensibilis lucet ac nascitur *quæ est Filius Dei:* et in ipsa videre incipimus."[55]

STUDIES IN THE PSYCHOLOGY OF THE MYSTICS

CONCLUSIONS

We propose, at the end of this discussion, to set forth a short summary of the most general reasons which explain the resemblances and dissemblances of mystical systems. This preliminary clearing of the ground of comparative mysticism may appear superfluous, so abstract is it; unhappily the strange confusion of ideas which one often meets with, even at the present day, in works on religious mysticism shows the practical necessity of unceasingly emphasising commonplace propositions, such as those which will serve as our summary and conclusion.

I. In the natural order—abstracting, that is to say, from a " supernatural " order of grace—the similarity of the various conceptions of mysticism should be explained: (a) By the inevitable identity of the series of psychological states which forms their common basis; (b) by the partially joint ownership of the metaphysical patrimony of mankind.

(a) *Psychological Foundation of the Resemblances in Comparative Mysticism.*—In all " natural " mystical life, of whatever kind (supernatural mysticism will be considered later), the common psychological conditions of human activity play their part; the general psycho-physiological mechanisms, natural inclinations and acquired tendencies, heredity, the influences of environment, etc. Moreover, the mystical states are everywhere arranged according to increasing degrees of interior concentration and mental simplification; it is not impossible to extract the general appearance of this ascent towards unity; to trace the inevitable, though partial and secondary, rôle that the subconscious has in it; to note the normal correlations between the kind of ascesis that is practised and the intrinsic quality of the states of psychological simplification that are obtained; to mark out the natural cross-roads of the mystic path, the culs-de-sac which branch off from it, the obstacles that arise therein; in short, to define a certain number of necessities and possibilities which dominate all mystical life without distinction, because they are reflections of the psychological make-up of mankind.

(b) *Doctrinal Basis of the Resemblances in Comparative Mysticism.*—Every mysticism, on its doctrinal side, is illuminated by a metaphysic. Here, also, the possible varieties are infinite; within each of the three or four great categories

332

of doctrines, the theoretical interpretation of the concrete facts of mysticism will be very similar; and everywhere, without exception, as the single root of the most varied conceptions, there will remain at least this presupposition; that the world of experience, and even the empirical *ego*, do not represent the highest values accessible to human activity. Every mystical system, even an agnostic one like that of Buddhism, claims the privilege of sovereignly " controlling " the *ego* and the world; and that means postulating an " absolute," by whatever name it may be called.

If we consider the various forms of mysticism, no longer in the abstract, but as related to the historical surroundings in which they developed, we shall evidently have to join with the necessary resemblances based on the identity of human nature the contingent resemblances that result from accidental imitation and more or less direct borrowing. For example, the problem of literary dependence, which is nowhere negligible, has, in the study of Western mysticism, a very special importance.

II. Abstracting always from a " supernatural order," the dissemblances between the various systems of mysticism depend: (*a*) Above all, on the divergence of the doctrinal elements which serve for the interpretation of religious states: as the metaphysic, so the mysticism; (*b*) secondarily and accidentally, on the mistaken attribution of a positive religious significance to aberrant or retrogressive forms of psychological activity.

(*a*) *Doctrinal Basis of the Dissemblances in Comparative Mysticism.*—Such imperfect metaphysical systems as animism or polytheism will hardly produce other than evil fruits in the " mystic garden "; abnormal states of imaginative and affective exaltation, or even states of psychological dissociation or automatism—" second states "—which may even go to the extent of the cessation of all distinct consciousness. If the contrary usage had not prevailed, we would avoid giving the name " mystical " to these inferior religious attitudes, in which as yet neither the doctrinal interpretation nor the psychological experience tends towards the unification of the whole soul beneath an absolute ideal.

In agnostic pessimism, as well as in Eastern idealist monism, the final end formally pursued is a kind of lived " acosmism," a state of complete indifference of the consciousness, of complete mental lethargy. It matters little then, from the psychological point of view, whether this state be defined negatively as deliverance, or positively as coincidence with a universal and formless self.

Let us, however, remark that the very effort expended in obtaining ecstatic unconsciousness *might* have accumulated precious potentialities in the subconscious, which on the return to normal consciousness would become the principle of a more intense religious life, a higher moral perfection, a more efficacious social action; and that the ecstasy itself *might*, like sleep, by procuring a beneficial relaxation, favour the harmonious adjustment of the psychological dispositions voluntarily introduced into the as yet unquieted consciousness. The presence or absence of these happy effects, which atone for the momentary unconsciousness of ecstasy, depends solely on the nature of the preparatory ascesis. Let us admit that an ascesis which looks directly and exclusively for the trance of unconsciousness runs a great risk of building up no appreciable good in the subconscious, and in the long run of impoverishing the soul. The mystical methods of Buddhism and Hinduism, taken literally, would tend rather to the creation of negativist and apathetic states.[56]

We do not, however, forget that a respectable margin almost always exists between the " theory of the practice " and the actual practice. A mind that is naturally upright, active, and generous, will often supply as if by instinct the lacunæ in the doctrine that guides it. Among the Eastern mystics we must consider, in addition to this, the positively organising function which is—or may be—performed during the first phases of their attraction for ecstasy by the rich symbolism with which they are in the habit of surrounding the most empty abstractions, and the very concrete personification which they willingly bestow, without ever becoming its dupes, on purely metaphysical apprehensions. So marked a sensible accompaniment will not fail to create new and permanent orientations of the affections, which will influence the ecstasy itself.[57]

In Neoplatonism and the Western Pantheistic systems, the symbolism of the senses is less exuberant; in revenge for this, the æsthetic and moral formation of the individual, and consequently also the progressive organisation of the subconscious, is undoubtedly favoured by the theoretical view-points of emanationism and evolutionism. When a contemplative life, regulated by these Pantheistic doctrines, leads to ecstatic paroxysms the extreme limit whereof seems, as in Hindu ecstasies, to be a total loss of consciousness, there are at least more chances that this unconsciousness will be " subconsciously polarised," void of perceived forms, but rich in potentialities. All, once more, depends on the nature of the methods of ascetical training.

In theism (we are concerned with it in its monotheistic expression alone) absolute Being is transcendent and distinct in substance from the creature; it is a personal God, who is at once Wisdom and Love. For a soul that represents to itself the nature of God after this fashion, the extreme point of the mystical union would not, as in monotheism, be the obscure apprehension of an ontological identity between the Creator and the creature, in the formless depth of consciousness; this natural identity does not exist. On the other hand, the extreme limit of contemplation cannot consist merely in some higher elaboration of the finite content of the consciousness; a gulf would always exist between this analogical contemplation of God, splendid as it would be, and the immediate union to which the mystic, at least confusedly, aspires. But immediate union with a personal God depends above all on the free co-operation of that infinite Being, solicited but not compelled by the humble yet bold yearning of the soul. Monotheistic mysticism, then, places its ideal in a positive and transcendent plenitude of consciousness, but this plenitude, it well knows, it is incapable of procuring by its own efforts; it can only *prepare* itself therefor indirectly, and expects its completion from the munificence of uncreated Love itself.

What kind of indirect preparation will this theistic conception of the mystical union inspire ? It essentially consists in freeing the soul from obstacles to the divine gift. Since God is subsistent Intelligence, and consequently sovereign Will, union with him presupposes on man's part, in the full measure in which the latter is at his own disposition, a conformity of intelligence and will with the creative Wisdom; for entire union between spirits is brought about, if one may so put it, by agreement of judgements and fusion of wills, by knowledge and love. This spiritual harmony, which mystical union carries to its highest degree, requires as its preliminary condition not, it is true, a destruction, but a revision and rectification of human values.

The monotheist ascesis, then, will be chiefly moral; it will be active, constructive, widely optimistic. Thus at least it should be by right, and most often it is so in fact. Apart from the very moment of ecstasy, if this latter be really divine, the monotheist ascetic remains, however, through ignorance or awkwardness, exposed to the danger of losing sight to some extent of his authentic ideal, and of misunderstanding the rules of ascesis which follow therefrom; even in Christianity there have been mental flights of Manichæan tendency and epidemics of false mysticism. These accidental deviations are not so much to be feared where an organised Church, watchful to protect its adherents from all extravagance, exercises control.[58]

(*b*) *Psychological Foundation of the Dissemblances in Comparative Mysticism.*—As long as the ascetic or devotee is still at the stage of taking for " divine " everything which appears to him as " unexplained," the capricious diversity of the concrete forms of mysticism has no necessary limits other than those of the peculiarities of the psychological life.

Later on, when the doctrinal lines become firmer and the critical sense is born, it is principally around the striving after unity that the characteristics of interior ascesis group themselves. But even there, beneath the accidental varieties, there subsists an irreducible diversity of types, due in part to the very easy confusion between the apparent unity which results from psychological dissociation and the real unity that is the fruit of a high organisation of both consciousness and the subconscious.

Whatever creed we may profess, it will readily be granted that mental disaggregation has never for its own sake any religious value. A psychological training which merely ended, when all was done, in sense-illusions or hallucinations, states of double personality or of shrinkage of consciousness, lethargic trances, automatisms of the mediumistic type or other manifestations of the kind, would not be directed even distantly towards any spiritual ideal, and would thus be lacking in an essential element of mystical activity. In order that a proceeding may have the value of a " mystical method," the least we can demand is that it approximate to the unity included in every religious end, that is, to the unity which corresponds to the higher faculties of the soul.

But if the truth of this remark cannot be contested in theory, the appreciation of concrete cases is frequently a very delicate matter. The normal ascesis itself, even though it tends to a higher end, often calls upon psychological automatism to contribute; the fixing of the attention, the obliteration of certain images, the banishing of certain tendencies, the very discipline of the action call forth dissociations in the mental content in some degree. These dissociations may become very deep, and even take on a pathological appearance, when the synthetic effort of the ascesis is intensified and concentrated. As long as they remain subordinate to the positive task of spiritual integration, of which they are, in the main, the natural effects, the price, if you will, which has to be paid therefor, nothing prevents them from being calmly faced as the inevitable jarrings of a psycho-physiological organisation not yet sufficiently adapted. Within certain limits, be it understood, the inconvenience is not so much that dissociations arise, but that having arisen they take on a religious significance which befits only the precious and wholly spiritual essence of the mystical union.

Unfortunately nothing is so frequent in the history of mysticism as illusions on this matter. Some merely betray an individual error; others are, so to speak, inherent in such or such a system of mysticism; we have referred to some of them in connection with Oriental mysticisms.

One may ask whether the high value of the intellectual ascesis in Neoplatonic mysticism suffices to protect it against the danger of illusion of which we are speaking. How should we characterise from a psychological point of view the ecstasy of a Plotinus or a Porphyry? How can the Alexandrine mystic recognise his supraconscious union with the supreme Good? In fact, apart from any miraculous intervention by a transcendent and personal God, the progressive overcoming of diversity of consciousness can only have two issues: a negative state of complete unconsciousness or the intellectual intuition of the essence of the *ego*. But the purely natural possibility of such an intuition, although it may be conceived in the Platonist dualism of body and soul, hardly fits in with those metaphysical theories which respect the strict unity of the human composite. Let us add that the inductive laws of psychology only show, in the essential intuition of the *ego*, a limit and not a possible term to the mind's activities. A natural intuition of the substance of the *ego*, therefore, is very improbable. Now it is in such an intuition that the Plotinian ἕνωσις must come to pass.

For these reasons we are inclined to think that the Alexandrian philosophers were victims of an illusion in interpreting as a beginning of unitive ecstasy the critical phase wherein, after a magnificent concentration of the soul's energies, the interior tension, carried too high, suddenly gave way; in reality,

Y

at this very moment, the dissociative forces till then held under control take a sudden revenge.

At the extreme point at which the mind's natural activity must give way in the boldness of its unitive effort, the theist philosophies give a glimpse of a new possibility; the benevolent and free initiative of the transcendent God, coming to afford his sovereign help to failing nature by bestowing his supernatural gifts, or even immediately revealing his Presence.

But this spontaneous response of uncreated to created Love already, in fact, belongs to supernatural mysticism.

III. The theistic metaphysical systems are alone in offering a perspective of the *possibility* of a supernatural mysticism. In fact, if absolute Being is personal and transcendent, the radical desire of the human soul, striving after the possession of that Being, cannot find an adequately satisfying object in a purely natural mysticism. The unsatisfied excess of the desire reveals the possible place for inserting a higher mysticism, in which all initiative would come from the divine grace.

To appreciate this mysticism in its doctrinal tenor it is evidently desirable to consult the revealed theology whereby it it inspired.

From the psychological point of view, monotheistic supernatural mysticism offers certain particular features which may usefully be recalled.

(1) It knows of no phase of complete unconsciousness. In ecstasy, where the empirical consciousness is wiped out and even the reflected consciousness of the *ego* ceases, a transcendent intuition is awakened, which offers a positive, non-conceptual content, of which the mystic retains the clearest memory.

(2) It passes in the first place through the same psychological stages as natural mysticism, and then surpasses it; for the influence of grace, which powerfully completes the task of ascesis, does not modify the psychological laws of interior unification. That is why the study of a supernatural mysticism can only benefit by a deeper knowledge of general psychology and a detailed comparison with the purely natural mystical systems.

(3) It tolerates certain secondary phenomena of psychological dissociation, and this in the exact measure in which it requires the always imperfect concurrence of human activity; the natural imperfections of this latter are not necessarily all in

opposition to the end of the mystical union. However, generally speaking, the unity of the contemplative soul tends to become more and more serene and harmonious; the perfection of the mystical state would be an intellectual contemplation of God apart from any ecstatic trance.

It would seem to be necessary to consider as indications of a state of psychological dissociation a series of secondary, and moreover inconsistent, phenomena, which are to be met with not only in supernatural, but also in natural mysticism, and even in forms of mysticism certainly abnormal; catalepsy or physical trance, suspension of the senses, levitation, lucidity and telepathy, hallucinatory or pseudo-hallucinatory visions, glossolalia, the sudden attacks or healing of certain diseases, etc. Other more or less frequent phenomena, such as prophecy, are more difficult of psychological interpretation; but divine or no, they do not belong to the essence of the mystical state, with which they have only an indirect and intermittent relation: not every mystic possesses the gift of prophecy—far from it; and not every prophet is a mystic.

To come back to the essential question, what is the legitimate attitude of a " positive and comparative science of mysticism " before the problem of supernatural mystical union? This problem it can neither set aside nor solve. It cannot set it aside, for it is *de jure* presented by every theist metaphysic, and is presented *de facto* by the mystical documents. Neither can it solve it. To answer it in the negative, that is, to deny the existence of a true supernatural mysticism, would be to go directly counter to the categorical affirmation of the monotheistic contemplatives, especially the Christian mystics, who claim to have had transcendental experiences, a claim nowise absurd in itself. But it cannot answer the problem in the affirmative, for, formal as the testimony of the mystics is, it remains uncontrollable by the means at the disposal of science. But it must faithfully record all the data of the problem—historical, psychological, philosophic, and theological—without pronouncing any affirmative or negative answer, for that is beyond the limits of its competence.[59]

STUDIES IN THE PSYCHOLOGY OF THE MYSTICS

NOTES

[1] Adapted from a conference given at Louvain.

[2] See the article entitled *Empirical Science and Religious Psychology* above.

[3] M. Haug, *Essays on the Sacred Language, Writings and Religion of the Parsis*, 4th ed. (London, 1907), p. 303 *et seq.*; Victor Henry, *Le Parsisme* (Paris, 1905).

[4] Extract from *Majjhima-Nikâya*, Sutta 63—after H. C. Warren, *Buddhism in Translations* (Cambridge, Mass., 1909), p. 122.

[5] L. de la Vallée Poussin, *Nirvâna* (Paris, 1925); Id., *Bouddhisme* (Paris, 1909); P. Oltramare, *L'Histoire des idées théosophiques dans l'Inde.* II, *La théosophie bouddhique* (Paris, 1923); S. Lévi, *Mahâyâna-Sûtrâlamkâra, Exposé de la doctrine du Grand Véhicule selon le système Yogâcâra*; Introduction et traduction (Paris, 1911); Max Walleser, *Die philosophische Grundlage des älteren Buddhismus* (Heidelberg, 1904).

[6] A. Schopenhauer, *Le Monde comme Volonté et comme Représentation*, French trans., Tome I, p. 431 (Paris, 1888); "The Concept of Nothingness is essentially Relative " (*ibid.*, p. 428).

[7] Chinese Buddhism, and even, through its intermediary, Taoism, are indebted to India. See, *e.g.*, Wieger, S.J., *Bouddhisme chinois* (Sienshien and Paris, 1910); Id., *Histoire des croyances religieuses et des opinions philosophiques en Chine, depuis l'origine jusqu'à nos jours* (Hokienfou, 1917); F. E. A. Krause, *Ju-Tao-Fo, Die religiösen und philosophischen Systeme Ostasiens* (Munich, 1924).—N.B. A good short bibliography on Hindu, Chinese and Japanese philosophies is to be found in R. Grousset, *Histoire de la philosophie orientale* (Paris, 1923).

[8] L. de la Vallée Poussin, *Le Brahmanisme* (Paris, 1910).

[9] P. Deussen, *Das System des Vedânta*, 3 Aufl. (Leipzig, 1921); P. Oltramare, *L'Histoire des idées théosophiques dans l'Inde.* I, *La théosophie brahmanique* (Paris, 1907); R. Guénon, *L'homme et son devenir selon le Védânta* (Paris, 1925).—N.B. The pantheistic monism of Samkara must not be understood in too simplifying a manner; for example, as M. Guénon observes, the Hindu theologian explicitly affirms the " irreciprocity of relation " between Brahma and the universe, which is logically the negation of monism. On the whole, however, we do not think that the metaphysics of Samkara is capable of bearing a theistic interpretation.

[10] P. Deussen, *Allgemeine Geschichte der Philosophie*, I, 3; *Die nachvedische Philosophie der Inder* (Leipzig, 1908), p. 586.

[11] Prabhu Dutt Shâstrî, *The Doctrine of Mâyâ in the Philosophy of the Vedânta* (London, 1911).

[12] At all times certain close affinities between the doctrine of Samkara and that of certain Buddhist sects have been emphasised. The recent *History of Indian Philosophy* (Cambridge, 1922) of Surendranath Dasgupta insists on this relationship (p. 165 *et seq.*).

[13] It is in this direction that the second of the great Vedantist doctors, Râmânuja (eleventh century) turns.

[14] R. Arnou, *Le désir de Dieu dans la philosophie de Plotin* (Paris, 1921); W. R. Inge, *The Philosophy of Plotinus*, 2 vols. (London, 1923, 2nd ed.).

[15] *Ennead* VI, vii, 34. *Plotini opera omnia*, ed. Creuzer (Oxonii, 1835).

[16] " Mentis amor intellectualis erga Deum est ipse Dei amor, quo Deus seipsum amat, non quatenus infinitus est, sed quatenus per essentiam humanae mentis, sub specie æternitatis consideratam, explicari potest; hoc est, mentis erga Deum amor intellectualis pars est infiniti amoris quo Deus seipsum amat." *Ethices* pars V, prop. 36, *B. de Spinoza Opera*, recognov. Van Vloten et Land, 3rd. ed., Tom. I (Hagae Comitum, 1914).

[17] After W. Radloff, *Das Schamanenthum und sein Kultus* (Leipzig, 1885), pp. 16-50.

[18] *Cf.* an extract from the *Milindapanha*; quoted in H. C. Warren, *op. cit.*, pp. 436 ff.

[19] P. Oltramare, *op. cit.*, II, *La théosophie bouddhique* (Paris, 1923), p. 366.

[20] R. Schmidt, *Fakire und Fakirtum im alten und modernen Indien* (Berlin, 1908); R. S. Copleston, *Buddhism Primitive and Present in Magadha and in Ceylon*, 2nd ed. (London, 1908); J. C. Oman, *The Mystics, Ascetics and Saints of India* (London, 1905); Id., *The Brahmans, Theists and Muslims of India*, 2nd ed. (London. s. d.).

[21] J. W. Hauer, *Die Anfänge der Yogapraxis* (Berlin, 1922).

[22] P. Masson-Oursel, *Esquisse d'une Histoire de la philosophie indienne* (Paris, 1923), p. 184.

[23] See the *Yoga-System of Patanjali* . . . , trans. J. H. Woods (Cambridge, Mass., 1914).

[24] *Yoga-sutras*, I, 2 and 3. After Deussen, *op. cit.*, I, 3, p. 511.

[25] *Yoga-sutras*, I, 51. *Ibid.*

[26] L. Massignon, *Essai sur les origines du lexique technique de la mystique musulmane* (Paris, 1922), p. 76.

[27] Samkara, *Âtmâ-Bodha*; quoted by R. Guénon, *op. cit.*, pp. 251-252.

[28] P. Oltramare, *op. cit.*, I, *La théosophie brahmanique*, pp. 312-313.

[29] This applies especially to the ancient Jewish religion. On the Alexandrian and Gnostic infiltrations in pre-medieval and medieval Jewish mysticism, see the article *Mysticism* in Hastings' *Encyclopaedia of Religion and Ethics*.

[30] L. Massingon, *op. cit.*, p. 84; see also the essay on *The Problem of Mystical Grace in Islam* in this volume. On Musulman mysticism in general, see R. A. Nicholson, *The Mystics of Islam* (London, 1914); on the connected philosophy: M. Horten, *Die Philosophie des Islam* (Munich, 1924).

[31] We use this word here without necessarily giving it the very strict acceptation which it receives in Catholic theology, where the name " supernatural " is applied to the Beatific Vision of God and the graces which are positively ordained thereto. Let us leave open the question as to whether a transcendental mysticism must on any hypothesis be supernatural in the strict sense.

[32] L. Massignon, *op. cit.*, p. 75.

[33] *Ibid.*, p. 248.

[34] See D. B. Macdonald, *The Religious Attitude and Life in Islam* (Chicago, 1912), who somewhat exaggerates his thesis.

[35] Hallâj, *Tawâsîn ;* quoted by L. Massignon, *La Passion d'Al-Hallâdj, martyr mystique de l'Islam*, Tome II (Paris, 1922), p. 517.

STUDIES IN THE PSYCHOLOGY OF THE MYSTICS

[36] Hallâj: *Mawâjida Haqq* ; quoted by L. Massignon, *op. cit.*, p. 529, note.

[37] After A. Bricteux, *Al-Djâmi, Salâmân et Absâl*, Traduit du persan (Paris, 1911), pp. 63-64.

[38] C. E. Wilson, *The Masnavî, by Jalâlu'd-Dîn Rûmî*, Book II, vol. i (London, 1910), pp. 283-8.

[39] If this simplification may take on the appearance of an annihilation, we must not be in a hurry to infer from this psychological destruction, absolute unconsciousness; it is not this that the authors have in view in their sometimes confused terminology. As concerns the Sufis, the shiek Al-Hujwiri rightly says: " The Shaykhs have discussed at large the terms by which unification is denoted. Some say that it is an annihilation that cannot properly be attained unless the attributes subsist, while others say that it has no attribute whatever except annihilation. The analogy of union and separation . . . must be applied to this question in order that it may be understood. I . . . declare that unification is a mystery revealed by God to his servants, and that it cannot be expressed in language at all, much less in high-sounding phrases." R. A. Nicholson, *The Kashf al-Mahjub, the Oldest Persian Treatise on Sufiism, by . . . Al-Hujwiri* (London, 1911), p. 285.

[40] See some remarks on the subject of these mystical schools in Mgr. L. Petit, *Les confréries musulmanes* (Paris, 1902); O. Depont and X. Coppolani, *Les confréries musulmanes religieuses* (Alger, 1897); E. de Neveu, *Les Khouan, Ordres religieux chez les musulmans de l'Algérie*, 3rd ed. (Alger, 1913).

[41] This spirit of apostolic universality is even one of the most marked features of Catholic mysticism. The majority of the great contemplatives approved by the Church devoted themselves with exceptional zeal, either to the corporal works of mercy, or to the ministry of souls, or to the government of important ecclesiastical institutions. There are none even among nuns vowed to contemplation and separated from the world by a severe enclosure who have not, by the resplendence of their sanctity, exerted a beneficent influence, often remarkably widespread.

[42] We may learn from the excellent work of Dom Cuthbert Butler: *Western Mysticism* (2nd ed., London, 1927), how necessary in comparative mysticism is an attentive exploration of the Fathers of the Church. Dom Butler methodically analyses the mystical teaching of St Augustine, St Gregory the Great, and St Bernard.

[43] That is, from Louvain.

[44] In the famous opuscule: *The Adornment of the Spiritual Marriage*. An analogous division is given in the treatise entitled *Regnum Dei amantium*. See the Latin translation of Surius (*D. Ioannis Rusbrochii Opera*, Coloniae, 1552).

[45] *Op. cit.*, I, 25, p. 310.

[46] *Op. cit.*, II, 3, p. 323.

[47] See, in the opuscule quoted, Book II, ch. 3.

[48] No guide through the theological doctrines of Ruysbroeck is surer than Mgr. G. F. Waffelaert, Bishop of Bruges. *The Union of the loving Soul with God ;* or, *Guide to Perfection*, according to the teaching of Blessed Ruysbroeck (Bruges, 1916).

[49] See a curious description of the quietism of the " false mystics " in *Adornment*, II, 76 *et seq.*

[50] *Op. cit.* (*De ornatu spiritualium nuptiatum*), II, 57, p. 351.

[51] *Op. cit.*, II, 54, p. 349.

[52] *Op. cit.*, III, 1, p. 369. English trans., *The Adornment of the Spiritual Marriage*, trans. C. A. Wynschenk Dom (London, 1916), p. 168.

[53] See the articles of L. Reypens, S.J., *Le sommet de la contemplation* (in Ruysbroeck's circle). *Revue d'ascétique et de mystique* (Rome and Toulouse, 1923).

[54] *De ornatu spirit. nupt.*, trans. Surius, III, 2, p. 369.

[55] *Ibid.* Many Catholic theologians, for theoretical reasons which may be appreciated in various ways, make the higher limit of the mystical states pass to the level of Ruysbroeck's " second degree." The latter, then, would in all good faith have erred by increasing the transcendental content of his experiences by an unconscious doctrinal interpretation. Without entering into the field of discussion, we may at least observe that the verdict passed on Ruysbroeck would reflect on other great Catholic mystics, whose point of view does not seem to differ in essentials from his.—N.B. In this question of the mystical union, Catholic teaching guards against two extreme positions: (*a*) On the one hand, the identification of the higher mystical union with the " beatific vision," the supernatural last end of man: the present life is the stage of *faith*, not of final beatitude. Yet we may admit that even on earth a vision of God is possible by " transitory," not " permanent," communication of that divine investiture which theologians call *lumen gloriæ*,—*faith* always co-existing at least as an active disposition (or *habitus*), if not as an act exercised at the moment. Would this explanation, which St Thomas proposes for some entirely exceptional cases of " rapture," be *demanded* also by the sublimest contemplation, *in divino lumine*, which Ruysbroeck describes ? We are not prepared to affirm it; other theological explanations are compatible with the text of the mystic of Groenendael. (*b*) The opposite excess consists in denying absolutely and universally the transcendental reality of the mystical states. However, as must be carefully noted, the Church has made no pronouncement as to their frequency and as to the degree of union with God which they suppose. The direction given in her name to souls who believe themselves to be on the mystic ways rests on the necessary principles of supernatural perfection and the general laws of prudence, which operate for eminent contemplatives as much as for the ordinary believer. This direction does not guarantee that the most sincere persuasions of any of the persons directed are well founded.

[56] When they do not end in this lamentable result (and we readily admit that exceptions are not very rare), is it not because they are unconsciously amended in a theistic direction ? It is observed, indeed, that agnosticism or pantheism—the foundation of so large a part of Eastern mysticism—is hardly adapted to the ordinary needs of the spiritual life save at the cost of compromises which deserve to be more emphasised. Agnosticism is almost always forced to return to metaphysical reality by way of " belief ", pantheistic monism is compelled to keep all the affective and moral values, and (in the practical order) even the language of theism. Even in the East, is not a sincere pantheistic mystic often a theist without knowing it, or one who expresses himself badly ?

[57] Of this imaginative uplift of feeling, concurrently with the most naked pursuit of samâdhi, a very clear example may be found in the filial cult of the Hindu mystic Râmakrishna (1833-1886) for the goddess Kali, who in his eyes personified the universal consciousness See Max Muller, *Râmakrishna, His Life and Sayings*, new impression London, 1910.

[58] Baron F. von Hügel, in his great work, *The Mystical Element o, Religion as studied in Saint Catherine of Genoa and her Friends* (2 vols., 2nd ed., London, 1923), has well shown that the " mystical element " of religion, to remain normal, needs to be tempered by an " institutional and historical " element. Protestant authors who treat of mysticism find an immense difficulty in understanding how beneficia! subjection to the Church's dogmatic and disciplinary authority is foɪ Catholic mystics, and how little it interferes with the freedom of their communications with God.

[59] But if the historians of religion or psychology desire, moreover, to judge of mysticism as metaphysicians or even as theologians, no one will complain, on condition that they consent to remember that they are then changing their ground and their methods. I have myself made use of this liberty elsewhere.